Map Legend

▬▬▬	Autoroute with Junction
= = = =	Autoroute (under construction)
═══════	Dual Carriageway
───────	Main Road
───────	Secondary Road
───────	Minor road
───────	Track
▬▬ ▪ ▬	International Boundary
─ ─ ─ ─	Province/State Boundary
─ • ─ ─	National Park/Reserve
─ ─ ─ ─	Ferry Route
✈✈	Airport
† ⸸	Church (ruins)
†	Monastery
◢ ▥	Chateau (ruins)
∴	Archaeological Site
∩	Cave
★	Place of Interest
▥	Mansion/Stately Home
☀	Viewpoint
↑	Beach
⊖	Border Crossing
═══════	Autoroute
───────	Dual Carriageway
─────── }	Main Roads
─────── }	Minor Roads
───────	Footpath
▬▬▬	Railway
▭	Pedestrian Area
▬	Important Building
▭	Park
❶	Numbered Sight
🚌	Bus Station
❶	Tourist Information
✉	Post Office
✝	Cathedral/Church
☪	Mosque
✡	Synagogue
⚑	Statue/Monument
▯	Tower
⚓	Lighthouse

PROVENCE

⅗ INSIGHT GUIDES

PROVENCE

Discovery
CHANNEL

APA PUBLICATIONS

Part of the Langenscheidt Publishing Group

L

2

INSIGHT GUIDE
Provence

Editor
Cathy Muscat
Art Editor
Ian Spick
Picture Editor
Hilary Genin
Cartography Editor
Zoë Goodwin
Production
Kenneth Chan
Editorial Director
Brian Bell

Distribution

UK & Ireland
GeoCenter International Ltd
Meridian House, Churchill Way West,
Basingstoke, Hampshire RG21 6YR
Fax: (44) 1256-817988

United States
Langenscheidt Publishers, Inc.
36–36 33rd Street 4th Floor
Long Island City, NY 11106
Fax: (1) 718 784-0640

Australia
Universal Publishers
1 Waterloo Road
Macquarie Park, NSW 2113
Fax: (61) 2 9888 9074

New Zealand
Hema Maps New Zealand Ltd (HNZ)
Unit D, 24 Ra ORA Drive
East Tamaki, Auckland
Fax: (64) 9 273 6479

Worldwide
**Apa Publications GmbH & Co.
Verlag KG (Singapore branch)**
38 Joo Koon Road, Singapore 628990
Tel: (65) 6865-1600. Fax: (65) 6861-6438

Printing

Insight Print Services (Pte) Ltd
38 Joo Koon Road, Singapore 628990
Tel: (65) 6865-1600. Fax: (65) 6861-6438

©2007 Apa Publications GmbH & Co.
Verlag KG (Singapore branch)
All Rights Reserved

First Edition 1989
Fourth Edition 2007

ABOUT THIS BOOK

The first Insight Guide pioneered the use of creative full-colour photography in guidebooks in 1970. Since then, we have expanded our range to cater for our readers' need not only for reliable information about their chosen destination but also for a real understanding of that destination. Now, when the internet can supply inexhaustible (but not always reliable) facts, our books marry text and pictures to provide that much more elusive quality: knowledge. To achieve this, they rely heavily on the authority of locally based writers and photographers.

How to use this book

The book is carefully structured to convey an understanding of Provence:
◆ To understand the region today, you need to know something of its past. The first section covers its people, history and culture in lively essays written by specialists.
◆ The main Places section provides a full run-down of all the attractions worth seeing. The main places of interest are coordinated by number with full-colour maps. Margin notes provide background information and tips on special places and events.
◆ A special section of photographic features highlights Provence wildlife and other aspects of Provençal culture, such as its major festivals.
◆ Photographs are chosen not only to illustrate the landscape and buildings but also to convey the moods of the region and the life of its people.
◆ The Travel Tips listings section provides a point of reference for information on travel, hotels, shops and festivals. Information may be located

changing cities like Marseille and Toulon, providing coverage on lesser-known inland areas and beauty spots, all accompanied by her reliable selection of local restaurants. She penned many new features on a wide variety of topics, from the new breed of chefs, wine and truffles to tropical gardens, perfumes, and the latest on the Avignon festival. She also planned and wrote the routes on the touring map that accompanies this guide.

Additional features on *Wild Provence* and *Architecture* were provided by London-based writer and editor, **Roger Williams**, who is knowledgeable on all things Provençal. He also co-wrote the *Provence Today* chapter and expanded the history section to bring it up to date.

The new edition was put together by Insight editor **Cathy Muscat** with invaluable editorial back-up from **Siân Lezard**. The Travel Tips section was comprehensively updated by **Lynn Parry**. Other contributors to previous editions include **Ingrida Rogal**, **Clare Peel**, **Peter Robinson**, **Peter Capella** and **Caroline Wheal**.

The majority of pictures were taken by regular Insight photographer **Gregory Wrona**, with additional images by **Catherine Karnow** and **Bill Wassman**. They have captured the timeless beauty of the Provençal landscape and its historic towns.

The book was proofread by **Neil Titman** and indexed by **Elizabeth Cook**.

quickly by using the index printed on the back cover flap – and the flaps are designed to serve as bookmarks.

The contributors

This latest edition of *Insight Guide: Provence* was completely revised and reshaped by Paris-based journalist and editor **Natasha Edwards**, who writes on travel, contemporary art and design for the *Independent* and *Condé Nast Traveller* among other publications. She is also a regular contributor to Insight's French titles. Building on the foundations laid down by contributors to previous editions, **Rosemary Bailey** (author of the chapter on Provençal Artists) and **Anne Sanders Roston**, Natasha revisited all corners of the region and compiled a wealth of new information, taking a fresh look at fast-

CONTACTING THE EDITORS

We would appreciate it if readers alerted us to errors or outdated information by writing to:

Insight Guides, P.O. Box 7910, London SE1 1WE, England. Fax: (44) 20 7403-0290. insight@apaguide.co.uk

NO part of this book may be reproduced, stored in a retrieval system or transmitted in any form or means electronic, mechanical, photocopying, recording or otherwise, without prior written permission of *Apa Publications*. Brief text quotations with use of photographs are exempted for book review purposes only. Information has been obtained from sources believed to be reliable, but its accuracy and completeness, and the opinions based thereon, are not guaranteed.

www.insightguides.com
In North America:
www.insighttravelguides.com

Route Touristique des Côtes du Rhône

THE BEST OF PROVENCE

Art, culture, nature, food and festivals... Here, at a glance, are our recommendations for your visit

CULTURAL HIGH SPOTS

- **Palais des Papes, Avignon**. Palatial 14th-century home of the popes, imposingly sited by the Rhône. *See page 60.*
- **Museon Arlaten, Arles**. This is where to see Provençal traditions, as preserved by Frédéric Mistral. *See page 135.*
- **La Vieille-Charité, Marseille**. View the exhibitions in this cultural space in a beautiful 17th-century hospice. *See page 102.*
- **Chapelle du Rosaire, Vence**. Matisse's spiritual masterpiece. *See page 208.*

- **Château Musée Grimaldi, Cagnes-sur-Mer**. Exquisite castle interior, in a Grimaldi fortress dating from 1300. *See page 240.*
- **Abbaye de Sénanque, Gordes**. A tranquil 12th-century Cistercian monastery. *See page 92.*
- **Musée des Beaux-Arts, Nice**. An overlooked museum in a Ukrainian palace. *See page 229.*
- **Musée de la Préhistoire, Quinson**. Ultra-modern museum of prehistory. *See page 159.*

NATURE, WILD AND TAMED

- **The Camargue**. Mysterious wetlands of flamingos, cowboys and wild horses. *See page 138.*
- **Prieuré de Salagon, Luberon**. Medieval plants and medicines in an ethno-botanical garden. *See page 94.*
- **Tortoise Village, Le Cannet-de-Maures** Last refuge of the Hermann tortoise. *See page 96.*
- **Colorado de Rustrel**. Colourful rock formations created by man and nature. *See page 93.*
- **Gorges du Verdon**. Enjoy adventure sports in this dramatic canyon. *See page 155.*
- **Domaine du Rayol**. Stunning gardens overlooking the sea.

See page 195.
- **Parc National du Mercantour**. Wild mountain landscape with prehistoric scratchings. *See page 216.*

TOP: the popes' dramatic palace in Avignon.
ABOVE: white-water rafting in the Gorges du Verdon.
LEFT: Abbaye de Sénanque among lavender fields.

BEST MARKETS

- **Covered market, Nîmes**. Enticing morning food market in the 15th-century Halles. *See page 151.*
- **Boulevard des Lices, Arles**. Saturday food market, spilling into boulevard Clemenceau *See page 134.*
- **Fish market, Vieux-Port Marseille**. This is where restaurateurs go to buy fish for their bouillabaisse. *See page 101.*
- **Flea Market, L'Isle sur la Sorgue**. The Sunday morning flea market is the largest outside Paris. *See page 90.*
- **Cours Lafayette, Toulon**. The daily Provençal market is one of the largest in the region. *See page 174.*
- **Street market, Apt**. This ancient Saturday-morning market is the most important in the Luberon. *See page 90.*
- **Le Lavandou**. Great Thursday market with crafts and bric-a-brac *See page 195.*
- **Cours Saleya, Nice**. In the heart of the old town, selling flowers, produce and antiques. *See page 226.*

FESTIVALS AND EVENTS

- **Feria de Nîmes**. Bullfights and costumes are the show-stoppers of these events. *See page 149.*
- **Festival d'Avignon**. Controversial, but still cutting-edge for theatre and dance. *See page 64.*
- **Festival International d'Art Lyrique, Aix-en-Provence**. Top international opera in splendid outdoor setting. *See page 116.*
- **Rencontres de la Photographie, Arles**. Photography's Oscars in the town with a commitment to the art. *See page 138.*
- **Transhumance at St-Rémy-de-Provence**. Traditional rural fete of the shepherds. *See page 147.*
- **Jazz à Juan**. Oldest, best and coolest of the Côte's many jazz festivals. *See page 238.*
- **Carnaval, Nice**. Mardi Gras is the winter highlight of the Côte d'Azur. *See page 229.*
- **Fête du Citron, Menton**. Three fragrant weeks of oranges, lemons and parades. *See page 249.*

BEST SEASIDE

- **The Calanques**. 20km of cliffs and coves in the massif west of Marseille. *See page 108.*
- **Sanary-sur-Mer**. Old-fashioned seaside charm. *See page 177.*
- **Plage de Pampelonne, St-Tropez**. Legendary for golden sands and people-watching. *See page 198.*
- **Côte d'Estérel**. Fine coves on the ruddy rocks mark this captivating coast. *See page 201.*
- **Plage de l'Estagnol, Cap Brégançon**. A tiny, paying public beach away from the crowd. *See page 195.*
- **Plage Mala, Cap d'Ail**. Small sandy Côte d'Azur beach. *See page 249.*

TOP: the Saturday market in Apt, the largest in the Luberon. Most towns and villages have a regular market day when local produce is on sale. **ABOVE RIGHT:** performers in the Avignon summer festival, one of the liveliest in Provence. Entertainment is laid on everywhere during the season. **RIGHT:** a beach on the attractive Côte d'Estérel.

WINE TRAILS

- **Bandol**. Great vintage reds in this pretty wine region. *See page 178.*
- **Beaumes Villages**. Home of the muscatel dessert wine. *See page 73.*
- **Bellet**. One of the smallest appellations in France. *See page 230.*

- **Côtes de Provence**. Light lunchtime rosés. *See page 200.*
- **Côtes du Rhône**. Excellent red wines, including Châteauneuf-du-Pape. *See page 71.*
- **Côtes du Ventoux**. Good drinkable wines. *See page 69.*

VILLAGES PERCHÉS

- **Les Baux-de-Provence**. The dramatic escarpment was once lorded over by counts and troubadours. *See page 125.*
- **Gordes**. A classic perched village with chateau and medieval arcaded alleys. *See page 92.*
- **Roussillon**. The extraordinary ochre earth colours are the signature of this beautiful village. *See page 93.*

- **Peillon**. A jumble of buildings make this fortified village behind the Côte d'Azur truly medieval. *See page 230.*
- **St-Paul-de-Vence**. A meeting place of 20th-century artists and now full of galleries. *See page 207.*
- **Eze**. An eagle's nest above the Mediterranean with views over Cap Ferrat. *See page 246.*

BEST RESTAURANTS

- **Une Table au Sud**. The domain of Lionel Levy, the south's most exciting new chef. *See page 111.*
- **Alain Llorca at the Moulin des Mougins**. True gourmet cuisine in a 16th-century mill. *See page 241.*
- **Bouillabaisse**. The famous fish stew from Marseille is best sampled in the port town and the immediate environs. Legendary address for bouillabaisse

is Bacon, Antibes. *See pages 100 and 241.*
- **La Merenda, Nice**. For authentic Niçois cooking in a tiny bistro. *See page 231.*
- **La Bastide de Capelongue**. New fief of creative chef Edouard Loubet in the Luberon. *See page 95.*
- **Joël Robuchon, Monaco**. The Parisian celebrity chef brings his brand of global tapas to Monaco. *See page 257.*

ABOVE: seafood. **RIGHT:** the *village perché* of Gordes.
FAR RIGHT: a Miró sculpture in Fondation Maeght.

ROMAN PROVENCE

- **Pont du Gard, Nîmes**. This astonishing aqueduct shows the Romans' technical genius. *See page 152.*
- **Les Arènes, Nîmes**. Wonderful Roman amphitheatre at the heart of city life. *See page 149.*
- **Orange, Théâtre Antique**. One of the best-preserved theatres in the Roman world. *See page 75.*
- **Vaison-la-Romaine**. The Quartier Villasse, with its shopping street and villas. *See page 76.*
- **Glanum, St Rémy**. Roman city on the site of a Celto-Ligurian settlement. *See page 124.*
- **Les Alyscamps, Arles**. Vast Roman necropolis painted by Van Gogh and Gauguin. *See page 137.*
- **La Turbie, La Trophée des Alpes**. Imposing triumphal monument above Monaco shows who was in charge. *See page 247.*

ABOVE RIGHT: the seafront at Cannes, the Riviera's glitziest resort.
RIGHT: St-Tropez fashionistas.
BELOW: the Roman theatre at Orange, still used for festival performances.

GLAMOUR SPOTS

- **Hotel de la Mirande, Avignon**. The former cardinals' palace is the hotel for special occasions. *See page 266.*
- **Old Port, St-Tropez**. Still fashionable and a good place for celebrity spotting. *See page 196.*
- **Cannes**. Go for the film festival – and for fun. *See page 233.*
- **Hotel Eden Roc**. The smartest hotel on the Riviera, with pedigree and class. *See page 276.*
- **Port Vauban, Antibes**. Where the most expensive yachts congregate. *See page 238.*
- **Promenade des Anglais, Nice**. Skate, jog, bike or just stroll and stare along one of the world's great promenades. *See page 228.*
- **Monte-Carlo Casino**. Have a flutter but don't lose your shirt. *See page 256.*

WHERE TO SEE...

Bonnard Look out for exhibitions in Espace Bonnard, Le Cannet. *See page 235.*

Cézanne His home and studio are outside Aix-en-Provence. *See page 117.*

Chagall His own museum of biblical paintings is in Nice. *See page 229.*

Cocteau His museum is in Menton and the exquisite Chapelle St-Pierre in Villefranche. *See page 245.*

Dufy His collection is housed in the Musée des Beaux-Arts, Nice. *See page 229.*

Klein Nice's Museum of Modern Art shows the town's artists. *See page 227.*

Matisse His main museum is in Nice. *See page 230.*

Miró The Spaniard's work can be seen at Fondation Maeght. *See page 209.*

Picasso The Picasso Museum is in Antibes, where he had a studio, and his presence is also felt in Vallauris. *See pages 236, 238.*

Renoir Pay a visit to Les Colettes, his evocative house and garden, in Cagnes. *See page 240.*

Van Gogh The inspiration for his work can be seen at Arles and at St-Rémy around the monastery. *See page 124.*

Vasarely The Hungarian-born artist's work can be seen in Aix. *See page 118.*

PROVENCE TODAY

"It was a pleasure to feel one's self in Provence again, the land where the silver-grey earth is impregnated with the light of the sky."
– **Henry James,** *A Little Tour in France*

Provence and the Côte d'Azur are the ultimate pleasure zone. No other region of Europe conjures up such familiar, enticing images, and few places live up to such continual hype. The region's unique combination of romance and glamour mixes a Mediterranean climate and a timeless Latin lifestyle with youthful dynamism and French ultra-chic. From beach resort to hill village, big city to nature park, it manages to embrace all these things.

France's sunny south is also a magical, mythical land where the ancient soil never seems far from the Romans who gave Provence its name. Long a poor, predominantly rural economy, it was not until it was "discovered" in the 19th century, first by foreign aristocracy and then by artists, that other Europeans, Russians and Americans began to turn their envious gaze towards this corner of the Mediterranean that was so benign in winter and so frolicsome in summer. They brought their millions with them and made it the world's most expensive coast.

A hard life

For the people of Provence, however, life is not one long holiday. Inland, the hills and the sparsely populated mountain areas of Mont Ventoux and the Alpine foothills of the Savoie, the soil is thin and the living hard. Here, the people are conservative and cling to traditions.

This rural landscape is imbued with a romantic quality, as immortalised in *Jean de Florette* and *Manon des Sources*, the books of Marcel Pagnol turned into haunting films. Cinema has also reflected the seedier side of life, particularly in Nice and Marseille, in such gangster movies as *Borsalino* with Jean-Paul Belmondo and Alain Delon, and *The French Connection* with Gene Hackman. Life here can have an edge.

Keeping traditions

The deep conservatism of the countryside, and the refusal to allow traditions to die, can nowhere better be seen than at Arles, where

PRECEDING PAGES: Ste-Agnès; Le Vieux Port, Cannes. **LEFT:** pavement cafés and beaches: the social hubs of Provence. **RIGHT:** on the beach at Nice.

the cowboys of the Camargue don their bright Provençal print shirts, and tenaciously traditional women pull on their shawls and full skirts at every festival.

Conservatism extends to food, too, in keeping the old ways, and some coming here year after year will wonder why the menus so seldom change. Many will be glad they don't. Even the new generation of talented young chefs remain faithful to authentic Provençal ingredients and seasonal produce.

Some parts of Provence seem to live in a nostalgia for lost glory, trying to keep a pre-industrial spirit alive, and for many visitors, this is how they want Provence to be. Many

Population

The population of Provence-Alpes-Côte d'Azur (PACA) is 4,600,000. Marseille, the administrative capital and a great Mediterranean port, is the largest city, with around 1.5 million inhabitants; Toulon, the naval port, has just over half a million. In between, with around a million, is Nice, the silicon valley of France, where opinion polls consistently reveal that French people would like to live more than anywhere else in their country.

Many other people not born in Provence would like to live here, too. Marseille, Nice, Toulon, Nîmes and Avignon are big multicultural cities with large immigrant popula-

like to come on courses, to cook in the traditional Provençal way, to paint as the artists before them have done. But they should not forget to look out for the active cultural scene, which includes prestigious festivals and a dynamic creativity that can spring from anywhere. There are adventurous dance and theatre companies in Marseille and Aix, theatre and opera in Nice, and a lively, often controversial annual festival in Avignon.

This creativity is propelled by a high student population. There are around 20,000 students in Marseille, and many of the foreigners who come to study in Provence inject a demand as well as a supply of new diversions.

tions, especially North and West Africans from former French colonies, as is evident in the local markets and street culture. Lying at a trade crossroads, Provence has long been multicultural, but this did not stop trouble flaring in towns and cities throughout the region during the civil unrest in 2005 that provoked long debates about immigration and integration.

Italians are also a large immigrant group, though they only come from next door and feel quite at home, owning many of the properties and restaurants around Nice and Menton, a municipality that is shared with Ventimiglia in Italy. Nice's most famous son is Garibaldi, founder of the Italian state, and the Italian flavour of the city is distinct.

In the 1980s the oil boom brought Arab money to the coast. Now it's the turn of the Russians, and Cyrillic script frequently appears in the menus of restaurants looking for a share of the wads of dollar bills that spill from the pockets of *nouveaux riches* Russians. In the restaurants of the Côte d'Azur, particularly in Nice and Antibes, English is frequently the majority language, as Britons make up the largest foreign resident population on the coast.

Immigration of retirement populations in search of warm winters, both from northern

turnover of around four billion euros, now bring in the same amount of revenue as tourism. The high-tech industries are centred on Sophia Antipolis near Cannes, and there is a burgeoning electronics industry near Aix-en-Provence, where a quarter of all France's components are produced. The pharmaceuticals sector is expanding, too. Agriculture and the food and drink sectors are major employers. Provence is an important producer of fruit and vegetables as well as wine in the Vaucluse and the Var – the Côtes de Provence is one of the few areas of French wine production that is actually flourishing. Provence is home to a number of food and

Europe and the rest of France, has given towns like Menton and Beaulieu the reputation of being France's *costa geriátrica*. But it also means that hill villages that were deserted half a century ago have been brought back to life and there is at least some work – building, maintenance, gardening – in the quieter months of the year.

Economy

The services industry is by far the largest employer, but technology companies, with a

drink groups, including Pernod-Ricard, Nestlé and Coca Cola.

Other less expected industries include salt in the Camargue, perfumes and food flavourings in Grasse, bauxite around Brignoles, nuclear research at Cadarache, and oil refining and petrochemicals companies around the Etang de Berre. People like to do business in Provence, and the large congress centres in Cannes and Nice are always popular.

Marseille, France's second city and the Mediterranean's largest port, has been undergoing a dramatic revival. This boom city of the 19th century that suffered so badly in the war, and long held a reputation

LEFT: girls about town in St-Tropez.
ABOVE: village life in the Provençal hinterland.

as France's crime capital, is now a lively cultural focus and a magnet for service industries and advertising and creative agencies. These are moving in to replace the traditional port industries.

Massive urban renewal programmes include the 310-hectare (766-acre) Euroméditerranée port district, where the passenger terminal is being renewed, and Zaha Hadid's 33-metre (110-ft) glass tower for a French shipping container company, which is set to dominate the waterfront, while the Belle de Mai Media Park, dedicated to film, TV and hi-tech media industries, opened in 2004 to add further glitz.

There are gangland killings over drugs and prostitution in the cities, and racketeering reverberates around slot machines. There are rich pickings for burglars along the coast, and the Cannes Film Festival and other glamorous events attract conmen and assorted small-time thieves. The gentlemen burglars of the Riviera are a breed that has passed.

Urbanisation

One would have thought that the authorities had learnt the lessons of *bétonisation*, the concreting-up of the coast at the risk of ruining the environment and the special beauty of the Riviera. But judging from the number of

Crime

Marseille may no longer be the crime capital of France, but it is not entirely redeemed. In fact, this whole area is spotted with dark areas where reputations are not always squeaky clean. Municipal corruption surfaces now and then in allegations, prosecutions and occasional shootings. Greedy property developers have been suspected to be behind the outbreaks of summer fires. Monaco continues to resist efforts by France to eliminate money laundering by making its banking rules more transparent. Its 45 banks produce a third of the nation's revenues, and fears have been voiced that these may fall under mobsters' control.

hoardings announcing new developments of "Grand Standing", it still seems as if nobody cares if all the land is cluttered up by apartment blocks, villas and garages, as long as everyone can have glimpse of the sea.

Incessant urbanisation threatens to make the coast between Cannes and Menton one continuous conurbation. It puts up prices and excludes locals who can no longer afford the rents. Elsewhere the demand for holiday homes and second residences has seen a new sprawl around rural villages, while villas in the tinder-dry woods of the Var add a further fire risk to an already charred landscape. Fire is aided when there is little water to quench it, and the risk of drought increases as expanding urban areas tap the finite reserves.

Sun and wind

One thing that all the *départements* share is dazzling light from a potent sun. There is twice as much sunshine here as in Paris, even if out of season the climate is not always perfect. Winter has its share of cool or cold days, and there are often spectacular thunderstorms at the end of August.

The months of hot weather appeal not only to tourists. Farmers and gardeners delight in the long growing season, and painters revel in the magical glow that surrounds the land.

thousands of hectares are destroyed in this way. Access routes and walking paths are closed at times of high risk. Areas of forest that have been burnt away are especially susceptible to erosion from the mistral.

Tourism

Coastal resorts and picturesque hill villages swing between seasonal extremes, from the summer, when populations increase tenfold, to winter, when it's quiet and there's little to do but watch the birds fly by. This has created a seasonal pattern of employment, too, and many who come here to work cannot afford to stay.

Another unifying characteristic is the infamous mistral. This wild, indefatigable northern wind sweeps across the region between late autumn and early spring, although the western and central sections, particularly down the Rhône valley and between Marseille and Toulon, are generally the worst hit. Its violent, chilling gales are created whenever a depression develops over the Mediterranean.

High winds and a dry, hot climate mean forest fires are a real hazard. Every summer

LEFT: Camargue cowboys preparing for the *feria*.
ABOVE: Marseille fisherman; vineyard owner of Châteauneuf-du-Pape.

Cheap flights, high-speed TGVs and the French 35-hour working week all help to extend the tourist season. Aix, Avignon or Nice can be ideal for out-of-season breaks. There have been efforts, too, to tempt visitors away from the crowded hot spots and lead them towards cultural centres and the developing "green tourism" with activity holidays in the less-frequented inland areas, such as the Var, the Gorges du Verdon and the Parc National du Mercantour. Even St-Tropez, which put on a major international contemporary art exhibition in summer 2006, is trying to restore its cultural image and prove there is more to it than nightclubs and sandy beaches. ❏

Comment mons̃ saint loys p̃int la seconde fois la croix pour
aler oultre mer : de son testus. vl̃ echappie.

annee dessus
mil et. lviii
le boy toy et
loys qui toute sa vie auoit

este amereux et entẽtif de
meur : de prisec de siur
adieu Aduint que la tie
sainte auoit le sõmg de

THE MAKING OF PROVENCE

Like most regions of France, Provence is a well-defined area with a history of independence and a strong identity. The Romans gave it shape by establishing Provincia, and it drew its colour from Renaissance troubadours, alternative popes, a cosmopolitan seaport and a dazzling coast

Through the ages, Provence's strategic position and climate have drawn wave upon wave of settlers and colonisers. Ligurians, Celts, Greeks, Romans, Visigoths, Franks and Arabs have all left their mark here.

Prehistoric rock carvings in the Grottes de l'Observatoire in Monaco, made over a million years ago, provide the earliest evidence of human habitation in the region, and are among the oldest carvings of their kind in the world. For thousands of years, Neanderthal hunters occupied the area, until modern man (Homo sapiens) made an appearance in 30,000 BC. Ancient sites all along the coast show significant traces of primitive settlements in the form of skeletons, rock carvings and paintings, standing stones and drystone dwellings. Among the most fascinating of these are the thousands of Bronze Age petroglyphs of the Alpine Vallée de Merveilles at the foot of Mont Bégo.

Between 1800 and 800 BC the area was inhabited and cultivated by Ligurians, an extremely tough people, who lived in small, disparate settlements and enjoyed a considerable degree of autonomy until the arrival of the Greeks.

Greeks and Romans

It could be argued that Marseille was the birthplace of Western civilisation on the European continent. It was to this marshy bay that

FONDATION DE MARSEILLE
Des Phocéens ayant abordé chez les Ségobriens, le roi

Greeks from Phocaea in Asia Minor set sail in the early 6th century BC. The peaceable Phocaeans formed a happy alliance with the locals and quickly set up a successful trading post. Their new colony, Massilia, soon became the most important commercial centre along the coast and a flourishing republican city-state in its own right. During its heyday in the mid-4th century BC, the Phocaean presence spread throughout the area. Among the cities founded were Nikaia (Nice), Antipolis (Antibes), Citharista (la Ciotat), Olbia (Hyères) and Athenopolis (St-Tropez). The Greeks introduced techniques for cultivating vines and the olive tree.

LEFT: scenes from the life of saintly king, Louis IX.
RIGHT: 19th-century engraving depicting the foundation of Marseille in 600 BC.

By the 3rd century BC, however, the indigents' ties with Greece were weakened, as a budding relationship with Rome began to develop. The friendship with Rome initially proved beneficial. The warlike Celts, Ligurians and Celto-Ligurians in the north of the region had been watching the prosperous Phocaeans with envy for some time, and banded together in 125 BC to seize the Massilian riches. Overwhelmed, the Phocaeans turned to the Romans for help, and, in response, the warrior Caius Sextius Calvinius brought in an entire Roman army. After a vicious three-year war the victorious Roman consul established the city of Aquae Sextiae (Aix-en-Provence).

Before long, the Romans had replaced the Phocaeans as lords of the region, which they called "Provincia Romana". Massilia, however, continued to thrive and to operate with a fairly high degree of autonomy. Now no longer just a trading post, the city became famous as an intellectual centre, with universities rivalling those of Athens.

The good times were not to last, however. Massilia made the fatal error of siding with Pompey against Caesar during Rome's civil war. After Caesar's victory, in 49 BC, the dictator punished the city by making it a Roman vassal. He further crushed the colony by strengthening the port of Arelate (Arles),

COUME VAI?

Today there are few speakers of Provençal, the language bequeathed by the Romans to this corner of their empire. In various dialects this Occitan language developed right across southern France from the Atlantic into Italy, unaffected by words from visiting Saracens or northern tribes.

The earliest surviving complete works in Provençal are poems designed to be sung, written by William IX, duke of Aquitaine (1071–1126). In fact, most of our knowledge of the development of the language comes through song, particularly through the ballads of troubadours who gathered at courts such as Les Baux (see page 125). This medieval period was the flowering of the language.

Some attempts are being made to keep the language alive, but it is an uphill battle. Road signs are occasionally written in Provençal (Aix-en-Provence is Ais de Provença), and street signs in the old town of Nice are translated into a local variant, Nissard or Nissart. Troubadour revivalists continue to reinterpret the medieval music, and world music performers have even tried mixing it with reggae.

In answer to the question coume vai? (how are you?), you might say balin-balan (so-so).

strategically located on the Via Aurelia – the Roman road linking Italy with Spain – and recruiting its inhabitants to besiege Massilia. With the fall of Massilia, Arles became capital of the Roman province, with a secondary city at Cimiez, just north of Nice.

The Romans remained in Provence for a further 600 peaceful and prosperous years, uniting the disparate trading posts and building roads, temples, bridges, aqueducts, baths and amphitheatres. One sign of this growing unity was the emergence of a regional language, Provençal, which was derived from Latin and is still spoken in the region (*see panel on opposite page*).

hills of Ste-Baume where she lived as a hermit until her death 30 years later. When the Western Roman Empire fell in AD 476, the entire region had been converted to Christianity.

Invaders and marauders

With the fall of the Western Empire, chaos reigned once again. The territory was invaded and occupied by Vandals, Visigoths, Burgundians, Ostrogoths and finally the Franks, who took control of the territory in 536. For the first two centuries under Frankish rule, Provence fared pretty well commercially. But the Franks ruled with an iron fist. Anti-Frankish rebellions in Marseille, Arles and Avignon between 732

The arrival of Christianity

According to legend, Provence was converted to Christianity in the 1st century after the miraculous landing of the boat from Judaea – the so-called Boat of Bethany – carrying, among others, Mary Magdalene, Martha and Martha's resurrected brother Lazarus. Buffeted by the waves, without sail or oar, this saintly company landed on the shores of a town that is now called Stes-Maries-de-la-Mer. Mary Magdalene found a cave up in the

LEFT: early map of Provence.
ABOVE: the French hero, Charles Martel, quashes the Arab army.

and 739 were brutally quashed. Great numbers of Provençals were slaughtered, and whole cities, including Avignon, were razed.

In the 8th and 9th centuries more marauders came from the sea. The Saracens, originating from North Africa and the eastern Mediterranean coast, appear to have been exceptionally violent, and devastated great swathes of the Mediterranean coastline. The terrified inhabitants were forced to flee to the hills where they set about building the *villages perchés* – fortified hill villages – Provence is so famous for. Not until 974 did Guillaume le Libérateur drive the Saracens from Provence once and for all, beating back the Arab forces at their fortress in La Garde Freinet. The providential hero took the title of marquis, thereby inaugurating the first Provençal dynasty, and at the same time marking a new era of prosperity for the region.

Feudal Provence

The lack of a strong central authority in the region promoted the rise of the feudal system. Towns such as Arles, Avignon, Nice, Tarascon and Marseille became independent, self-governing forces. Grandiose castles were built, and the church started a major expansion campaign using building material from structures that had stood for centuries. The construction

now the regional capital. After his death in 1245, his daughter Béatrice was married off a year later by the cunning Blanche of Castille to ambitious Charles of Anjou (brother of the French king, Louis IX) who became count of Provence. From that day onwards, the destiny of Provence was linked to that of the Angevins and, increasingly, to France. Two years later Louis IX (St Louis) set out from Aigues-Mortes on the Seventh Crusade which bolstered economic activity back home.

The popes in Avignon

In 1274 Comtat-Venaissin on the lower Rhône (roughly Carpentras and its Vaucluse

of Romanesque churches and chapels was also inspired by Roman building techniques. The arts found patronage within the various courts, and throughout the area cultural creativity reached unprecedented heights.

Agriculture developed and trade increased, and through the interplay of expedient marriages, control of the area was divided between the counts of Toulouse, who ruled the north, and the counts of Barcelona, who ruled the southern area stretching from the Rhône to the Durance and from the Alps to the sea, known as the Comté de Provence. Raimond Bérenger V in particular did much to organise and unify the province, and took up residence in Aix, by

hinterland) was ceded to Pope Gregory X in Rome. In 1309, Pope Clement V, a native Frenchman, decided that he had had enough of the anarchy that had gripped Rome, and when King Philippe the Fair of France invited him to return home, he transferred the papal court to Avignon. From a small provincial backwater, the town suddenly swelled into an important centre for diplomats and pilgrims, holy ecclesiastics and very unholy courtiers, who brought with them a sophisticated and *mondaine* way of life.

Six more popes were to follow, and a period called "the second Babylonian captivity of the Church" began. The third Provençal pope,

Benedict XII, had a reputation for being avaricious, egotistical and uncharitable. He instigated the construction of the vast Palais des Papes, as a symbol of the absolute power of the Church. Benedict's successor, Clement VI – who had bought Avignon from the reigning countess Jeanne of Provence for 80,000 gold florins – added a more ornate section to the palace, and had the Pont d'Avignon built in 1350.

The popes stayed in Avignon for almost 70 years. In returning to Rome, however, they started the "Great Schism" (1378–1417), when there were two popes: one in Avignon and one in Rome. This bitter rivalry continued for several decades. The popes in Rome and

the antipopes in Avignon excommunicated each other with monotonous regularity, and each of the powers in Europe chose their papal champion according to their current interests. The Schism was finally brought to an end in 1417 by the Council of Constance, which deposed the antipopes.

Good King René

Meanwhile, the rest of Provence had degenerated into a state of constant civil war. The area

LEFT: Giovanna, heirless queen of Naples, visits Pope Clement VI in Avignon, to surrender her lands.
ABOVE: Good King René (1409–80).

was already reeling from the devastation of the first great plague in 1348. A semblance of peace and order was restored by Louis II, a capable ruler. Louis fathered the most beloved count of Provence, René d'Anjou, popularly known as Good King René. René ushered in a new era of prosperity. A self-styled philosopher and humanist, he devoted himself to promoting the economic revival of Provence and its ports and to reinstating interest in the arts. He was a tolerant, amicable leader, whose steady control allowed cultural life to flourish.

After René's death, Provence passed to his nephew and heir, Charles III du Maine, who in 1482 bequeathed the entire region to Louis XI, king of France – a distant cousin. The conditions he attached for Provence's independence were confirmed by the Constitution Provençale in 53 "chapters", which the central government in Paris increasingly ignored. This caused constant friction between Provence and the French government, and there were numerous rebellions and attempts to secede. Angered by the constant friction, François I further curtailed the region's independence by strengthening the control of the hated Parlement over the local judiciaries and declaring French as the official language, supplanting the native Provençal dialect. Although the ancient dialect was not wiped out, the new law initiated its decline.

The Provençals fight back

Despite the repression by France during the early 16th century, noble Provençal families continued to thrive. Numerous chateaux were built, and small fortunes were amassed. Concerned that these wealthy inhabitants might try to rival the French nobility, the Parlement turned its Gallic eye towards their belittlement. Deciding that the chateaux, with their rounded corner towers, were potentially aggressive as well as presumptuous, they commanded that all towers be truncated to the level of the main roof. The stunted leftovers are still visible, dubbed *poivrières* ("pepper pots") by the locals.

However, the arts continued to flourish. There was a revival of native literature, mostly in the form of religious mystery plays; the period is sometimes called the "Provençal Renaissance". Many of the writers were scientific pioneers. Among them was the physician and astrologer Nostradamus *(see panel, below)*. A less sensational Provençal was Adam de Craponne (1527–76). Born in Salon-de-Provence amid the dry plains of the Crau, de Craponne designed and oversaw the construction of the irrigation canal that diverts water from the Durance River through the Lamanon gap, bringing water to the region.

War, rebellion and plague

The brutal Wars of Religion between the Catholics and the Protestants, brought on by the Reformation, lasted for most of the second half of the 16th century. One of the bloodiest campaigns in France's history was against the religious Vaudois sect from the Luberon area. The Vaudois were descendants of the Waldensians, who had formed in protest against the growth of papal wealth and property. Most controversial among Waldensian tenets were their beliefs that any layman could consecrate the sacrament and that the Roman Church was not the true Church of Christ. Despite all warnings, they persisted in their beliefs and resorted on occasions to violence. In 1545, François I ordered them to be disbanded by force. The result was that 2,000 were captured and hung, drawn and quartered, and hundreds of others turned into galley slaves.

Countless other atrocities took place in the region until, in 1582, a second bout of the plague caused the Provençal "heretics" to weaken; even fiercely independent Marseille finally submitted to Henri IV of France.

New dissension against the French emerged in the form of the Provençal Fronde, which pitted itself against royal absolutism. The Fronde was suppressed in 1653, but discontent persisted in Marseille. The defiant city revolted in 1659, only to be stripped of all its remaining rights after its defeat the following year.

In 1660, Louis XIV made one of his rare visits outside the royal palace, coming with great pomp to Marseille, whose strategic importance he recognised. His objective was to win over the opposition and anchor Marseille on his side. He ordered the construction of Fort St-Nicolas, from which both the town and port could be closely monitored, expanded the urban area threefold and encouraged the growth of maritime trade by making it a free port.

In all likelihood, it was the expansion of Marseille port which caused the third and deadliest of all the plagues to hit Provence. The epidemic that struck in the early 1720s was carried on trading vessels from the east, and more than 100,000 people – 38,000 from Marseille alone – died. Whole towns disappeared. Traces of a vast wall built in the desperate effort to contain the disease can still be seen near Venasque in the Vaucluse.

The French Revolution

The people of Provence embraced the ensuing Revolution with open arms and an extraordinary excess of blood-letting, even for that violent era. Their interest in the new constitution stemmed not so much from a desire for social reform as from the hope that it might offer a chance to regain lost powers. Marseille was an especially enthusiastic adherent. Before long, a guillotine graced la Canebière, the city's main street, and the cobblestones ran red with spilt blood.

On 11 April 1789, the Société Patriotique des Amis de la Constitution was formed on the rue Thubaneau in Marseille, and it was there that Rouget de Lisle's *Le Chant des Marseillais* – now the bloody national anthem for all of France – was sung for the first time. It was from the small nearby town of Martigues that the *tricolore* (now France's national flag) originated. Martigues consists of three boroughs, each with its own standard. Ferrières's is blue, Ile St-Genest's white, and Jonquières's red. United, they form the red, white and blue flag adopted by the Revolutionaries.

The Revolution did not, however, restore the autonomy Provence had enjoyed in earlier centuries. Instead, the region lost what little independence it had been able to retain. The local government was completely dissolved

in 1790, and the region was divided into three *départements*: the Bouches-du-Rhône, the Var and the Basses-Alpes. The Vaucluse was added three years later, after the French annexation of the papal territory in the Comtat-Venaisson.

Napoleon

Although the Provençals had embraced Napoleon the military genius, they were much less enthusiastic about Napoleon the emperor. This same people, such eager participants in the early years of the Revolution, soon became staunch supporters of the returning Bourbon monarchy. Blood flowed again in the streets, as those suspected of being anti-royalist were

slaughtered with the same intensity as the anti-Revolutionaries had been under Jacobinism.

The Provençal antipathy towards Napoleon proved to be justified, for his ever-escalating wars finally resulted in the ceding of much of the eastern territory (including Nice and the land as far north as the Var River) to Sardinia during the Congress of Vienna in 1814–15, after Napoleon's defeat. It was not until 1860 that these lands were returned to France.

The 19th Century

Nonetheless, the 19th century was probably the most peaceful period Provence had ever experienced. The French revolutions of 1830

LEFT: carts laden with the dead, outside Marseille town hall, during the plague of 1720.
RIGHT: *The Marseillaise*, by Gustave Doré, 1870.

and 1848 and the new regimes they heralded aroused little interest in the southern regions. With the Second Empire (1852–70) came a Provençal revival, led by Nobel Prize-winning poet and local hero, Frédéric Mistral. With a group of Provençal poets, he founded the Félibrige, a cultural and literary organisation that encouraged the local language and traditions, promoting literary works written in Provençal. He used his Nobel Prize money to found the Provençal museum in Arles.

Agriculture remained the economic mainstay, but the Industrial Revolution, which came fairly late to France, did not leave Provence untouched. Between 1876 and 1880

alone, the rural *département* of the Vaucluse lost some 20,000 inhabitants to the cities.

Aix-en-Provence languished through most of the 19th century as a provincial, if distinguished, backwater. Marseille, on the other hand, grew dramatically in size. Almost all trade with the French Maghreb (Algeria, Tunisia and Morocco) passed through the city, and the new industries it engendered drew waves of immigrant workers from Algeria, Armenia, Spain and Italy.

Another thriving new industry came in the form of tourism. A small community of English aristocrats had begun wintering on the Côte d'Azur in the late 1700s, but it wasn't

145 CANNES. — LA PROMENADE DE LA CROISETTE ET LE MONT CHEVALIER. — LL.

THE GLITTERING COAST

The "French Riviera", as the Italians dubbed this Mediterranean strip, was not always considered glamorous. When the Scottish novelist Tobias Smollett (1721–71) came to Nice in 1764 to cure his bronchitis, he wrote that it was a land of rude peasants and persistent mosquitoes. He did, however, admit that the gentle climate was remarkable. This praise encouraged a few brave Brits to visit, but the French stayed away, preferring fashionable Normandy.

In 1834, Lord Brougham, the English Lord Chancellor, and his daughter were detained in Cannes, while a bout of cholera spread through their favourite Italian winter playground. Eight days after his arrival in the tiny fishing village,

he bought land and ordered a villa to be constructed. The rage had begun. Within a year, a small but extant winter colony had sprung up in Cannes. Within three years, 30 new villas had been built, and the following year the harbourside avenue now called la Croisette was created. Five years later, the Promenade des Anglais was constructed in Nice for the newcomers' morning constitutionals.

In the second half of the 19th century the Côte d'Azur went into full swing. Any halfway fashionable Briton wintered in Nice, Cannes, Menton or Beaulieu. The elaborate Belle Epoque villas for which the Côte is still famous were built all along the coast, and immortal glamour was assured.

until Lord Brougham took a fancy to the town of Cannes in 1834 that tourism on the "French Riviera" really took off *(see page 233)*. The area became very popular with the aristocrats of Victorian England and European royals. Rich French, American and Russian tourists followed. Railway lines and roads were extended along the coast, and grand neoclassical buildings mushroomed.

The extraordinary quality of the light and intense colours of the landscape were captured on canvas by Monet, Renoir and Van Gogh, who were drawn to Provence, and by Cézanne, a native of Aix *(see pages 35–8)*.

Between the wars

Although thousands of soldiers conscripted from the south were killed in World War I, Provence was far from the battlefields of the north and remained unscathed. Post-war recovery was rapid. The period between the wars saw a boom in the tourist industry, particularly along the coast. In the 1920s and '30s Cannes and Nice became the playground for the rich and famous. The Scott Fitzgeralds, Noël Coward, Wallis Simpson, Gertrude Stein all made their mark on the Côte d'Azur, their hedonistic and liberal lifestyles centred on the casinos, jazz clubs, villas and outdoor pools. Sunbathing had been famously introduced by Coco Chanel, and the first nudist colony opened on the Ile de Levant. With the introduction of paid holidays in 1936, the south of France was no longer the preserve of the rich. French workers began flocking to the south, many of them to see the sea for the first time.

Provence continued to flourish as a centre of the avant-garde. Matisse, Picasso, Le Corbusier and other cutting-edge artists and architects continued to find inspiration here.

World War II

The Depression and World War II brought this carefree period to an end. Occupation by Italy in 1940 was followed by German occupation in 1942–3. When the Allies landed in North Africa in the winter of 1942, the Germans marched on Toulon and Marseille. Eager to get in on the deal, the Italians took over the Côte

d'Azur. After the collapse of the Italian regime ten months later, the Germans took possession of the entire area. The Provençals were swept into the thick of things. Those who had not already been conscripted into the French army banded into fierce local Resistance groups. Particularly active in the mountainous regions, their guerrilla tactics brought relentless reprisals from the occupying forces. Meanwhile, the US Air Force began to mount counter-attacks against the Germans, causing additional damage to once peaceful towns and destroying many historical monuments.

Finally, General de Lattre de Tassigny's 1st French and General Patch's 7th US armies

landed on the Dramont beaches just east of St-Raphaël on 15 August 1944. By 15 September, most of Provence had been freed from the occupying forces, and by April the following year, the enemy had been totally eliminated.

Post-war Provence

Glamour and optimism returned to the Riviera soon after the war. The first international film festival at Cannes in 1946 delivered Hollywood to the sunny Mediterranean shores, as the arrival of the likes of Clark Gable, Humphrey Bogart and Rita Hayworth heralded a return to the star-spangled tradition of the Côte d'Azur. Artists and writers continued to take up residence in

LEFT: La Croisette, Cannes, in the 1920s.
RIGHT: an Allied soldier and local demoiselle.

the area. Picasso moved to Antibes in 1946 and spent the rest of his life in Provence. Parisian bohemian stars like Juliette Greco and the writer Françoise Sagan followed in the footsteps of Colette and Anaïs Nin, and basked in the simple, sunny pleasures of the the little port of St-Tropez. By the late '50s, with the arrival of the bikini and the Brigitte Bardot phenomenon, the quiet fishing village had been transformed into a "metropolis of illicit pleasures".

Until the war Provence's economy had been almost entirely based on agriculture. After the war, farmers were encouraged to modernise their operations. The small-scale Provençal farms tried to adapt, going into debt to invest in modern machinery, but without any form of government support many were unable to survive. By the early 1980s only 10 percent of locals worked the land, compared to 35 percent 40 years earlier.

The 1960s were characterised by industrial expansion and the embracing of new technologies. The government pumped money into huge projects like Concorde and nuclear power. Hydroelectric plants were built on the banks of the Durance, and the area around the Berre Lagoon was turned into a huge petrochemical zone and industrial port with tanker docks and oil refineries. The traditional jobs of boat-building and fishing available to the locals were replaced by less interesting jobs in the industrial plants.

In 1969 the high-tech Sophia Antipolis Science Park, north of Cannes, was inaugurated. Hailed as Europe's answer to California's Silicon Valley, this centre for new technologies has been expanding steadily since its foundation. It now has 1,100 companies occupying an area a quarter the size of Paris, and is one of the most sought after business locations in Europe. More traditional heavy industry continues on more than 7,000 hectares bordering on the port of Marseille and Fos, which remains the country's main chemical and petrochemical centre.

Immigration and the far right

Following the creation of the Fifth Republic, General de Gaulle, its first president, set about tackling the unrest in the French colonies, negotiating independence with Algeria in 1962. Algerian independence was followed by a wave of immigrants from North Africa. Tens of thousands of *pieds noirs* (literally "black feet") – French settlers from Algeria – flooded into France, many settling in the large southern cities like Marseille and Nice. A steady flow of immigrant workers (legal and illegal) from the former colonies added to the ethnic mix.

With economic recession and growing unemployment at the end of the 20th century, the extreme right Front National party gained enormous popularity in the region among those less than content with the growth of a multi-ethnic society. Its xenophobic leader, Jean-Marie Le Pen, was not born in Provence, nor does he embody any particularly Provençal

ET DIEU... CRÉA LA FEMME

SCANDALOUS

Political scandals are part of life in Provence. Most infamous was Jacques Médecin, mayor of Nice from 1965 to 1990, who was imprisoned for financial corruption. Throughout the region, mayors and public officials have been indicted and imprisoned for underworld dealings. Hyères became known as the "Chicago of the Côte" after a series of bomb attacks and the assassination of a local official campaigning against corruption. The mayor of Cannes was brought to trial over a casino scandal, and the mayor of Fréjus was investigated for financial irregularities. In 2005 officials in Nice were accused of accepting bribes for contracts on the new tramway.

attributes, and yet he has found a remarkably large following in the region. The Front National polled 22 percent in 2004, and the riots across France the following November, which errupted in Nice and Marseille, added fuel to the xenophobia, but it also showed how difficult the immigrant population has found it to integrate. There are significant Muslim communities in towns across the region.

The 21st century

It has taken a while for Provence, which for so long has been deeply rooted in agricultural life, to come to terms with modernisation. However, prosperity in the region is now

region have boomed, and plans are under way to extend the track to Nice.

Tourism continues to dominate the economy. An increase in the number of low-cost flights is bringing more and more visitors to Provence – and not just to the big cities and coast. The more rural, further-flung corners are attracting increasing numbers of tourists looking to escape the crowds. The rural economy is experiencing a significant boost, with foreigners buying and renovating run-down farmhouses and other properties. Whole villages have been rejuvenated as a result of well-to-do British and German tourists buying holiday homes in the countryside, while multimillionaires, particu-

growing, and unemployment continues to fall. The European Fund for Regional Development is currently involved in supporting scores of minor rural enterprises and agricultural projects which benefit the regional economy. The TGV has been extended to Avignon, Nîmes, Marseille and Aix-en-Provence, making Provence only a comfortable three-hour journey from Paris. Property prices in the

larly Russian oligarchs, have pushed up prices so dramatically in the Côte d'Azur that a lot of old French money is moving out.

But Provence continues to be the most popular holiday spot for the French themselves. They make up 80 percent of the 34 million visitors who bring 10 billion euros to the region's economy and account for 11 percent of its GDP. Such an influx obviously creates ecological problems, both on land and in the sea. Global warming brings the increased risk of annual fires, and many tourist attractions, especially hiking trails, are now closed during high-risk periods, but by and large the region continues to look after its visitors very successfully. ❑

LEFT: Roger Vadim's *And God Created Woman*, shot the director's then wife, Brigitte Bardot, to fame.
ABOVE: the opening years of the 21st century were marked by natural disasters, as swathes of Provence were ravaged by floods and forest fires.

Decisive Dates

Pre-Roman and Gallo-Roman era

c.1 million BC Earliest evidence of humans in Provence in the Vallée des Merveilles, Monaco.
1800 BC Ligurians occupy Mediterranean coast.
600 BC Marseille is founded by Greek traders.
121 BC The Romans conquer southern Gaul and establish Aquae Sextiae (Aix-en-Provence).
102 BC The Romans defeat invading Germans.
58–51 BC Subjugation of Gaul by Julius Caesar.
27 BC–AD 14 Reign of Caesar Augustus. Provence begins to flourish.
AD 12 Romans occupy the settlement at Vaison.

AD 19 Construction of the Pont du Gard.
AD 3rd–5th centuries Christianity spreads.
395 Arles becomes the administrative capital of the western provinces (Gaul).
476 Fall of the Western Roman Empire. Vandals, Visigoths, Burgundians, Ostrogoths and Franks invade the coastal zones.

The Middle Ages

8th–10th centuries Provence becomes part of the Carolingian Empire. Arabs from the Iberian peninsula invade and settle by the coast, staying for 200 years until expelled by Guillaume le Libérateur.
1096–9 The First Crusade.
1032 Provence annexed to the Holy Roman Empire.
1178 Frederick I (Barbarossa) is crowned king of Provence in Arles.
1246 Provence becomes part of the Angevin dynasty through marriage.
1248 Louis IX embarks on the Seventh Crusade.
1274 Comtat-Venaissin (east of Avignon) is ceded to the pope.

The Renaissance

1308 The Genoese Grimaldi family acquires Monaco.
1309 Clement V of France given the papal crown.
1316 Pope John XXII moves papacy to Avignon.
1320 Carpentras is made capital of the region.
1348 Pope Clement VI buys Avignon. Plague strikes.
1377 The papacy returns to Rome.
1388 Eastern Provence (the Comté de Nice) falls under the rule of the House of Savoy (Italy).
1409 The University of Aix is founded.
1471 Good King René (1434–80) moves to Aix.
1482 Charles du Maine hands Provence over to the king of France.
1501 The founding of the parliament in Aix.
1503 Nostradamus born in St-Rémy-de-Provence.
1545 Massacre of the Vaudois.
1539 French replaces Provençal as the official language.
1545 Destruction of Protestant villages in the Luberon during the Wars of Religion.
1598 Under the Edict of Nantes, the Huguenots are granted the right to worship in freedom, ending the Wars of Religion.
1577 First soap factory is founded in Marseille.
1685 The Edict of Nantes is revoked, and thousands of Huguenots emigrate.
1691 The French conquer Nice, but the town is handed back to Savoy in 1715 after the Spanish War of Succession.
1718 Nice becomes part of Sardinia.
1720 Plague spreads from Marseille into Provence and more than 100,000 people die.

The Revolution and Napoleon

1789 The storming of the Bastille.
1790 Provence is divided into three *départements*: Basse-Alpes, Bouches-du-Rhône and Var.
1791 France annexes both Avignon and the Comtat-Venaissin.
1793 End of the siege of Toulon, which sparks Napoleon Bonaparte's rise to glory.

The Belle Epoque

1815 End of the Napoleonic Wars; the English aristocracy begins to winter in the south of France.
1830 Frédéric Mistral, Provençal champion and poet laureate, is born at Maillane near Avignon.
1834 Lord Brougham settles in Cannes and the south French coast becomes the preferred winter residence of the English nobility.
1839 Cézanne is born in Aix-en-Provence.
1854 Mistral founds the Félibrige, a cultural association to promote the Provençal language.
1860 Nice is returned to France.
1863 Monte Carlo casino opens its doors.
1869 The Suez Canal opens, and Marseille gains in importance as a Mediterranean port.
1887 The term Côte d'Azur is coined by the writer Stephen Liégeard.
1888 Van Gogh settles in Arles.
1892 Paul Signac moves to St-Tropez.
1906 Renoir settles in Cagnes.
1924 F. Scott and Zelda Fitzgerald visit the Riviera.
1925 The writer Colette moves to St-Tropez. Coco Chanel visits the Côte d'Azur.
1928 Jean Médecin becomes mayor of Nice. The Médecin dynasty rules Nice for 62 years.
1929 Monaco holds its first Grand Prix.
1936 Introduction of the paid holiday in France.

World War II

1939 The Cannes Film Festival is inaugurated but the onset of World War II causes the first festival to be delayed until 1946.
1940 Italians occupy Alpes Maritimes.
1942 German troops occupy southern France.
1944 The Allies land between Toulon and Esterel on 15 August. Toulon and Nice recaptured.

Tourism booms

From 1945 Mass tourism. The coastal strip is no longer a playground for the rich and famous only.
1946 First Cannes Film Festival. Picasso in Antibes.
1952 Le Corbusier's now iconic housing block, the so-called "Cité Radieuse", is built in Marseille.
1956 Fairy-tale marriage of American film star Grace Kelly to Prince Rainier III of Monaco. Brigitte Bardot hits St-Tropez, starring in the film *And God Created Woman*.
1960 Opening of the dam at Serre-Ponçon.
1962 Many French Algerians settle in Provence

after the Algerian war of independence.
1964 The Fondation Maeght art gallery opens.
1966 Jacques Médecin succeeds his father as mayor of Nice.
1969 Sophia Antipolis Science Park is founded.
1972 The Provence-Alpes-Côte d'Azur region is created with reorganisation of local government.
1975 Opening of the dam at Sainte-Croix.
1982 Princess Grace of Monaco dies in a car crash.
1990 Jacques Médecin, mayor of Nice for 25 years, flees to Uruguay to avoid trial for corruption.
1992 Floods in Vaison cause havoc.
1994 Jacques Médecin returns to face trial and serves two years of a three-and-a-half-year sentence. In 1998 he dies of a heart attack in Uruguay.

1995 Jacques Chirac elected president.
1998 France wins the World Cup.
1999 The Front National is split by internal feuding and an extreme-right breakaway party forms.
2001 High-speed TGV rail network reaches Marseille, cutting journey times to the Riviera.
2002 The euro replaces the French franc. Chirac is re-elected president.
2003 Heatwave and fatal forest fires create major problems for the region.
2005 Prince Rainier of Monaco dies, Prince Albert II enthroned. French voters reject EU constitution. Avignon and Nice affected in nationwide riots.
2006 The planned TGV link Marseille–Toulon–Nice is confirmed. ❑

LEFT: Roman arch, Orange.
RIGHT: anti-racist march on the streets of Marseille.

ARTISTS IN PROVENCE

**"The whole future of art is to be found in southern France,"
Van Gogh told Gauguin. He was right. With such intense
light, inspirational landscapes and azure bays,
no other part of the world has had such
a dramatic effect on modern art**

Our image of Provence has been largely created by modern artists, and they in turn have given the history of modern art a distinctly southern flavour. Familiar images include Cézanne's *Mont Ste-Victoire*, Van Gogh's tortured olive trees, Picasso's nymphs and sea urchins, the iron tracery of Matisse's balconies and Bonnard's red-tiled roofs and palm trees, seen through an open window.

Today Provence and the Côte d'Azur are among the best places in the world to see modern art in the setting in which it was created, to enjoy still the sensual pleasures and luminous light that inspired Cézanne, Van Gogh, Matisse and Picasso, and also to see many of the masterpieces that resulted.

Van Gogh

Vincent Van Gogh (1853–90) was one of the first artists to be inspired by the intense bleached light and brilliant colours of the south. Today his image and work are slapped on everything from wine bottles to ash trays, but few people wanted to know him when he arrived in Arles in 1888 at the age of 35. Yet this was where, in just three years, all his great paintings were executed. Here he found a power and vitality that inspired him almost beyond endurance.

"The Midi fires the senses, your hand is more agile, your eye sharper, your brain clearer..." he wrote in one of his many letters to his brother, Theo. Interiors, sunflowers, irises, night skies and the harvest fields all

LEFT: *Café Terrace, Place du Forum, Arles*, by Van Gogh, 1888. **RIGHT:** Renoir painting in his garden, *c.*1910.

charged his brush with colour – "The olive trees look like silver, at times bluer, at times greener, bronze-coloured, whitening on a soil that is yellow, purple or orange pink or even deep ochre red."

Van Gogh had been painting for only six years before he arrived in Arles. He was born in the Netherlands, the son of a Protestant pastor, and although he began work as an art dealer, he became obsessed with evangelical Christianity. Determined to become a preacher, he spent a year living in poverty in a mining community in Holland. Slowly the inspiration to paint took over, and after training in Antwerp, he went to Paris where Theo worked as an art dealer at Goupil & Cie. Inspired by what he saw of the Impressionists, he then headed for Provence and immediately began working furiously. Wanting to share his experience, he wrote to his friend Paul Gauguin, saying "The whole future of art is to be found in southern France."

In preparation for Gauguin's arrival, he rented four rooms in the Yellow House at 2 Place Lamartine in Arles as a studio and began painting sunflowers. Impoverished, his health was deteriorating and he was drinking excessively. When Gauguin arrived he found Vincent impossible to tolerate and they fell out. This was the cause of Van Gogh slicing off part of his ear lobe, which he wrapped in newspaper and gave to a prostitute in the local brothel, asking her to keep it safely.

A series of mental breakdowns followed as epilepsy and syphilis took their toll, exacerbated by heavy drinking and a meagre diet. Finally he entered the Asylum for the Alienated in St-Rémy-de-Provence, and although he suffered further breakdowns, he continued to paint, producing more than 150 works, among them some of his best paintings. He then travelled to Auvers-sur-Oise just outside Paris to consult a physician recommended by Pissarro. Here he ended his life by shooting himself, even though by this time he was

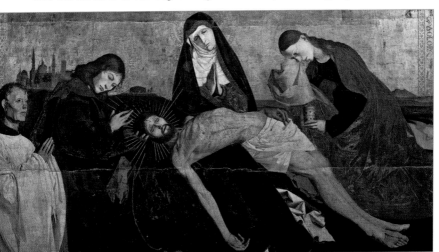

THE SCHOOLS OF AVIGNON AND NICE

The patronage of the papal palace helped to establish a school of Avignon painters led by Simone Martini of Siena, who arrived in 1335, and his successor Matteo de Giovanetti from Viterbo. They worked on the palace and in surrounding secular buildings, and some of their frescos can still be seen. One of the finest works to emerge from the school is the *Avignon Pietà* (1457) by Enguerrand Charonton, now in the Louvre. Nicolas Froment (1435–86), another member of the Avignon school, was court painter to Good King René. He came from northern France where, he had been a follower of Jan van Eyck, and both he and Charonton are credited with infusing Flemish naturalism into

French art. Froment's major surviving work is the triptych in the cathedral of St-Sauveur in Aix, which depicts René in the left-hand panel.

In the 15th and 16th centuries a painting school flourished in the county of Nice, where many churches and even the humblest chapels were decorated with murals. The school's principal painter was Louis Bréa (1450–1523), the "Provençal Fra Angelico", who provided the altarpiece for Monaco cathedral and three fine works for the Franciscan monastery in Cimiez. His work can also be seen in the main church in Grasse, where that town's own painter, Jean-Honoré Fragonard, is also represented.

becoming appreciated as a major talent. The only original Van Gogh to be seen in Provence is in Avignon, but around the Asylum *(see page 124)* you can follow a trail to see the scenes that he painted. The landscape that inspired him remains largely unchanged, and it is hard to see it all without being moved by his spirit.

Cézanne and Braque

Although many painters came to Provence, one of the most famous was born there. Paul Cézanne (1839–1906) was the son of a banker from Aix-en-Provence, where he went to college with his friend the novelist Emile Zola.

lived until his death in 1906. He painted the Provençal landscape, the gnarled olive trees and lavender terraces, and countless versions of his beloved Mont Ste-Victoire, determined to capture the structure of nature on canvas. "To paint a landscape well", he wrote, "I must first discover its geological characteristics."

You can tour around Mont Ste-Victoire, which was declared an international treasure by UNESCO in 1993 and, in Aix, visit Cézanne's atelier *(see page 117)* as well as the Musée Granet *(see page 117)*, which shows eight of his works including *Les Baigneurs (The Bathers)*.

Cézanne was highly influential. His paintings of the bay and sea at l'Estaque, just out-

In spite of a desire to paint he struggled for a while to become his father's successor. Eventually his family realised that it would be better to allow him to pursue his painting, and in 1863 he went to join Zola in Paris. Once there, Cézanne's distaste for the "old school" led to his association with the revolutionary group of painters now known as the Impressionists. But he eventually went his own way, believing that the Impressionists' work lacked an understanding of the "depth of reality".

In 1870 Cézanne returned to Aix, where he

LEFT: *Avignon Pietà*, by Enguerrand Charonton, 1457.
ABOVE: *Mont Ste-Victoire*, by Cézanne, 1900.

side Marseille, inspired Georges Braque (1882–1963) to visit the port in homage to the master. The Cubist's key painting *Les Maisons de l'Estaque (Houses at l'Estaque*, 1908) was the result. Although the port is now overwhelmed by industry, the little houses that were transformed into revolutionary blocks and planes of colour can still be seen.

Renoir

The Impressionists came to Provence and the Côte d'Azur, fascinated by what Claude Monet (1840–1926) described as "the glaring, festive light", which made colours so intense that he claimed no one would believe that they were real. In 1883 Monet brought Pierre Auguste Renoir (1841–1919) on his first visit to the area; Renoir returned increasingly often to paint the filtered golden light, the olive trees and the soft terracotta roofs that are characteristic of Provençal villages.

Suffering from arthritis, he settled in the south for his health, buying up a 500-year-old olive grove and building a house, Les Colettes, there for his family. This proved the ideal setting for Renoir's final period; he had a glassed-in studio built among the olive trees, with curtains to control the light, providing a perfect solution to the choice between working from nature and in a studio. He even found

the strength, with the help of an assistant, to sculpt. "Under this sun you have a desire to see marble or bronze Venuses among the foliage," he said. And here among the olives you can still see his bronze *Venus Victrix*. Today Les Colettes is a museum *(see page 240)*, surrounded by the magnificent shady olive grove. Inside the house are 10 original paintings as well as the master's studio, with chair, easel and palette just as he left them.

Picasso and his influence

The south of France belongs in large part to Pablo Picasso (1881–1973), and nowhere is his presence more palpable than the Musée

THE APPEAL OF ST-TROPEZ

Although many of the ports and coastal towns beyond Marseille, such as Toulon, la Ciotat, Cassis and Hyères, became favoured destinations for artists, St-Tropez had the greatest pull. Paul Signac (1863–1935), a keen sailor, was one of the first artists to move here, although the place was then only accessible by sea. In 1892 he bought a villa just outside St-Tropez, which at that time was no more than a tiny fishing port. He invited many of his fellow artists, including Georges Seurat (1859–91), Maurice Utrillo (1883–1955), André Derain (1880–1954) and Raoul Dufy (1877–1953), who all painted the little harbour, the ochre cottages and the shimmering sea. Henri Matisse

visited Signac in St-Tropez in 1904, producing his own experiment with pointillism – *Luxe, Calme et Volupté (Luxury, Calm and Delight)* – and the liberation from traditional techniques that led him to Fauvism. In 1909 Pierre Bonnard (1867–1947) also rented a villa in St-Tropez. He too was stunned: "Suddenly I was hit with a Thousand and One Nights; the sea, the yellow walls, the reflections which were as brightly coloured as the lights..."

The work of many of these artists, including Signac's *St-Tropez au Soleil Couchant (St-Tropez at Sunset)* and Matisse's *La Gitane (The Gypsy)*, is on show at the Musée de l'Annonciade in St-Tropez *(see page 197)*.

Picasso *(see page 238)* in Antibes. Here a glittering sea reflects strong sunlight into the windows of the chateau, providing a superb backdrop for the sculptures on the terrace.

Picasso's love affair with the Riviera began in 1920, when he spent the summer in Juan-les-Pins, and he was a frequent visitor to the coast over the following summers. When World War II broke out in 1939, he was in Antibes, painting *Pêche de Nuit à Antibes (Night Fishing at Antibes)*, a luminous nocturnal seascape inspired by watching the fishermen and their boats illuminated by white acetylene lamps. The painter returned to Antibes in 1946 with Françoise Gilot, whom

> ### MATISSE ON NICE
>
> "What made me stay are the great coloured reflections of January, the luminosity of daylight."

collection that includes paintings, drawings, sculpture, engravings and ceramics. The Musée Grimaldi also has the largest collection of work by Nicolas de Staël, as well as works by César, Yves Klein and Joan Miró.

In Vallauris Picasso single-handedly revived the town's pottery industry. In Cannes he painted the *Las Meninas* series (1957), after Velázquez's painting of the Spanish court. The pleasure he took in the environment is partic-

he had met in 1943, and he was given the Grimaldi Palace to use as a studio.

After the grim war years in Paris, Picasso was inspired by the light, colour and antiquity of the Mediterranean; his nymphs, centaurs, goats, sea urchins and monumental women running on the beach have a pagan innocence that expresses the inspiration the painter derived from the hard shadows and bright colours of sea, beach and mountains. These paintings and drawings resulted in a major work, *Joie de Vivre (Joy of Life)*, the gem of a

ularly evident in the wonderful dove paintings, *Els Colomins* (1957), which feature exuberant yellows and oranges with views of turquoise sea and black-and-purple palm trees.

Droves of painters followed in Picasso's footsteps, including Fernand Léger (1881–1955), whose interest in developing large architectural ceramic sculpture and murals attracted him to Biot *(see page 239)*, which, along with Vallauris, became the centre of a revival of ceramic art. Shortly before Léger died in 1955 he bought a plot of land just outside Biot on which to build a studio, and his wife subsequently created the Musée National Fernand Léger *(see page 239)* to

LEFT: *The Harbour at St-Tropez,* by Paul Signac, *c.*1905. **ABOVE:** Picasso's *Joy of Life,* 1946.

house his personal collection. Its exterior is dominated by his massive, brilliantly coloured ceramic panels.

Matisse

Henri Matisse (1869–1954) spent much of his life on the Côte d'Azur, eventually settling in Nice. For a year he lived in the Hôtel Beau Rivage, painting the great sweeping bay of the Promenade des Anglais fringed with palm trees, and then bought an apartment on the Place Charles Félix, where he painted his famous *odalisques* – harem slaves – framed by shuttered windows and flowers, capturing forever the voluptuous ease of the Riviera.

One of the most moving examples of his work is the Chapelle du Rosaire *(see page 208)*, just outside Vence, an exquisite blue-and-white chapel designed and decorated by Matisse at the end of his life, when he was unwell. The tiled roof, the blue-and-yellow stained glass, and the appliquéd vestments are all a poignant testimony to the artist's genius. He once observed that if there was a heaven, he would want it to be "a Paradise where I paint frescos". In the Cimiez area of Nice is the Musée Matisse *(see page 230)*, which houses his personal collection. The museum has works from every period of Matisse's working life, as well as the vases, mask, pots, shell furniture, Moroccan wall hangings and even the giant cheese plant that he so often included in his paintings.

Chagall, Dufy and Cocteau

The Russian artist Marc Chagall (1887–1985) settled on the Côte d'Azur towards the end of his career, finding inspiration in the light and colour of the south. The Musée Chagall in Nice *(see page 229)* is home to the largest collection of Chagall's work; it was built to house his masterpiece, *Message Biblique (Biblical Message)*. Many local churches, including the cathedral in Vence, feature his mosaics.

Raoul Dufy (1877–1953) often came to the south of France, and his sensual paintings convey the delights of the region – the food, wine, palm trees and grand hotels – perhaps more than those of any other artist.

Jean Cocteau (1889–1963) was another frequent visitor, both to the grand villas of St-Jean-Cap-Ferrat and to the seedy sailors' bars of Villefranche-sur-Mer. In Villefranche, the candy-coloured Chapelle St-Pierre has an interior designed by Cocteau, and Menton has the Musée Jean Cocteau *(see page 249)*, which houses self-portraits, abstracts, the *Inamorati (Lovers)* painting series, mosaic floors and tiling by the artist. Also in Menton is the Salle des Mariages, which he decorated with murals. It's a seriously recherché wedding location.

Nouveaux Réalistes and beyond

In the 1950s Nice produced its own school of artists, the Nouveaux Réalistes. They are well represented at the Musée d'Art Moderne et d'Art Contemporain in Nice, and include Yves Klein (1928–62), Arman (1928–2005), Martial Raysse (b.1936), all from Nice, and César (1921–98), born in Marseille. These artists' fascination with everyday material surfaces, packaging and industrial waste is evident in Arman's transparent containers packed with trash and flock of birds created from pliers. There are many works by Klein, who took the inspiration of the Riviera to its limit with his startling blue paint IKB (International Klein Blue). The Fluxus artist Ben (b.1935), whose 1985 piece *Il y a Trop d'Art (There is Too Much Art)* is reproduced all over Nice, may have a point. ❏

LEFT: Jean Cocteau seated by one of his paintings.

Architecture

The terracotta earth colours, the rich ochres that can be seen in such variety around the town of Roussillon, give Provence its civilised and inviting air. From the drystone bories at Gordes to abbeys, farms and city mansions, this earthy hue gives Provence its architectural richness.

It was the Romans who set the building style. Nowhere outside Italy is there such a collection of Roman remains – arenas, theatres, temples, cemeteries and triumphal arches depicting abject, naked Gauls in chains. Even from this distance we can see how their power was made obvious through their buildings, through the great gladiatorial arenas at Nîmes and Arles, the theatre at Orange and, most significantly, the astonishing Pont du Gard. The Romans invented the arch, and nowhere can its function be better appreciated than in the three tiers that support this vast aqueduct.

For their roofs, the Romans used tiles made of clay moulded over the tilers' thighs, and this shape is still used today, giving towns and villages their overarching appeal. Planning laws continue to insist that all new houses have these terracotta roofs, pitched at 30 degrees.

Farmhouses (*mas* in Provençal) have changed little since Roman times. Built against the heat and the cruel mistral wind, their walls are thick, their windows small and shuttered.

From the Romans' rounded arches and barrel vaults came Romanesque, the style of medieval church architecture that combines spaciousness with bulk. Great ecclesiastic buildings were established in this style, some in secluded surroundings like the Abbaye du Thoronet. Others were highly ornamented; the figures on the façade of Saint-Trophime in Arles and the abbey church of St-Gilles-du-Gard are exquisite examples.

A Renaissance flair embellishes the streets of many *villages perchés,* fortified

hill towns, where from the late 16th century mansions were built side by side, often in streets too narrow to be able to appreciate them properly. An additional flourish was the ironwork belltower, a speciality of Provence. Castles, too, such as Château Grimaldi and the Palais des Papes at Avignon, were built in, or adapted to, the Renaissance style.

Grand town houses in the 17th and 18th centuries were built where life prospered, notably in the Cours Mirabeau in Aix. In less sympathy with the townscapes were the 19th-century neoclassical manor houses, but the Belle Epoque

set a new pace with a lavish casino and splendid hotels in Monaco and the Côte d'Azur where the rich came to play with their fantasy homes.

Modern architecture begins with Le Corbusier and his Unité d'Habitation in Marseille. Courageous leaps of the imagination are rare in a region where strict planning laws aim to keep the townscapes as visitors like them. But Norman Foster, famous for his Viaduc de Millau in neighbouring Languedoc, has snuck in with a glass art gallery in Nîmes, and the world's largest museum of prehistory in the Gorges du Verdon. ❑

RIGHT: grand-scale buildings: the Pont du Gard aqueduct and Le Corbusier's Unité d'Habitation.

PROVENÇAL CUISINE

The secret to Provençal cooking, one of the simplest, yet most flavoursome of French cuisines, is its total reliance on fresh natural ingredients and the fragrant herbs that are so abundant in this fertile region

I f there's one thing that truly distinguishes Provençal cuisine it's the sheer wealth and variety of local produce. To get an idea of what's best at the moment, head to one of the region's food markets *(see Best Markets, page 7)*, where you'll find countless varieties of tomatoes, different colours and shapes of courgettes, bundles of purple artichokes, cherries, Cavaillon melons and figs in summer, wild mushrooms, pumpkins and even truffles in winter, as well as appealing displays of cheeses, sausages, oils and much more.

The magic ingredients

The real essence of Provençal cuisine is based on simplicity and quality, the respect for seasonal produce and recipes that maximise individual flavours, and an emphasis on vegetables and fish that are perfectly adapted to today's demands for healthy eating.

Cooking here is characterised by the use of olive oil – with none of the rich butter and cream sauces of northern France – and herbs. This may be a *herbes de Provence* mix (various combinations of rosemary, thyme, marjoram, sage, savory and bay leaves) but is often just a single herb chosen to go with a specific ingredient: *daurade* (sea bream) or *loup de mer* (sea bass) baked with fennel, rabbit or lamb roasted with rosemary, a meaty *daube* infused with thyme and bay leaves, chicken roast with whole heads of garlic, even crème brûlée flavoured with lavender.

LEFT: putting the finishing touches on a bouillabaisse.
RIGHT: ripe and juicy summer fruits.

If many restaurants, especially tourist-oriented ones, continue to perpetuate age-old recipes, a new generation of young chefs is also revitalising southern cuisine, intelligently dusting off old recipes, experimenting with new techniques and foreign influences.

A cornucopia of vegetables

Tomatoes, aubergines, courgettes, onions and peppers all get into the classic Provençal ratatouille. Elsewhere one vegetable is privileged: *tomates à la provençale* are simply tomatoes halved horizontally, topped with a sprinkling of chopped garlic and breadcrumbs, and baked in a slow oven until succulent and almost caramel sweet. Red peppers are grilled and served cold marinated in olive oil. Small purple artichokes are braised *à la barigoule*, or sliced thinly and served raw dressed with olive oil and lemon. Courgettes and aubergines are baked as *tians*, gratins named after the rectangular earthenware dish in which they are cooked. A speciality of Nice are the *petits farcis* – assorted vegetables each with their own stuffing (variants on rice, leftover meat and onion bound with egg or bread), served lukewarm as a starter, legacy of a long frugal tradition of using up leftovers.

A hearty rustic speciality found around Grasse and St-Paul-de-Vence is *lou fassum*,

cabbage stuffed with a mixture of sausage meat, rice, swiss chard and onion and boiled in a *fassumier*, a sort of cotton net, to hold it together. More refined are courgette flowers, either stuffed or dipped in egg and deep fried.

A variety of *crudités* (chopped raw vegetables) might be served with an *anchoïade* or *bagna caouda*, to be dipped in a warm anchovy, garlic and olive oil sauce, while all sorts of vegetables accompany the *grand aioli*, the classic Friday feast of salt cod, whelks and lashings of garlic mayonnaise.

Today's chefs make the most of this vegetable bounty. For a tomato tartare, Reine Sammut of La Fenière in the Luberon uses no

THE OLIVE

The Phocaeans are believed to have introduced the olive tree to Provence around 600 BC, and harvesting and milling methods have changed little since then. Whole olives are milled and repeatedly pressed, producing about a litre (1¾ pints) of oil per 5 kg (11 lb) of fruit. Only the results of initial pressings may be called virgin oils (look for "huile d'olive extra vièrge, première pression à froid" on the label). The cooking qualities and health benefits of this precious golden liquid have made it one of Provence's most prized exports. Varying from pale gold to deep green in colour, some olive oils are produced from just one variety of olive, others are blends of several varieties.

The main production areas with their own *appellation contrôlée* are in the Alpilles around Les Baux-de-Provence, in the Alpes-Maritimes around Grasse and Opio and around Sospel, near Aix-en-Provence, around Nîmes, and at Nyons in the southern Drôme. With the harvest beginning at the end of September, pressing generally takes place between November and February, but many of the area's mills and co-operatives have shops open all year round. Table olives are rinsed and soaked in lye (a brine solution), then stored for up to a year prior to consumption, to be served with aperitifs, pounded into purées and *tapenades*, cooked in stews or baked in bread.

less than six different varieties of tomato grown in her own vegetable garden. She describes her cooking as "a cuisine of love and tolerance".

Fish and shellfish

Ugly *rascasse* (scorpion fish), tiny *girelle* (wrasse), *rouget de roche* (red mullet) and silvery *congre* (conger eel) are just some of the *poissons de roche* (literally "rock fish") that hide in the shadows of the indented Mediterranean coastline, caught at night from the little wooden boats called *pointus*. In Marseille, locals jostle for position and are prepared to pay high prices for the still flapping fresh fish

the Côte Bleue west of Marseille and mussels cultivated in the bay of Toulon. Today the region's top restaurants often reserve the best of the artisanal catch, but overfishing of the Mediterranean means that much of the fish served in restaurants may well come from Brittany or the Channel ports.

At its best, fish may be simply chargrilled at a beach-side restaurant – the waiter will often present a basket of fresh fish for you to select the one you like the look of, which will then be paid for by weight. Other preparations include sea bream stuffed with fennel, red mullet cooked with basil or fish baked *à la provençale* (with white wine and tomatoes).

at the daily fish market on the Vieux Port. In towns such as Beaulieu-sur-Mer, where the fishing fleet caters to at least a dozen restaurants, the competition is fierce; restaurant chefs position themselves on the quays to get the pick of the night's catch.

Other species include prized *loup de mer*, *daurade* and its cousins *pagre*, *pageot* and *sarde*, or shoals of sardines and anchovies. Shellfish include *langouste* (spiny lobster), little crabs, sea urchins collected by divers off

LEFT: olives and tomatoes, cornerstones of Provençal cuisine; stuffed courgette flowers.
ABOVE: catch of the day, Marseille.

BOUILLABAISSE

Bouillabaisse is *the* dish of Marseille, and you'll find it all along the Riviera coast. Several types of fish (in particular gurnard, scorpion fish, john dory and conger eel) are simmered with onion, leek, tomatoes and saffron, with mussels and potatoes added just before the end. It is traditionally served in two courses, first the broth accompanied by *rouille*, toasted baguette and grated cheese, then the pieces of fish and potatoes.

Originally a humble dish made by fishermen from the leftovers of the catch they couldn't sell, bouillabaisse is now a luxurious – and expensive – dish; be prepared to fork out at least €45 for a good one *(see page 100)*.

The New Southern Chefs

A generation of new young chefs in their twenties and thirties are revitalising southern cooking. Chefs like Alain Llorca, Lionel Levy, inventive young Finn Journi Tourmanen at the tiny Atelier du Goût in Nice, Christophe Petra at Le Sud in Le Lavandou or Edouard Loubet in the Luberon. Some might follow the back-to-nature approach of forgotten vegetables and the search for authentic, seasonal produce. Others are not afraid to bring in the scientific techniques of molecular cuisine,

with its foams, jellies and suspensions inspired by Ferran Adria and Pierre Gagnaire, to Mediterranean ingredients, or to show off their talents with a wealth of daring and even witty preparations.

A native of Cannes, Alain Llorca took over the weighty legacy of Roger Vergé at the Moulin des Mougins in 2004, after presiding at Le Chantecler at the Negresco in Nice, and has quickly stamped his own identity on the place. As well as cleverly reworking Provençal cuisine, he also brings in memories of his Catalan grandfather, such as a "Catalan-style" salad of white cocoa beans with chorizo, mussels and

fish or a brilliant langoustine "paella". Llorca's trademark is the "ronde de tapas", a series of eleven small tasting dishes, which might include a pot-au-feu jelly or chip mousse. Alain Llorca works with his brother Jean-Michel, who is responsible for the excellent desserts. He experiments with low-sugar and low-butter concoctions, and creates exotic fruit and coconut combinations alongside wickedly childlike caramel chocolate bars.

Lionel Levy opened his Marseille restaurant, Une Table au Sud *(see page 111)*, in 1999, after working as Alain Ducasse's number two at Parisian world food pioneer Spoon, Food & Wine. Levy is part of the new generation of chefs who have struck out on their own. He is also an active member of the young chefs' movement Génération C, championed by exclusive foodie magazine *Omnivore*, which is seeking to defossilise French cuisine. His cooking is light, creative and fun. While inspired by his adopted home Marseille, elements of his native southwest creep in, such as *espelette* pepper, foie gras or *piperade*. Sometimes surprising associations might include a foie gras crème brûlée, grey mullet and ginger crumble, or a dessert of strawberry and black olive tart. The technique is impeccable, but the style of the restaurant has also adapted to today's lifestyles, with contemporary setting and an atmosphere that is convivial and relaxed.

At La Bastide de Moustiers, up in the mountainous Gorges du Verdon, another Alain Ducasse protégé, Eric Santalucia, relies heavily on his own kitchen garden to produce dishes that are at once rustic and refined, such as his translucent ravioli – delicate skeins of fresh herbs sandwiched between wafer-thin pasta. Edouard Loubet at the Bastide de Capelongue also focuses on local produce. Along with other leading chefs, he has rediscovered *épeautre*, a wild wheat grown on the Sault plateau at the foot of Mont Ventoux, and incorporates it into his inspired recipes along with wild herbs and flowers picked in the meadows. ❏

LEFT: Alain Llorca, the inventive chef who combines Provençal and Catalan influences.

Two dishes that involve much heated debate are the bouillabaisse of Marseille *(see box on page 45)* and the fish soup of Nice. A first-rate *soupe de poisson* can take hours to prepare. Traditionally, the fish is crushed, then hung in linen sheets from the kitchen's rafters to squeeze out the rich juice. Nowadays, the sheet is often replaced by a sieve that presses the juice out more efficiently.

Meat and game

Provence's quintessential meat dish is the *daube de boeuf*, chunks of beef marinated overnight in red wine and cooked slowly with bay leaves, thyme and a twist of orange peel

Provence, where *transhumance*, the twice-yearly moving of the flocks between summer and winter grazing, is still an important ritual, and its tough mountain lifestyle gives lean meat with an incomparable herby flavour. Another widely used meat is rabbit, simply baked with herbs or stewed with white wine, tomatoes and herbs. Then there are plentiful terrines and *caillettes*, round patties of minced pork and chopped chard or spinach leaves.

Départemental differences

Within the region, different *départements* or even different villages proudly cling on to their own specialities. The cuisine of Nice

until it is a deep, almost black colour; in Avignon, it is more usually made with lamb, and in Nice, the leftovers go to stuff ravioli. The rustic dish of *alouettes sans têtes* are not the headless skylarks the name might suggest but beef or veal olives – slices of meat stuffed and rolled up. In the Camargue and nearby Nîmes and Arles you'll find *viande de taureau*, the meat of the area's little black bulls, grilled as steaks or on skewers or stewed with wine and olives as *gardiane de boeuf*. The best lamb comes from Sisteron in the Alpes de Haute-

reflects its Italian past. Here you'll find gnocchi, pasta and ravioli – which the Niçois like to claim originated here – typically filled with rich, meaty *daube de boeuf*, and the street snacks of *socca* and *pissaladière (see page 227)*. Another Niçois speciality is *estocaficada* (stockfish), made from dried cod, soaked in water for several days, then cooked with onions, leeks and tomatoes. In Nîmes, *brandade* is a speciality; salt cod is soaked and then beaten up into a purée with lashings of olive oil and a little milk and served piping hot, often with croûtes, while *pieds et paquets* is a dish typical of Marseille: stuffed sheep's tripe stewed with sheep's feet.

ABOVE: the *transhumance*, when thousands of sheep are herded through St-Rémy to summer pastures.

Cheese, fruit and desserts

Provence is not a major dairy region, but along with the familiar French cheeses you will find local cheeses mainly made from goat's or sheep's milk. Banon, produced in the mountains around Forcalquier, is easily recognisable: the creamy goat's cheese is wrapped in a chestnut leaf, which gives it a distinctive tangy flavour. Other goat's cheeses vary from moist fresh cheeses eaten a few days after they are made to mature, hard *crottins*; they may be rolled in herbs or marinated in olive oil.

Brousse is a soft, ricotta-like fresh cheese made from goat's or sheep's milk depending on the season, the best coming from Rove near

Marseille, which is stirred into soups or sweetened with honey and nuts for dessert.

Desserts – served after the cheese course in France – make the most of the region's wonderful fruit. St-Tropez's Tarte Tropezienne is a rich patisserie comprising brioche filled with vanilla cream and strawberries or raspberries. Menton's lemons go into lemon tart, with or without a meringue topping. In late summer fresh figs come into their own, to accompany cheese or ham, stewed or baked in gratins. And as well as tarts and jams, all sorts of fruits are made into sweet treats, from the candied fruits of Apt and *calissons* of Aix to the marrons glacés of Collobrières.

As for crêpes Suzette – crêpes flambéed in orange liqueur and named in honour of 19th-century actress Suzanne Reichenberg, a mistress of the Prince of Wales – they supposedly arose from a culinary mishap at the Café de Paris in Monte-Carlo: a face-saving exercise when famous chef Auguste Escoffier (or one of his kitchen boys) accidentally set a crêpe on fire.

Destination restaurants

In small villages the best place to eat may well serve as shop, newsagent and tobacconist as well as restaurant, but still be packed with diners hungry for genuine home cooking and a taste of local gossip. In recent years, there has been a trend for top chefs to open less expensive annexes. Globe-trotting chef-entrepreneur Alain Ducasse is at the head of an empire that includes the renowned Louis XV at the Hôtel de Paris in Monte-Carlo, but also his simpler (yet highly sophisticated) country inns, the Bastide de Moustiers, Abbaye de la Celle and Domaine des Andéols, not forgetting summer Bar et Boeuf (sea bass and beef) at the Sporting Club in Monte-Carlo and Spoon Byblos in St-Tropez. Others who have opened less formal offshoots include Bruno Cirino of the Hostellerie de Jérôme in La Turbie, who recently took over the village café, giving a top chef's touch to inexpensive, traditional fare, and Reine Sammut of La Fenière in Lourmarin, who has opened the trendy, cosmopolitan La Passage in Aix-en-Provence, while the Pourcel twins of Montpellier have one of their Compagnie des Comptoirs offshoots in Avignon.

For the best restaurants you may have to book weeks ahead; even for simpler places it's generally worth ringing up ahead, especially in high season, to check if there's a table. It's often easier to get a table at lunch than dinner, and lunch can also be a good time to sample a top chef's style for a fraction of the price by night, as many offer excellent-value lunch menus.

Lunch is generally served from around noon to 2pm. After 2pm, you may find it difficult to get served, except in cafés and brasseries. Dinner is served from around 8pm to 9.30pm, and often later in big cities and trendy resorts, with some brasseries staying open until 1 or 2am. ❑

LEFT: a generous selection of local cheeses.

Regional Wines

Vines were introduced to Provence by the Phocaeans when they established trading posts up the Rhône valley some 2,600 years ago. The high-living Avignon papacy gave winemaking a further boost when it established its vineyards around its summer residences at Châteauneuf-du-Pape and in the Luberon. Today, most of the wines in the Vaucluse and Bouches du Rhône fall within the numerous appellations of the southern Côtes du Rhône. These include the illustrious, full-bodied reds of Châteauneuf-du-Pape, grown on flat pebble-covered terrains and made from a complex variety of grape *cépages*, dominated by syrah, mourvèdre and cinsault. Other wines grown around Orange include Gigondas, Vacqueyras, Rasteau, Lirac and Côtes du Ventoux, while further south you'll find the Côtes du Luberon, Coteaux de Pierrevert and Costières de Nîmes. Lesser wines will often come under the Côtes du Rhône and Côtes du Rhône Villages labels. Look out also for the rarer but highly regarded white Châteauneuf-du-Pape, the rosés of Tavel and the golden-coloured, sweet white dessert wines of Beaumes-de-Venise, made with the tiny muscat grape.

The wines of Les Baux-de-Provence have a growing reputation. Cultivated by a dozen or so *vignerons* in tiny vineyards scattered around the white limestone Alpilles hills beneath Les Baux, most are produced according to organic or even biodynamic principles, a holistic philosophy that involves the whole ecological system and the phases of the moon and planets; red wines have an appellation AOC Les Baux-de-Provence, white wines come under the neighbouring Coteaux d'Aix-en-Provence label. The white wines of Cassis, east of Marseille, are perfect for drinking with fish or shellfish at one of the restaurants that line Cassis's harbour.

In the Var, by far the largest Riviera appellation is the Côtes de Provence, principally producing vast amounts of easily quaffable dry rosés, that go well with eating out in the hot climate, but also small quantities of white and some good-quality reds. The main vineyards are concentrated around La Londe-des-Maures, around Ramatuelle on the St-Tropez peninsula, where they grow virtually up to the sea, and inland around Les Arcs-sur-Argens and Draguignan. Further west, you'll find the Coteaux Varois around Brignoles and the St-Baume massif. Bandol, produced in eight communes around the seaside resort of Bandol, is the *département*'s most prestigious appellation, notably for its excellent though pricey reds, made using the mourvèdre grape, the best

of which can be kept for several years, unlike the drink-young rosés. The only wine appellation in the Alpes-Maritimes *département* is the ancient but tiny Bellet appellation outside Nice, with just 60 hectares of precariously sloped vineyards under cultivation, producing white, red and rosé wines.

Another famous Provençal tipple is pastis – a strong aniseed-flavoured spirit, which was created in Marseille in the 1930s. Pastis is served with ice and a carafe of water for mixing – when the clear yellow liquid turns cloudy – and is stereotypically enjoyed by elderly male boules players on hot Sunday afternoons. ❏

RIGHT: bottles of golden Beaumes-de-Venise, a fine dessert wine.

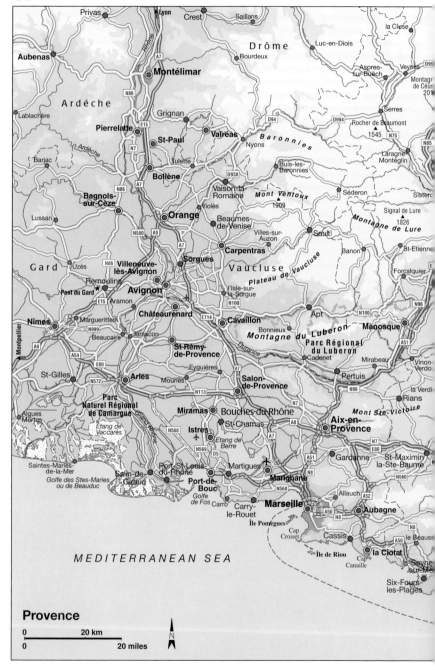

Provence

0	20 km
0	20 miles

N

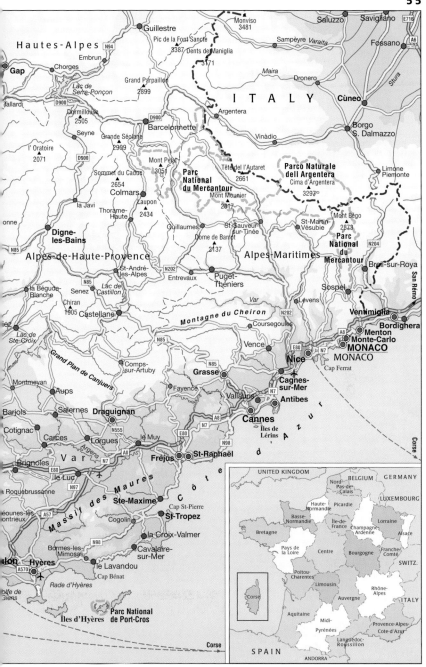

Guillestre
Pic de la Font Sancte
3387 Dents de Maniglia
3171
Monviso
3481
Saluzzo
Savigliano
E716

Hautes-Alpes **N94**
Embrun
Chorges
Gap
Maira
Dronero
Sampèyre *Varaita*
Fossano **A6**
Stura

Grand Parpaillon
2899
Lac de
Serre-Ponçon
Tallard
D900

I T A L Y
Cùneo

Dormillouse
2505
D900
D900
Barcelonnette
Argentera
Vinàdio
Borgo
S. Dalmazzo

Seyne
Grande Séolane
2909
Mont Pelat
3051
D900
l' Oratoire
2071

Sommet du Caduc
2654
**Parc
National
du Mercantour**
Tête del l'Autaret
2661
**Parco Naturale
dell Argentera**
Cima d'Argentera
3297
Limone
Piemonte

Colmars
la Javie
Laupon
2434
Mont Mounier
2817
Thorame-
Haute
onne

**Digne-
les-Bains**
Guillaumes
St-Sauveur-
sur-Tinée
Dôme de Barrot
2137
St-Martin-
Vésubie
Mont Bégo
2873
**Parc
National
du
Mercantour**
N204

Alpes-de-Haute-Provence
St-André-
les-Alpes
N202
Entrevaux
Puget-
Théniers
Alpes-Maritimes
Breil-sur-Roya

N85
Senez
Lac de
Castillon
Var
Lévens
Sospel
San Rémo

la Bégude-
Blanche
Chiran
1905 Castellane
Montagne du Cheiron
Courségoules
N202
Ventimiglia
Bordighera

iez
Lac de
Ste-Croix
Vence
E80
Nice
Menton
Monte-Carlo
MONACO
A8
N7
MONACO

Montmeyan
Grand Plan de Canjuers
Comps-
sur-Artuby
N85
Grasse
**Cagnes-
sur-Mer**
Cap Ferrat

Aups
Fayence
Vallauris
N7
Antibes

Bariols
Salernes
Draguignan
N555
A8
Cannes
Îles de
Lérins

Cotignac
Carces
Lorgues
le Muy
A8
E80
N7
N98
St-Raphaël
Corse

Brignoles
E80
N7
A8
Argens
Fréjus
d' *Azur*

le Luc
N97
Ste-Maxime
Côte

Roquebrussanne
A57
Massif des Maures
Cap St-Pierre
St-Tropez

éoures-les-
ontrieux
Cogolin
la Croix-Valmer

lon
Hyères
A570
Bormes-les-
Mimosas
N98
le Lavandou
Cavalaire-
sur-Mer
Cap Bénat

Rade d'Hyères

olfe de
iens
**Parc National
de Port-Cros**
Îles d'Hyères

Corse

V a r

UNITED KINGDOM
BELGIUM GERMANY
Nord-
Pas-de-
Calais
LUXEMBOURG
Haute-
Normandie Picardie
Basse-
Normandie
Île-de-
France
Champagne-
Ardenne
Lorraine
Alsace
Bretagne
Pays de
la Loire
Centre
Bourgogne
Franche-
Comté
SWITZ.
Poitou-
Charentes
Corse
Limousin
Auvergne
Rhône-
Alpes
ITALY
Aquitaine
Midi-
Pyrénées
Provence-
Alpes-
Côte d'Azur
Languedoc-
Roussillon
SPAIN
ANDORRA

PLACES

In this detailed guide to the region, the principal sites
are cross-referenced by numbers to the maps.
A supplementary touring map inside the back cover
describes eight scenic routes through the region

This guide covers the south of France from the delta of the River Rhône to the Italian border. Most of this falls within the modern administrative region of Provence-Alpes-Côte d'Azur (commonly abbreviated to PACA), and it includes the *départements* of Alpes de Haute-Provence, Alpes-Maritimes, Bouches-du-Rhône, the Var and the Vaucluse. It also sneaks across the Rhône into the Gard *département* in order to take in Nîmes, for without this glorious Roman city and its extraordinary aqueduct, the story of Provence would be incomplete.

The vigour with which Provence clings to its traditions means that each region has a distinct flavour, a landscape, a speciality that makes you know at once where you are. In the Camargue you will find bullfights to remind you of Spain, in Nice you will eat socca pizza to make you think of Italy; in Avignon you will feel yourself on the world stage in the papal palace; in Les Baux you will hear lute strings in the wind and imagine troubadours of medieval times.

Getting around is no problem. Motorways swoop through the region, as does the high-speed TGV, but there are also local buses and trains. You don't need a car if you make a city a base of your visit, but you might consider hiring one for a day or two, as driving through the hills is a wonderful motoring experience. At every twist and turn the landscape changes, villages come and go, vistas open and close; the extraordinary light moves through ilex, oak, the silver olive and dark cypress, and the heady scrub of lavender and rock roses, thyme and rosemary intermingle with the rich ochres and glinting granites of this harmonious land. The landscape is clearly labelled: Van Gogh's sunflowers, Cézanne's Mount Ste-Victoire, Picasso's Antibes, Matisse's Nice. The familiarity adds comfort to a sense of well-being. Stop for roadside water melons, peaches, honey, pots, to have a drink or to watch an unfolding game of *pétanque*. Or take to the road and follow any or all of the routes on the enclosed touring map.

On the Côte d'Azur the Corniches are the famous coastal roads, famous now for their summer traffic. If you are lazing you might not want to stray far from the beach, but prefer instead to read about what else can be seen in Provence – places to save up for another trip. ❏

PRECEDING PAGES: classic landscapes: lavender and sunflowers in bloom.
LEFT: café terrace in the picturesque hill village of Gordes.

AVIGNON

Contained within a ring of perfectly preserved walls, Avignon's architectural wealth is a legacy of its papal rulers. But Avignon is no staid and dusty museum city. It is as proud of its contemporary cultural scene as its history, and a thriving student population, plus the world-famous July festival, keep things lively

trategically situated at the confluence of the Rhône and Durance rivers, the medieval city of Avignon glowers behind the serrated teeth of its city walls. It was first established by the early Gauls as a tribal capital, and it was known to the Greek traders of Marseille. During the Roman period, however, it became overshadowed by Orange and Arles.

Avignon's moment of glory came in the 14th century, when French-born Pope Clement V fled to France in 1309 to escape the papal power struggles in Rome, eventually settling in Avignon. It was the start of 70 years of the "second Babylonian captivity of the Church", which saw the city ruling Christendom under nine successive popes (see box page 62).

Avignon's 4.3-km (2½-mile) fortifications still enclose its inner core. A walk around these ramparts, which are broken up by 39 towers and seven gates, reveals a cornucopia of historic buildings, churches and palaces. The French writer Rabelais called Avignon "la ville sonnante" because of the number of steeples that adorned its skyline. Less poetic are the views of the modern suburbs which fan outwards from under the shadow of the wall. This is where the majority of the city's 90,000 inhabitants live.

Orientation

It's best to explore the town centre on foot, leaving your car outside the ramparts or in one of the car parks by the Palais des Papes or Place Pie. If you are coming by train, the main station is at the Porte de la République, south of the centre.

From the station, the tree-lined cours Jean Jaurès and its continuation, the rue de la République, divide the town through the middle, leading into the **place de l'Horloge**, a lively brasserie-filled square sitting roughly

Map on page 60

LEFT: Le Pont St-Bénézet – the Pont d'Avignon of nursery-rhyme fame.
BELOW: the Palais des Papes, seen from across the Rhône.

on the site of the original Roman
forum. On it stand the **Hôtel de
Ville** with its Jacquemart Tower and
the ornate **Théâtre Municipal**.

Behind the square, the **Palais des
Papes** looms over a large sloping
square, while the **Jardin des Doms**
crowns the rocky promontory that
saw Avignon's Neolithic beginnings.

To the west of rue de la République, the circular sweep of **rue
Joseph Vernet** contains Avignon's
smartest shops, along with the Musée
Calvet and other mansions housing
trendy restaurants. At the southern
end of the street, towards the Rhône,
is a quiet district with antiques shops
and the venerable **Hôtel de l'Europe**
on place de Crillon.

To the east, towards place Pie and
place St-Didier, is an area of ancient
narrow streets, many of which contain often crumbling former noble
residences. **Place Pie** is home to the
city's covered market (every morning except Monday), topped by an

unsightly multi-storey car park – partially disguised by a "vegetal wall"
by botanist Patrick Blanc. Many of
the town's chefs come here to stock
up. Further east towards the Porte St-
Lazare lies the **university quarter**.

Home of the papacy

As the local saying goes, all roads
lead to the **Palais des Papes** Ⓐ
(Papal Palace; place du Palais; open
daily summer 9am–7pm, winter
9.30am–5.45pm; admission charge;
tel: 04 90 27 50 74; www.palais-des-
papes.com), the monumental symbol
of papal Provence. The original city
walls, which were built by popes
Innocent VI and Urban V, were not
strong enough to ward off attack by
the bands of wandering knights that
plagued the countryside, so the palace
was designed to double as a fortress.

Step through the **Porte des Cham-
peaux** and into the **Cour d'Honneur**
and you get an instant sense of the
palace as a city within a city. It's a

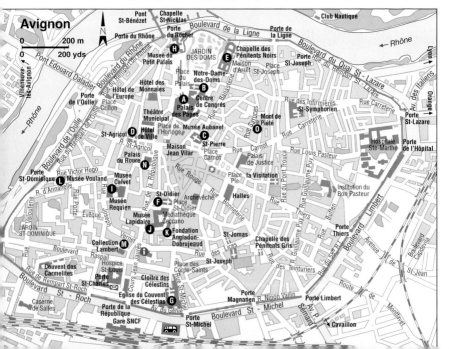

veritable labyrinth of vaulted halls, echoing assembly rooms, small chapels and narrow staircases, illustrating the palace's multiple functions as residence, place of worship, fortress and administrative centre.

The palace is divided into two sections: the "old" palace (**Palais Vieux**), built by Pope Benedict XII between 1334 and 1342, and the "new" palace (**Palais Neuf**), begun under Benedict's successor, Pope Clement VI, and completed in 1348. The old palace has a monastic simplicity and austerity that reflect the minimalist tastes of Benedict XII. The new palace, on the other hand, is brightly decorated with elaborate frescos and flamboyant ceilings, the hallmarks of Clement VI, patron of the arts and lover of the high life.

The first rooms, beginning with the **Grande Trésorie**, present the history of the building and some of the papal bulls and other artefacts discovered here. Frescos by the Sienese artist Simone Martini, originally from Notre-Dame-des-Doms, now hang in the **Salle du Consistoire**, where the pope held assemblies with his cardinals or received kings and ambassadors. The sheer size of the vaulted **Grande Audience** and **Grande Chapelle** is awe-inspiring. The ornately decorated **Chambre du Pape** and **Chambre du Cerf**, where you can feast your eyes on the frescos painted by Matteo Giovanetti in 1343, reveal the sumptuous tastes of Clement VI. These lively scenes of hunting, fishing, falconry and youths picking fruit and bathing give valuable insight into life at the papal court during the 14th century.

Around the place du Palais

In contrast to the grand Palais des Papes, Avignon's cathedral, **Notre-Dame-des-Doms** ❸ (open daily 8am–6pm), is a more sombre affair. This 12th-century building has undergone many structural changes over the years, but despite the 19th-century addition of a gilded Madonna to the tower, it retains its original spiritual simplicity.

Across the place du Palais is the lavishly sculpted façade of the **Hôtel des Monnaies** (the old mint), home

Ringed with appealing pavement cafés, Avignon's main square, the place de l'Horloge, is a hub of social activity. It is named after the 14th-century Gothic Tour de l'Horloge, the last remnant of the original town hall.

BELOW: the Palais des Papes.

to the municipal music school, while
at the north end of the square, the former bishops' palace contains the
Musée du Petit Palais (see page 63).

Rising behind the cathedral overlooking the Rhône is the **Jardin des
Doms**, site of the earliest settlement
of Avignon. A vineyard was planted
here at the end of the 1990s, sym-
bolising Avignon's status as capital
of the Côtes du Rhône wines.

City of churches

Several other edifices testify to the
wealth and power of the Church. A
couple of streets south of the Palais
des Papes stands the **Eglise St-
Pierre**  (open Thur 2–5pm, Fri–
Sat 2–6.30pm) with its pyramidal
spire, flamboyant Gothic façade and
carved walnut doors. Just west of
the place de l'Horloge, the **Eglise
St-Agricol** (open Sat 4–5pm) is
another fine Gothic church.

The richly decorated interior of
the **Chapelle des Pénitents Noirs**
(open Sat 2–5pm, plus Fri in summer) on rue de la Banasterie is rarely
open, but worth a detour to see the
façade, which has an exquisite

sculpted relief of cherubs emerging
from clouds bearing the head of
John the Baptist on a dish – the
emblem of this charitable brotherhood which tended prisoners sen-
tenced to death and the mentally ill.

Consecrated in 1359, the **Eglise
St-Didier** (open daily 8am–6.30pm)
owes much of its elegant clean-
lined appeal to the influence of Pope
Benedict XII. The first chapel contains an early Renaissance work by
Francesco Laurana entitled *The Way
of the Cross*. Another notable feature
is the imposing Gothic pulpit standing in the centre of the church.

On place des Corps-Saints stands
the unfinished **Eglise du Couvent
des Célestins** – the apse and
transept were completed but the
nave was hurriedly truncated and
shored up at the end. In summer the
square is filled with café terraces.

East of here, picturesque **rue des
Teinturiers** was once the dyers'
street supplying local weavers, and is
lined with mill wheels along a branch
of the River Sorgues that flows down
one side. At No. 8, the **Chapelle des
Pénitents Gris** (open daily 3.30–

The Papal Legacy

In 1348 pope Clement VI bought Avignon from Jeanne, countess
of Provence. The popes built not only the massive Palais des
Papes; they also built cardinals' palaces, enlarged churches and
gave the city an extensive new set of city walls. A lavish court grew
up and cultural life flourished around the poet Petrarch and
painters such as Matteo Giovanetti and Simone Martini. From
1378, during the Great Schism there were two popes – one in
Rome, and one the "anti-pope" in Avignon – the last, Benedict XIII
(or Benoît XIII), was besieged in the Palais des Papes for five years
before escaping one night in 1403.

Even after the popes had eventually returned to Rome, Avignon
retained its independent status ruled by a papal legate – along with
the nearby Comtat-Venaissin. The paper, publishing and textile
industries flourished, the city's prosperity seen in fine residences
put up in the 17th and 18th centuries. Avignon was reunited with
France only in 1791 after the French Revolution. It remained an
intellectual centre, where the Félibrige, the movement founded by
Mistral and like-minded poets to preserve the Provençal language,
printed its newspaper, *Aioli*.

5.30pm), which still belongs to a penitent order, has paintings by Parrocel and Nicolas Mignard.

Galleries and museums

Avignon has several good museums covering everything from archaeology to contemporary art. At the northern end of the place du Palais is the **Musée du Petit Palais** (open Wed–Mon 10am–1pm, 2–6pm; admission charge; tel: 04 90 86 44 58). The Gothic palace, built around 1318, later became the bishops' palace and was given an elegant Renaissance façade. Today it houses a superb collection of medieval and Italian Renaissance painting and sculpture, including a *Madonna and Child* by Botticelli.

Art and archaeology

The **Musée Calvet** (65 rue Joseph Vernet; open Wed–Mon 10am–1pm, 2–6pm; admission charge; tel: 04 90 86 33 84; www.fondation-calvet.org) is Avignon's museum of fine art, housed in a beautiful 18th-century mansion with a stunning forecourt paved in russet-coloured pebbles

from the Durance. Jacques-Louis David, Théodore Géricault, Eugène Delacroix, Camille Corot and Edouard Manet are just a few of the painters represented here. There is also a good modern section, showing work by Chaïm Soutine, Alfred Sisley, Albert Gleizes, Maurice Utrillo, Raoul Dufy and Camille Claudel.

The Musée Calvet's archaeological collection can be seen in the **Musée Lapidaire** (27 rue de la République; open Wed–Mon 10am–1pm, 2–6pm; admission charge; www.fondation-calvet.org), a former Jesuit chapel on the main street. The collection of Egyptian, Greek, Roman and Gallic antiquities includes carved sarcophagi, Roman glass, painted Greek vases and the 1st-century Tarasque de Noves, a statue of the mysterious amphibian beast that once terrorised the region.

Other museums in Avignon worth visiting include the **Fondation Angladon-Dubrujeaud** (5 rue Laboureur; open summer Tues–Sun 1–6pm, winter Wed–Sun 1–6pm; admission charge; tel: 04 90 82 29 03; www.angladon.com) with a fine

Map on page 60

TIP

Papalines, sweets made from chocolate filled with oregano liqueur, have been an Avignon delicacy since 1836. They can be found at most patisseries, but those from Mallard (13 rue des Marchands) are particularly reputed.

BELOW: rue des Teinturiers.

Avignon Festival

For three weeks each July since 1947, French theatre has migrated to the south of France. That was the year Jean Vilar of the Théâtre National Populaire first put on a production in the grandiose setting of the Cour d'Honneur in the Palais des Papes. Originally just three shows and an art exhibition, it marked the birth of the Avignon Festival. In the spirit of post-war idealism, Jean Vilar's ambition was to bring first-rate adventurous theatre to the people of the provinces. He remained festival director until 1971.

Sixty years on and Avignon Festival has become an unmissable rendezvous for the theatre world. While the Cour d'Honneur remains the most prestigious venue, the festival has expanded to numerous other theatres, churches, courtyards and schools, including the Théâtre Municipal and Cloître des Célestins, as well as some dramatic stone quarries outside town. Over the years it has seen actors like Gérard Philippe, Jeanne Moreau, Philippe Noiret, Michel Piccoli, Isabelle Huppert and Kristen Scott Thomas, directors like Ariane Mnouchkine and Matthias Langhoff, grand classics by Molière, Shakespeare, Brecht and Chekhov,

or revealed new playwrights like Olivier Py. In the late 1960s Maurice Béjart introduced contemporary dance, now an important element of the festival, for the first time.

How much it is still a festival for the people is a contentious issue. Debate rages as to the artistic quality and intended audience of the festival, now often accused of elitism, in a conflict between accessibiity and the highbrow avant-garde. In 2003 the festival was cancelled at the eleventh hour when the *intermittents du spectacle* (the union of performing artists and backstage staff) went on strike, spelling disaster not only for all those putting on shows but for the town's hotels and restaurants, which are usually fully booked at this time of year. The appointment of young directors Hortense Archambault and Vincent Baudriller in 2004, to be joined each year by a guest "associated artist", was intended to inject new blood but has proved controversial.

The festival reached an all-time artistic low in 2005, when several shows, reaching the limits of nudity, scatology, provocation or the plain absurd, were severely attacked by critics and booed or walked out of by the public. For its 60th edition in 2006, the Festival was back on a more moderate course, with the multi-talented Hungarian-born choreographer, director and artist Josef Nadj as guest artist, the arrival of new names like young Swiss director Stefan Kaegi and the return of veteran Peter Brooke, and a recentring of the festival's original focus on theatre.

Many of the people who flock to Avignon during the festival don't even come to see the official shows, but to absorb the atmosphere in the streets, pick up the thespian gossip in the cafés and catch some of the hundreds of productions in the "Off", the more anarchic fringe festival that has overtaken its mother in size. Any available space is taken over by street theatre, one-man comedy shows and radical plays. The Off is still a springboard for many young acts hoping to be discovered.

Avignon Festival: tel: 04 90 14 14 60; www.festival-avignon.com. Festival Off: tel: 04 90 25 24 30; www.avignon-off.org ❑

LEFT: dancers at the 60th Avignon Festival.

collection of 17th-century Dutch oils and furniture, and Post-Impressionist and modern French art. The only painting by Van Gogh in Provence, *Les Wagons du Chemin de Fer*, hangs alongside works by Modigliani, Cézanne, Picasso and Degas.

There are more decorative arts in the **Musée Louis Vouland** (17 rue Victor Hugo; open May–Oct Tues–Sat 10am–6pm, Sun 2–6pm, Nov–Apr 2–6pm; admission charge; tel: 04 90 86 03 79; www.vouland. com), set in a prim 19th-century villa. The contents, amassed by a wealthy industrialist, focus on fine 18th-century marquetry furniture, ormolu clocks, faience from Moustiers and Marseille and paintings by 19th-century regional artists.

Fans of contemporary art will delight in the cutting-edge **Collection Lambert** (Hôtel de Caumont, 5 rue Violette; open Tues–Sun 11am–6pm, daily 11am–7pm in July; admission charge; tel: 04 90 16 56 20; www.collectionlambert.com). The beautifully renovated 18th-century *hôtel particulier* alternates between a revolving display from the private collection of Paris art dealer Yvan Lambert, which includes such artists as Sol LeWitt, Jenny Holzer, On Kawara, Thomas Hirschhorn and Douglas Gordon, and temporary loan exhibitions.

Local history

The **Palais du Roure** (3 rue Collège du Roure; guided visits Tues 3pm or by appointment; tel: 04 90 80 80 88) contains a library and research centre of Provençal culture. Its eclectic display includes a collection of bells, Provençal furniture and costumes, the stagecoach which once transported Mistral and Daudet, and the printing press on which Mistral and Co. printed their journal *Aioli*.

Another oddity is the **Mont de Piété** (6 rue Saluces; open Mon–Fri 8.30–11.30am, 1.30–5pm; free; tel: 04 90 86 53 12), a charitable institution which functioned as the local pawnshop, offering credit to the city's poor. Its history is recounted in this small museum alongside an exhibition relating to the silk-conditioning industry.

The 17th-century Cloître St-Louis has been converted into an upmarket hotel with a modern extension by Jean Nouvel (www.cloitre-saint-louis.com). It also houses the Avignon Festival offices.

BELOW: inside the Musée Calvet.

Map on page 60

Both the Fort St-André and the Tour Philippe le Bel offer excellent views over the papal city. On a clear evening you can watch the mesmerising twilight colours, as the sun sets on Avignon's golden stone.

BELOW RIGHT: views from the Fort St-André.

Villeneuve-lès-Avignon

Away from the hustle and bustle of Avignon, on the west bank of the Rhône lies attractive **Villeneuve-lès-Avignon**. Much smaller than Avignon, Villeneuve nevertheless has a rich history of its own. The French king founded the town to keep a beady eye on what was going on in Provençal and later papal territory across the river. As the papal court increased in importance, the number of adjunct cardinals rose. Finding that Avignon had no more suitable space available, many of these cardinals chose to build their magnificent estates across the water in Villeneuve.

Towering over the town is the 14th-century **Fort St-André** (west tower open daily 10am–noon, 2–6pm, to 5pm in winter; admission charge), which guarded the frontier of France when Avignon was allied to the Holy Roman Empire. Inside the crenellated ramparts are the gardens of the **Abbaye St-André**, a restored Romanesque chapel, and the ruins of the 13th-century church (closed Jan and Mon; admission charge; tel: 04 90 25 55 95).

The isolated **Tour Philippe le Bel** was once the starting point of the Pont St-Bénézet *(see box below)*.

The **Chartreuse du Val de Bénédiction** (rue de la République; open daily Apr–Sept 9am–6.30pm, Oct–Mar 9.30am–5.30pm; admission charge; tel: 04 90 15 24 24; www.monum.fr) was founded in the mid-14th century by Pope Innocent VI (whose tomb lies in the adjacent church). A small vaulted chapel features beautiful frescos by Matteo Giovanetti. The Chartreuse now functions as a centre for playwrights.

The **Musée Pierre de Luxembourg** (rue de la République; closed Feb and Mon; admission charge; tel: 04 90 27 49 66) contains some wonderful works of art, including a carved ivory *Virgin and Child* and the *Coronation of the Virgin* (1453) by Enguerrand Quarton, which shows an exquisitely detailed medieval view of the world.

Just south of the museum is the 14th-century church of Notre-Dame, home to paintings by Mignard and Levieux, a fine 18th-century altarpiece and a 14th-century cloister. ❑

Sur le Pont d'Avignon

Immortalised in the popular children's song "Sur le pont d'Avignon", the Pont St-Bénézet *(pictured on page 58)* is one of the region's most famous landmarks. Hearing a voice from heaven, a young shepherd boy, Bénézet, left his mountains in the Ardèche and travelled to Avignon to build a bridge. At first the inhabitants mocked him, but when they saw him lift a massive rock and throw it into the river they were convinced that divine power was at work and helped to build the bridge in just eight years between 1177 and 1185. The bridge was destroyed a first time in 1226 during the Crusades and reconstructed in 1234. During the Avignon papacy, it provided a vital link between the town and the many cardinals who had chosen to live across the river in less-polluted Villeneuve. A chapel dedicated to St Nicholas, patron saint of sailors, was added on top of the Chapelle St-Bénézet, which stands halfway along the remaining structure. The Rhône's frequent floods took their toll, the town gradually gave up on costly maintenance, and the bridge collapsed bit by bit during the 17th century, leaving only four of its original 22 arches at the Avignon end and the lonely Tour Philippe le Bel on the far bank.

RESTAURANTS, BARS AND CAFÉS

Restaurants

Christian Etienne

10 rue de Mons. Tel: 04 90 86 16 50. Open: L & D Tues–Sat (daily in July). €€€€
www.christian-etienne.fr

Avignon's top chef is renowned for his creative cuisine using different varieties of tomato or épeautre (wild wheat) and saffron from Mont Ventoux. The setting is a splendid medieval residence with painted beams and frescoed walls niched behind the Palais des Papes.

La Compagnie des Comptoirs

83 rue Joseph Vernet. Tel: 04 90 85 99 04. Open: L & D Tues–Sat (daily in July). €€
www.lacompagniedes comptoirs.com

The trendy offshoot of the Pourcel twins of Montpellier is located in the cloister of a former Benedictine monastery. The cosmopolitan modern cooking, inspired by the concept of a French colonial trading post, spans the Mediterranean and Asia, and there's a lounge bar with DJs open in the evening.

L'Endroit

10 place Saboly. Tel: 04 90 82 15 15. Open: L Mon–Tues, Thur–Fri; D Thur–Tues. €€
A relaxed, friendly bistro serving refreshing modern fare where North African influences blend with Provençal flavours.

Pleasant pavement terrace.

L'Extramuros

44 boulevard St-Michel. Tel: 04 32 74 22 22. Open: L Mon–Fri, D daily. €
A trendy, recently opened address in an airily converted building just outside the city walls, serving steaks and other brasserie classics. Good cocktails and live jazz some evenings. Open until midnight.

La Fourchette

17 rue Racine. Tel: 04 90 85 20 93. Open: L & D Mon–Fri. €€
This cheerful bistro is a local favourite for its good-value gastronomic take on daube avignonnais, pieds et pacquets and other traditional Provençal specialities.

Hiely Lucullus

5 rue de la République (1st floor). Tel: 04 90 86 17 07. Open: L & D daily. €€€
www.hiely.net.
This Avignon institution changed management four years ago and has been revitalised in the hands of young chef Sébastien Giraud, whose beautifully prepared blend of modernity and Provençal tradition is one of the best deals in Avignon at the moment. Try dishes like duck fillet with artichokes and pesto or a gâteau d'agneau (lamb with aubergine). Charming old-fashioned service.

La Mirande

4 place de la Mirande. Tel: 04 90 14 20 20. Open: L daily, D Thur–Mon. €€€€
www.la-mirande.fr
A magnificent tapestry-hung dining room and summer terrace are the setting for grand classical cuisine inspired by seasonal local produce. The desserts are excellent, as is the wine list centred on Côtes du Rhône. On Tuesday and Wednesday evening there's a less formal table d'hôte served in the old kitchens. La Mirande also runs cookery courses hosted by some of the region's top chefs.

Numéro 75

75 rue Guillaume Puy. Tel: 04 90 27 16 00. Open: L & D Mon–Sat (daily during Avignon Festival). €€
www.numero75.fr
Another fine hôtel particulier – this one used to belong to the pastis-producing Pernod family – is now the place for modern Provençal and Med-wide cooking.

Piedoie

26 rue des Trois Faucons. Tel: 04 90 86 51 53. Open: L Tues, Thur–Sun, D Thur–Tues (daily in July). €€
www.piedoie.com
Chef Thierry Piedoie concentrates on keeping his market-inspired cooking light and well balanced at his small, serious restaurant near St-Didier. The lunch menu is a bargain. Quite formal service, modern paintings; wines from most of Côtes du Rhône.

Bars and Cafés

Place de l'Horloge and place des Corps-Saints are awash with café terraces. Trendy designer Opéra Café is the pick of the cafés on place de l'Horloge, either for a simple lunch or DJs by night, while Le Cid is a popular gay haunt. Other favourites include La Comédie on place Crillon, while an arty intellectual crowd frequents the La Manutention (4 rue Escaliers Ste-Anne) at the Utopia cinema, which is a sleekly designed café and salon de thé by day and provides more elaborate dining by night. Studeny bars congregate around rue Carnot, with the Red Zone popular for live music, salsa evenings and DJs.

ORANGE AND THE MONT VENTOUX

Bordered by the flat plains of the Rhône valley in the east and the windswept Mont Ventoux in the west, with the filigree peaks of the Dentelles de Montmirail in between, this picturesque corner of the Vaucluse is an easy place to while away the days

The northern Vaucluse stretches from the Rhône valley north of Avignon across the scenic peaks of the Dentelles de Montmirail to the bald summit of Mont Ventoux. There's plenty to see and do in this area, from exploring Roman remains and seeking out France's oldest synagogue to wine-tasting and hill-walking.

Capitals of the Comtat

As you approach **Châteauneuf-du-Pape ❶**, rows of green vines rise out of what looks like a pebbled beach on either side of the road. In fact, this land was once washed by the waters of the Rhône. The stones are said to radiate back the heat from the sun, thus "cooking" the grapes on the vine. This curious landscape marks the beginning of a wine-growing area of 55 vineyards all classified under the Châteauneuf-du-Pape *appellation (see box on page 71).*

Vines have been cultivated here since the days of the Avignon papacy (bottles bear the papal coat of arms). The town is named after the summer palace built by Pope John XXII in the 14th century. The **Château des Papes** is now a ruin. Its strategic importance led to its near total destruction in 1944, when German troops fought a scathing battle against Resistance forces. From the ruins, however, there are fine views over the tiled rooftops across the vineyards towards Avignon.

The **Musée des Vins** (Cave Brotte, place du Portail; open summer daily 9am–1pm, 2–7pm, winter 9am–noon, 2–6pm; free; tel: 04 90 83 70 07; www.brotte.com) is dedicated to the history and traditions of wine-making in the region. It also offers the opportunity to taste and buy a good selection of the local wine.

Like Châteauneuf-du-Pape, the market town of **Carpentras ❷** was

Map on page 70

LEFT: lavender fields, Sault. **BELOW:** walking through wine country.

St-Siffrein cathedral, Carpentras.

once part of the Comtat-Venaissin, the papal territory that roughly spanned the land between the Rhône, the Durance and Mont Ventoux. The peculiar mix of architectural styles – from Roman to rococo – reflects the town's history.

Before the Roman conquest, the settlement was tribal capital of the Celto-Ligurian Memini. The conquest itself is recorded in the carvings on the monumental gate in the courtyard of the **Palais de Justice**. By the 4th century, Carpentras had become a bishopric. Between 1320 and 1797 it was capital of the Comtat-Venaissin

and therefore part of the Holy See.

During the Middle Ages, a thriving Jewish community, known as the *juifs du pape* ("papal Jews"), enjoyed freedom of worship here. Behind the Hôtel de Ville, France's oldest **synagogue** (open Mon–Thur 10am–noon, 3–5pm, Fri 10am–noon, 3–4pm, closed Jewish holidays) is a testament to this singular period of religious tolerance. It was founded in 1367, but rebuilt in the 18th century when the prayer room was given its elegant interior. Sadly, the Jewish cemetery outside town was desecrated some years ago.

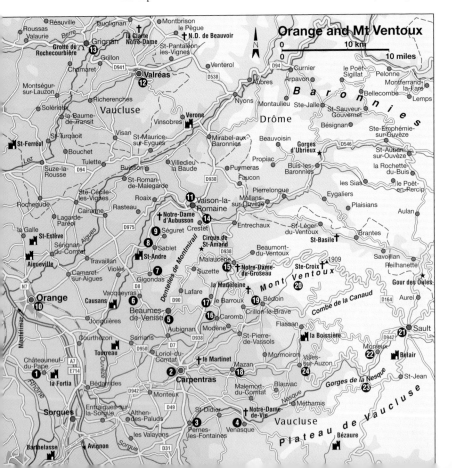

Further evidence of the Jewish presence can be seen in the 15th-century **Cathédrale St-Siffrein** in the centre of the old town. The south portal is known as the Porte Juive, probably because it was used by Jewish converts to Christianity.

One man who was less than tolerant of the Jewish population, however, was the Bishop d'Inguimbert. In the 18th century, he decreed that the Jewish community must remain segregated within their own ghetto. Intolerance aside, the bishop played a major role in the cultural and architectural development of Carpentras. He ordered the building of the rococo **Chapelle Notre-Dame-de-Sainte** and founded the **Hôtel-Dieu** in 1750. The well-preserved pharmacy of the former hospital is lined with faience jars and decorated with panels by court painter Duplessis. The rest of the building is being restored to house an ambitious new cultural centre (due to open in 2012), incorporating most of the town's museums.

Most notable among Carpentras's many museums is the **Musée Comtadin et Duplessis** (234 boulevard A. Durand; open summer Wed–Mon 10am–noon, 2–6pm, winter by appointment; admission charge; tel: 04 90 63 04 92). It covers the customs and history of the region and features works by Hyacinthe Rigaud, Joseph Vernet and local painters. Across the courtyard is the magnificent **library**, bequeathed by Bishop d'Inguimbert, which contains more than 150,000 volumes, including some rare editions of works by Petrarch.

The **Musée Sobirats** (rue du Collège; open summer Wed–Mon 10am–noon, 2–6pm, winter by appointment; admission charge; tel: 04 90 63 04 92) preserves the atmosphere and furnishings of an 18th-century mansion.

Every Friday, an excellent **market** takes over the town centre. Local specialities include strawberries and the stripy caramel sweets called *berlingots*, but Carpentras is most famous for its truffles *(see page 72)*.

Pernes and Venasque

Baking on the plain 6 km (4 miles) south of Carpentras, the lively little agricultural town of **Pernes-les-Fontaines** ❸ preceded Carpentras as

Map on page 70

👁 **TIP**

On 27 November, every year since 1525, Carpentras has celebrated the feast day of St Siffrein with the Foire St-Siffrein, a huge agricultural and craft market with hundreds of stalls selling local produce and hand-crafted goods. There's also a horse fair and the first truffle market of the season.

BELOW: Châteauneuf-du-Pape vines are planted amid heat-absorbing stones.

Châteauneuf-du-Pape

The vineyards of Châteauneuf-du-Pape are planted with 13 different grape varieties, predominantly Grenache, followed by Mourvèdre, Syrah and Cinsault. The best wines achieve their complexity and character from skilful blends of these grapes. The end product is a supple, warm and full-bodied wine that goes well with strongly flavoured dishes such as game and red meat and pungent cheese. The writer Alphonse Daudet (1840–97) praised Châteauneuf-du-Pape as "the king of wines and the wine of kings". This noble wine can be sampled at countless local vineyards that line the little lanes around here.

Black Diamonds

The Foire St-Siffrein on 27 November marks the start of the truffle season and augurs the weekly truffle auction held in Carpentras each Friday morning until March, near the Café de l'Univers on place Aristide Briand opposite the Hôtel-Dieu. The auction itself is a somewhat cloak-and-dagger affair. Sellers discreetly unveil their precious black treasures from jute sacks, and bidding starts promptly at 9am as chefs, merchants and conserveries compete to carry off the lots.

A delicacy prized by leading chefs – and in ancient times reputed to have aphrodisiac qualities – the pungent black truffle, known in Provence as the *rabasse* (also dubbed the "black diamond" or "black pearl of Carpentras") is the result of an unusual symbiosis between a tree, generally an oak, and the parasitic underground fungus *tuber melanosporum*, which lives on its roots. Although tuber melanosporum is also known as the truffle du Périgord, today 80 percent of French truffles come from southeast France, and of those 70 percent come from the Carpentras area. The Carpentras market serves as a reference to determine the

weekly rate per kilogram for the other truffle markets in the region, such as the Saturday market at Richerenches, the Tuesday market at Vaison-la-Romaine and the Wednesday market at Valréas.

Should you buy truffles yourself (there is also a small unregulated market for individuals), you are advised to keep them in olive oil or to store them with eggs in a closed box in the fridge, where they will help to perfume the eggs for a future *brouillard aux truffes* (scrambled egg with truffles).

Truffles were once so widespread that Parisians ate them as interval snacks at the opera, and even peasants could scoff them down as vegetables. But climate change and over-exploitation means that truffle yields have been declining in recent years.

The first conscious attempt to cultivate truffles – as opposed to simply finding them in appropriate woods – began in the 19th century with the deliberate planting of oak trees in suitably chalky soils. Today new research is attempting to work out how best to create the conditions for truffle cultivation. At Carpentras, the local agricultural college even offers courses in how to plant your own (hopefully) truffle-bearing oak.

Truffles often leave tell-tale rings in the ground under the trees where they might be found. But don't be tempted to go foraging for them yourself when out for a stroll in the country – truffle orchards are privately owned, and individuals pay high prices when truffle-collecting permits are auctioned every five years.

As to how truffle-hunting – or the art of *rabassage* – is done, both dogs and pigs have their fans. Pigs are the traditional method, as they will hunt truffles naturally, but they also adore eating them. Dogs have to be trained for the purpose, but are happier to give up their trophy in return for a piece of cheese.

The Office de Tourisme at Carpentras (place Aristide Briand, 84200 Carpentras; tel: 04 90 63 00 78; www.carpentras.fr) can provide information on truffle-hunting weekends, cookery courses and restaurants serving special truffle menus. ❏

LEFT: a truffle pig at work.

capital of the Comtat Venaissin from 1125 until 1320. With its ramparts and fortified gateways, it's like an Avignon in miniature. The town boasts a medieval tower, the **Tour Ferrande** (visits booked through the tourist office; tel: 04 90 61 31 04), decorated with vivid frescos depicting the victory of Charles II of Anjou over the Emperor Frederick II near Naples in 1266. But the most remarkable thing about Pernes is its multitude of sculpted fountains, most installed in the 18th century. Among the most beautiful of these is the "Gigot" next to the Tour Ferrande and the Cormoran by the covered market.

A few kilometres further up the Nesque River, perched on a rocky spur and bordered to the east by a dense forest, stands **Venasque ④**, the very first capital of the Comtat Venaissin and one of the prettiest villages in the region. From its strategic position, it offers commanding views of the Carpentras plain. At one end are the impressive remains of medieval **ramparts**. The other historic highlight here is **the baptistery** within the Eglise de Notre-Dame.

Founded in the 6th century and remodelled during the 11th, it is one of France's oldest religious buildings.

Wine villages

North of Carpentras, the D7 links a string of picturesque wine-producing villages. Take a short detour along the D90 to **Beaumes-de-Venise ⑤**, noted for its sweet white dessert wine made from the tiny Muscat grape, before heading to the hamlet of **Vacqueyras ⑥**, home of the troubadour Raimbaut de Vaqueiras, who died while on Crusade.

The beautiful medieval village of **Gigondas ⑦** has fragments of ramparts and numerous works of modern sculpture dotted around the streets. The best wines here fetch high prices, but there are still several lesser-known *caves de dégustation* where you can pick up a bottle or two without breaking the bank.

Continuing along the D7 will take you towards the prototypically Provençal village of **Sablet ⑧**, which in turn leads into **Séguret ⑨**. The latter is a charming village, with steep paved streets, an old gateway,

Venasque comes alive in early summer as a market centre for cherries grown in the surrounding area. It's particularly beautiful in spring when the cherry orchards are blossoming.

BELOW: drinking from one of Pernes-la-Fontaine's many fountains; out and about in Beaumes-de-Venise.

Nine scenic colour-coded wine routes cross the Côtes du Rhône wine region: the Azur route takes in vineyards and co-operatives around Avignon and Château-neuf-du-Pape, the Indigo route meanders between Orange and Vaison-la-Romaine west of the Ouvèze River, and the Tur-quoise route covers Beaumes-de-Venise and the Dentelles de Montmirail east of the Ouvèze River. www.vins-rhone.com

BELOW: the Dentelles de Montmirail.

a fountain, lavoir, belltower, Romanesque chapel and, high above the village, some castle ruins.

The sharp limestone peaks that frame the area are known as the **Dentelles de Montmirail**. The jagged forms that pierce the clear blue sky present an irresistible challenge to climbers. More accessible pathways through the hills make this an excellent area for gentle rambles through the surrounding pine and oak woods and stunning countryside.

Orange

Founded in around 35 BC by retirees of the Second Roman Legion, the historic town of **Orange** ❿ is famous for its two outstanding Roman monuments – the Arc de Triomphe and the Théâtre Antique (both UNESCO-listed heritage sites).

For centuries, Orange remained an independent principality, ruling over a domain about 12 km (7½ miles) from north to south and 25 km (15½ miles) east to west. By the 14th century, numerous religious foundations had been established, and the town had its own university. The city's name has nothing to do with the fruit but is a derivation of the town's Roman name *Arausio*. It was subsequently adopted by the Dutch royal family, the House of Nassau, who inherited the city in 1559 from the Chalon family (the Queen of Holland still bears the honorary title of Princess of Orange). The population of Orange was largely Protestant, making it a target during the Wars of Religion, when hundreds of Huguenots were massacred.

In the 1670s, when France was at war with Holland, ruled by William of Orange (later William III of England), Louis XIV ordered the destruction of the magnificent chateau built by Prince Maurice de Nassau in the 1620s on the hill behind the theatre. Its ruins in the **Colline St-Eutrope** now make for a pleasant strolling ground. Control of Orange was finally ceded to France in 1713 by the Treaty of Utrecht.

With a population of 28,000, Orange is a busy town all year round, and its proximity to the *autoroute* makes it a popular stopping-off point. However, its reputation has been

tarnished in recent years with the election of a Front National town council under mayor Jacques Bompard in 1995; re-elected in 2001, Bompard has since defected to the extreme-right MPF (Mouvement Pour la France) party.

Roman treasures

The magnificent **Arc de Triomphe** that once straddled the Via Agrippa between Lyon and Arles now stands at the centre of a roundabout north of Orange town centre. Erected in 21 BC, the decorative friezes and carvings of battle scenes, enslaved Gauls and naval equipment, celebrate Roman supremacy on land and sea.

At the heart of the town is Orange's other great Roman monument, the **Théâtre Antique** (open daily 9am–7pm, winter until 5pm; admission charge; tel: 04 90 51 17 60; www. theatre-antique.com). Built in the 1st century BC, it is the best-preserved theatre of the ancient world, and the only one in Europe with an intact stage wall. This is where the renowned Chorégies d'Orange opera festival and other cultural events are held *(see right)*. Time and the weather have taken their toll, but an ingenious new high-tech glass-and-steel roof erected in 2006 protects the theatre without putting pressure on the structure.

Housed in a fine 17th-century mansion, the **Musée Municipal** (rue Madeleine Foch; open daily; admission charge included with Théâtre Antique; tel: 04 90 51 17 60) sheds light on Roman goverment policy in Gaul. The collection includes fragments of a marble tablet on which land holdings were recorded in AD 77. This early form of land registry not only reveals what areas were settled but also to whom the better plots belonged, providing insight into early property ownership and social dynamics. The museum also contains a reconstructed atelier demonstrating how its famous indiennes fabrics were once manufactured here. The museum's art collection has portraits of members of the Royal House of Orange and some paintings by British artist Sir Frank Brangwyn.

Behind the museum the streets of the old town give way to some

Map on page 70

TIP

The Roman Theatre in Orange is the main venue of the acclaimed Chorégies d'Orange summer opera festival (www.choregies. asso.fr). Thanks to its intact stage wall, the acoustics are excellent, but don't forget to bring a cushion to a performance here, as the stone seats are hard and cold.

BELOW: the Théâtre Antique, Orange.

TIP

Epitomised in the 1950s *chanson* by Charles Trenet, the Route Nationale 7 was the mythic holiday road south between Paris and Menton before the construction of the motorway. Today it has its own museum at Piolenc, 6 km (4 miles) northwest of Orange (tel: 04 90 29 57 89; www.memoire nationale7.org).

BELOW RIGHT: the prayer room, Carpentras synagogue.

pretty squares and fine architecture. **Place Clemenceau** (often called place de la Mairie), home to the Thursday morning market, is graced by the handsome 17th-century Hôtel de Ville with its wrought-iron belfry and arcades and, near by, the restored **Cathédrale Notre-Dame**.

Vaison-la-Romaine

The Vaucluse's second great Roman town, **Vaison-la-Romaine** , was built on the east bank of the Ouvèze River, 28 km (17 miles) northeast of Orange. The modern town has developed around the Roman remains, while on the other side of the river sits the medieval Haute Ville (upper town). With the fall of the Roman Empire, the villagers no longer found it safe to live on the exposed river bank and retreated to the more easily defensible hill.

Two areas have been excavated. The upper site, known as the **Quartier Puymin** (open summer daily 9.30am–6.30pm; winter 10am–5pm, closed Jan; admission charge), is a pleasant park dotted with cypress trees and the excavations of several

Roman buildings, most notably the House of Laureled Apollo, where a marble head of Apollo was unearthed, the House of the Messii, a patrician villa, a colonnade known as Pompey's Portico and a nymphaeum. Reproductions of statues housed in the adjacent museum decorate the park's promenade.

The **Musée Théo Desplans** has a helpful map of the province of Gallia Narbonensis and a varied collection of mosaics, jewellery, weapons, coins and ceramics. The imposing statue of Tiberius and two larger-than-life marbles of the Emperor Hadrian and Empress Sabina speak volumes about the power and arrogance of Rome.

Built into the hillside at the top of the Puymin site, the 1st-century **Théâtre Antique** could seat 6,000 spectators. Like the amphitheatre in Orange, this well-preserved theatre is the main venue for the town's summer arts festival *(see page 75)*.

Southwest of the Puymin site, and separated from it by a road, the **Quartier Villasse** (open summer daily 10am–noon, 2.30–6.30pm; winter 10am–noon, 2.30–5pm,

The Papal Jews

When Jews were expelled from France in the 13th century, they were allowed to remain in Avignon and the Comtat Venaissin, which were subject to papal rule rather than that of the French crown. The ancient Jewish populations of cities like Marseille and Aix took refuge in the papal territories. This tolerance has given Provence a Jewish heritage unique in France. Gradually the laws became stricter: Jews were excluded from practising many trades or owning land, and they were forced to live cramped together in the *carrière* or ghetto, which was locked by gates at night. By the 17th century, the Jewish communities were concentrated in four ghettos in Avignon, Carpentras, Cavaillon and L'Isle-sur-la-Sorgue. Nonetheless, the Jews enjoyed a certain prosperity, especially during the 18th century, as the rules relaxed and merchants often had the freedom to trade in neighbouring towns.

The French Revolution brought an end to the official exclusion of Jews from France, allowing them full citizenship, and the ghetto disappeared. Two beautiful synagogues survive at Carpentras and Cavaillon.

closed Jan; admission charge) contains the extensive ruins of two Roman villas, a bathing complex and the rue des Boutiques, a paved Roman street lined with shops, which leads to the arch of a former basilica.

Near the exit of the Villasse site, the **Cathédrale Notre-Dame-de-Nazareth** has a fine 12th-century cloister (open daily 10am–12.30pm, 2–6.30pm, 5pm in winter, closed Jan; admission charge), featuring pillars with beautifully decorated capitals.

Cross the **Pont Romain** (Roman Bridge), heavily restored following severe flood damage in 1992, to reach the Cité Médievale or **Haute Ville** (upper town). From the fortified gate, a cobbled street climbs to a dilapidated church and ruined chateau that was once the country seat of the counts of Toulouse. Looking east from the top of the upper town will give you one of the best views over the valleys and foothills that lead to Mont Ventoux.

Valréas

An excursion from Vaison will take you across the Aigues River northwards to **Valréas** ⓬. Valréas marks the northernmost frontier of the Vaucluse, despite being surrounded on all sides by the Drôme *département*. It was once part of the Comtat-Venaissin territory, hence the sobriquet "l'Enclave des Papes".

The legendary salon hostess and prolific letter-writer, Madame de Sévigné (1626–96), spent a considerable amount of time here, and eventually built a chateau in nearby **Grignan** ⓭. Although she was critical of the climate – the mistral is particularly virulent here – she was full of praise for the food and landscape, which is brightened in summer by the fields of sunflowers.

Hill villages

One of the simplest and best pleasures of touring Provence is persevering to the end of a tortuously winding road, for the reward of seeing a tranquil village perched at the crest of a hill and enjoying the view from a church or castle at its highest point. **Crestet** ⓮, south of Vaison-la-Romaine, is one of many such villages tucked away in the Dentelles

Map on page 70

Each autumn the villages around Vaison-la-Romaine get all souped up for the Festival des Soupes, as the Confrérie des Louchiers (brotherhood of ladlers) elects the best soup from a panoply of veloutés, potages *and* bouillons. *Tastings and recipes for all.* http://soupes84.free.fr

BELOW:
Quartier Puymin, Vaison-la-Romaine.

BELOW: Bédoin.

de Montmirail and foothills of Mont Ventoux. Set above olive groves, Crestet is, at times, eerily quiet. A climb up the cobbled alleyways brings you to a 12th-century church and, after a further ascent, to the castle. The former residence of the bishops of Vaison-la-Romaine is now privately owned, but there are some stunning views across the valleys and to the peak of Mont Ventoux.

If you return to the D938 and head south, the road will take you to the small town of **Malaucène** ⓰, a good base for hiking and biking in the nearby Mont Ventoux. The lively main street bustles with cafés and restaurants.

Heading west from here towards Mont Ventoux will take you along the very route that Petrarch followed in 1336 when he undertook to climb the mountain. First, however, you might want to make a detour south to Caromb. This route (the D938 to the D13) takes you along a scenic backroad, offering glimpses of small fortified villages on either side.

Caromb ⓰ is another medieval hilltop village. Long famed for its vines, its well-preserved exterior walls enclose another typical feature of the area: a church topped with a wrought-iron cage, designed to protect the bell from the fierce mistral. The interior is decorated with frescos and woodcarvings.

The base of Mont Ventoux is surrounded by many other pretty villages. Fortified **Le Barroux** ⓱, with its chateau and fine Romanesque church, **Mazan** ⓲, where the former chateau of the de Sade family is now a comfortable hotel, **Crillon-le-Brave**, **St-Pierre-de-Vassols** and **Bédoin** ⓳, a popular starting point for hikes up Mont Ventoux. All have their own individual charm.

Windy mountain

After you've had your fill of picturesque hilltop villages, rejoin the D974 at Malaucène for the best route to **Mont Ventoux** ⓴, the "Giant of Provence" that dominates the landscape. The road passes through lavender fields and meadows dotted with cedars of Lebanon. You can take a refreshment stop at the waterfall and café beyond the **Chapelle**

Notre-Dame du Groseau, before beginning the climb to the Observatory. It's possible to drive all the way to the top except when the road is blocked by snow.

En route you'll doubtless pass cyclists doing it the hard way. Mont Ventoux ("windy" mountain) is frequently included as one of the stages in the Tour de France cycle race, and it was on these steep slopes that the English rider Tommy Simpson suffered a fatal heart attack in 1967. Countless amateurs attempt to follow in the tracks of the professionals *(see right)*. Words of encouragement are painted in white on the road surface.

If you've time and energy it's perfectly possible to walk to the summit (detailed information on the best routes can be obtained from the tourist office in Bédoin).

Below the ski resort of Mont Serein, the lower slopes of the mountain are ferny and forested, with many scenic spots where you can stop to enjoy a packed lunch. As you approach the wind-blown summit, the temperature drops (the peak is snowcapped for at least two-thirds of the year) and the greenery gives way to harsh white limestone, where nothing grows. When the sun reflects off the bald white top, the glare is blinding. From this elevated point, at 1,909 metres (6,263 ft), it is easy to appreciate why the Vaucluse has always been such an important crossroads. On a clear day – although mist and haze are more typical – you can see the Rhône, the Alps and the Mediterranean from here. Some people even claim to have caught sight of the Pyrenees from this spot.

Once below the tree line, the drive downhill on the D164 in the direction of Sault takes you through a nature reserve of particular interest to botanists. The Mont Ventoux has been designated a "Réserve de Biosphère" by UNESCO for the rarity and diversity of its flora, ranging from Mediterranean to Alpine species as the altitude mounts; panels at various stopping points indicate some of the flora and fauna found here. Pine trees give way to oak, followed by fields of wild thyme and, in the lower valleys, rolling fields of lavender.

Map on page 70

TIP

Should you wish to try the gruelling Mont Ventoux ascent yourself, bicycles can be hired from Bédoin Location (tel: 04 90 65 94 53) in Bédoin and Albion Cycles (tel: 04 90 64 09 32) in Sault.

BELOW: ascending Mont Ventoux the hard way.

The Association des Routes de Lavande (www.routes-lavande.com) proposes five itineraries through the main lavender-producing areas of southeast France, with information on lavender distilleries to visit, restaurants, places to stay and traditional lavender fairs and parades.

BELOW: Gorges de la Nesque; the summit of Mont Ventoux.

Sault and the Gorges de la Nesque

Sault ㉑, which curls tightly up a mound on the flanks of Mont Ventoux, is the capital of the largest area of true lavender *(lavande vraie)* production in Europe. It is also at the heart of the revival of *épeautre*, a sort of hardy, primitive wild wheat that has been rediscovered by many of Provence's leading chefs and is also brewed here in a *bière blanche* (white beer). The only remnants of the town's former glory as a baronial seat are the towers of a 16th-century castle. The Romanesque Eglise de St-Sauveur stands guard over the town, which acts as a lively marketplace for the surrounding lavender distilleries.

South of Sault between Mont Ventoux and the Plateau de Vaucluse, the drive along the D942 (towards Carpentras) to the lively village of **Monieux** ㉒ is lush, green and lined with fields of lavender.

Monieux marks the start of the **Gorges de la Nesque** ㉓, which offer breathtaking views and a sensational display of colours all year round. The river itself is often dry, but the gorges

are impressive, plunging in some spots to depths of over 300 metres (984 ft), and scrub and rocks camouflage deep caves. A couple of kilometres along, the **belvédère de Castelleras** looks across to the **Rocher du Cire**, a steep, wax-covered rock climbed by Frédéric Mistral in 1866 to collect its honey.

The Nesque Gorges are sprinkled with attractive Provençal villages, surrounded by vineyards, olive groves and cherry trees. **Villes-sur-Auzon** ㉔ has had its fair share of disasters in the form of invaders, sieges and plagues. Today, the close-knit community lives off the cultivation of the vineyards that surround the town. Stop at one of the town's *caves de dégustation* to sample the local Côtes du Ventoux, best drunk when young.

To the south, set on a rocky spur overlooking the gorges, **Méthamis** is dominated by its surprisingly large Romanesque church.

Like many mountainous areas in Provence, the Gorges de la Nesque is wonderful climbing and hiking country.   ❑

RESTAURANTS AND BARS

Châteauneuf-du-Pape

La Mère Germaine
Place de la Fontaine. Tel: 04 90 83 54 37. Open: L Thur–Mon, D Thur–Tues. €€€
www.lameregermaine.com.
Landmark restaurant in the heart of the village, with views over the vineyards from the dining room. Founded in 1922 by Germaine Vion, former cook to the French president, it has fed a parade of celebrities and politicians over the years. The classical cuisine includes dishes such as snail *feuilleté*, venison stew and guinea fowl, designed to go with the excellent range of Châteauneuf-du-Pape wines.

Monteux

Saule Pleureur
145 chemin de Beauregard. Tel: 04 90 62 01 35. Open: L Tues–Fri and Sun, D Tues–Sat. €€€€
www.le-saule-pleureur.com
Young chef Laurent Azoulay, who has worked for many of the top chefs in France, has recently taken over this well-reputed restaurant near Carpentras. A native of Provence, he shows off his talent in dishes like a "barigoule" of langoustines, sea bream with artichokes and anchovies, rabbit

prepared in four different ways, or a dessert combining raspberries and red peppers. A good-value weekday lunch menu lets you try out his style. Closed last week Aug, 1–15 Nov.

Orange

La Table Vigneronne
Palais des Vins, Route Nationale 7. Tel: 04 90 51 76 50. Open: L Mon–Sat. €€
Located at the motorway exit just south of town, the Palais des Vins was created by a group of independent wine producers. In addition to the restaurant serving well-presented Provençal dishes, there is a shop which stocks around 600 different wines from 150 domaines in the Côtes du Rhône. Wine courses are also on offer.

Le Yaca
24 place Silvain. Tel: 04 90 34 70 03. Open: L Thur–Tues, D Thur–Mon. Closed: Nov. €
Tasty dishes are offered at a good price in attractive wood-beamed surroundings near the Théâtre Antique. Friendly welcome.

Séguret

Le Mesclun
Rue des Poternes. Tel: 04 90 46 93 43. Open: L and D Wed–Sun. €€
www.lemesclun.com

Sit on the shady terrace with view over the vineyards or in one of the dining rooms of this attractive 16th-century house. Young chef Christophe Bonzi's artistically presented creations draw on both Mediterranean and local traditions. The desserts are irresistible.

Vaison-la-Romaine

Hostellerie Le Beffroi
Rue de l'Evêché, Cité Medié-vale. Tel: 04 90 36 04 71. Open: L Sat and Sun, D Wed–Mon. €€
www.le-beffroi.com
This picturesque hotel-restaurant in the medieval upper town serves proficient Provençal and French classics. Closed Nov–Mar.

Venasque

Auberge La Fontaine
Place de la Fontaine. Tel: 04 90 66 02 96. Open: D Thur–Tues. €€
www.auberge-lafontaine.com
At this stylish inn overlooking the fountain of this pretty village, Christian Soehlke concocts a daily-changing menu, much of it using organic produce. In winter, truffles are a central feature.

PRICE CATEGORIES

Prices for a three-course meal without wine. Note that many restaurants have a less expensive lunch menu.
€ = under €25
€€ = €25–€40
€€€ = €40–€60
€€€€ = more than €60

RIGHT: café on place Clemenceau, Orange.

THE LUBERON AND PLATEAU DE VAUCLUSE

With its sensuous landscape of wooded limestone hills, rolling vineyards and orchards, peppered with picturesque hill villages, historic châteaux and country farmhouses, the Luberon has become one of the most fashionable areas of the Vaucluse

Map on page 84

The chic Luberon is a favourite with France's champagne socialists, American actors and a torrent of international tourists in search of the idyllic corner of France evoked by the English expat Peter Mayle's best-selling book, *A Year in Provence*. But the area's wealthy second-homers remain a more discreet breed than on the show-off Riviera. A dedicated year-round local population ensures that it remains a lived-in area, with an economy based on agriculture – notably fruit-growing and increasingly respectable wines – as well as tourism.

This area of the Vaucluse has gone through several waves of fortune. It was decimated by the Black Death and ravaged by the Wars of Religion and the plague. Then it prospered as a centre for silkworm farming and the paper, glass, ochre and faience industries. It became severely depopulated after World War I, but was rediscovered by writers and artists (among them Camus, De Staël, Vasarely), who helped restore and repopulate its historic villages.

Orientation

In 1977, a large section of the Luberon was designated a protected area. The 100,000-hectare (247,000-acre) regional park stretches between Cavaillon in the west and Manosque in the east, taking in villages such as Gordes and Roussillon on the Plateau de Vaucluse, as well as the main mountain ridge.

The main roads run either side of the Montagne du Luberon: the N100 runs along the northern side, and the D973 along the Durance valley to the south. The D943, which runs from Cadenet and Lourmarin along the Aigue Brun River, is the only road that crosses the massif, dividing it into the Petit Luberon to the west and the Grand Luberon to the east.

LEFT: Apt market.
BELOW: Abbaye de Sénanque.

Created in 1171, the Canal St-Julien, which runs alongside the River Durance, is the oldest irrigation canal in Provence and centrepiece of a complex network of channels and sluices that ensure the water table is high even in summer. Originally the canal served both for irrigation and as a source of energy for numerous water mills. Cavaillon tourist board (tel: 04 90 04 52 94) organises guided visits around the canal, its offshoots, a 15th-century aqueduct and a pumping station.

The Luberon offers plenty of opportunities for walking, cycling, riding and rock-climbing, and is crossed by numerous footpaths, including stretches of the GR4, GR6, GR9 (and offshoots GR92 and GR97) long-distance footpaths.

Cavaillon

Cavaillon ❶, the main town on the western edge of the Luberon, is known as the melon capital of France. Melon-growing here dates back to the days of the Avignon papacy, when cantaloupe melons were introduced from Italy and flourished thanks to irrigation from the medieval Canal St-Julien *(see left)*.

Although the modern town sits on the heat-baked plain, its history began on the hill up above – the **Colline St-Jacques**. A footpath climbs up the hill from behind a Roman triumphal arch on place du Clos (Cavaillon was an important Roman settlement), past traces of ramparts to the top of the hill, where there is an ancient hermit's chapel and a fine view over the plain.

On Monday morning a lively **market** fills the town centre, but the more serious business goes on at the edge of town, where the daily wholesale fruit-and-vegetable market (not open to the public except on guided tour by the tourist office) is one of the most important in France.

The melon is not the only thing that is legendary in this town. Popular mythology suggests the area around Cavaillon was once flattened by a monster called the "Coulobie". Basically an oversized lizard, he was chased away by St Véran, a hermit from nearby Fontaine-de-Vaucluse and later bishop of Cavaillon. The Coulobie is the subject of a painting that hangs in the **Cathédrale Notre-Dame et St-Véran** on place Joseph d'Arrard. Go round the side of the cathedral to see its unusual octagonal tower and carved sundial, and to admire the fine old houses on shady

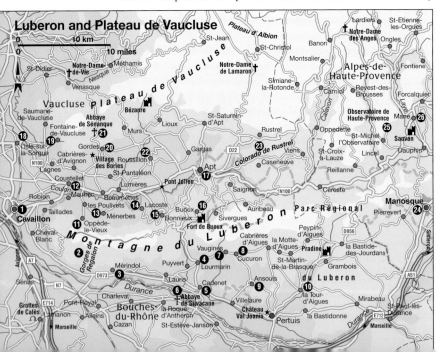

square **Philippe de Cabassole**. From here a covered passage leads to the elegant 18th-century **Hôtel de Ville** (town hall).

The **Musée Archéologique de l'Hôtel-Dieu** (Porte d'Avignon; open May–Sept Wed–Mon, Oct–Apr Wed–Fri, Mon; admission charge; tel: 04 90 76 00 34), a collection of local archeological finds, is housed in the chapel of the former hospital.

As part of the papal Comtat Venaissin, Cavaillon, like Carpentras, "tolerated" a significant Jewish community when Jews were being expelled from the rest of France *(see page 76)*. The present **synagogue** was built in 1772, a time of new prosperity and increasing freedom for the Jews. It has a splendid interior in pastel pink and blue with fine rococo carving and a beautiful wrought-iron gallery. Below the prayer room, the former bakery now houses the small **Musée Juif-Comtadin** (rue Hebraïque; open May–Sept Wed–Mon; Oct–Apr Wed–Fri, Mon; tel: 04 90 76 00 34), containing Jewish prayer books, tombstones and Torahic relics, as well as the original bread oven. Just out-side, an archway across the street marks the former gate into the ghetto, which was locked at night.

Gorges de Regalon and the Mérindol memorial

East of Cavaillon, the D973 runs through orchards and melon fields between the Durance River and the Canal St-Julien. About 13 km (8 miles) from Cavaillon, a lane leads to the **Gorges de Regalon ❷**. The high walls of the limestone gorge make this a refreshing walk in summer.

Modern **Mérindol ❸** has little of interest, but the town remains the symbol of the horror of the religious massacres of 1545 *(see box page 86)*. A memorial footpath climbs amid olive trees, rosemary and evergreen oak through the still partly ruined old village to the top of the hill, where a simple memorial plaque on the battered castle ruins remains extraordinarily evocative. From here there is good access to several footpaths over the Petit Luberon, and an orientation table points out the views stretching to the Alpilles, the Mont Ste-Victoire and the Sainte-Baume.

TIP

The Espace Tourisme, Création et Terroir at Cheval-Blanc, 5 km east of Cavaillon, is an information centre on crafts and regional produce in the Luberon, with temporary exhibitions, information on potters, sculptors and other craft studios open to the public, and a selection of artisanal produce. Tel: 04 90 04 52 94; www.cavaillon-luberon.com

BELOW: Cavaillon melons; inside the synagogue.

Busy markets are held on different mornings around the Luberon: Monday in Cadenet and Cavaillon, Tuesday in Cucuron, Gordes, Lacoste and La Tour d'Aigues, Thursday in Roussillon, Friday in Bonnieux, Lourmarin and Pertuis, Saturday in Apt and Manosque. Expect printed Provençal fabrics and pottery as well as tempting fruit and veg, goat's cheeses, dried sausages, olives and tapenades.

BELOW RIGHT: Château de Lourmarin.

Southern Luberon chateaux

Chic but not showy, **Lourmarin ❹** is a pleasant place to stop off, with a choice of good restaurants and lively cafés. Existentialist author Albert Camus (1913–60) bought a house here in 1958 and is buried in the cemetery outside the village.

At the opposite edge of the village, the **Château de Lourmarin** (open summer daily 10–11.30am, 2.30–5.30pm; winter 10–11.30am, 2.30–4pm, Jan Sat and Sun afternoons only; admission charge; tel: 04 90 68 15 23; www.chateau-de-lourmarin. com) bridges the period between medieval fortification in the 15th-century "old" wing and the new, more comfortable lifestyle of the 16th-century Renaissance wing – seen in the large mullioned windows, Italianate loggia and cantilevered staircase. Note the unusual fireplace with carved Corinthian columns below and column figures of Native American Indians above, inspired by the recent discovery of the Americas.

The chateau was rescued from delapidation in the 1920s and turned into an arts foundation with resi-

dences for writers and musicians in summer, when it is also used for classical concerts.

Nearby **Cadenet ❺** is a more workaday village, with a good market which fills its streets and squares on Mondays. It was once a centre of *vannerie* (basket-making), using willows from the nearby river bank.

Northwest of the city, near the south bank of the Durance River in a lovely peaceful setting, is the austerely elegant **Abbaye de Silvacane ❻** (Apr–Sept: open daily; Oct–Mar: closed Tues; admission charge; tel: 04 42 50 41 69). Completed in 1144, it is considered the finest of three Cistercian abbeys in Provence (the others are Sénanque and Le Thoronet).

East of Lourmarin, a web of lanes runs through vineyards and olive groves under the eastern flank of the Montagne du Luberon. At minuscule **Vaugines ❼** many of the houses are built into the rock.

There's much more to explore at **Cucuron ❽**. At the foot of the pretty village you'll find the **Moulin à Huile Dauphin** (tel: 04 90 77 26 17), whose olive oil is used by many of

The Massacre of Mérindol

The Vaudois or Waldensian sect was founded in Lyon in 1180 by Pierre Valdes, who preached the virtues of poverty. The Vaudois took refuge in the Alps of Savoie and northern Italy, then spread to the Luberon, encouraged by local landlords looking to repopulate the area after the Black Death. Then came the Reformation and its subsequent condemnation by the Catholic Church. Being associated with Protestantism, the Vaudrois suffered a brutal repression that was particularly violent in the Luberon. The Wars of Religion split the region in two: some villages such as Mérindol, Lourmarin and La Motte d'Aigues had large Vaudois populations; others, such as Cucuron, Bonnieux and Oppède, remained staunchly Catholic. On 16 April 1545, Jean de Meynier, Baron of Oppède, sent in his troops to implement the Decree of Mérindol, which condemned the Vaudois as heretics. Within six days 22 villages were pillaged and burnt and an estimated 2,500 were killed. Mérindol was razed to the ground. The route des Vaudois *(see above)* climbs up through the still partly ruined village to the top of the hill, where the bleak ruins of the citadel, now bearing a memorial plaque, are a potent reminder of the bloodshed.

the area's top chefs, and the Etang, a rectangular pool of water surrounded by plane trees, around which the weekly market is held on Tuesday mornings. Above, still contained within fragments of ramparts and fortified gateways, the old village is scattered with fine doorways, fountains and traces of medieval and Renaissance windows.

Further east beneath the ridge, tiny, sleepy villlages like **Cabrières d'Aigues** and **La Motte d'Aigues** with tall houses, painted shutters and narrow alleyways seem to be have been bypassed by the fashionable revival of much of the Luberon.

The D56 south of Cucuron heads to the village of **Ansouis ❾**, which spirals up around a small hill to the **Château d'Ansouis** (open July–Sept daily 2.30–6pm, Easter–June, Oct Wed–Mon 2.30–6pm, Nov–Easter Sun 2.30–6pm, closed Jan; admission charge; tel: 04 90 09 82 70; www.chateau-ansouis.com). It has a fortified gateway and an elegant 16th-century classical façade overlooking terraced gardens with topiaried hedges. The interior likewise

reflects different periods, including the panelled dining room, the chapel and the big old-fashioned kitchens. The village church, reached via an impressive semicircular stairway, is attached to the side of the chateau.

In one old village house, the **Musée Extraordinaire de Georges Mazoyer** (Rue du Vieux Moulin; open Mar–Dec Wed–Mon 2–5pm; admission charge; tel: 04 90 09 82 64) is a somewhat eccentric one-man show created by a painter with a passion for marine life and now run by his widow. It includes a recreated underwater cave in the cellars.

The third of the great chateaux of the southern Luberon at **la Tour d'Aigues ❿** (open summer 10am–1pm, 2.30–6pm, winter 10am–noon, 2–5pm, daily July–15 Aug, rest of year closed Mon and Sun am, Tues pm; admission charge; www.chateaulatourdaigues.com) is only a shadow of its former self. The pedimented entrance with its crisply carved friezes and the remains of the central pavilion and two towers only hint at what must have once been the finest Renaissance chateau in the

Map on page 84

The Luberon à Velo is a 235-km (146-mile) waymarked cycle route taking in many of the area's prettiest villages. It runs between Cavaillon and Forcalquier, via Oppède-le-Vieux, Lacoste and Apt on the north side of the Montagne de Luberon and Manosque, Lourmarin and Lauris by the southern route.

BELOW: picking *tilleul*, which is used for tea.

TIP

The wine-producing Domaine de la Citadelle, near Ménerbes, is also home to the Musée du Tire-Bouchon, a collection of corkscrews ranging from historic items to novelty pieces. Tel: 04 90 72 41 58; www.musee dutirebouchon.com.

BELOW: characteristic wrought iron bell tower, Lacoste.

Luberon if not all Provence, until it was pillaged by the revolutionary mob in 1792.

The town, which sits amid rolling vineyards, has a busy wine co-operative. Towards Pertuis, the **Château Val Joanis** (gardens open Apr–Oct daily 10am–7pm; free; tel: 04 90 79 20 77; www.val-joanis.com) is known both for its wines and its imaginative formal gardens, which are open to the public.

From la Tour d'Aigues, the D956 continues northeast across the eastern flank of the Luberon towards Manosque and Forcalquier, through unspoilt villages such as **Grambois** and the **Bastide-des-Jourdans**.

The northern villages

A string of old villages runs along the northern side of the Petit Luberon. At the western end, the quiet villages of **Taillades** and **Robion** were once important for stone-quarrying. Taillades's castle and houses are strangely perched on rectangular blocks of rock. At the foot of the village stands an imposing 18th-century watermill.

Further east, **Oppède-le-Vieux**  is a symbol of the Luberon revival. Largely deserted in the 19th century when the population moved down to a new village on the plain, Oppède has since been resettled, often by writers, craftsmen and artists, who have restored some of its ancient houses and the village church. A footpath climbs up a cobbled street, still romantically overgrown, to the **Collégiale Notre-Dame d'Alidon** (open Easter–June, Sept–Oct Sat–Sun 10am–7pm, July and Aug daily 10am–7pm, closed Nov–Easter), a fine Romanesque church where gargoyles leer from a hexagonal bell-tower. Above it is the ruined château of mercenary Baron Meynier d'Oppède who ordered the massacres of the Vaudois in 1545 *(see page 86).*

Starting from the car park below the village, a footpath has been created through the vineyards, with panels explaining the soils and different grape varieties cultivated here for both wine and the table.

Back down on the plain, **Coustellet** is known for its farmers' market held in the main square beside the N100 on Sunday mornings (May–Nov). Near by, the **Musée de la Lavande** (Lavender Museum; open daily June, Sept 9am–noon, 2–7pm, July–Aug 9am–7pm, Oct–May 9am–noon, 2–6pm; admission charge; tel: 04 90 76 91 23; www.museedela lavande.com) has a collection of archive photos and a film explaining distillation processes.

The village of **Ménerbes** (the central focus of Peter Mayle's *A Year in Provence*) stretches out along a spur. From the main street an archway leads through to a small square where you'll find the elegant town hall, the clocktower with campanile and the fine 17th-century Hôtel d'Astier de Montfaucon, recently restored as the **Maison de la Truffe et du Vin** (open daily 9am–noon, 3–6pm; tel: 04 90 72 52 10). Here you can join a truffle and wine-tasting workshop or visit the *oenothèque*, which sells the three different wine appellations found in the Luberon (Côtes du Luberon, Côtes du Ventoux and Coteaux de Pierrevert).

The scenic D109 passes the remote **Abbaye St-Hilaire** (visits by appointment; tel: 04 90 75 88 83), the remains of a Carmelite priory restored by its owners as a residence.

Views of **Lacoste** begin to appear from afar. The village sits beneath the imposing ruins of the castle that once belonged to the notorious Marquis de Sade, who lived here from 1771 until his arrest in 1778 for sodomy and other nefarious deeds. The chateau now belongs to veteran fashion designer Pierre Cardin, who has established a summer opera festival here.

The village itself is an intimate place, with a ruined gateway leading to some tastefully restored houses and an overgrown tangle of old arches and stairways. Despite the increased glamour quotient some semblance of ordinary village life continues down below, where the inevitably named Café de Sade is still the sort of place where you can pick up a newspaper, stop by for a sandwich or a *plat du jour* and eavesdrop on local gossip.

Zigzagging up a hillside further east, **Bonnieux** is an archetypal Provençal hill village. It was once a property of the Knights Templar and later part of the papal enclave and home to a powerful clergy. Several elegant carved doorways and two churches hint at a village that was rather grander than it is today.

From Bonnieux you can head south towards the Combe de Lourmarin, or north towards the N100 via **Pont Julien**, a remarkably well-preserved Roman bridge from the 1st century BC, or northeast towards Apt.

One detour worth making is to **Buoux**. Its crags are popular with rock-climbers, and at the entrance to the valley are the scattered ruins of the **Fort de Buoux**, a Protestant stronghold until dismantled under the orders of Cardinal Richelieu. The main attraction, however, is the quiet valley of L'Aigrebrun, where there is a simple hotel with friendly

Map on page 84

TIP

The award-winning jams produced by Confiturerie La Roumanière in Robion are made out of every conceivable fruit. The factory is a rehabilitation project employing disabled adults, who also run the shop and offer guided tours. Place de l'Eglise, Robion; tel: 04 90 76 61 21; www.laroumaniere.com

BELOW: Bonnieux.

Apt is known for two distinctive styles of faience: the historic creamy yellow monochrome wares and more modern Aptware, characterised by the swirling multicoloured patterns that result from mixing white, red, ochre and green clays. If you're interested in buying some faience visit Atelier du Vieil Apt, 6 place Carnot, tel: 04 90 04 03 96; www.faiencedapt.com

BELOW RIGHT:
antiques fair, Isle-sur-la-Sorgue.

buvette bar. This is a good starting point for several walks up towards the Mourre-Nègre or across to the isolated hamlet of **Sivergues**.

Apt

Apt ⑰, the Roman city of Apta Julia and an ancient bishopric, is the main town of the northern Luberon, and headquarters of the regional park. Apt comes to life on Saturday mornings, when its food market, one of the best in Provence, fills the old town from place de la Bouquerie up to the **Ancienne Cathédrale Ste-Anne**. For centuries, this curious Baroque and Gothic structure was a place of pilgrimage for the relics of St Anne, mother of the Virgin Mary, buried in the crypt. In 1660 the Baroque Royal Chapel was added when Anne of Austria, wife of Louis XIII, came here to give thanks for the birth of her son Louis XIV.

Apt's past prosperity, however, came from the three industries of faience, ochre production and crystallised fruit *(fruits confits)*. Its history is traced in the interesting **Musée de l'Aventure Industrielle**

(open summer Mon–Sat 10am–noon, 3–6.30pm, Sun 3–7pm, winter Mon, Wed–Sat 10am–noon, 2–5.30pm; admission charge), housed in a converted crystallised fruit factory just behind the cathedral. Near by, an 18th-century *hôtel particulier* contains the **Maison du Parc** (place Jean Jaurès; tel: 04 90 04 42 00) which focuses on the Luberon's fauna, flora and geology.

Four km (2½ miles) southwest of Apt, **Saignon** sits on a magnificent escarpment, with a cluster of fine houses under some impressive crags, a Romanesque church and a rocky belvedere with the ruins of a castle.

L'Isle-sur-la-Sorgue and Fontaine-de-Vaucluse

Watery **L'Isle-sur-la-Sorgue** ⑱, 12 km (7 miles) north of Cavaillon, was once a marshy island in the middle of the Sorgue River. The old town was built on piles some time in the 12th century, and the river's numerous branches were channelled to surround it in a double – in places triple – ring of canals. There are still canals everywhere, and countless dripping

The Antiques Trail

Ever since a *brocante* was first held in L'Isle-sur-la-Sorgue in 1966, antiques dealers, bric-a-brac-ers and cosmopolitan collectors have been arriving in ever-growing numbers to give the town the largest concentration of antiques dealers in France outside Paris. There are four main arcades open Monday to Saturday. Le Quai de la Gare (4 avenue Julien Guigue), by the station, and Hôtel Dongier (9 place Gambetta), an 18th-century coaching inn, home to 30 or so *antiquaires*, are rather upmarket. Many items reflect the south – carved Beaucaire mirrors, faience from Apt and Moustiers, marriage wardrobes and elaborate openwork bread cupboards. The Village des Antiquaires de la Gare (2bis avenue de l'Egalité), in a ramshackle old carpet factory, and the Isle-aux-Brocantes (7 avenue des Quatre Otages), reached across its own little canal, are more bohemian in mood, and the goods tend more towards 20th-century items and collectables, such as art-deco furniture, vintage toys, garden furniture and old bar and hotel fittings. Every Sunday, the permanent shops and arcades are joined by a flea market that sprawls along avenue des Quatre Otages, and for the big Easter and 15 August fairs, stalls take over the local park and meadows as well.

waterwheels remain from the mills that once supplied silks, wools and paper to the Avignon court.

Today L'Isle-sur-la-Sorgue is famous for the biggest antiques and flea market (Sat–Mon) outside Paris *(see box opposite)*, but the old centre, sprinkled with fine Renaissance doorways and old town houses, is worth exploring. On a square in the centre stands the church of **Notre-Dame des Anges**. Its stern Romanesque exterior is in marked contrast to the exuberant Baroque interior, awash with cheerful angels: frescos with cherubim over the west door, and sculpted pairs of gilded virtues and graces flying over the arches along the nave.

Seven km (4 miles) up the Sorgue River, **Fontaine-de-Vaucluse** ⑲ (beware, the D25 road can be very busy in summer) is named after the mysterious spring that surges out of the bedrock into an incredibly deep pool a few minutes' walk from the village – the mysterious Vallis Clausa (closed valley) that has given its name to the Vaucluse *département*. Despite diving trips and exploratory robots, no one has yet discovered the

base of the pool, which is fed by rainwater that drains through the Vaucluse Plateau. In winter and spring the flow rate can be so great that water does indeed bubble out like a fountain. Along the footpath to the pool, the **Monde Souterrain de Norbert Casteret** (tel: 04 90 20 34 13), dedicated to a famous potholer, has displays of potholing and cave systems, and attempts to explain the Fontaine-de-Vaucluse phenomenon.

Although full of souvenir shops and tourist restaurants, the town is spectacularly situated, with the ruins of a castle on rocky cliffs, surrounded by a bowl of mountains, and the remains of several paper and glass factories that once flourished here. One water-powered paper mill, **Vallis Clausa Moulin à Papier** (open daily; tel: 04 90 20 34 14), continues to produce handmade paper. Visitors are allowed in to watch the process.

Near the entrance to the village, the Romanesque **Eglise de St-Véran** is dedicated to the 6th-century bishop of Cavaillon, who is said to have freed the area of the Coloubie monster *(see page 84)*, and who is buried

Map on page 84

The Sorgue River is a popular spot for kayaking.

BELOW: festival at L'Isle-sur-la-Sorgue.

Outside the Eglise de St-Véran in Fontaine-de-Vaucluse, a column commemorates the Italian poet Petrarch, who lived in the town from 1337 to 1353. It was here that he composed the famous sonnets to the love of his life, Laura.

in the crypt. It has an unusual 11th-century open altar table made from an antique tombstone.

On the other side of the river, the **Musée Bibliothèque Pétrarque** (Quai du Château Vieux; open Apr–Oct Wed–Mon 10am–noon, 2–6pm, closed Nov–Mar; admission charge; tel: 04 90 20 37 20) is a small museum devoted to the life of Italian poet and scholar Petrarch *(see left)*.

A narrow road runs out of Fontaine-de-Vaucluse over a bleak mountainside to Cabrières d'Avignon. One of the curiosities here are the fragments of the **Mur de la Peste**, a long drystone wall built in 1721 in an attempt to keep out the plague.

Gordes and the Plateau de Vaucluse

With its pristine drystone walls and elegantly renovated houses, smart hotels and interior-decoration shops, **Gordes** ⑳ epitomises the Luberon's social rise. During the summer, the town is one of the most popular tourist spots in the Vaucluse. Climbing up the side of the Plateau de Vaucluse, Gordes is dominated by its

Château (open daily 10am–noon, 2–6pm; admission charge; tel: 04 90 72 02 75), a medieval castle, transformed during the Renaissance, which houses the tourist office and an exhibition of paintings by Belgian artist Pol Mara.

The majority of tourists, however, come here to see the **Village des Bories** (open daily 9am–sunset; admission charge; tel: 04 90 72 03 48), a cluster of 20 restored beehive-shaped *bories* (drystone huts) that lies just below the town. The curious, wind-resistant dwellings are believed to date from the 16th to 19th centuries, but may have replaced much earlier structures. Similar drystone huts are found scattered throughout the area, some used as sheep pens, others as holiday homes or incorporated in chic hotel conversions.

The winding D177 Vénasque road leads from Gordes across the plateau to the **Abbaye de Sénanque** ㉑ (open Feb–Dec, guided visits in French only, ring for times; admission charge; tel: 04 90 72 05 72; www.senanque.fr), one of the three great 12th-century Cistercian abbeys

of Provence (along with Thoronet and Silvacane), a typically austere structure, which sits in calm isolation amid lavender fields.

Ochre country

With its colourful ochre-washed houses set off by the green landscape that surrounds it, the hill village of **Roussillon** ㉒ is the most visible reminder of the ochre industry that once thrived here, thanks to a 50-km (30-mile) seam of ochre-bearing rock that runs through the area. The only industrial-scale mine still in operation today is in Gargas. Roussillon's economy is now driven by tourism, and it can get suffocatingly overrun in summer. On the edge of the village, the **Sentier des Ochres** (admission charge) is a waymarked trail through the red-and-orange landscape.

Even more spectacular than Roussillon, though more difficult to find (look for signs from the D22), is the **Colorado de Rustrel** ㉓, situated south of the village of Rustrel to the northeast of Apt. From the car park, various footpaths lead through a surreal landscape of orangey-red rocks sculpted into strange chimneys, turrets, bowls and narrow valleys, by a combination of ochre-quarrying and natural erosion.

Manosque and the eastern Luberon

At the eastern edge of the Luberon, on the border with the *département* of Alpes de Haute-Provence, the town of **Manosque** ㉔ occupies a prime site. Sitting on a small hill overlooking the River Durance, at the edge of the Luberon and the Plateau de Valensole, and on the motorway to Aix-en-Provence, the once sleepy town has become a thriving economic axis. Agriculture in the Durance valley (Manosque is known for its peaches) is blossoming, while the proximity of the Cadarache nuclear research centre has drawn scientists and their families to settle here, and the global success of cosmetics and skincare group Occitane means it is now the town's largest employer.

Within the urban sprawl of housing and industrial estates, the central core of Manosque, ringed by busy boulevards that replaced the ancient

Map on page 84

The Manufacture des Ochres Okhra (open for guided visits Apr–Sept daily, Oct–Mar Tues–Sun; admission charge; tel: 04 90 05 66 69; www.okhra.com), 2 km (1 mile) outside Roussillon, a former ochre-washing plant, explains the process of extracting ochre and making pastels and pigments.

BELOW:
Colorado de Rustrel.

Map on page 84

TIP

Visits to the l'Occitane factory to see the production of traditionally made perfumes, soaps and cosmetics using natural ingredients can be arranged through L'Occitane, ZI St-Maurice, Manosque, tel: 04 92 70 19 00, www.loccitane.com.

BELOW RIGHT:
Montagne de Lure: Giono country.

ramparts, has changed little from the "tortoiseshell in the grass" described by the town's own Jean Giono *(see box below)*. Two imposing gateways – the tall crenellated **Porte Saunerie** and the **Porte Soubeyran** topped with a wrought-iron campanile – stand guard at either end of the **Vieille Ville**. Between them runs the old town's main artery, the Grande Rue, and a pedestrianised web of narrow streets, small squares and honey-coloured churches.

Continue north towards Frocalquier to find the hilltop village of **Dauphin**. Northwest of Manosque is the perched village of **Reillane**.

A surreal sight above the pretty village of **St-Michel l'Observatoire** is the mushroom-like silhouette of the **Observatoire de Haute-Provence** ㉕ (open July–Aug Wed, Thur 1.15–4.15pm, Apr–June, Sept Wed 2–3.30pm, Oct–Mar Wed 3pm; admission charge; www.obs-hp.fr). The state observatory is located here because of the clarity of the night air.

The beautiful monastic complex of the **Prieuré de Salagon** (open May–Sept daily 10am–12.30pm,

2–7pm, Oct Sat–Sun 2–6pm; admission charge; tel: 04 92 75 70 50; www.musee-de-salagon.com) is just outside the village of **Mane** ㉖. The former priory buildings contain an ethnographic collection, including a blacksmith's forge, a display about beekeeping and photographic archives of rural life in the Luberon. The most interesting aspect, though, is the series of themed gardens: a garden of medicinal plants used in local remedies, a perfume garden, and a medieval garden based on plants found in medieval manuscripts, including a kitchen garden, where the pulses and root vegetables that formed the staple diet in medieval times, before the arrival of tomatoes or aubergines, are a far cry from the typical Provençal cuisine of today.

While at Salagon, you can pay a visit to the **Château de Sauvan** (open July–Aug daily from 3.30pm, Sept–June Thur, Sun from 3.30pm; admission charge; tel: 04 92 75 05 64), an 18th-century neoclassical mansion, inspired by the Petit Trianon at Versailles and known locally as the *"Petit Trianon Provençal"*.❏

Jean Giono

Writer Jean Giono (1895–1970) was a lifelong resident of Manosque. An ecologist and pacifist, he was imprisoned by the Nazis for his beliefs at the start of the occupation, and by the French at the end of the war because his philosophical love of nature had been twisted to support Nazi propaganda. He made his name with a series of novels on village life in the Alpes-de-Haute-Provence, including the swashbuckling *Hussard sur le Toit*. Giono's Provence has little in common with the sunny region of Pagnol or even Daudet. His main themes were the abandonment of the mountain villages, the destruction of the traditional patterns of rural life and the rough sensuality of man's communion with nature. A plaque marks the writer's birthplace at 14 Grande Rue, above his parents' shoe shop. Outside the old town, the **Centre Jean Giono** (open Tues–Sat 2–6pm; admission charge; tel: 04 92 70 54 54) puts on temporary exhibitions and has a permanent display about the writer's life and work. Giono's house, **Lou Parais** (Montée des Vrais Richesses; tel: 04 92 87 73 03), north of the Old Town, is open for guided visits by appointment on Friday afternoons.

RESTAURANTS AND BARS

Apt

Café de France
Place de la Bouquerie. Tel: 04 90 74 22 01. Open: L & D Tues–Sat. €
Charming, old-fashioned bistro, where the friendly patron serves up a generous *anchoïade*, autumn game or the winter treat of scrambled eggs with truffles.

Bonnieux

La Bastide de Capelongue
Tel: 04 90 75 89 78. Open: L & D daily. Closed: mid-Nov–mid-Mar. €€€€
www.capelongue.com
Edouard Loubet mans the stoves at this luxurious hotel. His style is modern, spontaneous and inventive, often using wild herbs or flowers and plants from his garden.

Le Fournil
5 place Carnot. Tel: 04 90 75 83 62. Open: L & D Wed–Sun. Closed: Dec–Jan. €€
This troglodyte restaurant draws a fashionable set with its good-value updated Provençal cuisine.

Cavaillon

Prévôt
353 avenue de Verdun. Tel: 04 90 71 32 43. Open: L & D Tues–Sat. €€€
Jean-Jacques Prévôt is obsessed with Cavaillon melons. Melon memorabilia fill the dining room, and there's an "all-melon" menu in summer. But Prévôt is also a good

classical southern cook, as seen in dishes such as a *barigoule* of vegetables or local lamb with spices.

Restaurant Pantagruel
5 place Philippe de Cabassole. Tel: 04 90 76 11 98. Open: L Tues–Sat, D Mon–Sat. €€
You're in for a Rabelaisian feast at this laid-back restaurant on a shady square. In winter meat is cooked on the open fire.

Coustellet

Maison Gouin
N100. Tel: 04 90 76 90 18. Open: L & D Mon, Tues, Thur–Sat. €€
Small bistro within an upmarket butcher and deli. At lunch it's simple bistro fare, with a more elaborate menu by night.

Cucuron

Restaurant de l'Horloge
55 rue Léonce Brieugne. Tel: 04 90 77 12 74. Open: L Thur–Tues, D Thur–Mon. €
www.horloge.netfirms.com
Traditional Provençal cooking served in a pretty vaulted stone cellar.

Goult

Café de la Poste
Place de la Libération. Tel: 04 90 72 23 23. Open: L Tues–Sun. €
An institution where local families, chic second-homers and international tourists pile in for no-nonsense home cooking.

L'Isle-sur-la-Sorgue

Le Jardin du Quai
91 avenue Julien Guigue. Tel: 04 90 20 14 98. Open: L & D Thur–Mon. €€
Reputed chef Daniel Hébert opts for a simpler, bistro style and mood. Daily menu based on excellent fresh produce.

Joucas

Le Mas des Herbes Blancs
Tel: 04 90 05 79 79. Open: summer L & D daily, winter L & D Thur–Mon. Closed: Jan–Feb. €€€€
www.relaischateaux.fr/masherbes
This elegant *mas* near Gordes has a reputation as one of the best restaurants in the Luberon.

Lourmarin

Auberge La Fenière
Route de Cadenet. Tel: 04 90 68 11 79. Open: L Wed–Sun, D Tues–Sun. Closed: mid-Nov–mid-Dec & Jan. €€€€
www.reinesammut.com
Leading chef Reine Sammut produces stylish food at this modern *mas* between Cadenet and Lourmarin. Near by, La Cour de la Ferme serves a less expensive *menu du jour* and spit-roast meats.

Restaurant Michel Ange – Maison Ollier
Place de la Fontaine. Tel: 04 90 68 02 03. Open: summer L & D daily, winter L & D Thur–Mon. €€
Med-wide flavours including Sisteron lamb and excellent grilled fish.

Ménerbes

Hotellerie du Roy Soleil
Route des Beaumettes, D103. Tel: 04 90 72 25 61. Open: L & D daily. Closed: mid-Nov–mid-Mar. €€€
www.roy-soleil.com
Refined Provençal cooking by Richard Baima served in the calm dining room of an 18th-century manoir or on its terrace.

Robion

Lou Luberon
Avenue Aristide-Briand. Tel: 04 90 76 65 04. Open: L & D daily, winter L only. €
A simple roadside restaurant, serving carefully prepared salads and Provençal dishes, such as lamb with garlic.

Vaugines

Hostellerie du Luberon
Cours St-Louis. Tel: 04 90 77 27 19. Open: L Thur–Tues, D daily. Closed: Dec–Jan. €€
www.hostellerieduluberon.com
Family-run hotel-restaurant where good-value menus feature personalised Provençal dishes, such as squid with broad beans. Children welcome.

PRICE CATEGORIES

Prices for a three-course meal without wine. Note that many restaurants have a less expensive lunch menu.
€ = under €25
€€ = €25–€40
€€€ = €40–€60
€€€€ = more than €60

WILD PROVENCE

However crowded the cities and coast, the countryside isn't far away. Here, among mountains and rivers, you can seem miles from civilisation

This swallowtail butterfly is a common visitor to Provence and is just one small component in the colourful landscape which runs from the salt marshes of the Rhône delta, pink with flamingos, to the Alpine summits along the Italian border. It includes seven nature parks and 20 nature reserves. The *maquis* scrub of rock rose and lavender, myrtle and thyme is the enduring attraction of the region, typified by the Luberon, where an abundance of wild flowers and herbs is looked down on by eagles and vultures while beavers are busy in the Durance and Calavon. Haute-Provence lies at the heart of the region, with escarpments and mountains providing constantly changing views, meadows cropped by sheep and valleys filled with fruit. The Valensole plateau in the Parc Natural Régional du Verdon is the place to head for in June and July to see and smell the lavender fields and buy honey. Mushroom- and boar-hunting are autumn pursuits when chestnut-gatherers roam the Maure Massif. Wildest of all is the Mercantour National Park (*see below*), while the Ecrins National Park has 100 peaks above 3,000 metres (9,850 ft), glaciers and tarns. Finally, the Queyras Park in the upper Alps enjoys Mediterranean sunshine 300 days a year, but its wooden houses and a traditional way of life seem a century away.

ABOVE: Camargue horses live wild in the marshy delta of the Rhône. Harnessed as working horses by *gardians*, they are used for farm work and herding cattle. There are 30 herds; each year they are rounded up and the foals are branded.

ABOVE LEFT: this prehistoric ammonite fossil comes from near Dignes. The fossil record of the region can be seen at the new museum in Quinson.

LEFT: the bee eater, relative of the kingfisher, is often seen around vineyards and meadows, in pairs and on telephone lines. They are just one of several colourful birds – look out for roller birds and, near woodlands, hoopoes.

LEFT: Alpine flowers in the Mercantour National Park show the diversity of the region. The sparsely inhabited park has some 2,000 plant species, all protected. Among them are Alpine columbine, edelweiss and gentians. Look out, too, for ibex, mouflon, marmots and even recently introduced wolves.

BELOW: Hermann tortoises, the only native French tortoise, were once plentiful in the Maures Massif, but now they are endangered. Helping to keep them alive is the Village des Tortues at Le Cannet, which has specimens from around the world.

GET OUT AND GET ACTIVE

Provence's wonderful landscape provides endless opportunities to enjoy the outdoors. For the sedate and leisurely, it's great walking country, and for the more energetic there are well-marked long-distance routes *(grandes randonnées)*, including the Route Napoléon from Golfe-Juans to Grenoble. Cycling can be leisurely or demanding. The Luberon is a popular place for bikers, while Mont Ventoux is one of the arduous climbs on the Tour de France. The local rivers run swiftly, particularly the Verdon *(above)*, making canoeing, kayaking and white-water rafting a possibility, and because its gorge is so deep you can go bungee jumping from bridges. The rivers also offer a chance for some trout-fishing. Mountains and escarpments present opportunities for climbing at every level, and of course there are the well-tried ski resorts of the Alps *(see page 170)*. There are few more evocative places to go horse-riding than the Camargue *(see left)*, where the local horses are perfect for a day's hack in the marshes. There are equestrian centres *(centres equestres)* throughout the region.
See Travel Tips – Activities, page 281 for details.

ABOVE: diving presents a chance to explore the underwater life along the coast, particularly around the islands of Lérins and Porquerolles *(pictured above)*, where there are numerous wrecks, clear water and a sandy seabed. Anemonies, coral, sponges, conger and moray eels, moonfish and dolphin can be seen. The Calanques near Marseille are another diving area; in Cosquer Cave, 38 metres (125 ft) below sea level, 27,000-year-old cave paintings of bisons, horses and penguins were discovered in an air-filled chamber in 1985. Scuba diving was invented on this coast, by Jacques Cousteau, in Toulon, and today all the resorts have diving schools *(écoles de plongée)* and facilities.

BELOW: the Dentelles de Montmirail, named after their lace-like jagged peaks, climb to 734 m (2,400 ft). They support oak and pine woods and are yellow with broom from April to June. Vineyards flourish at the mountains' feet.

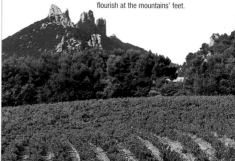

MARSEILLE AND THE CALANQUES

France's oldest and second-largest city is a
gloriously gutsy multicultural port, where
tower blocks jostle with historic monuments

France's oldest city and leading port, **Marseille ❶** is a magnificent mix of urban and marine, the grandiose and the intimate. With 2,600 years of history, the town abounds in historic monuments, fine churches, old fortresses, interesting museums and some icons of modern architecture. Ancient tenements, fishermen's cottages, Haussmannian boulevards, Belle Epoque villas and modern tower blocks alternate with docks, beaches and tiny coves, and steep stairways look out over dingy alleyways or sparkling sea views. Some 40 km (25 miles) of seaboard stretch from the fishing port and industrial suburb of L'Estaque in the north, past the docks, ferry terminal, fishing inlets and the long expanse of the Prado beach to tiny Les Goudes. Even the remote, fjord-like Calanques which stretch east between Marseille and Cassis largely fall within the urban limits of Marseille itself.

Birth of a city

It was 2,600 years ago that Greek sailors from the Ionian city of Phocaea first sailed into the harbour at Marseille, establishing a prosperous trading post called Massilia. The new settlement set up a string of outposts including Hyères, Antibes and Nice, and was also a thriving intellectual

centre, home to one of the principal universities of the Greek Empire. Over the centuries, the Massilians developed a strong and independent character still apparent in their modern descendants. A major Roman port, Marseille was an early centre of Christian monasticism around the important abbey of St-Victor. The city briefly set itself up as an independent republic in 1214, until it was taken by Charles d'Anjou in 1256. Along with the rest of Provence, the city became part of France in 1481,

Maps:
City 101
Area 106

LEFT: Marseille's Vieux Port. **BELOW:** Port-Miou, Les Calanques.

TIP

Bouillabaisse is the quintessential Marseille dish, originally made out of the unsold leftovers of the day's catch. Its name is supposed to come from "quand ça bouille... abaisse" – when it bubbles lower the heat – in an instruction in how to cook it without the fish disintegrating. To find a truly memorable bouillabaisse in Marseille, avoid the tourist traps around place Thiers behind the Vieux-Port and choose one of the restaurants that adheres to the bouillabaisse charter.

BELOW:
selling the daily catch.

but guarded its spirit of independence. As a vital part of Louis XIV's maritime strategy, he built the star-shaped Fort St-Nicolas and enlarged the Fort St-Jean, on either side of the Vieux-Port, as much to control the unruly citizens as to protect the port.

In 1720, an outbreak of the plague – the worst of several epidemics that hit the city – wiped out half the population, and despite efforts to isolate the city spread to the rest of Provence.

Unsurprisingly, the Marseillais were active in the Revolution. In 1792, 600 Marseillais *fédéralistes* marched towards Paris singing the song that has since become France's national anthem, known as la Marseillaise. In the 19th century Marseille became the most powerful port on the Mediterranean, serving the expanding French Empire, its new wealth reflected in the construction of grand hotels, the Docks de la Joliette, the new cathedral and Palais du Pharo.

Today, France's second city is still a major port, and adminstrative capital of the Bouches-du-Rhône *département* and the Provence-Côte d'Azur region. This is one of the most invigorating cities in France: a place where most of the city's residents proudly consider themselves Marseillais before being Provençal.

The arrival of the TGV high-speed train in 2001, bringing Marseille to within three hours of Paris, and massive investment in urban regeneration have tranformed the city's image. The refurbishment of the 19th-century Joliette docks, flagship of the larger Euroméditerranée redevelopment project, illustrates the transformation of the local economy, as design and advertising agencies and service companies replace shipping ones and the dockworkers of old. It has long been an entry point for immigrants – Italians, Greeks, Spanish and, more recently, North and West Africans have all contributed to a melting pot where France's often uneasy racial mix for once largely seems to work.

The Vieux-Port

Any visit to Marseille should begin at the **Vieux-Port** Ⓐ (old port), the heart of the city, with its yachts, fishing boats and café-lined quays framed

by forts at either end. There's a lively fish market each morning along the quai des Belges, as crates of wriggling fish are unloaded and sold off by vociferous fishmongers. This is also where boats leave for trips to the Calanques, the Château d'If and the Iles de Frioul *(see page 107)*. A tiny passenger ferry runs across the Vieux-Port between the Quai du Port and Quai du Rive Neuve.

The Quai du Port was heavily bombed by the Germans during World War II, but was sensitively rebuilt in the 1950s by architect Fernand Pouillon, whose housing in tinted reinforced concrete frames one of the rare buildings to survive, the ornate 17th-century **Hôtel de Ville ⓑ** (town hall). From here various stairways lead up to Le Panier district. Just beside the Hôtel de Ville, newly landscaped terraced gardens climb up to the **Hôtel-Dieu**, the city's old hospital, designed in the 18th century by Mansard. On the

other side of the town hall stands the **Maison Diamantée ⓒ**, built in the 16th century and one of the oldest surviving houses in Marseille, so called because of the unusual diamond-faceted façade. Long the **Musée du Vieux-Marseille** (tel: 04 91 55 28 58), it is currently used for temporary exhibitions.

A little further along the quai, look in on the **Musée des Docks Romains ⓓ** (place du Vivaux; open June– Sept Tues–Sun 11am–6pm, Oct–May 10am–5pm; admission charge; tel: 04 91 91 24 62; www.marseille.fr), which shelters a series of uncovered Roman docks on the site of their excavation. The open amphorae once stored grain, olives and wine for the Romans. At the end of the quay, the medieval Fort St-Jean will form the centrepiece of the future **MUCEM** (Musée National des Civilisations de l'Europe et de la Méditerranée; tel: 04 96 13 80 90; www.musee-europemediterranee.

Map on page 101

TIP

The City Pass, available for one or two days, gives free access to 14 museums in Marseille, free travel on the bus, metro and tram network, the tourist train, and discounts on selected shops, shows and city tours. Information from the Office de Tourisme: 4 rue de la Canabière; tel: 04 91 13 89 00; www.marseille-tourisme.com. Note that all municipal museums are free on Sunday.

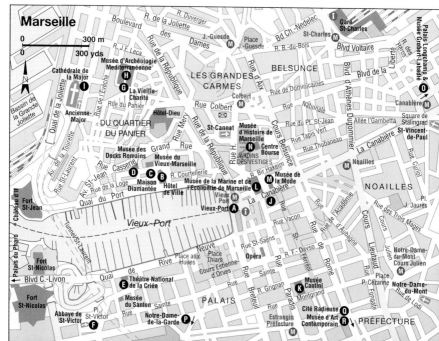

First created in 1781 in Le Four des Navettes (136 rue Sainte), navettes are biscuits flavoured with orange-flower water cooked in the shape of the boat that is said to have brought Mary Magdalene and her saintly crew to the shores of Provence 2,000 years ago. These biscuits are the special mark of the Fête de la Chandeleur on 2 February.

BELOW:
sunset over the port.

org), alongside a new building by Rudy Ricciotti, an ethnographic and folk art collection centred on Mediterranean cultures.

On the opposite side of the Vieux-Port, the quai de Rive Neuve leads towards the star-shaped Fort St-Nicolas (now occupied by the French Foreign Legion) and the Jardins and Château de Pharo, the palace built for Napoléon III. At 33 quai de Rive Neuve, the old fish market is now Marseille's highly renowned **Théâtre National de la Criée Ⓔ**.

Behind the quai, **place Thiars**, place aux Huiles and cours d'Estienne d'Orves are busy with restaurants, fashion boutiques and galleries, many of them in converted warehouses and arsenal buildings, such as the elegant Les Arcenaulx, now a restaurant, bookshop and kitchen shop. Just down the street is an enclave of Marseillais tradition, the Four des Navettes bakery *(see left)*.

Rue Sainte ends at the **Abbaye de St-Victor Ⓕ** (open daily 9am–7pm; admission charge for crypt; tel: 04 96 11 22 60). The basilica was built on the site of an ancient burial ground in

the 5th century and is named after local martyr St Victor, patron saint of sailors, millers (Victor was ground to death between two millstones) and Marseille. Throughout the Middle Ages, the abbey's power was felt across the Mediterranean as it set up daughter houses from northern Spain to Italy. What remains is the extraordinary two-storey fortified church – the original 5th-century church in the crypt and the lofty 11th- to 13th-century church above. In the crypt, ancient sarcophagi, some hidden in candlelit alcoves, line the walls; in the centre stands the sombre tomb of two slain martyrs over which the basilica was built. In a rocky alcove is the 3rd-century tomb of St Victor.

Le Panier

Climbing up the hill behind the quai du Port on the northern side of the port is the **Quartier du Panier**, characterised by colour-washed houses, narrow streets, flights of stairs and little squares, such as place de Lenche, where there is a small morning market on the site of the original Greek agora. Traditionally the immigrant quarter, where first Italians, Greeks and Spanish, then North Africans and Africans washed up, it has also recently been colonised by artists and craftsmen and Parisians in search of a southern pied-à-terre.

At the heart of Le Panier is **La Vieille-Charité Ⓖ** (2 rue de la Charité; open June–Sept Tues–Sun 11am–6pm, Oct–May 10am–5pm; admission charge; tel: 04 91 14 58 80). Erected as a charity hospital in the 17th century, it is the masterpiece of Marseille-born architect and sculptor Pierre Puget (1620–94), who also created several sculptures for Louis XIV at Versailles. The three storeys of galleried arcades are amazingly serene and beautiful for a building originally destined to round up beggars, fallen women and other social rejects. The restored buildings now contain the

Musée d'Archéologie Mediterranéenne ⓗ, which features local archaeology and a small but well-presented Egyptian collection, and the **Musée d'Arts Africains, Océaniens et Amerindiens**, particularly strong on American Indian art and artefacts. At the centre of the courtyard, the **Chapelle**, which has an unusual oval dome, makes a striking setting for temporary exhibitions.

More contemporary art can be found down the hill at the gallery of the **FRAC-PACA** (Fonds Régional d'Art Contemporain Provence-Alpes-Côte d'Azur, 1 place Francis-Chirat; open during exhibitions Mon–Sat 10am–12.30pm, 2–6pm; free; tel: 04 91 90 28 50). Looming over the coast is the neo-Byzantine **Cathédrale de la Major ❶** (open Tues–Sun 9am–noon, 2–5.30pm). Built 1852–93, its interior is a riot of coloured marble and porphyry.

Adjacent to la Major is the 11th-century Romanesque **Ancienne-Major**, the earlier cathedral, which was undermined by the construction of the new cathedral and the flyover below it, and is closed for restoration.

Around La Canabière

Running inland from the centre of the Vieux-Port is the legendary **Canabière ❿**, Marseille's equivalent of the Champs-Elysées. It was laid out in 1666 as part of Louis XIV's expansion of the city, but its heyday came in the 19th century when its smart hotels, banks, cafés and department stores were a symbol of Marseille's booming port economy at the height of the French Empire. It has since gone downhill, but nonetheless has some interesting museums and vestiges of its glorious past.

Just near the port, at No. 4 is the tourist office. Behind here a garden square leads up to Marseille's art-deco **Opéra**, which is used for both opera and ballet. Near here, amid Marseille's smartest shops on rue Paradis, rue St-Férreol and rue Grignan, is the **Musée Cantini ❿** (19 rue Grignan; open June–Sept Tues–Sun 11am–6pm, Oct–May 10am–5pm; admission charge; tel: 04 91 54 77 75; www.marseille.fr), a notable collection of Fauve, Surrealist, early abstraction and post-war art, including paintings and sculptures by

At 47 rue Neuve Ste-Catherine is the Atelier Marcel Carbonel, one of Provence's best-regarded santon makers. Visitors can watch figures being made and view M. Carbonel's personal collection of Christmas cribs from around the world.

BELOW: streets in the Quartier du Panier, Marseille's oldest quarter.

The massive 9.7-metre (32-ft) high statue of the Virgin that crowns Notre-Dame-de-la-Garde was a technical feat, sculpted by Lequesne and cast in bronze at the Christofle workshop near Paris, covered in gold leaf and installed on the church in 1870. Inside the church are numerous marble ex-voto plaques, which make fascinating reading if you can understand French, as they give thanks to the Virgin for saving loved ones from cyclones, cholera and, more recently, a postal hold-up.

BELOW: Notre-Dame-de-la-Garde.

Derain, Signac, Léger, Kandinsky, Ernst, Arp, Brauner and Bacon.

Almost opposite the tourist office, the Palais de la Bourse – the ornate 19th-century stock exchange (note the ship carvings on the façade) – contains the **Musée de la Marine et de l'Economie de Marseille** (9 La Canabière; open daily 10am–6pm; admission charge; tel: 04 91 39 33 33), which documents Marseille's maritime history. Next door is the **Musée de la Mode** (11 La Canabière; open June–Sept Tues– Sun 11am–6pm, Oct–May 10am– 5pm; admission charge; tel: 04 96 17 06 00; www.marseille.fr), a fashion museum that puts on adventurous exhibitions, generally focusing on 20th- and even 21st-century style.

Between here and the Vieux-Port, against a backdrop of modern tower blocks, excavations during the construction of the **Centre Bourse** shopping centre in the 1960s unearthed Greek and Roman fortifications, wharfs, wells and a road, dating from between the 3rd century BC and the 4th century AD. These now lie exposed in the **Jardins des Vestiges**.

The adjoining **Musée d'Histoire de Marseille** (1 square Belsunce; open Mon–Sat noon–7pm; admission charge; tel: 04 91 90 42 22) presents some of the finds and the city's subsequent history.

Behind here, running north of La Canabière, is the **Cours Belsunce**, a broad promenade laid out in the 17th century. It has a souk-like atmosphere with its stalls and street traders, and is home to a garlic festival in July. A recent arrival is the striking new municipal library.

On the opposite side of La Canabière, the busy shopping street of rue de Rome leads towards the Préfecture. Rue d'Aubagne is lined with North African grocers, with sacks of couscous, spices, nuts and dates and hanging loofahs. Steps climb up the hill to Notre-Dame-du-Mont and the colourful **Cours Julien** with its fountain, cosmopolitan restaurants, morning produce market (Mon–Sat), book and record shops and music venues.

Crowning the top of boulevard de Longchamp, the **Palais Longchamp** is a glorious confection of foun-

tains and waterfalls, with a winged colonnade around a central fountain. It is in fact a grandiose water tower that celebrated the arrival of a much-needed drinking-water supply to the city in 1869. The pavilions on either side house two museums: the **Musée des Beaux-Arts** (closed for renovation; tel: 04 91 14 59 30; www.marseille.fr) has sculptures by Pierre Puget and old master paintings, and **Muséum d'Histoire Naturelle** (open June–Sept Tues–Sun 11am–6pm, Oct–May 10am–5pm; admission charge; tel: 04 91 14 59 50; www.marseille.fr) features a variety of zoological and geological exhibits.

A little way down the street is the **Musée Grobet-Labadié** (140 boulevard de Longchamp; open June–Sept Tues–Sun 11am–6pm, Oct–May 10am–5pm; admission charge; tel: 04 91 62 21 82; www.marseille.fr), the restored private mansion of a couple of avid 19th-century collectors, filled with the treasures they amassed: Northern and Italian Renaissance paintings, French 18th-century paintings, Provençal furniture and faience and a unique array of Flemish, Beauvais and Gobelins textiles.

Euroméditerranée

In contrast to the bourgeois homes around boulevard de Longchamp, the quartier de la Belle de Mai is much more run-down, but it is now one of the key zones in Marseille's ambitious Euroméditerranée urban regeneration project, centred on the arty **Friche de Belle de Mai,** a former tobacco factory, now home to artists' studios, recording studios, a local radio station and dance and theatre companies. The development district stretches from the main station, Gare St-Charles, to the beautifully renovated 19th-century warehouses of the **Docks de la Joliette**.

The Good Mother

Perhaps the best-loved site in all Marseille is the church of **Notre-Dame-de-la-Garde ❿** (open daily summer 7am–7pm, winter 7.30am–5.30pm; tel: 04 91 13 40 80), dubbed "la Bonne Mère" (the Good Mother) by the Marseillais. Erected on a bluff of 162 metres (530 ft), no

Map on page 101

Mansion on corniche J.F. Kennedy.

BELOW: relaxing in the Cours Julien district.

Cafés and Bars

Naturally the Vieux-Port is first port of call if you're pausing for a drink or a snack. Elegant **La Samaritaine** (2 quai du Port), with its corner vantage point, is a favourite meeting place; the **OM Café** (3 quai des Belges) is the rallying point for supporters of Olympique de Marseille football team. **Le Crystal** (148 quai du Port), with its '50s decor and terrace, is a cocktail hotspot, as is **La Caravelle** (34 quai du Port), on the first floor of the Hôtel Bellevue. Across the harbour, the **Bar de la Marine** (15 quai de Rive Neuve) is a local classic. Up the hill east of the Canabière, place Jean Jaurès and the bars and music venues around cours Julien draw a younger, bohemian set.

One art form that remains a vital part of Provençal life, is the santon, *clay figures displayed in cribs at Christmas. The main production centres are Marseille, Aix-en-Provence and Aubagne. The two-week Foire aux Santons, dating to 1803, is held in Marseille in December.*

matter where you go in Marseille, you can't miss the extravagant 19th-century basilica with its stripy marble walls and massive gilded statue of the Virgin atop the campanile. The terrace in front offers the best view over the city. Supposedly a lookout post since prehistoric times and later a fort, it also became a place of worship for seafarers.

Along the corniche

The Château du Pharo and the tiny plage des Catalans, a small sandy beach (admission charge), and little harbour of the Anse des Catalans, mark the start of the **corniche Président-John-F.-Kennedy**, the 5-km (3-mile) stretch of road that follows the coastline east of the Vieux-Port past fishermen's cottages, small coves and palatial 19th-century villas, with constant perspectives over the sea, the offshore islands and the winding shore ahead. Take a little detour up the picturesque **Vallon des**

Auffes, with its colourful *pointu* fishing boats, old fishermen's *cabanons* and renowned bouillabaisse restaurants *(see right)*.

The road eventually leads to the **Plages du Prado**, a large area of lawns, sports facilities and mainly pebble beaches on artificial land created with landfill from the construction of the Marseille metro system. The beach here has been split into two parts, the first half being pebble and the second sand, and the water is quite clean. This area is a lively and chic place to dine at night.

On the avenue du Prado, **Parc Borély** is Marseille's largest park, with its landscaped *jardins à l'anglaise*, French formal gardens, botanical garden with tropical greenhouse and racetrack, laid around the Château Borély, most elegant of all the *bastides*, a huge 18th-century neoclassical country house put up by the Borély family in 1766 and now used for cultural events and exhibi-

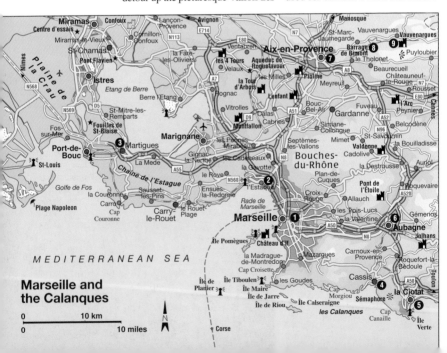

Marseille and the Calanques

tions. Near here another *bastide*, the Château Pastre, now houses the **Musée de la Faïence** (Earthenware Museum; 157 avenue de Montredon; open June–Sept Tues–Sun 11am–6pm, Oct–May 10am–5pm; admission charge; tel: 04 91 72 43 47; www.marseille.fr). Pride of place goes to Provençal faience from Moustiers, Apt, Tour d'Aigues and, of course, Marseille, but the collection ranges from ancient Neolithic pottery to early art pottery and ceramics by contemporary designers.

The coast road continues on past the **Plage de la Pointe Rouge**, a sandy beach that is known for its restaurants and watersports facilities, notably windsurfing and water-skiing, past La Madrague de Mondredon to finish at Les Goudes and tiny Callelongue. You're still technically in Marseille, but with the bare white rock, glittering blue sea and whirling seagulls you could well be on a Greek island.

Modern monuments

Heading inland up avenue du Prado from the beaches past the giant replica of Michelangelo's *David* in the south of the city on boulevard Michelet are two modern shrines. At No. 3, the **Stade Vélodrome**, is the stadium of Marseille's much-loved football team, Olympique de Marseille. At No. 280, a must-see for modern architecture enthusiasts is the **Cité Radieuse ⓠ** by the French Modernist architect Le Corbusier. Built 1947–52 as a model for mass housing, the 165-metre (540-ft) long, 56-metre (180-ft) high block illustrated Le Corbusier's principles of mass housing with its reinforced concrete structure built on *pilottis*, apartments with balconies and built-in furniture, use of colour, and sculptural roof. As well as 337 apartments, it contains a supermarket, rooftop theatre, gym and infant school. It is open for guided tours run by the tourist office (tel: 04 91 13 89 00), but you can also stay in the hotel or eat in the restaurant (tel: 04 91 16 78 00).

Near by is the **Musée d'Art Contemporain** (MAC) **ⓡ** (69 avenue d'Haïfa; open June–Sept Tues–Sun 11am–6pm; Oct–May 10am–5pm;

Map on page 101

Although locals nicknamed it the Maison du Fada (madman's house), Le Corbusier's Cité Radieuse is much loved by its residents.

BELOW: Chateau d'If.

Château d'If and the Iles de Frioul

The Iles de Frioul, a rocky archipelago off the shore of Marseille, are just minutes from the frenetic Vieux-Port activity, yet miles away in mood. Regular boat trips leave from the quai des Belges out to the tiny Ile d'If, site of the Château d'If (open summer daily 9.30am–6.30pm; winter Tues–Sun 9.30am–5.30pm; admission charge), France's version of Alcatraz. It was built by François I in the 1520s to keep an eye on the unruly Marseillais, and later used for the internment of Protestants and political prisoners. Its most famous inmate was fictional – Edmond Dantès, hero of Alexandre Dumas's novel *The Count of Monte-Cristo*. As well as visiting the fortress, you can enjoy a great view of the city, and even take a swim off the rocky shores.

You can combine the trip with a visit to the Iles de Frioul, two rocky, sparsely vegetated islands linked by a causeway. Near the quay there are a few cafés and apartments, and some little creeks for swimming, or you climb up the hill to the ruins of the Hôpital Caroline, an 18th-century quarantine hospital, today used for Les Nuits de Caroline outdoor theatre festival in July.

Les Calanques

Stretching for 20 km (12 miles) southeast of Marseille, between Cap Croisette and Cassis, lies a stunning landscape of long, finger-like rocky inlets, sheer white cliffs, sparse *garrigue* vegetation and tiny beaches, offering superb opportunities for walking, rock-climbing, birdwatching and swimming. Although most of the area is actually within the city limits of Marseille, it remains a haven of unspoilt nature, largely because most of it is accessible only by foot or boat. Often compared to the Norwegian fjords, the Calanques are technically *rias* – valleys flooded by the rising of the sea level by 80 metres (260 ft) or more at the end of the Ice Age some 10,000 years ago. Over 700 species of plant, including 14 types of orchid, grow here; birdlife includes the rare Bonelli's eagle, the peregrine falcon and huge colonies of seagulls.

You can reach the Calanques by boats from the Vieux-Port in Marseille and the harbour in Cassis, which stop at some of the main Calanques, or by walking along the GR98 footpath between Marseille and Cassis. Certain roads offer access across the massif out of season and at night for those with restaurant reservations. Note that in high summer from July to mid-September, access to the Calanques is severely restricted due to fire risk. Most footpaths are closed; only the GR98 (indicated in red and white) remains open. The rest of the year, the Marseille tourist office organises walks in the Calanques on Friday afternoons and Saturday mornings (reserve on 04 91 13 89 00). If walking alone, be sure to take a good map, sun cream and water with you.

The Marseille coast road trickles out just beyond the little village of Les Goudes at Cap Croisette and Calanque de Callelongue, a starting point for the GR98, which follows the coast to the Calanque de Cortiou and the series of little Calanques of the Massif de Marseilleveyre. The broad Calanque de Sormiou, with its small beach, and Morgiou, with its fishing harbour, are two of the most picturesque Calanques, still lined with some of the old *cabanons* – simple rickety shacks that were put up by fishermen or as weekend homes by the ordinary workers of Marseille and are now considered part of the region's architectural heritage. Further east, Sugiton, accessible by foot from Luminy in the northeast of Marseille, sits under a sheer cliff face favoured by rock-climbers, while its flat, waterside rocks are popular with nude bathers.

From Cassis the first inlet, the only one reachable by car, is Port-Miou; this is dedicated to harbouring yachts. The second is Port-Pin, so named for the shrubby pines that decorate its rocky walls, and with a small sandy beach. Port-Pin must be approached either by boat or on foot, as must the breathtaking Calanque d'En-Vau, about an hour's walk further on with a difficult descent at the end. Here sky-high white cliffs cut directly down into water of the deepest blue-green imaginable. A sandy white beach adorns one end. The view from the top is unforgettable, but be warned – getting there isn't easy and neither is getting down, and finding the paths can be difficult.

The Calanques are also favourite with divers. The Grotte Cosquier, an underwater cave covered with prehistoric paintings, is closed to the public, but expeditions can be organised from both Marseille and Cassis to other underwater caves and shipwrecks. ❏

LEFT: sailing in to Port-Miou.

admission charge; tel: 04 91 72 01 07; www.marseille.fr), Marseille's hangar-like contemporary art museum, which has an impressive international collection, including artworks by Robert Rauschenberg, Marseille-born César, Andy Warhol, Dieter Roth, Martial Raysse, Daniel Buren and Nan Goldin, shown in rotation along with temporary exhibitions. A huge bronze cast of César's sculpture *La Pouce* (the thumb) stands in the centre of the roundabout just down the street.

L'Estaque

For all its air of unassuming fishing village, **L'Estaque ❷**, on the north-western tip of Marseille, is one of those places that changed art history. When he came here in the 1870s, Cézanne painted its red-roofed houses, the chimneys of its tile factories, its railway viaduct and the view across the bay to Marseille. In 1906–8, Georges Braque, whose Cubism was highly influenced by Cézanne, André Derain, Raoul Dufy and Othon Friesz, painted the coast here, appreciating its authenticity and the variety of subject matter. Dubbed the Fauves – or wild animals – by the critic Vauxcelles for their savage use of colour at the Salon d'Automne in Paris in 1905, they used colours that no longer sought to capture the changing times of day or weather of the Impressionists, instead using colour for its expressive value.

Along the Côte Bleue to Martigues

West of l'Estaque, the attractive Côte Bleue is a popular weekend jaunt for the populations of Aix and Marseille, less known yet more accessible than Cassis and the Calanques (*see left*) to the east. Set against the backdrop of the red hills of the Chaîne de l'Estaque, villas hide up on the hillsides, and a succession of tiny harbours and small resorts includes **Niolon**, **Carry-le-Rouet**, famed for its *oursinades* (sea urchin feasts in February), **Sausset-les-Pins** and **Carro**, a small fishing port and beach popular with windsurfers.

North of Carro, bridging the mouth of the heavily industrialised and polluted Etang de Berre lake, **Martigues ❸** is a surprisingly picturesque place consisting of three ancient fishing villages linked by a network of canals and bridges. There's a striking contrast between the modern Théâtre des Salins and the pretty fishermen's cottages along quai Brun and quai Baron, while the main sight is the ornate Baroque **Chapelle de l'Annonciade** (rue du Dr Sérieux, Jonquières), with its *trompe l'oeil* walls and gilded altarpiece.

Nineteenth-century marine and orientalist painter Félix Ziem was so seduced by the light of the little port that he set up his studio here. His works form the centrepiece of the **Musée Ziem** (boulevard du 14 Juillet, Ferrières; open July–Aug Wed–Mon 10am–noon, 2.30–6.30pm,

Maps:
City 101
Area 106

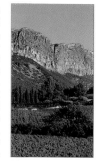

The vineyards of Cassis produce some very quaffable wines.

BELOW:
L'Estaque, by Cézanne.

Map on page 106

Provençal writer Marcel Pagnol was born in Aubagne in 1895. Pagnol captured the spirit of the region in works such as Manon des Sources *and* Jean de Florente, *both turned into successful films. Drive through Cuges-les-Pins and up to Riboux, where the pastoral scenes were shot. The tourist office in Aubagne can give details of the Circuit Pagnol, which covers many of the sites mentioned in his works.*

BELOW: Cassis harbour.

Sept–June Wed–Sun 2.30–6.30pm; tel: 04 42 41 39 60), installed in the old customs house, along with paintings by Dufy, Picabia and Manguin, contemporary artists and a statue of St Pierre (St Peter), patron saint of fishermen, which comes out for a procession down to the harbour every June.

Cassis

20 km (14 miles) east over the bleak Col de la Gineste is **Cassis ❹**. First of the Riviera resorts, Cassis possesses none of the glamour or urbanity of St-Tropez or Cannes, and therein lies its special charm. It is blessed with the coolest water along the French Mediterranean, thanks to a series of mainland streams. Numerous modern painters spent many summers in this delicate port, and it is easy to see why, with its pretty old town and a lively harbour front, lined with shops and restaurants and diving stores; you can take boat trips from the harbour to the Calanques *(see page 108)*. The town has three beaches, the best being the **Plage de la Grande Mer**.

La Ciotat and Aubagne

Looming over Cassis to the east is **Cap Canaille**, which at 416 metres (1,400 ft) is the highest cliff in all of continental Europe. For a panoramic thrill, take a drive along the **Route des Crêtes**, which climbs up, over and down to the neighbouring city of **La Ciotat ❺**. From summer homes to clinging vineyards to rubble, the road seems to disappear up into the sky. The giddy view is fabulous.

Down on the other side of the cliff, La Ciotat has a very different character. A genteel Belle Epoque resort and long an important ship-building centre, it now rather resembles a resort in Florida, with a long flat beachfront lined with souvenir shops, and a harbour where you can take boat trips to the tiny Ile Verte out in the bay. Among summer residents were the Lumière brothers, who shot the world's first moving picture here, showing a train pulling into La Ciotat station. It was projected at the Eden cinema in 1895. At the time, the spectators fled in horror, afraid they would be crushed by the oncoming train. The **Espace Lumière-Simon** (20 rue Foch; Sept–June closed Mon, Tues and Sun, July–Aug closed Mon, Tues and Sun pm; tel: 04 42 71 61 70) has photographs, posters and a film archive in their honour.

Travelling inland along the A50, north of La Ciotat and east of Marseille, will bring you to **Aubagne ❻**, home town of writer and film director Marcel Pagnol. The house where he was born, **Maison Natale de Marcel Pagnol** (16 cours Barthélemy; open daily 9am–12.30pm, 2.30–6pm; admission charge; tel: 04 42 03 49 98) is now open to the public. Long a centre for everyday pottery, there are still several workshops turning out high-quality garden and plant pots, such as the family-run Poterie Ravel, as well as a number of *santon* makers. ❑

RESTAURANTS AND BARS

Carro

Le Chalut
Place Joseph Fasciola. Tel: 04 42 80 70 61. Open: L & D Wed–Sun. Closed: Christmas–late Jan. €
Unpretentious, family-run restaurant serving excellent local fish and shellfish, fresh from the morning's catch, simply prepared, with views over the little harbour.

Cassis

Le Jardin d'Emile
23 avenue Amiral Ganteaume. Tel: 04 42 01 80 55. €€
This hotel-restaurant in a lovely pine-tree-shaded garden by the Plage de Bestouan serves what is perhaps the best Provençal – both land and sea – cuisine in Cassis.

La Presqu'île
Route de Port-Miou. Tel: 04 42 01 03 77. €€€
www.restaurant-la-presquile.com
This place on the way to the Calanques offers great views of the sea and Cap Canaille cliff across the bay. The inventive menu changes every month, though some consider it pretentious.

Marseille

Les Arcenaulx
25 cours d'Estienne d'Orves. Tel: 04 91 59 80 30. Open: L & D Mon–Sat. €€
www.les-arcenaulx.com
This stylish restaurant-cum-tearoom-cum-bookshop and deli is located within the renovated arsenal buildings behind the Vieux-Port. Draws a dressy crowd for upmarket Provençal fare. Excellent desserts.

La Baie des Singes
Cap Croisette, Les Goudes. Tel: 04 91 73 68 87. Open: Apr–Sept. €€€
You have to scramble over rocks or take a boat to this seafront restaurant. It draws a showbizzy crowd for wonderfully fresh fish, brought raw to table in a basket for you to select, and then chargrilled to order. Private sunbathing terrace.

Chez Fonfon
140 vallon des Auffes. Tel: 04 91 52 14 38. €€
www.chez-fonfon.com
A good fish restaurant and classic address for bouillabaisse, in a picturesque little harbour just off the Corniche.

Chez Michel
6 rue des Catalans. Tel: 04 91 52 64 22. €€€
A classic destination for bouillabaisse and other fish dishes served by navy-dressed waiters.

La Côte de Boeuf
35 cours d'Estienne d'Orves. Tel: 04 91 54 89 08. Open: L & D Mon–Sat. Closed: mid-July–mid-Aug. €€
After all the fish restaurants, this is one for carnivores: the speciality is a gigantic chargrilled côte de boeuf for two. Grilled steaks, duck and chops are also on the menu, while wine buffs come here for one of the most extensive wine lists anywhere in the world.

L'Epuisette
156 Vallon des Auffes. Tel: 04 91 52 17 82. €€€€
This venerable restaurant perched at the end of a fishing inlet is now in the hands of a young chef who masters bouillabaisse and adventurous modern creations.

Lemongrass
8 rue Fort Notre-Dame. Tel: 04 91 33 97 65. Open: D Mon–Sat. Closed: Aug. €€
On a side street just off the Vieux-Port. Imaginative modern Asian-inspired fusion cooking with a calm, dimly lit zen setting to match.

Le Lunch
Calanque de Sormiou. Tel: 04 91 25 05 37. Closed: mid-Oct–mid-Mar. €€€
Fish restaurant with an idyllic setting hidden in one of the loveliest calanques. Pricey food but fabulous views.

Le Miramar
12 quai du Port. Tel: 04 91 91 10 40. Open: L & D Tues–Sat. €€€
www.bouillabaisse.com
This fish institution on the Vieux-Port changed hands a couple of years ago, but new chef Christian Buffa continues to prepare its famous bouillabaisse (ideally order 24 hours in advance) and even runs courses in how to cook it. Lots of other options, too.

Le Péron
56 corniche J.F. Kennedy. Tel: 04 91 52 15 22. Open: L & D daily. €€€
Stylish contemporary restaurant with stunning sea views. Cooking is accomplished and inventive. A Marseille hotspot.

Pizzeria Etienne
43 rue de Lorette. No telephone. €
A reminder that Le Panier was once the Italian quarter, this ever-busy corner restaurant is renowned for the best pizza in town.

Une Table au Sud
2 quai du Port. Tel: 04 91 90 63 53. Open: L & D Tues–Sat. Closed: Aug. €€€
Young chef Lionel Levy is the rising gastronomic star of Marseille, making brilliantly inventive use of southern produce – a "deconstructed" bouillabaisse, squid in its ink, a foie gras crème brûlée – in a modern dining room overlooking the Vieux-Port. He recently opened a simpler bistro annexe.

For bars and cafés in Marseille, see page 105.

PRICE CATEGORIES

Prices for a three-course meal without wine. Note that many restaurants have a less expensive lunch menu.

€ = under €25
€€ = €25–€40
€€€ = €40–€60
€€€€ = more than €60

AIX-EN-PROVENCE

Handsome, aristocratic Aix-en-Provence, is a city of fountains and tree-lined avenues, and seat of one of Europe's most prestigious universities. With its elegant town houses, smart shops and lively café society, it remains one of France's most desirable cities to live in

Aix-en-Provence
Marseille

R oman spa and garrison town, former capital of the counts of Provence and historic university city, **Aix-en-Provence** ❼ is still the epitome of civilised aristocratic Provence. The Romans first founded Aquae Sextiae – so named for its hot springs – in 122 BC, after conquering the nearby Ligurian settlement of Entremont. It was overshadowed, however, by Marseille and Arles until the 15th century when the beloved "Good" King René, count of Provence and Anjou, made it his city of preference, and a cultural as well as political capital. René's death brought Provence under the rule of the French crown, and Aix was made the seat of a parliament designed to keep the region under Gallic control.

Much of Aix's renowned architecture dates from this period of prosperity, as the parliamentarians and wealthy burghers built themselves fine town houses and lavish country *bastides*. During the Industrial Revolution, Aix fell back under Marseille's shadow. In the 20th century, however, new industries managed to find a niche here: the city remains the European capital for prepared almonds, but it has also attracted a growing high-tech industry sector, and whole new university, business and residential districts

have grown up around the historic centre. Today, Aix is particularly renowned as a university town (of its 150,000 inhabitants around 40,000 are students).

Maps:
Area 106
City 114

Cours Mirabeau

The best place to begin exploring the city is the **cours Mirabeau** ❹, which marks the dividing line between Vieil Aix ("Old Aix") , the commercial heart of the city, with its largely medieval plan of narrow streets and irregular squares, and the

LEFT: 18th-century *hôtel.* **BELOW:** Les Deux Garçons, cours Mirabeau.

Every Tuesday, Thursday and Saturday morning the Marché d'Aix takes over the centre of town, joining the daily fruit and vegetable stalls of place Richelme. The food and produce heart is on place de la Madeleine, but stalls of household goods, textiles and second-hand goods take over streets and squares towards the Palais de Justice and flower stands by the Hôtel de Ville.

BELOW:
busking on the Place de l'Hôtel de Ville.

aristocratic Quartier Mazarin. Laid out in the 17th century as a carriageway on the trace of the old ramparts, the long, wide, tree-lined avenue with its noble residences is flanked by café terraces on the sunny side, and punctuated by fountains: the Fontaine du Roi René with a 19th-century sculpture of the king by David d'Angers, the Fontaine des Neuf Canons, the Fontaine d'Eau Chaude, a mossy lump which burbles out water at a constant 34°C (93°F), and at the western entrance to the avenue, the ornate **Fontaine de la Rotonde B**, on place du Général de Gaulle.

About two-thirds of the way up the cours, **the Café des Deux Garçons**, affectionately dubbed "les Deux Gs", is an Aix institution, an intellectual hub since 1792; the café's terrace is still the place for people-watching today, while the interior has beautifully preserved Consular-period decor. Just a couple of doors

up at No. 55 once stood the *chapel-lerie* – hat shop – of Cézanne's father Louis Auguste, where the young Paul Cézanne lived as a small child.

Vieil Aix

North of the cours Mirabeau, the narrow streets of **Vieil Aix** are the beating heart of the city: a tangle of small squares and ancient buildings, many with carved heads looming over doorways or sticking out of niches, and busy with fashion shops and snack stalls.

On rue Espariat you can see the Baroque church of St-Esprit and the belfry of a former Augustinian monastery. At No. 6, the **Musée d'Histoire Naturelle C** (open daily 1–5pm; admission charge for over 25s; tel: 04 42 27 91 27) is located inside a fine 17th-century *hôtel particulier*, built according to the Parisian fashion with the main building at the rear of a fine entrance courtyard. The collection

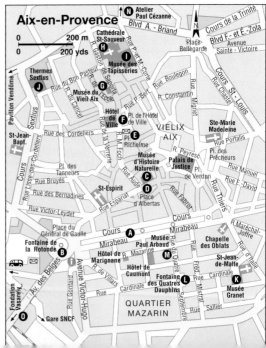

Map on page 114

includes thousands of dinosaur eggs found on the Mont Ste-Victoire as its star attraction.

Almost opposite is the delightful semicircular **place d'Albertas** . When the parliamentarian Albertas built his home in the 1720s, he also bought all the land in front of it – to "protect his view". The four contiguous buildings that now enclose the square were not constructed until 1740. Just near by, **rue Aude** and **rue Fabrot** are home to many of Aix's most fashionable stores. Rue Aude runs into **place Richelme** , with an excellent morning fruit-and-vegetable market, which adjoins the more genteel **place de l'Hôtel de Ville** , a good place to stop and have a drink or a bite to eat.

On the western side of this square is Aix's **Hôtel de Ville** (town hall), built 1655–78, originally the regional assembly of the Etats de Provence. If you go into the town hall, glance up at the beautiful wrought-iron gateway, which fans out in a representation of the sun. Crossing the pretty paved courtyard will lead you into the foyer, where an elegant staircase leads up to the Salle des Etats de Provence, where regional taxes were voted, hung with portraits and mythological paintings.

On the south side of the square is **la Poste** (post office), built in the 18th century as the splendid corn exchange. Note the cavorting figures, intended to represent the Rhône and Durance Rivers, that drape themselves around the pediment. West of the town hall, small streets lead towards the place de la Madeleine, with a gigantic obelisk in the centre, and the large Baroque church of **Ste-Marie Madeleine**, containing an *Annunciation* attributed to 15th-century Flemish painter Barthélemy Van Eyck.

On the north side of the Hôtel de Ville is the whimsical **Tour de l'Horloge**, dating from 1510. This tall clock tower houses four statues, each of which marks a season; in the summer, you'll see a woman holding wheat; autumn shows the wine harvest; winter has a wood-bearer, and spring appears as a woman carrying fruit and a young salmon. Originally part of the city wall, the

TIP

Aix's culinary speciality is the white diamond-shaped *calisson d'Aix*, made out of a mixture of sugar, almonds and preserved melon. You'll find them at most patisseries and chocolate shops.

BELOW: Vieil Aix.

TIP

Aix's presitigious international summer opera festival features top-rate performers and directors. The main venue is the courtyard of the Palais de l'Evêché, but other venues include the Jeu de Paume theatre, a park and even quarries by the Mont Ste-Victoire. Festival International d'Art Lyrique; box office, 11 rue Gaston de Saporta; tel: 04 42 17 34 34; www.festival-aix.com.

BELOW: Cathédrale St-Sauveur. **RIGHT:** detail from one of the tapestries depicting Don Quixote's exploits, Musée des Tapisseries.

tower marked the division between the count's city and that of the clergy around the cathedral to the north. Continue up rue Gaston de Saporta with its string of fine 17th-century *hôtels particuliers*. Several of them are linked to the university or theatres, so you can often wander in on weekdays to see the magnificent entrance stairways.

At No. 17, the Hôtel Estienne de St-Jean contains the **Musée du Vieil Aix** (tel: 04 42 21 43 55; open Tues–Sun 10am–noon, 2.30–6pm; 5pm in winter; admission charge). The collection focuses on local folk art, including an array of mechanised puppets *(marionnettes)*.

The **Cathédrale St-Sauveur** (place de l'Université; open daily but closed to tourists during services; cloister closed Sun; tel: 04 42 21 10 51) is an eclectic structure; its façade combines the 12th century with the 16th, the belfry belongs to the 15th, and there are three naves in Romanesque, Gothic and Baroque styles. The highlight inside is Nicolas Froment's 15th-century triptych, *Le Buisson Ardent* (The

Burning Bush). Off the right-hand nave is the 5th-century **baptistery**, one of the rare surviving Merovingian baptisteries in Provence (others being in Fréjus and Riez). South of the cathedral are fine, Romanesque cloisters.

The Baroque **Palais de l'Ancien Archevêché** (Archbishop's palace) contains the **Musée des Tapisseries** (Tapestry Museum; open Wed–Mon 10am–noon, 2–6pm; admission charge), which includes a rare series depicting the adventures of Don Quixote, from 1735. There's a section dedicated to performance arts, and the opera festival in particular. The courtyard is used for the most prestigious opera productions in Aix's Festival d'Art Lyrique.

Rue du Bon Pasteur leads towards the **Thermes Sextius** , now a luxury glass-and-marble spa but originally a series of 1st-century BC Roman baths (these can be seen to the right of the present entrance), fed by the water from the *Source Impériatrice*. The baths were expanded in the 18th century, and a fountain from this period is still on view to visitors.

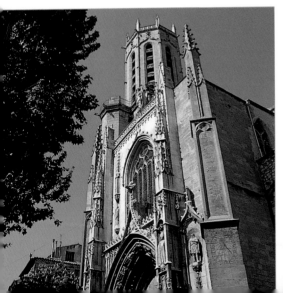

The Quartier Mazarin

Back across the cours Mirabeau, the Quartier Mazarin was a speculative property venture laid out in the 17th century on a geometric grid plan. It still has a calmer, more discreet residential atmosphere than Vieil Aix, with its 17th- and 18th-century *hôtels particuliers*, now often housing antique shops, as well as Aix's two main museums. The **Musée Granet** Ⓚ (place St-Jean-de-Malte; tel: 04 42 38 14 70; open Wed–Sat and Mon noon–6pm; free), in the former monastery of the Knights of Malta, recently reopened after restoration; it has one of the best fine art collections in Provence. Archaeological finds from the Oppidum at Entremont and from Roman Aix, 18th-century statues and portrait busts are on display, along with French painters from the 16th to the 20th centuries, and Dutch, Flemish and Italian art, including Ingres's extraordinary and disturbing *Jupiter and Thetis*. There are also eight paintings by Cézanne.

Next door is the 13th-century **St-Jean-de-Malte**. The long single-naved building was Aix's first Gothic church; note the Maltese cross carved over the door. Further down the street at No. 41 is the Collège Mignet (then Collège Bourbon), where Cézanne went to school and became friends with the young Emile Zola.

East down the rue Cardinale lies the **Fontaine des Quatre-Dauphins** Ⓛ. Dating from 1667, it was the first fountain in Aix to be placed in the middle of a street rather than against a wall, giving it an unprecedented decorative purpose.

The **Musée Paul Arbaud** Ⓜ (2 rue du Quatre-Septembre; tel: 04 42 38 38 95; open Mon–Sat 2–5pm; admission charge) has a fine collection of Provençal faience (pottery) from Moustiers, Marseille and Apt.

Just beyond the Thermes Sextius, past a remaining turret of medieval wall, is another architectural gem, the **Pavillon Vendôme** (*see right*).

Cézanne and Vasarely

Up the chemin des Lauves, north of Vieil Aix, is the **Atelier Paul Cézanne** Ⓝ (9 avenue Paul-Cézanne,

Map on page 114

The Pavillon Vendôme (tel: 04 42 21 05 78; hours vary; admission charge). Louis de Mercoeur, duke of Vendôme and governor of Provence, built this home in 1665 so he could meet his lover here in secret.

BELOW: in the courtyard of the Atelier Paul Cézanne.

Artistic Aix

New districts are transforming the area south of the station and Vieil Aix, where university buildings, a landscaped espalanade and several important arts buildings are giving new all-year facilities to a city long dominated by its summer festival. Marked by a sculpture of a giant open book, the **Cité du Livre** (tel: 04 42 91 98 88) is a vast complex of library, cinema, performance and exhibition spaces, housed in a converted match factory. Just next door stands the striking black glass skeletal structure of the new **Centre Chorégraphique**, opened in autumn 2006. Near by, the new **Salle des Spectacles** will serve for opera productions and concerts.

Maps:
Area 106
City 114

TIP

A terrible episode of Provençal history can be traced at the **Mémorial des Milles** (tel: 04 42 24 34 68), a former tile factory to the south of the city which was used as an internment camp during World War II. Thousands of Jewish and foreign prisoners passed through here on the way to concentration camps; the refectory is painted with moving murals made by the prisoners showing the daily atrocities of internment.

BELOW:
Fondation Vasarely.

tel: 04 42 21 06 53; open daily; admission charge), built by the artist in 1902; it was here that Cézanne painted his last works. The scrupulously preserved studio is an atmospheric place, still cluttered with easels, palettes and objects familiar from Cézanne's still lifes (*see picture story on Cézanne, page 120*). A steepish 15-minute walk further up the hill brings you to the plateau where Cézanne painted many of his views of the distant Mont Ste-Victoire – or "the motif" as he called it (*see page 120*).

The manor house at **Jas de Bouffan** (reserve at tourist office; www.aixenprovencetourism.com; closed Jan, Feb, Mar) gives a sense of the country residence it was when bought by Cézanne's father in 1859. Cézanne had a studio in the attic and painted many works directly on the walls, all since dispersed to museums around the world; here you have to make do with a multimedia presentation in their place, but outside you can still recognise the long avenue of chestnut trees and other features from Cézanne's paintings.

Another artist who left his mark on Aix was Hungarian-born Victor Vasarely. The **Fondation Vasarely** ❼ (1 avenue Marcel-Pagnol, Jas de Bouffan; open daily; admission charge; tel: 04 42 20 01 09; take bus No. 8 from la Rotonde), on the Jas de Bouffan, is unmistakable, with its bold black-and-white Op Art design. All of the works were painted directly onto the high walls in 1975.

Outside Aix

If you head east along the D10, you come to the **Barrage de Bimont** ❽. This dam makes for a pleasant afternoon trip, with its dramatic waterworks and large nature reserve. Hikers will find numerous trails to choose from, several of which lead to the Barrage Zola, designed by Emile Zola's father in 1854. Further along the D10 is the pretty village of **Vauvenargues** ❾, famous for its Renaissance chateau, inherited by Picasso in 1958. He died here in 1973, aged 91, and is buried in the grounds; neither the chateau nor the park is open to the public, but it's a stunning spot. ❑

RESTAURANTS, BARS AND CAFÉS

Restaurants

Antoine Côté Court
19 cours Mirabeau. Tel: 04 42 93 12 51. €€
www.antoine-cote-court.com
With its conservatory-style setting in a courtyard off cours Mirabeau, this long-standing local favourite draws a fashionable crowd for plentiful Italian food.

Bistro Latin
18 rue de la Couronne. Tel: 04 42 38 22 88. Open: L Tues–Fri, D daily. €
This small-budget bistro in Vieil Aix serves real cooking at remarkable prices. Try southern dishes like pork fillet with honey, and a trio of *tapenade*, chickpea terrine and *brousse*, accompanied by decent Coteaux d'Aix wines.

Brasserie Léopold
2 avenue Victor Hugo. Tel: 04 42 26 01 24. Open L & D daily. €€
A classic brasserie near la Rotonde with excellent old-fashioned service. Vintage photos reveal that the art-deco interior was once a garage.

Chimère Café
15 rue Brueys. Tel: 04 42 38 30 00. Open: D daily. €€
This fashionable old-town haunt has a colourful Baroque interior and a star-spangled cellar for well-prepared market-inspired cooking.

Le Clos de la Violette
10 avenue de la Violette. Tel: 04 42 23 30 71. Open: L & D Tues–Sat. €€€€
At Aix's long-standing gastronomic address chef Jean-Marc Banzo offers light and healthy Provençal cuisine and some exceptional desserts. Dine in the garden under the chestnut trees.

Les Deux Frères
4 avenue de la Reine Astrid. Tel: 04 42 27 90 32. Open: L & D daily. €€
www.les2freres.com
The success story of the Bouchérif brothers, who moved to larger premises in summer 2006. With a pared-back contemporary design, spacious terrace and a screen on which images of the excellent mod Med food are projected.

Le Formal
32 rue Espariat. Tel: 04 42 27 08 31. Open: L & D Tues–Sat. Closed: 3 weeks in April. €€€
Hidden away on one of Vieil Aix's busiest streets, haute-cuisine-trained chef Jean-Luc Le Formal modernises classic ingredients with gastronomic flair.

Le Passage
10 rue Villars. Tel: 04 42 37 09 00. Open: L & D daily. €€
www.le-passage.fr
Reine Sammut, one of France's leading female chefs, is behind fashionable Le Passage, in a dramatically converted sweet factory. The accomplished modern Provençal cooking is based on first-rate ingredients.

Bars and Cafés

All the great and good from Cézanne to Colette or Churchill have frequented **Les Deux Garçons** (53 cours Mirabeau, tel: 04 42 26 00 51), or "les Deux Gs". This intellectual hub, founded in 1792, has a perfect people-watching terrace for an aperitif and a Consular-period interior where you can eat brasserie food. Almost as venerable is the **Café Grillon** at No. 49, with another fine terrace and an elegant period dining room on the first floor. The laidback **Le Verdun** on place de Verdun near the Palais de Justice is very popular with the town's student population. A more recent arrival is **La Rotonde**, a *branché* cocktail haunt with a cosmopolitan menu, overlooking the Rotonde fountain.

PRICE CATEGORIES

Prices for a three-course meal without wine. Note that many restaurants have a less expensive lunch menu.
€ = under €25
€€ = €25–€40
€€€ = €40–€60
€€€€ = more than €60

RIGHT: Aix's many patisseries are irresistible.

CÉZANNE

Paul Cézanne, born in Aix-en-Provence in 1839, was a post-Impressionist painter whose work laid the foundations for Cubism and modern art

Cézanne's work is inextricably linked with the landscape of his native Provence, and above all the countryside around Aix-en-Provence. In the 1860s and '70s he alternated between Paris, Auvers-sur-Oise and Aix, meeting Pissarro (*see below, Pissarro on the left*), being part of the circle of the Impressionists, with whom he exhibited in 1874 and 1877, and remaining in touch with the latest artistic currents and developments in the capital. Paradoxically though, for an artist seen as one of the forerunners of modern art, Cézanne mistrusted modernity and industrialisation.

Cézanne's favourite *motif* or subject was the Mont Ste-Victoire. A tireless walker, he spent many hours walking on the mountain, first as a schoolboy with his friend Emile Zola, later carrying up his easel and bag or painting it from his various studios. He depicts it in over 80 oils and watercolours, searching the key to its structure: "To paint a landscape well, I must first discover its geological characteristics," he wrote. In the mountain, Cézanne found the geometrical ordering of nature – "Nature must be treated by the cylinder, the sphere, the cone..." – that would lead him towards a new conception of perspective, moving away from the Impressionists' moulding through light and colour to a more structural resolution of two-dimensional canvas and three-dimensional nature, a relationship with landscape that approaches abstraction and prefigures the Cubism of Braque and Picasso.

ABOVE: Cézanne's subject par excellence was the Mont Ste-Victoire, seen here in a painting from 1900. The barren triangular white limestone peak that dominates the Aixois landscape from afar is instantly recognisable, and today it's almost impossible to look at the mountain without thinking of Cézanne.

ABOVE: Cézanne had a studio built at chemin des Lauves, north of Vieil Aix, which has been scrupulously preserved, with its clutter of easels and palettes, jugs and bowls of fruits from his still lifes (*see pages 117–18*). For the last four years of his life (1902–6), Cézanne painted here in a period of intense creativity.

THE CÉZANNE TRAIL

A Cézanne trail around Aix picks out numerous spots associated with the artist. Take a leaflet from the tourist office (2 place du Général de Gaulle; tel: 04 42 16 11 61; www.aixenprovencetourism.com) or follow the brass medallions inserted in the pavement; you'll see the building where he was born on rue de l'Opéra, the site of his father's hat shop on 55 cours Mirabeau where he lived as a small child, the Café des Deux Garçons at No. 53, where he would often stop for an aperitif, the Collège Mignet (then Collège Bourbon) in the Quartier Mazarin where he went to school, and the Hôtel de Ville where he got married in 1886.

RIGHT: *Pears and Peaches* (c.1895–1900). Cézanne found a wealth of possibilities within the convention of the still life; using layers of colour, he altered traditional perspective expressed in terms of successive planes of depth by emphasising the foreground – a revolutionary development later taken up by the Cubists.

The Jas de Bouffan, the family estate bought by his father, is also open to the public *(see page 118)*, and although now surrounded by modern housing you can still see several of the elements painted by the artist, including the long avenue of chestnut trees *(see below, Chestnut Trees at the Jas de Bouffan, c.1885–7)*. His celebrated *Card Players (see opposite, top left)* portrays two of the gardeners.

The Carrières de Bibémus, atmospheric disused quarries that for centuries provided stone for the construction of Aix, can also be visited with a route taking you past views depicted by the artist, and the simple drystone cottage he rented to store his materials. As you clamber through this rocky universe, works you previously thought of as stylised proto-Cubism suddenly seem almost realist, and in the ochre rocks you can see the varying hues of yellow, cream and orange that dominated Cézanne's palette.

BELOW: *Bathers* (c.1900–6). As well as the paintings of Mont Ste-Victoire, Cézanne is also known for his series of naked female nudes, in which the groups of almost abstract, geometric figures are paralleled by a vault of overhanging trees. This painting became an inspiration for the nascent Cubist movement; both Picasso and Matisse took a strong interest in it.

ST-RÉMY AND LES ALPILLES

At a maximum height of 500 metres, Les Alpilles may not reach Alpine heights, but the jagged crags and ravines of these miniature mountains are nonetheless impressive. It was here, amid the dazzling limestone, pine woods and olive groves, that Van Gogh was inspired to paint some of his best-known works

South of Avignon, hemmed in by the Durance River on one side and the Rhône on the other, the white limestone of the Alpilles mountain range dazzles against blue skies and the pine woods, vines and olive trees on its slopes.

St-Rémy-de-Provence

The mini-capital of the Alpilles, **St-Rémy-de-Provence ❶**, makes a good base for exploring the area with its combination of archaeological remains, fine architecture, chic boutiques and a thriving café society. As in many Provençal towns, the dense network of narrow streets that makes up the old city is ringed by broad, plane-tree-shaded boulevards which trace the line of the former ramparts.

On boulevard Marceau, the cavernous **Collégiale St-Martin** was rebuilt in neoclassical style in 1821 after the previous church collapsed. The ceiling is decorated with faded blue paint and a sprinkling of gold stars, and lit by numerous stained-glass windows. An enormous organ dominates the interior (recitals every Saturday at 5.30pm, July–Sept).

Behind here lies the old town, full of cafés, art galleries and smart interior-design shops, and some remarkable Renaissance houses. The 16th-century Hôtel Mistral de Mondragon, on the corner of the main

thoroughfare, rue Carnot, is home to the recently refurbished **Musée des Alpilles** (place Favier; tel: 04 90 92 68 24; open Nov–Feb Tues–Sat and first Sun of month 2–5pm, Mar–Oct Tues–Sat and first Sun of month 10am–noon, 2–6pm, July and Aug until 7pm; admission charge). The superb Renaissance mansion has an ornate façade decorated with Ionic pilasters, carved friezes and a tower with rams and lions heads. An arcaded courtyard is graced by a bust of Van Gogh by Zadkine. The

Map on page 124

LEFT: Les Baux-de-Provence. **BELOW:** Daudet's windmill.

When Van Gogh left the hospital at St-Rémy a year after checking himself in on 8 May 1889, he had painted some 150 canvases. Twenty-one of these are now reproduced on enamel plaques around town in a trail of the main sites he painted. Enquire at St-Rémy tourist office for more information.

museum focuses on history and folk art, with displays on quarrying in the Alpilles, pottery and tile-making, agriculture, costumes and festivities, and collections of *santons*.

Across the square the Renaissance **Hôtel de Sade** and the **Mairie** (town hall), housed in a former convent, are worth a look. On Tuesday and Thursday evenings in summer, a craft market is held beneath the arcades fronting the square.

The Van Gogh trail

Many people come to St-Rémy on the trail of Vincent Van Gogh, who spent a year here painting many of his most famous works, including *Irises* and *Starry Night*. He checked himself into the local asylum in May 1889, after an argument with Gauguin during which he sliced off part of his ear. Follow the avenue Vincent Van Gogh south of the centre to the **Monastère St-Paul-de-Mausole** (open daily Apr–Oct 9.30am–7pm, Nov–Mar 10.15am–4.45pm; admission charge), the medieval monastery that houses the clinic where he painted some of his best works. The pretty cloisters and the Romanesque chapel can be visited, as can a reconstruction of Van Gogh's room; but the still active psychiatric home cannot. Today, art plays a part in the therapy received by the psychiatric patients.

The Hôtel Estrine, an elegant 18th-century residence, houses the **Centre d'Art Présence Van Gogh** (rue Estrine; open Apr–Dec Tues–Sun 10.30am–12.30pm, 2.30–6.30pm; admission charge). The works are Van Gogh reproductions (very few of his Provençal paintings remain in Provence), but temporary exhibitions of modern art share the same space.

Glanum

Ancient **Glanum** lies just south of here en route to Les Baux. Marking the entrance are two particularly well-preserved monuments, an arch and a

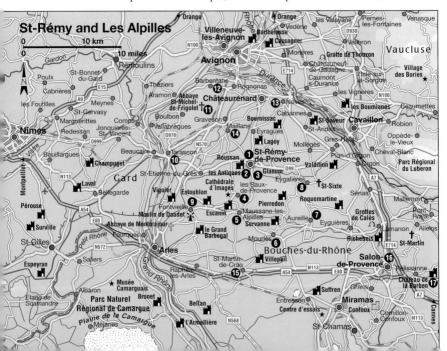

mausoleum, known collectively as **Les Antiques ❷**. The **triumphal arch** straddles what was once the Via Domitia, the Roman road connecting Spain to Italy. It was built during the reign of Augustus to mark the entrance to the city of Glanum, and decorated with reliefs illustrating Caesar's conquest of Gaul. The **Mausolée de Jules**, dated 30–20 BC, is a funereal monument built by members of a powerful Roman family in honour of their patriarchs.

Slightly further up the road is the archaeological site of **Glanum ❸** (tel: 04 90 92 23 79; www.monum.fr; open Apr–Aug daily 9am–7pm, Sept–Mar Tues–Sun 10.30am–5pm; admission charge). A Celto-Ligurian sanctuary city built beside a sacred spring was succeeded during the Gallo-Greek era by a flourishing Phocaean trading post that served as a commercial and religious centre. This role continued under the Romans, until the city was virtually destroyed by invaders in the 3rd century.

The remains of baths and villas around a paved main street have been unearthed, as has a separate district of temples, where a couple of facsimile columns provide a sense of scale. Even if it is not easy to work out what the different remains represent, the setting – a hollow in the mountains where white stone glints against blue sky – is remarkably beautiful.

Les Baux-de-Provence

For a change of scenery, take the D5 south from St-Rémy and then the D27A, climbing up through wooded hills and the award-winning vineyards of the Mas de la Dame towards the spectacularly situated **Les Baux-de-Provence ❹**, perched high above rocky outcrops that tumble into deep valleys (the name Baux comes from *baou*, Provençal for rocky spur).

The site of Les Baux has been inhabited for 5,000 years. Its fame, however, derives from the period between the 11th and 14th centuries when the bold and arrogant lords of Baux made their presence felt throughout the region.

Today, more than 1½ million tourists a year come to see where the lords raged and troubadours once roamed. Les Baux has become the ultimate in tourist traps, with craft shops and ice-cream parlours spilling out of old buildings. In high season, the place becomes unbearably crowded, but visit in early spring, autumn or on a crisp winter's day, and you can enjoy this extraordinary place in relative calm.

The site divides into two parts: the "Château", which contains the ruins of the feudal court, and the partially ruined "Village" below it, an attractive mixture of shops and galleries set in medieval and Renaissance houses, many with delightful gardens.

The village has several museums. The **Musée Yves Brayer** (Hôtel Porcelet, rue de l'Eglise; open Apr–Sept daily 10am–12.30pm, 2–6.30pm, Oct–Mar Wed–Mon until 5.30pm, closed Jan–mid-Feb; admission charge) contains oil paintings of

TIP

St-Rémy is a good place to come for those interested in herbalism and aromatherapy. There are many charming shops selling essential oils, soaps and more. The boutique Florame also has a small museum, the Musée des Arômes, with distillation of lavender on site between mid-July and mid-August. 34 boulevard Mirabeau; tel: 04 32 60 05 18; www.florame.com

BELOW: Glanum.

The feudal life of Les Baux presents a fascinating paradox. Here, amidst these "impregnable fortresses, inhabited by men whose roughness was only matched by that of their suits of armour, the 'Respect of the Lady' and ritual adoration of her beauty was born." The patronage of the troubadours by these lords gave rise to the chivalric code, and much of France's literary tradition emerged from the bloody citadel.

BELOW: Les Baux.

the region by the well-known artist, while the **Fondation Louis Jou** (Hôtel Brion, Grande Rue; tel: 04 90 54 34 17; open Apr–Dec Thur–Mon 11am–1pm, 2–6pm; admission charge) offers guided tours of typographer and publisher Louis Jou's collection of antiquarian books, engravings, presses and woodblocks.

Best-preserved of all the monuments in the old city is the **Eglise St-Vincent**, which has a central nave dating back to the 12th century and stained glass that is a striking *mélange* of ancient and modern. Across the road is the lovely 17th-century **Chapelle des Pénitents Blancs**, painted with Nativity scenes by Brayer in 1974.

The castle and its ramparts

The "Cité Morte" or **Château des Baux** (open daily summer 9am–7.30pm, winter 9.30am–5pm/6.30pm; admission charge; www.chateau-baux-provence.com), stronghold of the lords of Baux, is entered through the rectangular Tour de Brau, dating from the late 14th century. Beside it lies a small modern cemet-

ery filled with fragrant lavender, and the 12th-century **Chapelle de St-Blaise**. Press on to the highest point of the ruins, where there is a round tower from which the Baux family must have surveyed the valley with watchful eyes. The view from here is incredible: on one side, the crags of the Alpilles, on the other, a sheer drop to the rolling vineyards and olive groves nestling below.

There are more fortifications along the northern ramparts. If you've energy enough, climb them for wider-ranging views or to investigate what is left of the 15th-century castle, the 10th-century keep and the Paravelle tower, as well as some troglodyte dwellings.

For more breathtaking views head northwards out of Les Baux on the D27, which winds along a perilous precipice overlooking the **Val d'Enfer** (valley of hell). At its start, just outside Les Baux, stop off at the **Cathédrale d'Images** (Val d'Enfer; open Mar–early Jan daily 10am–6pm; admission charge; tel: 04 90 54 38 65; www.cathedrale-images.com), a former limestone quarry where a

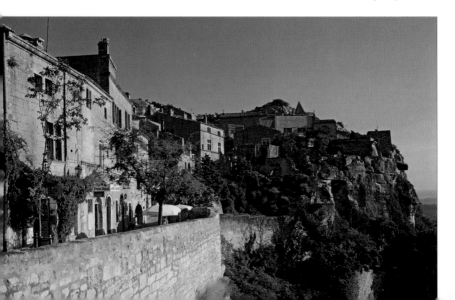

sophisticated *son et lumière* show, which changes each year, is projected onto the rocky walls and crevasses.

Olive country

Head south of Les Baux and you're in vine and olive country. Gentrified **Maussane-les-Alpilles** ❺ and more workaday **Mouriès** ❻ vie for the title of the village with the most olive trees in France, and both have reputable olive mills. Others swear by the olives of **Aureille** ❼, a half-forgotten town a little further east in the midst of grassy plains and vast olive groves. Aureille is a simple, pleasant enough place, with a friendly central bar and the ruins of an 11th-century castle rising above it on a hill that is only accessible on foot. For those in search of the "real" Provence, it can come as a relief.

North of here, **Eygalières** ❽ provides some of the prettiest perspectives in the Alpilles with its cluster of old houses climbing up a small hill and, 1 km (½ mile) outside the village, the quaint Romanesque Chapelle St-Sixte, ringed by cypresses.

Daudet's Windmill

Towards Arles and west of Maussane-les-Alpilles, the picturesque town of **Fontvieille** ❾ is notable for its series of modest oratories, erected in 1721 in thanksgiving for an end to the plague. The town's primary attraction is the **Moulin de Daudet**, immortalised in Alphonse Daudet's (1840–97) *Letters from My Windmill*. The fact that the windmill actually belonged to Daudet's friends and witnessed little penmanship has done little to deter the hordes of tourists that crowd its tiny interior. The mill does enjoy a picturesque location and contains some interesting features, such as a circular ceiling inscribed compass-fashion with the names of the winds that sweep the hill. However, the narrow underground museum is rather disappointing.

Tarascon

Bordering the Rhône, 14 km (6 miles) west of St-Rémy, the historic town of **Tarascon** ❿ became the stuff of Provençal legend in AD 48 when its resident monster, the Tarasque, was tamed by St Martha *(see page 128)*. By the Middle Ages the town had become an important place of pilgrimage thanks to the saint's relics, which are held in the crypt of the **Collégiale Ste-Marthe**. Countless paintings and sculptures of Martha and the Tarasque exist, including paintings in the Collégiale Ste-Marthe and the marble Tarasque de Noves, in the archaeological museum in Avignon.

The feudal **Château du Roi René** (open Apr–Aug daily 9am–7pm; Sept–Mar Tues–Sat 10.30am–5pm; admission charge) on the banks of the Rhône is a grandiose affair. The castle was begun in 1400 by Louis II d'Anjou and completed by his son Good King René, who turned it into a sumptuous Renaissance palace. The building proudly rivals the Château de Beaucaire on the opposite bank, built from the same white limestone.

TIP

Olive oil AOC Les Baux-de-Provence is made from a blend of oils. Two mills making high-quality oil according to traditional methods are the 17th-century Moulin Jean-Marie Cornille (rue Charloun-Rien, Maussane-les-Alpilles; tel: 04 90 54 32 37; open Mon–Sat), and the recently constructed Moulin de Calanquet (vieux chemin d'Arles, St-Rémy-de-Provence; tel: 04 32 60 09 50; open daily).

BELOW: olive grove, Vallée des Baux.

According to legend a scaly amphibious monster had for years terrorised the people of Tarascon, drinking the Rhône dry and devouring villagers. In the 1st century, Martha, member of the saintly boat from Bethany crew (see page 23) tamed the beast, then converted the grateful and hitherto pagan Tarascon-nais to Christianity. Tarascon celebrates the legend with the annual Fête de la Tarasque (see page 146).

The interior of the Château du Roi René is mostly empty, apart from six magnificent 17th-century Flemish tapestries and the reconstructed interior of an old pharmacy.

Architectural highlights in the old town itself include the three fortified gateways, the Renaissance cloisters of the former Couvent des Cordeliers and the arcaded rue des Halles. On rue Proudhon, the fine Hôtel d'Aiminy now contains the **Musée Soleïado** (open May–Sept daily 10am–6pm; Oct–Apr Tues–Sat 10am–5pm; admission charge; www.souleiado.com), with a the collection of woodblocks, printed *indiennes*, costumes, pottery and objects belonging to the Tarascon textile house *(see box below)*.

Across the Rhône sits Tarascon's twin and historic rival **Beaucaire**, once a stop on the Via Domitia between Italy and Spain. The massive **castle ruins** (open mid-Mar–Oct Thur–Tues) are used as a site for eagle and falconry displays. The town's main appeal resides in the fine 17th- and 18th-century town houses and the lively port at its heart, with its quayside cafés and companies offering boat trips to the Camargue or along the canal to Sète.

La Montagnette

From Tarascon, travel north along the D970 towards Avignon to reach the **Abbaye St-Michel-de-Frigolet** ⓫. Parts of the abbey are used for religious retreats, and there are also two churches and a simple hotel and restaurant (open daily 8–10.45am, 2–6pm; www.frigolet.com). The land seems slightly less forbidding here than around Tarascon, as the Alpilles meld into the gentler Montagnette. These hills cover the area between the curve of the Rhône and the east–west stretch of the Alpilles, and harbour numerous groves of cypress and poplars, olive, apricot and almond trees, straggly pines and fragrant herbs. Note that footpaths are closed from July to mid-September.

Barbentane ⓬ is a little town just north of the abbey with a warm, laid-back atmosphere. Worth visiting here is the handsome 17th-century **Château** (open Apr–Oct Thur–Tues 10am–noon, 2–6pm; daily July–

Provençal Textiles

Today no Provençal hotel or restaurant seems to be without its colourful Provençal print curtains and tablecloths, still called *indiennes* after the woodblock-printed textiles first imported from India in the 17th century. The prints soon became a craze adopted by the latest fashions and copied by local manufacturers in kaleidoscopic floral and geometric patterns, including the Indian paisley motifs still popular today. But in 1686, Louis XIV's minister Colbert banned their production in France to protect the Compagnie des Indes, as well as French silk- and wool-makers, and local manufacturers moved to Orange within the Comtat Venaissin. When the law was repealed in 1759, production once more flourished in Provence.

Two companies continue to produce quality traditional *indiennes*, although even they are no longer printed by hand: Les Olivades, at St-Etienne-des-Grès in the Alpilles, which produces furnishing fabrics, tablecloths and clothes from both modern designs and those based on 17th- and 18th-century fabrics; and Soleïado ("the rays of sun that pierce through clouds" in Provençal), which uses motifs from its huge archive of old woodblocks and is based in Tarascon, where it has also opened a museum *(see above)*.

Sept; admission charge; tel: 04 90 95 51 07), just off the main street. An impressive collection of antiques and objets d'art fill the interior.

The Petite Crau

Between Avignon and St-Rémy, **Châteaurenard** is a quiet Provençal town – except during its colourful horse-drawn wagon parades *(see page 146)* – set amid a network of 17th-century canals that turned the Petite Crau plain into a major centre for market gardening.

Just to the east, you may want to make a quick sweep through **Noves** ⓭. The town today has little to attract tourists (all that remains of its chateau are segments of the 14th-century ramparts), but it was here that Petrarch first laid eyes on his beloved Laura, about whom he would later write some of the world's most famous love poems. The wine grown on the neighbouring hillsides is called the *Cuvée des Amours* (love's vintage).

Another town of literary significance crops up on the D5 between St-Rémy-de-Provence and Graveson. **Maillane** ⓮ was both the birth

and burial place of Frédéric Mistral *(see page 28)*. The house where the poet lived from 1876 until his death in 1914 has been turned into a museum, the **Museon Mistral** (11 avenue Lamartine; open Tues–Sun; admission charge; tel: 04 90 95 84 19), containing his desk and gloves just as he left them. He is buried in the cemetery down the street.

Salon-de-Provence and the Grande Crau

South of the Alpilles, the landscape changes radically as you cross the Grande Crau plain, an area of sheep pasture and hay cultivation centred around the market town of **St-Martin-de-Crau** ⓯. Here, a small Eco-musée (open Mon–Sat 9am–noon, 2–6pm) in an old sheepfold explains the local habitat and agriculture.

Situated on the eastern edge of the Crau, the sprawling, dusty traffic-filled **Salon-de-Provence** ⓰ has been dubbed the "crossroads of Provence" for its central location. Its role in the olive oil trade, aided by the arrival of the railway at the end of the 19th century, turned it into the heart

Map on page 124

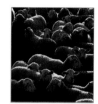

Transhumance is the moving of sheep flocks between their winter grazing on the Crau plain and summer grazing up in the Alps. Traditonally this was done on foot, but now the herding is done with a lorry. The practice is celebrated each year with a festival in St-Rémy.

BELOW: horse-drawn wagon parade, Châteaurenard.

Map on page 124

Nostradamus died in Salon in 1566. His tomb is marked with a plaque which reads: "Here lie the bones of Michel de Nostradame, alone at the judgement of humans worthy of knowing the stars of the future. He lived 62 years, 6 months and 17 days."

BELOW:
Château de l'Emperi.

of the soap industry. A few of the elaborate villas built by the soap barons survive, mostly on and around rue de la République, though only two companies still make soap. Marius Fabre has been in operation here since 1900. You can see how the traditional cubes of soap are made on tours of the factory every Monday and Thursday at 10.30am. There is also a small museum (open Mon–Fri; tel: 04 90 53 82 75; www.marius-fabre.fr).

The town is dominated by the forbidding turrets of the **Château de l'Emperi**, built between the 10th and 16th centuries as a residence of the bishops of Arles – clearly a militant lot – and around which Salon originally sprang up. Inside, through an elegantly arcaded Renaissance courtyard, the **Musée de l'Emperi** (place des Centuries; open Wed–Mon 10am–noon, 2–6pm; admission charge) showcases one of France's largest collections of militaria, dating from 1700 to 1918. Several rooms are dedicated to the Napoleonic era, with the diminutive general's short blue bed among the treasures.

The hub of the town below is the tree-lined cours Gimon, where you'll find the 17th-century Hôtel de Ville and tourist hotspot, the **Maison de Nostradamus** (13 rue Nostradamus; open Mon–Fri 9am–noon, 2–6pm, Sat–Sun 2–6pm; admission charge), where the renowned physician-turned-astrologer wrote his famous book of predictions. It has been turned into a colourful waxworks experience, with 10 scenes recounting episodes from his life.

Also in the old town is the beautiful early Gothic **Eglise St-Michel**, dating from 1220 to 1239. Lying outside the old town walls, **St-Laurent**, built between 1344 and 1480 in characteristically sombre Provençal Gothic style, presents a much grander spectacle than its forerunner.

A second famous inhabitant of Salon, Adam de Craponne, is commemorated by a statue on a small square across from the Hôtel de Ville. De Craponne was the 16th-century engineer who brought fertility to the region by building an irrigation canal from the Durance River through the dry plains of the Crau and out into the sea.

Château de la Barben

Eleven km (7 miles) east of Salon-de-Provence on the D572/D22, the impressive **Château de la Barben** (guided visits daily 11am, 2pm, 3pm, 4pm; admission charge; tel: 04 90 55 25 41) is yet another of Good King René's castles. Its formal gardens were laid out by the landscape gardener of Versailles, Le Nôtre. In the centre is a fountain in which Napoleon's sister, Pauline, liked to bathe *au naturel*.

Outside the chateau, the **Zoo de la Barben** (open daily 10am– 6pm; admission charge; tel: 04 90 55 19 12; www.zoolabarben.com) is the largest zoo in the region, where some 120 species of animal have the run of 33 hectares (82 acres) of grounds. ❑

RESTAURANTS AND BARS

Les Baux-de-Provence

Hostellerie de la Reine Jeanne
Grande Rue. Tel: 04 90 54 32 06. Open: L & D daily. €
www.la-reinejeanne.com
Les Baux's chic eateries hide out in the hills, but if you want to eat in the village itself, then this place offers reliable traditional Provençal cooking and lovely views. Garlicky lamb from the Alpilles is a speciality.

L'Oustou de la Baumanière
Val d'Enfer. Tel: 04 90 54 33 07. Open: L & D daily (closed Wed and L Thur in winter). Closed: Feb. €€€€
www.oustoudebaumaniere.com
This luxurious *bastide* is the place for a gastronomic splurge. Owner Jean-André Charial uses home-grown vegetables, and there is an all-vegetable set menu. Talented chef Sylvestre Wahid, previously chez Ducasse, produces dishes like gently spiced spider crab, and desserts are concocted by his brother Jonathan, dessert "champion de France" of 2005.

Eygalières

Bistrot d'Eygalières
Rue de la République. Tel: 04 90 90 60 34. Open: L Wed–Sun, D Tues–Sun (closed D Sun in winter). Closed: Jan–mid-Mar. €€€€
www.chezbru.com
Flamboyant chef Wout Bru has made this village

house one of the most sought-after tables in Provence and a favourite with the showbiz set. His trademark is a light, inventive blend of flavours and textures and sweet-and-sour mixes. Book well ahead. He also owns the more affordable Petit Bru (18 avenue Jean Jaurès, tel: 04 90 95 98 89).

Fontvieille

Auberge La Regalido
Rue Frédéric Mistral.
Tel: 04 90 54 60 22. Open: L Tues–Sun. Closed: Jan–Feb. €€€
www.laregalido.com
Grand classic cuisine is served in the vaulted dining room of a restored olive-oil mill. Dishes such as monkfish in Châteauneuf-du-Pape wine sauce are a culinary and aesthetic treat.

La Paradou

La Petite France
55 avenue de la Vallée-de-Baux. Tel: 04 90 54 41 91. Open: L & D Fri–Tues. Closed: mid-Oct–early Dec. €
Haute-cuisine trained chef Thierry Maffre-Bogé has forsaken grand cuisine for a simpler bistro style. His blackboard menu is remarkably good value.

St-Rémy-de-Provence

Alain Assaud
13 boulevard Marceau. Tel: 04 90 92 37 11. Open: L Fri, Sun–Tues, D Thur–Tues. Closed: Nov–Mar. €€

It may look like no more than a stone-walled café, but the food here is surprisingly sophisticated. Try the *aioli* with fresh cod and the excellent desserts and sorbets.

Les Ateliers de l'Image
36 boulevard Victor Hugo.
Tel: 04 90 92 51 50. Open: L & D daily. €€
www.hotelphoto.com
St-Rémy's arty design-hotel has an appropriately stylish restaurant where you can choose between modern Provençal cuisine (dinner Thur–Sun) or excellent sushi (D Tues–Sat, and L Thur–Sun in season). At the more casual Resto' Bar, in an airy former cinema, salads and light dishes are served (L & D daily 11am–midnight). A large terrace overlooks the landscaped garden.

Bistrot Découverte
19 boulevard Victor Hugo.
Tel: 04 90 92 34 49. Open: L Tues–Sun, D Tues–Sat (L & D daily in high season). €€
www.bistrotdecouverte.com
Wine sommelier Claude and his wife Dana opened this attractive little bistro in 2005. Dishes might include an accomplished risotto with *girolles*, the fish of the day or roast veal with seasonal veg, accompanied by well-chosen wines. The cellar contains a wine shop and can also be used for tastings.

La Maison Jaune
15 rue Carnot. Tel: 04 90 92 56 14. Open: L Wed–Sun, D Tues–Sat. Closed: Jan–Feb. €€€
In a dressed-up bistro in the old town, chef François Perraud puts his own deft spin on carefully chosen local produce. Try dishes such as purple artichokes in a herb stock or marinated anchovies with chickpeas.

PRICE CATEGORIES

Prices for a three-course meal without wine. Note that many restaurants have a less expensive lunch menu.
€ = under €25
€€ = €25–€40
€€€ = €40–€60
€€€€ = more than €60

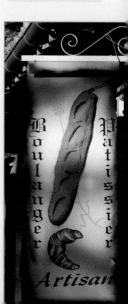

ARLES AND THE CAMARGUE

Arles is the soul of Provence. In among the nests of red roofs and maze of narrow streets are superb Roman remains, Romanesque churches and sun-dappled cafés. Arles is also gateway to the Camargue, an area of desolate beauty, famed for its white horses, pink flamingos and cowboys

Arles ❶ captures the essence of Provence. Despite its grand past and impressive architectural heritage the town still has an intimate, villagey atmosphere that makes it easily accessible to the visitor. While the Arlesiens are fiercely proud of their past and dedicated to upholding Provençal and, especially, Camarguais traditions, the town also has an active cultural scene: home to a world music festival as well as the annual Rencontres Internationales de la Photographie and one of France's most respected publishing houses, Actes Sud.

Arles in its heyday

Founded by the Massilians as a trading post in the 6th century BC, Arles's position at the crossroads of the Rhône and the Roman Via Aurelia made it a natural choice for development by the Romans. The town grew slowly for several hundred years, cementing its position as a river and maritime port. Then, during the struggle for power between Caesar and Pompey, Arles got its lucky break. Marseille made the fatal error of showing friendship towards Pompey, and Caesar turned to Arles, known for its skilled boatbuilders, with the request that 12 war vessels be built for him within 30 days. The city complied, and Arles's good fortune was

sealed. Caesar designated Arles as the first city of Provence, leading to the construction of temples, baths, the amphitheatre, theatre and circus.

The city continued to prosper, and was briefly capital of the 10th-century kingdom of Bourgogne-Provence. Although its predominance would wane over the following centuries, Arles enjoyed a new period of prosperity in the 16th and 17th centuries when the local landowners built themselves fine Renaissance and classical town houses. It remained a

Maps:
City 134
Area 140

LEFT: flamingos in the Camargue. **BELOW:** Théâtre Antique, Arles.

TIP

If you're planning to do a lot of sightseeing, invest in the Pass Monuments, which gives access to all the ancient monuments and museums in Arles. Available from the tourist office, museums and monuments. For more information, contact, www.arles tourisme.com.

BELOW:
portal sculptures,
St-Trophime.

key maritime and river port right until the advent of the steam engine, when transportation by train overtook the tugboat method, spelling disaster for the Arlesian economy.

As gateway to the Camargue (top producer of rice in France), Arles has managed to recoup some of its status as a trading centre, but it does rely heavily on its past for its livelihood.

The Vieille Ville

At the heart of Arles is the **Vieille Ville** (old town), an attractive maze of narrow stone streets where crumbling Roman edifices mingle with sturdy medieval stonework. The old town is bordered to the south by the wide boulevard des Lices, to the east by the remnants of ancient ramparts and to the north and west by the grand sweep of the River Rhône.

Most visitors will first arrive in Arles via the boulevard des Lices. If you have a car, it's a good idea to leave it in the car park on the street's

south side. Almost all of the city's tourist sites are within easy walking distance of each other. Although often traffic-clogged, the boulevard des Lices is a lively spot with many cafés and the local tourist office (esplanade Charles de Gaulle; tel: 04 90 18 41 20; www.tourisme.ville-arles.fr). Its high points come on Saturday morning during the extensive produce market and every first Wednesday of the month, when a fabulous flea market spills over its streets.

Eglise St-Trophime

The cobbled rue Jean Jaurès will bring you to the spacious **place de la République 🅐**, with an ancient obelisk in the middle and the splendid **Hôtel de Ville** (town hall) at one end. The most impressive building in the square, however, is the **Eglise St-Trophime 🅑**, named after the saint credited with bringing Christianity to Provence. The richly carved doorway is a glorious example of the

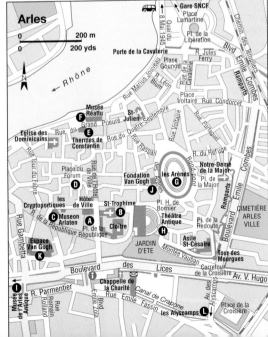

Provençal Romanesque style. Built between 1152 and 1180, its intricate tympanum shows the Last Judgement overseen by a barefoot and crowned Jesus, while dozens of winged angels soar over the archway. The church's barrel-vaulted nave is, at over 20 metres (60 ft), the highest in Provence. To the left of the entrance, a 4th-century sarcophagus serves as a baptismal font. Further in, the life of the Virgin is depicted on a huge 17th-century Aubusson tapestry.

St-Trophime's **cloisters** (open winter daily 10am–4.30pm, summer 9am–6pm; admission charge) are more cheerful. The sound of birds fills the air as you enter, and in warm weather pink flowers dot the bright courtyard, which is enclosed by solemn 14th-century figures posted as columns. Up on the roof, the sun reflects off the white stone and birds circle the lofty belltower. Delicate columns and the stone tiles used for eaves round off an exquisite picture.

Tribute to Provence

A couple of blocks down the rue de la République, in an imposing Renais-sance mansion, is the **Museon Arlaten ⒞** (open July–Aug daily 9.30am–12.30am, 2–6.30pm, Sept–Jun closed Mon, until 5pm in winter; admission charge). Regional poet Frédéric Mistral founded this ethnographic museum and funded it with the money he was awarded when he won the Nobel Prize for literature in 1904, with the proviso that it be dedicated to all things Provençal. Accordingly, the name is Provençal (for "Musée d'Arles"), all the documentation within is in dialect (as well as in French) and the *gardiennes* are dressed in traditional costume. One hall is filled with costumes and explanations of how they should be worn, others feature amulets and charms, *tambours* and other instruments, nautical and agricultural equipment, wall hangings and paintings.

Towards the river

The *museon* is not the only mark left on the city by the poet. A formidable **bust of Mistral** looks down over the **place du Forum ⒟**, once the commercial heart of the Roman city. A couple of columns from an ancient

Map on page 134

Traditional Arlesienne dress is still worn for local festivals and for the feria*, when Arlesi-ennes parade around the arena prior to the bullfighting. Fine examples can be seen at the Museon Arlaten.*

BELOW: old town, Arles.

Bullfights of various types are still held in the Arènes, as are concerts and other shows. Saturday afternoons find locals munching peanuts and drinking sodas as they watch their favourite cocarde *champions cavort in front of snorting bulls. The first of May welcomes the Fête des Gardians, when cowboys from the Camargue gather for an extravaganza. More annual bullfights take place during the Feria Pascale at Easter and the Prémices du Riz in mid-September.*

BELOW: festivities at the Arènes.

temple can be spotted in the façade of the Grand Hôtel Nord-Pinus. Much of Arles' nightlife is concentrated on this lively square. Several cafés, including the Café de la Nuit, done up in homage to Van Gogh's painting, make it a great place to enjoy a drink or a laid-back meal. Bullfighting aficionados frequent the Tambourin, where the walls are lined with autographed photos of local champions.

If you continue towards the river, you will come to the **Thermes de Constantin** ❺. These 4th-century baths were once the largest in Provence, but not much remains. The **Musée Réattu** ❻ (10 rue du Grand Prieuré; open Nov–Feb daily 1–5pm, Mar, Apr, Oct daily 10am–noon, 2–5pm, May–Sept daily 10am–noon, 2–6.30pm; admission charge) across the street is far more interesting. Many of the rooms are devoted to historical paintings by Jacques Réattu (a local artist who bought the former priory in 1790) and his collection of 17th-century paintings. Much more worthwhile, however, are the collections of modern sculpture – including works by Zadkine, Richier and

Toni Grand – photography, and the Picasso Donation, a collection of 57 Picasso sketches and two paintings.

If the inevitable press of tourists has begun to get to you, steal a quiet moment exploring the antiques shops around here or walking down the ramparts lining the Rhône.

The Arènes and Roman Arles

At the very heart of the old city, the **Arènes** ❼ (rond-point des Arènes; open daily Nov–Feb 10–11.30am, 2–4.30pm, Mar–Apr, Oct 9–11.30am, 2–5.30pm, May–Sept 9am–6pm, closed during Féria; admission charge; tel: 04 90 49 38 20) is another place to chase Roman ghosts. This vast amphitheatre measures an impressive 136 by 107 metres (440 by 345 ft) and holds more than 20,000 spectators. Built in the 1st century AD, it is larger and older than its counterpart in Nîmes. A climb up one of the remaining medieval towers offers a view over the red-roofed expanse of the old city, its modern environs, the Rhône and the Alpilles hills beyond.

Follow the Arènes round and you'll come across another trace of ancient Arles, the neighbouring **Théâtre Antique** ❽ (rue de la Calade; open winter daily 10–11.30am, 2–4.30pm, summer 9am–6pm; admission charge; tel: 04 90 49 36 74). By day, this 1st-century BC theatre equates to little more than a few piles of rubble, a siding of worn stone seating and two half-standing columns; but it makes a romantic setting for summer concerts.

Once you've seen the monuments, you can learn about the former splendour of Roman Arles at the **Musée de l'Arles et de la Provence Antique** ❾ (avenue de la Première Division Française Libre; open Nov–Mar daily 10am–5pm, Apr–Oct daily 9am–7pm; admission charge; www.arles-antique.cg13.fr), outside the old town by the banks of the Rhône. Inside the striking blue triangular building,

designed by Henri Ciriani, models of Roman Arles complement ancient statues, jewellery and richly carved marble sarcophagi. Outside is the partially excavated **Circus**, used by the Romans for chariot-racing.

The legacy of Van Gogh

Visitors who come to Arles with the intention of making a pilgrimage to Van Gogh's old haunts may be disappointed. The house where he and Gauguin lived, worked and argued no longer stands, and the Café de la Nuit on Place du Forum is a reconstruction. However, you can visit the **Fondation Van Gogh** ❶ (Palais de Luppé, 24 bis rond-point des Arènes; open Apr–Sept daily 10am–6pm, Oct–Mar Tues–Sun 11am–5pm; admission charge; tel: 04 90 49 94 04), which has a collection of work by contemporary artists in tribute to Van Gogh. Otherwise, you can see some of the sites the artist painted, such as the copious fields of sunflowers, and the fabulous quality of the light that imbues them.

The **Espace Van Gogh** ❸ (place du Docteur Félix Rey, open daily 9am–6pm; admission varies; tel: 04 90 49 38 05) is housed in the 16th-century hospital building where Van Gogh was treated, restored to look as it did when the artist was there. The building, set around a garden courtyard, incorporates a bookshop, library and temporary exhibition space.

One place that still looks very much as it did when Van Gogh painted it in October 1888 is **Les Alyscamps** ❶ (open daily; admission charge; tel: 04 90 49 38 20), the atmospheric ancient necropolis on the avenue des Alyscamps. The cemetery was begun by the Romans, but by the 4th century it had been taken over by Gallic Christians. As you walk down the tomb-lined lane, look for the plaque that reads: "Van Gogh. Here, struck by the beauty of the site, he came to set up his easel." There is a solemn tranquillity under the poplars that makes it a favourite place for afternoon walks.

Abbaye de Montmajour

Just 5 km (3 miles) northeast of Arles stands the **Abbaye de Montmajour** ❷ (route de Fontvieille; open

Maps:
City 134
Area 140

Four separate colour-coded walks around Arles allow you to discover different aspects of the town's heritage: blue for ancient Arles, green for medieval Arles, red for Renaissance and classical Arles, and yellow for Van Gogh. You can pick up a brochure at the tourist office.

BELOW:
the Espace Van Gogh.

LE JARDIN DE LA MAISON DE SANTÉ A ARLES
"... C'est un galerie à arcades comme des bâtiments arabes, blanchie à la chaux. Devant ces galeries un jardin antique avec un étang au milieu et huit parterres de fleurs, des myosotis, des roses de Noël, des anémones, des renoncules, etc. Et sous la galerie des orangers et des lauriers-roses.
... l'ai tout droit des fleurs et de verdure printanière."

Every summer, the highly respected Rencontres Inter-nationales de la Photographie bring together photo-graphers from around the world for a panorama of shows, held in Arles' monuments, chapels and museums, includ-ing the Théâtre Antique, the Espace Van Gogh and Abbaye de Montma-jour. For more details and dates, contact: www.rencontres-arles.com

BELOW: flat plains of the Camargue.

Sept–Apr Tues–Sun 10am–5pm, May–Aug daily 10am–6.30pm; admission charge; www.monum.fr). It was founded in the 10th century by Benedictine monks who turned the island refuge, surrounded by marsh-land, into an oasis, by draining the swamp and building an abbey. By the Middle Ages it became rich with the thousands of pilgrims who flocked here to buy pardons. However, the abbey fell on hard times in the 18th century, when the head abbot, Cardi-nal de Rohan, became embroiled in a scandal involving Marie Antoinette. In the 1790s, the property was bought and stripped by antique dealers. Restoration didn't begin until 1872.

The enormous 12th-century **Eglise de Notre-Dame** is a Romanesque masterpiece. The central crypt forms a perfect circle, and the restored clois-ter has some remarkable capitals carved with beasts, plants and little figures. For stunning views, climb to the top of the 14th-century tower.

The Camargue

Arles is the gateway to the Camargue, a wild place of lagoons, rice fields, cowboys riding white horses, herds of black bulls and thousands of flamingos that turn the waters pink in summer. Bordered to the west by the Petit-Rhône, which flows to the sea past Stes-Maries-de-la-Mer, and to the east by the Grand-Rhône, which runs down from Arles, the marsh-lands of the Rhône delta form an unusual natural environment that has helped shape the Camargue's unique history. The setting for one of France's greatest wildlife reserves also provides a spiritual home for the country's gypsies, stages a national windsurfing championship, and offers a range of historic towns and churches to visit as well as the joys of riding across beaches and salt plains.

The celebrated horizons that inspired the poet Frédéric Mistral and the light that fascinated Van Gogh have also encouraged an onslaught of tourism resulting in pseudo-rustic hotels, brash campsites, and piles of debris generated by holidaymakers. To get the best from the area, which covers more than 800 sq. km (480 sq. miles), takes careful planning *(see tip page 140)*.

The curious blend of marsh, swamp, salt plain and paddy fields, which have led to the establishment of numerous wildlife parks, means that you'll have to abandon your car and choose from a variety of options. You can get around by boat, in a 4WD, on horseback or by bicycle. Some areas are best discovered on foot. Even if you spend only a few days in the region, visits to two or three well-chosen spots can reveal an amazingly rich variety of wildlife.

Getting to know the area

For a good introduction to the region, take the D570 southwest from Arles to the **Musée de la Camargue ❸** (Mas du Pont du Rousty; open Apr–Sept daily 9.30am–6pm, Oct–Mar Wed–Mon 10am–5pm; admission charge; tel: 04 90 97 10 82). This sheep farm-cum-regional museum contains an exhibition illustrating the history, agriculture and traditional way of life of the Camargue.

A signposted footpath to the rear of the museum leads to the beginning of the marshes. The walk will take you about an hour and give you a feel

for these strange flatlands. You will see a wide variety of birds: the curious black-winged stilts with their long pink legs, herons, and all sorts of wading birds. Spring is the ideal season for birdwatching, as this is when the migrants visit the Camargue on their journey back north.

Once you've left the Mas du Pont du Rousty, continue along the D570 through paddy and wheat fields, towards the Camargue's main town, Stes-Maries-de-la-Mer *(see page 140)*. En route, you'll pass numerous advertisements for roadside ranches which run half- or full-day pony-trekking and trips into the marshes.

Just before Stes-Maries, you may want to stop at the information centre at **Ginès ❹**. Here, an excellent exhibition gives information on the indigenous flora and fauna. Next door to the information centre is the **Parc Ornithologique de Pont de Gau** (ornithological park; route d'Arles, 4 km/2½ miles from Stes-Maries; open Apr–Sept daily 9am–7pm, Oct–Mar daily 10am–5pm; admission charge; tel: 04 90 97 82 62), where you can see bird species

TIP

The Musée de la Camargue's explanations of the different terrains in the region – how the wildlife of freshwater marshes differs from that of the salt lagoons and from that of the coastal dykes – sums up the contrasts central to the enduring allure of this region. Don't be surprised to suddenly see, for example, a flock of marshland pink flamingos in full flight over an industrial salt plant.

BELOW: Camargue cowboys gathering bulls for a bullfight.

Cowboy Country

The Camargue cowboys *(gardians)* cling passionately to their traditional way of life, herding the small black bulls destined for the arenas of Nîmes or Arles, and riding their fine white horses in costume – flat black hat, leather chaps, high leather boots and shirts in Provençal fabric. Many still live on *manades* (bull-breeding ranches) in the Camargue, in traditional cabins, low white houses with reed-thatched roofs and rounded north ends as a protection against the blasts of the mistral wind. If you enquire about the *manades* that offer horse riding or demonstrations, you will be able to see *gardians* at work, or they can be seen before the bullfights and festivals in Arles and Nîmes.

of the region in aviaries and also follow birdwatching trails.

A saintly city

Situated at the southern tip of the Camargue, **Stes-Maries-de-la-Mer** ❺ is something of a mirage after the flat landscape. The flourishing resort owes its name to a group of travellers that landed on this shore. According to legend, these early Christians had set out to sea from Palestine around AD 40 in a small boat without sails. They were miraculously washed ashore, safe and sound, at this spot. Among the saintly company were Mary Jacoby (sister of the Virgin Mary), Mary Magdalene, Mary Salome (mother of Apostles John and James), Martha and the miraculously resurrected Lazarus, along with their Egyptian servant Sarah. After their deaths, the two Marys who had stayed in the Camargue gained a cult following among newly Christianised gypsies and nomads. The town has been a place of pilgrimage ever since.

In the 9th century, the **Eglise de Notre-Dame-de-la-Mer** was built in place of the simple chapel that existed on that site and was fortified against invading Saracens. Excavations beneath this structure, begun in 1448 under the behest of Good King René, led to the discovery of a well and a spring filled with "the fragrances of sweet-scented bodies". The remains of the saints were uncovered in this same spot and their tomb was placed in the church's Chapelle de St-Michel. The stones on which the bodies had rested are kept below in the crypt and have become "miracle" stones, said to have the power to cure infertility and heal sore eyes.

Climb to the roof of the church for stunning panoramic views across the sand hills and down to the waves splashing against the sunlit shore.

Stes-Maries-de-la-Mer is a thriving resort during the holiday season,

TIP

Because of the lay of the land, exploration of the Camargue inevitably entails a certain amount of zigzagging, so it's worth considering basing yourself at its edge, near Arles, and making a series of day trips. Bear in mind that it is not always possible to wander off the main track without a permit. If you hate crowds, avoid July and August, when the mosquitoes are also out in force.

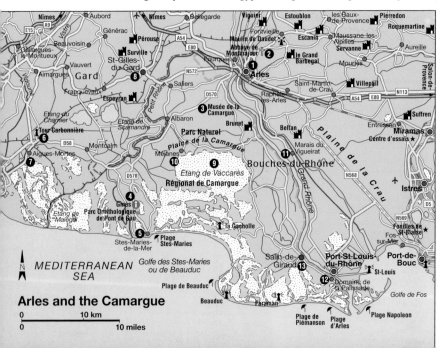

Arles and the Camargue

and the many reasonably priced hotels and campsites do well here. There are numerous places where you can rent horses and boats, swim or play tennis. Bullfights *(see page 136)* are held in the local arena. The little **Musée Baroncelli** (currently closed for renovation; tel: 04 90 97 87 60 for information) contains material on bullfighting and Camargue traditions donated by Marquis Folco de Baron-celli-Javon, aristocratic champion of the *gardians*.

Along the Petit-Rhône

Escape the bustle by booking a boat trip along the Petit-Rhône. Excursions leave at regular intervals from the landing stage near Baroncelli-Javon's tomb. These boat trips also offer the opportunity to get close to Camargue wildlife – birds wading through the water and herds of bulls and horses running along the shore.

The beaches close to town can get very busy at certain times of year. Frédéric Mistral, who set the tragic end of his famous work *Mireille* (*Mireio* in Provençal) on these sandy shores, would no longer be able to write of it "no trees, no shade and not a soul".

If you venture a bit further west of Stes-Maries-de-la-Mer, there are some lovely quiet beaches, but you'll need to brave the weathered tracks off the main road to reach them. Find a suitable spot to park to climb over the sand dunes, and you'll be rewarded with some empty stretches away from the crowds. Van Gogh painted his *Bâteaux de pêche de Stes-Maries* (fishing boats at Stes-Maries) on these beaches.

The western Camargue and Aigues-Mortes

West of the Petit-Rhône, the D58 takes you across the plain of Aigues-Mortes, a part of the Camargue that has hardly changed in decades. Every so often an authentic *cabane de gardian* comes into view – a single-storey whitewashed cabin with a thatched, mistral-defying roof.

The plain borders a rich agricultural area that produces grapes and cereals. At the end of the drive along the D58, the **Tour Carbonnière 6** offers a splendid view over these

Map on page 140

In May, gypsies flock to Stes-Maries-de-la-Mer to celebrate the cult of Sarah *(see page 140)*, and on the last Sunday of October, the feast day for Mary Salome is commemorated by colourful processions around the church *(above)*.

BELOW: Camargue horses near Stes-Marie-de-la-Mer.

The white horses that some say are descendants of the wild horses that populated prehistoric Gaul, and others claim are either of North African or Tibetan origin, have also been woven into one of the legends surrounding Aigues-Mortes. Children are told that if they misbehave they will be dragged off by "Lou Drape" – a horse whose back can supposedly lengthen to carry away as many as 100 naughty children into the marsh, where it then devours them.

BELOW:
Aigues-Mortes.

fields to the foothills of the Cévennes in the northwest, the Petite Camargue in the east and across the salt flats of Aigues-Mortes to the south. Built as a watchtower for the garrison of Aigues-Mortes during the Crusades, the tower guards what was once the only route in and out of town.

The area around **Aigues-Mortes** ❼ is made up of salty lagoons and channels, where the Rhône meets the sea. The town itself was built amidst the marshes, salt flats and lagoons in 1241 by King Louis IX (St Louis), who wanted a port on the Mediterranean from which to launch the Seventh Crusade in 1248.

Laid out on a square grid plan, the new town, built on the site of an earlier Roman settlement, was named for its location (Aigues-Mortes means "dead waters") as it contrasted with the town of Aigues-Vives ("living waters") that lay in the hills about 20 km (12 miles) further north. Aigues-Mortes flourished under its royal patronage, but the incorporation of Marseille and Provence into the French kingdom and the recession of the sea meant it didn't last long as a

major port – although it is still connected to the sea by a canal that leads to the fishing village and beach resort of Grau-le-Roi.

Today Aigues-Mortes is still contained within its remarkably intact city wall. The ramparts, punctuated by 20 defensive towers, trace a fabulous silhouette over the salt marshes. Once you've passed through the gateway, attractive narrow streets crisscross the town. They lead to place St-Louis, the main square, lined with cafés and restaurants – although you will get a better meal by wandering down the more secluded side streets in search of local specialities, such as *gardiane de taureau* (a delicious beef stew with olives) or seafood. The town also has two fine 17th-century chapels, open only by prior arrangement with the tourist office on the main square.

Tour de Constance

Dominating the town is the circular **Tour de Constance** (open May–Aug daily 10am–7pm, Sept–Apr daily 10am–5.30pm; admission charge; tel: 04 66 53 61 55; website

www.monum.fr). The defensive keep, built by Louis IX, served as both watchtower and lighthouse. It looks over the Renaissance Logis du Gouverneur, which replaced the royal palace burnt down in the 15th century. Later, the tower became an infamous prison where Protestant women were held during the 16th-century Wars of Religion. The visit to the tower also gives you access to the walk along the ramparts, with views out to the marshes and vineyards.

Aigues-Mortes is still a centre for salt production, vine-growing and the cultivation of asparagus and carrots. In summer, the Salins du Midi (route du Grau du Roi; tel: 04 66 73 40 24; www.salins.com) organises tours in a little train or bus around the crystallisation tables and evaporation basins.

Back inland towards Arles, **St-Gilles-du-Gard ❽**, a busy little agricultural town hemmed in by canals, is also well worth visiting, chiefly for the carvings on the western front of the town's 12th-century abbey church – a masterpiece of Provençal Romanesque architecture with a fine stone spiral staircase.

Marshes and lagoons

If you turn off the D570 at Albaron, onto the D37 and then the D36, you skirt around the **Etang de Vaccarès ❾**, a huge brackish lagoon, and head deep into the regional park. Travelling in this direction offers excellent sightings of pink flamingos and other waterfowl, even from a car. On foot, a sharp eye should be able to spot beavers, turtle or lime-green tree frogs. Remember that the lagoon is a protected area. Hunting, fishing and the picking of plants and flowers are all prohibited.

The black bulls of the Camargue also roam here, and sometimes (but not as often as postcards may have you believe) you will see a *gardian* (*see page 139*) astride his white horse. Twilight is particularly lovely here, when the setting sun casts its colours over the lagoon.

To get a closer look at the famous white horses of the Camargue, you may want to check in at one of the Camargue's "ranches", where the *gardians* take you out on horseback for a tour of the marshes. The *mas* belonging to Paul Ricard (of pastis

All year round, a system of *bacs*, miniature ferries, carries both vehicles and horses across the Rhône. The Bac de Barcarin crosses the Grand Rhône between Salin-de-Giraud and Port St-Louis-du-Rhône; the Bac du Sauvage crosses the Petit-Rhône near Stes-Maries-de-la-Mer.

BELOW: practising for the *course camarguaise*.

Course Camarguaise

The *course camarguaise*, in which the bull is chased but not killed, is the style of bullfighting practised in towns and villages all over the Camargue and the nearby Crau and Alpilles. It is more light-hearted than Spanish-style bullfighting (although you will also find the latter at the big *ferias* in Arles and Nîmes). The *course* began as a game with lions, dogs, bears and men chasing bulls. Now the real competition is between the *manades* (bull-breeders), who raise the bulls, and the *raseteurs*, who take the animals on. In Arles, the fighting season starts with the April *feria*, when the Queen of Arles is crowned. It ends at the beginning of July with the awarding of the *Cocarde d'Or*.

Map on page 140

The D36 leads from Salin-de-Giraud to the Plage de Piémanson, a nudist beach. For the more modest, the Plage d'Arles (above) is located on the same stretch of coast.

BELOW: the flat terrain is ideal for leisurely bike rides.

fame) at **Méjanes** , (tel: 04 90 97 10 10; www.mejanes.camargue.fr) is especially well publicised. Around the fortified medieval buildings of a Templar *commanderie*, you will find an efficient pony-trekking centre, and some particularly knowledgeable *gardians* willing to show off their skills, such as calf-branding.

Two further areas of protected marshland, managed by the Conservatoire du Littoral (the French coastal conservation trust) are open to the public, with footpaths and observation posts. The **Marais du Vigueirat** ⓫ (open Feb–Nov daily 10am–5pm; tel: 04 90 98 70 91; www.marais-vigueirat.reserves-naturelles.org) at Mas Thibert sits at the junction of two remarkable ecosystems: the marshy Rhône delta and the Crau plain. Access is free, but ring ahead if you want to join one of the guided walks, visit in a horse-drawn cart or fish for crayfish. Located on the eastern bank of the Grand-Rhône, it is most easily reached by the D35 from Arles, although you can cross the river by the Bac de Barcarin *(see tip page 143)* at Salin-de-Giraud.

On the edge of the salt flats, south-east of Salin-de-Giraud along the D36D, the **Domaine de la Palissade** ⓬, (open daily 9am–5pm; tel: 04 42 86 81 28) is rare in that it subsists in its quasi-natural state. Continually affected by the tides, it has never been controlled by the dykes that separate the Rhône from the sea nor cultivated for agriculture, disturbed only by hunters and grazing horses. Again, several footpaths and bridleways have been created, and the reed beds and remains of dunes that trace the former coastline provide a habitat for rare plants, eels, herons and egrets.

Southeast of the Etang de Vaccarès, the landscape changes to one of powdery white hills and salt pans. This corner of the Camargue, around **Salin-de-Giraud** ⓭, is the French capital for salt production, and over half of the country's supply comes from here. From March to October you can visit the salt flats by tourist train, the last stop being the **Musée du Sel** (tel: 04 42 86 71 80; www. salins.com). This area is also the gateway to the Camargue's dune-backed beaches *(see left)*. ❏

RESTAURANTS AND BARS

Aigues-Mortes

Restaurant Marie-Rose

13 rue Pasteur. Tel: 04 66 53 79 84. Open: D only Thur–Sun. €€
A lively restaurant in an old presbytery, with dishes such as rabbit with *tapenade* or little fillets of sole with *pistou*, to be accompanied by local gris de gris wine.

Arles

L'Atelier de Jean-Luc Rabanel

7 rue des Carmes. Tel: 04 90 91 07 69. Open: L Wed–Sun, D Tues–Sun. €€€
www.rabanel.com
Innovative chef Jean-Luc Rabanel runs this intimate modern bistro in the centre of Arles, serving only organic produce.

Brasserie Nord Pinus

14 place du Forum. Tel: 04 90 93 44 44. Open: L Tues–Sat, D Tues–Sun. €€
www.nord-pinus.com
This elegant, grandly styled brasserie belongs to the cult hotel frequented by Cocteau and Picasso. It's a place to enjoy grilled meats and seasonal food, such as artichoke salad.

Café de la Nuit

Place du Forum. Tel: 04 90 96 44 56. €
This brightly painted re-creation of the café immortalised by Van Gogh has a lively atmosphere and a good terrace

on the square. Decent food includes pasta and Camargue bull *daube*. Touristy but fun.

La Caravelle

1 place Constantin. Tel: 04 90 96 39 09. Open: D Tues–Sat (plus Mon and L July & Aug). €
www.lacaravelle.net
Expect cosmopolitan dishes and a trendy young crowd at this restaurant and cocktail bar near the Rhône. Food ranges from local oysters to ostrich steak.

Le Jardin de Manon

14 avenue des Alyscamps. Tel: 04 90 93 38 68. Open: L Thur–Tues, D Thur–Mon. Closed: 2 weeks Oct/Nov and 2 weeks Feb. €€
This little Provençal house near Les Alyscamps has a lovely garden for eating alfresco. Good-value, fresh market cooking might include rabbit stuffed with goat's cheese, roast sea bass or *daube d'agneau*.

Lou Caleu

27 rue Porte de Laure. Tel: 04 90 49 71 77. Open: L & D daily. Closed: mid-Jan–mid-Feb. €–€€
A reliable bet among the cluster of little restaurants near the Théâtre Antique for carefully prepared Provençal cooking.

Le Sambuc

La Chassagnette

Route du Sambuc. Tel: 04 90 97 26 96. Open: L & D

Thur–Tues (daily in July & Aug). Closed: Wed except in July and Aug. €€€€
www.chassagnette.fr
This spacious, stylishly converted barn southeast of Arles serves dishes using organic produce from the restaurant's own kitchen garden, along with local fish and meat from the Camargue.

St-Gilles

Le Cours

10 avenue François Griffeuille. Tel: 04 66 87 31 93. Open: L & D daily. Closed: mid-Dec–mid-Mar. €
www.hotel-le-cours.com
With its shady terrace under the plane trees and its good-value menus, the restaurant at this friendly Logis de France hotel is very popular.

Stes-Maries-de-la-Mer

Rostellerie du Pont de Gau

Route d'Arles. Tel: 04 90 97 81 53. Open: L and D daily (closed Wed in winter). Closed: Jan–mid-Feb. €€
www.pontdegau.camargue.fr
Right next to the bird reserve is this serious restaurant, serving expertly prepared classic and regional dishes – foie gras, eel stew, local bull's meat and hare, wild boar and other seasonal game.

PRICE CATEGORIES

Prices for a three-course meal without wine.
€ = under €25
€€ = €25–€40
€€€ = €40–€60
€€€€ = more than €60

RIGHT: Café de la Nuit.

FESTIVALS

Merrymaking activities take place across Provence all year round. Everything is celebrated, from saints and cowboys to lavender and lemons

Though religious observance has declined, the Christian history of Provence still influences the *fêtes* that are part of the cultural life of every village. Some are clearly part of the Christian tradition, such as the *fêtes* on Christmas Eve, when the Nativity is enacted by members of the village (one of the best-known of these is in the village of Séguret in the Vaucluse). In many cases the Christian foundations of a festival have been forgotten or overlayed with new meaning, and the *fête* has become a popular celebration. The rowdy Bravade of 16 May in St-Tropez, originally to commemorate its martyred patron saint, is one example; another is the gypsy *fête et pèlerinage* to Stes-Maries-de-la-Mer. The 700-year-old pilgrimage to the town where the Boat of Bethany (carrying Mary Magdalene) landed is now famous for its energetic two-day festival *(see right)*.

Summer arts festivals abound: Avignon is known for its theatre festival, as is Cannes for film, and there is also the opera festival of Orange and the jazz festivals of Nice and Juan-les-Pins.

From February to September Nîmes, Arles and St-Rémy demonstrate their historical links to Spain with annual *ferias* and *corridas*.

ABOVE: on 24 and 25 May, gypsies from the surrounding regions descend on the town of Stes-Maries-de-la-Mer for two days of horse-racing, bull-running and general celebrations. In the evenings the spirit of the fiesta runs wild, and the frenzied excitement of gypsy music and dancing fills the air.

LEFT: though Mardi Gras celebrations have been going on in Nice since medieval times, the Carnival in its modern incarnation, with costumes and parades, began in 1873. On the last night vast papier-mâché floats are set on fire in the sea.

BELOW: Fête de la Tarasque, Tarascon. On the last weekend in June, Tarascon celebrates the legend of an amphibious monster that once terrorised the town *(see page 128)*. A costume parade featuring characters from the story is led by a papier-mâché monster. This festival was inaugurated by Good King René in 1474.

BELOW: the Fête des Charrettes Ramées, Châteaurenard in July is a colourful horse-and-cart parade, part of the festival of St Eloi, patron saint of farriers.

ABOVE: each February, for three weeks the normally sedate retirement town of Menton hosts a lively lemon festival to celebrate the area's main crop. Floats decorated with thousands of lemons parade the streets on the Sundays. The rest of the time during the festival, they are displayed in the Jardins Boivès.

ABOVE RIGHT: the Fête de la Transhumance, marking the traditional moving of the flocks between their winter grazing on the Crau plain and summer grazing up in the Alps, is celebrated each Pentecost Monday in St-Rémy-de-Provence. In the morning, shepherds and their dogs circled by thousands of sheep, parade through the streets.

FOOD AND WINE

There are countless festivals across the region celebrating the amazing richness and variety of Provençal produce: truffles, rice, mushrooms, olives, chestnuts, cherries, lemons, not to mention the many Provençal wines, are all fêted with parades, bands, fairs, fireworks and, of course, plenty of eating and drinking. Most, but not all, of these festivals take place in the autumn around harvest time. Here is a selection of the best:

● *Mid-September: Prémices du Riz, Arles.*
Rice has been cultivated in the Camargue for centuries. This annual rice festival includes colourful costume parades, folkloric dances and bullfights.
● *October: Fête de la Châtaigne, Collobrières.*
Celebration of the chestnut harvest with a craft market and opportunities to sample chestnuts in countless guises. Last three Sundays of the month.
● *End October–early November: Journées Gourmandes, Vaison-la-Romaine.*
A five-day festival of feasting on regional specialities in the Roman town.
● *Mid-November: Festival of the Côtes du Rhône primeurs, Avignon.* Celebration of the first wines of the year, with lots of opportunities for tasting.
● *December–February : Les Oursinades, Carry-le-Rouet.*
Tastings of sea urchins and other shellfish that thrive in the shallow waters of la Côte Bleue.
● *December: Fête du Millésime, Bandol.*
Lively wine festival in the port of Bandol. First Sunday of the month.

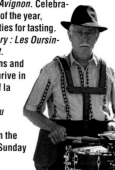

NÎMES AND THE PONT DU GARD

Nîmes is a far-sighted city which combines the ancient with the avant-garde. Alongside the 2,000-year-old amphitheatre and ancient temple stands Sir Norman Foster's Carré d'Art, a steel-and-glass tribute to Roman architectural flair. The nearby Pont du Gard aqueduct is another unmissable marvel on the Roman trail

Map on page 150

BELOW: the Pont du Gard.

Nîmes may rival Arles as the ancient Rome of France, but far from being a museum city, here ancient monuments – some of the best-preserved in Europe – coexist with high-tech architecture and contemporary works of art typical of a modern multicultural city. Its lively streetlife mingles Provençal traditions with a Spanish-tinged love of bullfighting. High unemployment and some dodgy housing estates have given the outskirts a slightly rough reputation, but new biotechnology companies are bringing employment opportunities and sensitive rehabilitation, and ongoing renovation programmes are keeping the old centre alive.

A good introduction to the city is to take a ride on La Citadine, a little bus which runs in a loop from Nîmes railway station, taking in many of the principal sights. For information on this and Nîmes in general, contact the tourist office (6 rue Auguste; tel: 04 66 58 38 15; www.ot-nimes.fr).

The Arènes

Originally a staging post on the road to Spain, Nîmes was the first French city to be colonised by the Romans. A number of impressive Roman structures were built here, several of which still stand. The most outstanding monument is the amphitheatre, the **Arènes** Ⓐ (Boulevard des Arènes; open daily June–Aug 9am–7pm, Mar–May, Sept–Oct 9am–5.30pm, Nov–Feb 9.30am–4.30pm, hours vary during *feria* and concerts; admission charge but free audioguide; tel: 04 66 21 82 56; www.culturespaces.com), built between AD90 and 120, roughly at the same time as the Colosseum in Rome.

Ringed by busy brasseries, it is still a focal point of the city. Today, the amphitheatre has been restored to something approaching its former glory, and a clever glass-and-steel roof structure, removable in summer, allows the arena to be used for a variety of activities all year round. Most famous are the bullfights, both the traditional Spanish *corrida* (in which they do kill the bull) and the more light-hearted, Provençal-style *course camarguaise* (in which they don't – *see page 143*).

Several shops selling bullfighting souvenirs and toreadors' costumes can be found in the streets around the arena, and the **Musée des Cultures Taurines** Ⓑ (6 rue Alexandre Ducros; open Tues–Sun 10am–6pm; admission charge; tel: 04 66 36 83 77) contains an eclectic array of posters, costumes and miscellaneous *tauromachie* – bullfighting memorabilia.

The Maison Carrée

Behind the amphitheatre, the heart of old Nîmes lies within the shield-shaped ring formed by boulevards Victor Hugo, Gambetta and Amiral Courbet. Nîmes' second-most important Roman sight is the **Maison Carrée** Ⓒ (open daily June– Aug 9am–7pm, Mar–May, Sept–Oct 9am–5.30pm, Nov–Feb 9.30am–4.30pm; admission charge; tel: 04 66 21 82 56; www.culturespaces.com), further up boulevard Victor Hugo on the western side of the old town.

The most important of Nîmes' ferias is the Feria de la Pentecôte, held on Pentecost weekend in June, when bodegas fill the streets, the sangria flows and the whole town is in high festive spirits. For more information, contact the tourist office (see page 148).

BELOW: a bullfight in the Nîmes arena.

Sir Norman Foster's Carré d'Art complements the forms of the Roman temple opposite.

Known as the "square house" despite being twice as long as it is wide, the 1st-century BC structure is generally considered to be the best-preserved Roman temple in existence. It is entered up a flight of tall steps and surrounded by a set of fluted columns with crisply carved Corinthian capitals.

Its original dedication has long been debated – some say it was dedicated to Juno, others cite Jupiter or Minerva. Like the amphitheatre, it underwent several incarnations, serving as a stable, the town hall and a monastery church temple. Inside,

a 3D film presents daily life in ancient Nîmes, medieval Nîmes and during the *feria*.

Statues, frescos and other Roman and Iron Age archaeological finds can be seen at the **Musée d'Archéologie ⊙** (13bis boulevard Amiral Courbet; open Tues–Sun 10am– 6pm; admission charge; tel: 04 66 76 74 54) housed in an old Jesuit college.

A superb Roman mosaic, uncovered here in 1883, holds centre stage amid the eclectic painting collection of the **Musée des Beaux-Arts ⊜** (20–22 rue de la Cité Foulc; open

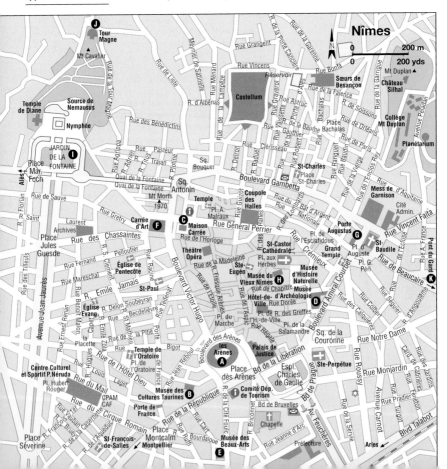

Tues–Sun 10am–6pm; admission charge; tel: 04 66 67 38 21).

The Carré d'Art

Opposite the temple is the **Carré d'Art** (place de la Maison Carrée; open Tues–Sat 10am–6pm; admission charge; tel: 04 66 76 35 80), a contemporary art museum and public library in a glass-and-steel building, designed by the British architect Sir Norman Foster, which brilliantly echoes the form of the ancient temple opposite (*see margin picture, left*). The collection focuses on European art since 1960, with particular emphasis on avant-garde movements such as Arte Povera and New Realism, and work by French and Mediterranean artists. Artists well represented include Martial Raysse, Christian Boltanski and Arman.

This mix of the ancient and the modern is typical of Nîmes. There are commissioned artworks all over the city, notably a Philippe Starck bus stop (Abribus on avenue Carnot) and a fountain by Martial Raysse in the place du Marché.

The origins of denim

From the Maison Carrée, rue du Général Perrier leads to Les Halles, Nîmes' excellent covered market (mornings daily). At the far end of the market, rue Nationale follows the traces of the Via Domitia to **Porte Augustus** on boulevard Gambetta, which was one of the original Roman gates of the city. It has two large arches that provided a dual carriageway for carts and chariots, while the two smaller arches took pedestrian traffic. South of the market, explore the old town with its mix of 18th-century façades, Renaissance courtyards and medieval vaults.

On the place aux Herbes, the elegant 17th-century former bishops' palace now houses the **Musée du Vieux Nîmes** (open Tues–Sun 10am–6pm; free; tel: 04 66 76 73 70), which has rooms furnished with regional furniture, pottery and paintings, and an interesting display on the famous hard-wearing, blue cotton serge "de Nîmes" that has since conquered the world under the name of… denim.

Map on page 150

TIP

The culinary speciality of Nîmes is *brandade de morue* – dried salt cod soaked in milk and then whipped into a purée with olive oil, served piping hot. The tourist office can supply a list of restaurants serving *brandade*, or you can buy a jar to take home: two reputable addresses are F. Nadal on rue Castor and Brandade Raymond on rue Nationale.

BELOW: the 1st-century BC Maison Carrée.

Map on page 150

Perrier, the naturally sparkling mineral water, comes from a spring southwest of Nîmes at Vergèze. Hannibal and his 30 elephants supposedly discovered the spring in 218 BC, and in 1863, Napoleon III decided that the water should be bottled "for the good of France". However, it was an Englishman, St John Harmsworth, who first bottled and marketed the water in 1903. Guided tours of the bottling plant Feb–Nov; tel: 04 66 87 61 01.

BELOW RIGHT: walking on the Pont du Gard.

The neighbouring **Cathédrale** was severely damaged during the Wars of Religion, particularly violent in this town which was a major centre of Protestantism in the 16th century. The town's Protestant heritage can still be seen in the imposing Grand Temple and Petit Temple in the **Îlot Littré**, the recently renovated former dyers' district situated near the tourist office.

Jardin de la Fontaine

Just west of the old town, the quai de la Fontaine leads along a canal lined with patrician houses to the **Jardin de la Fontaine ❶** (open daily). The park was laid out in the 18th century with gravel paths, canals, terraces and sculptures. On one side the so-called Temple de Diane are the ruins of a Roman sanctuary. At the top of Mont Cavalier, the ancient **Tour Magne ❷** (open July and Aug daily 9am–7pm, Sept–June daily 9am–6pm; admission charge; www.culturespaces.com) is a watchtower built by the Celtic Volques tribe and later enlarged and incorporated within the Roman ramparts.

The Pont du Gard

The extraordinary three-storey aqueduct of **Pont du Gard ❸** dates from the 1st century AD and stands 19 km (12 miles) northeast of Nîmes. A testament to the Romans' engineering prowess, it remains in excellent condition and stood firm against devastating floods in 1988 and 2002, when several nearby bridges collapsed. The structure spans the Gardon valley and was built to bring water along a 50-km (31-mile) long channel when the growing city's water requirements were no longer met by the Nemausus spring. At 360 metres (1,200 ft) long and 48 metres (157 ft) high, it was the tallest bridge that the Romans ever built.

The aqueduct is at its most stunning early in the morning or at dusk. Car parks (open daily 6am–1am; parking fee) are on both banks. A visitor centre (open daily summer 9am–7pm, winter 9.30am–5.30pm, closed Mon morning and 2 weekends in Jan; admission charge; tel: 08 20 90 33 30; www.pontdugard.fr), complete with cinema and café, is located on the left bank. ❑

The Arena – 2,000 Years of History

Slightly smaller than its counterpart in Arles, the two-tier arcaded oval amphitheatre could originally seat nearly 24,000 spectators, with a complex system of stairways providing access to the tiers of seats and *vomitoria* (exit tunnels). The structure was used for gladiatorial combat, wild-animal shows and the public executions of Christian martyrs, condemned slaves and foreigners, who would be thrown into the arena with wild beasts. It could also be flooded for aquatic events. The seating plan respected the social hierarchy: the lower tiers were reserved for notables, with citizens in the middle and the populace and slaves far up at the top.

Over the centuries, the amphitheatre was subjected to a variety of indignities. Visigoths substantially altered its form for use as a fortress, and it suffered further changes to accommodate a village for 2,000 poor people, with many houses and a chapel added. In the 19th century, when attempts were finally begun to unearth the original structure, it was by then concealed under 8 metres (25 ft) of rubble.

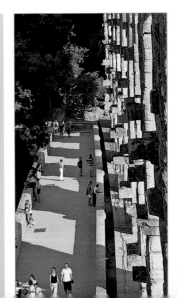

RESTAURANTS, BARS AND CAFÉS

Restaurants

La Bodeguita
3 boulevard Alphonse Daudet. Tel : 04 66 58 28 29. Open: D Mon–Sat. €€
The trendy restaurant of the arty Royal Hôtel serves up tasty tapas by night accompanied by both Nîmois and Spanish wines. A *feria* hotspot.

La Casa Don Miguel
18 rue de l'Horloge. Tel: 04 66 76 07 09. Open: L & D daily (closed Mon in winter). €
Typical of the Spanish influence in bullfighting-crazy Nîmes, this lively tapas bar in a vaulted medieval building in the old town serves up both hot and cold dishes, along with the occasional live music show at weekends. Open until 3am.

Le Chapon Fin
3 place du Château Fadaise. Tel: 04 66 67 34 73. Open: L Mon–Fri, D Mon–Sat. €€
This popular, convivial bistro, plastered with Bardot posters, is a Nîmes stalwart. The tasty traditional food includes piping hot *brandade de morue*, Alsatian *choucroûte* and a smattering of south-western classics, such as cassoulet.

Le Ciel de Nîmes
Carré d'Art, 16 place de la Maison Carrée. Tel: 04 66 36

71 70. Open: L Tues–Sun. €
The café at the top of the Carré d'Art is a laid-back place for a light lunch, and has the benefit of superb views.

Le Jardin d'Hadrien
11 rue de l'Enclos Rey. Tel: 04 66 21 86 65. Open: L Thur–Tues, D Mon, Thur–Sat. €€
Good traditional regional cooking – with offerings along the lines of beef in red-wine sauce, *pieds et pacquets*, or courgette flowers stuffed with *brandade* – is served in the spacious beamed dining room. In summer, you can opt to dine outside in the lovely courtyard garden.

La Lisita
2 boulevard des Arènes. Tel: 04 66 67 29 15. Open: L & D Tues–Sat. €€€
www.lelisita.com
Nîmes' gastronomic destination of choice is a collaboration between young chef Olivier Douet and sommelier Stéphane Debaille. Trained with Bernard Loiseau, Roger Vergé and at the Gavroche in London, Douet's stylishly presented modern French dishes, which include roast john dory with spring vegetables and a flaming red beetroot sauce, are colourful works of art based on fresh market produce.

There is a good selection of regional wines.

Aux Plaisirs des Halles
4 rue Littré. Tel: 04 66 36 01 02. Open: L & D Tues–Sat. €€
www.auxplaisirsdeshalles.com
An upmarket establishment with a spacious contemporary dining room. Chef Sébastien Granier turns out excellent modern Mediterranean fare, sampled in dishes such as scorpion fish with black olives, meats and fish grilled *a la plancha* and innovative desserts.

Restaurant Nicolas
1 rue Poise. Tel: 04 66 67 50 47. Open: L Tues–Fri, Sun; D Tues–Sun. €
This totally unpretentious, family-run bistro offers home cooking at

prices that add up to good-value dining. Dishes are served amid exposed stone walls festooned with the obligatory bullfighting photos.

Bars and Cafés

Place aux Herbes, place du Marché and the western side of place de la Maison Carrée buzz with café life.

PRICE CATEGORIES
Prices for a three-course meal without wine. Note that many restaurants have a less expensive lunch menu.
€ = under €25
€€ = €25–€40
€€€ = €40–€60
€€€€ = more than €60

LA GRANDE BOURSE

RIGHT: café outside the Arènes.

THE GORGES DU VERDON

The immense canyon of the Gorges du Verdon – the largest in Europe – provides spectacular views of dramatic cliffs and sheer drops to the blue-grey river below. This is a favourite area for hiking, white-water sports, paragliding and birdwatching

Cutting through the limestone, the River Verdon leaves a breathtaking, sweeping gorge in its wake. It flows from its source near the Col d'Allos at 2,200 metres (7,220 ft) into the Durance River, 175 km (108 miles) further west near Gréoux-les-Bains, marking the boundary between the *départements* of Alpes-de-Haute-Provence to the north and the Var to the south. Despite the rise in tourism, many of the villages here retain a rustic authenticity, and there are opportunities aplenty for walking, rock-climbing and white-water sports.

Grand Canyon du Verdon

The most spectacular section of the gorge is the **Grand Canyon du Verdon ❶**, the area roughly between Aiguines and Rougon. Statistics only hint at the Grand Canyon's magnificence. Around 21 km (12½ miles) in length and up to 700 metres (2,300 ft) deep, the vertiginous limestone cliffs were gouged out by the Verdon River when the Mediterranean receded some five million years ago. In the early 20th century the canyon was largely deserted, but by the late 1940s the construction of the Corniche Sublime opened access. Tourism has now moved in wholesale, and the area is best avoided in August, when the roads become

clogged with tour buses. Out of season, most of the restaurants and hotels will be closed, but you'll have the views and wildlife pretty much to yourself. Autumn puts on a particularly breathtaking display, when the ochres and russets of nearby trees contrast dramatically with the turquoise waters. Whenever you travel it's worth checking with the tourist board which route they recommend, as the roads on either side of the Canyon are regularly closed for maintenance.

Map on page 156

LEFT: Grand Canyon du Verdon. **BELOW:** white-water rafting.

With a wingspan of 2.5–2.8 metres (8–9 ft), the griffon vulture is an impressive sight as it glides on the air currents high above the Gorges du Verdon. Easily recognisable by its white-ruff and buff plumage with darker wing tips, the bird was once wide-spread in the mountains of southern France, but had died out. It has now been successfully reintroduced, with the 90 birds released in the Verdon Regional Park between 1999 and 2004 having formed a breeding colony in the crags of the Grand Canyon.

Moustiers-Ste-Marie

First stop on the Canyon trail is **Moustiers-Ste-Marie ❷**, where an astonishing backdrop of craggy cliffs offers a taste of what's to come. Moustiers is an attractive small town perched above a narrow torrent on the sides of a ravine. High up behind the town, the two sides of the ravine seem held together by a massive chain 225 metres (740 ft) long from which a man-sized gilded star is suspended. The story goes that it was placed there by a knight fulfilling a religious vow on his return from the Crusades. The star has been replaced on a number of occasions after being blown down during storms, most recently in 1957.

During the 16th century, tanneries, paper mills and potteries flourished here. Moustiers' major claim to fame, however, is its faience (*see box, opposite*). Established in the late 17th century by Antoine Clérissy, the recipe for the white tin glaze was believed to have come via an Italian monk from Faenza. The village streets are crammed to bursting with shops and studios producing this decorative glazed pottery, though quality is not always what it should be. It is still possible to seek out good examples from the vast range on offer, but perhaps more rewarding is a visit to the **Musée de la Faïence** (open Apr–Oct Wed–Mon 9am–noon, 2–6pm, Nov–Mar Wed–Mon 2–5pm; closed Jan; admission charge; tel: 04 92 74 61 64) on the ground floor of the Mairie. It has a good collection of historic wares by the Clérissy and Olerys families, on whom Moustiers built its reputation.

It's an energetic walk to the chapel of **Notre-Dame de Beauvoir** high above the village. The approach is from the eastern side of the stream, up 365 steps punctuated by a couple of ancient oratories and the 12 stations of the Cross.

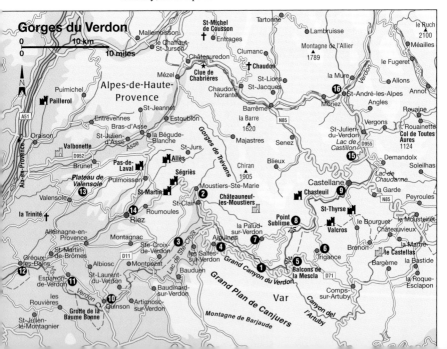

On the other side of the river, crossed by a small bridge, the village church on the main square has a three-storey Romanesque belfry and fine carved choir stalls.

Less than 3 km (2 miles) south of Moustiers, a fork in the road offers a choice of two routes along the Grand Canyon du Verdon. Both have their virtues and require at least a half-day trip – the distance may not be long but the roads are narrow and winding.

The Corniche Sublime

Along the southern route, the D957 first skirts the glorious, man-made **Lac de Ste-Croix ❸**, an 11-km (7-mile) stretch of azure water created in the 1970s by the installation of a hydroelectric dam. It is now a popular spot for canoeing, sailing and pedalos, and has several beaches where you can bathe in summer. The small village of **Les Salles-sur-Verdon** was submerged by the creation of the lake and reconstructed on its eastern edge.

The D19 then dog-legs east via the village of Aiguines, continuing along the D71 to follow the southern ridge

of the canyon, known as the **Corniche Sublime**. The village of **Aiguines ❹** itself is a tranquil spot, where houses and narrow *ruelles* cluster around an attractive turreted chateau. There are many opportunities near by for climbing and rafting.

The Corniche Sublime offers consistently spectacular views, most notably those at the **Balcons de la Mescla ❺**, where the Verdon converges with the smaller canyon formed by the Artuby River. The single-span, concrete **Pont de l'Artuby** (Artuby Bridge) is a favourite spot for bungee-jumpers.

East of here you can opt either to quit the Verdon and go south towards Draguignan, or head back towards the Verdon via the village of **Trigance ❻**, which sits under a vast 11th-century fortress, now a romantic hotel.

La Palud-sur-Verdon

Alternatively, the northern route along the Grand Canyon snakes along the old road to Castellane (the D952). On the plain between the gorges and the Montdenier and Mourre de

Map on page 156

TIP

Tourist information:
Castellane: rue Nationale; tel: 04 92 83 61 14; www.castellane.org
Gréoux-les-Bains: 5 avenue des Marronniers; tel: 04 92 78 01 08; www.greoux-les-bains.com
Moustiers Ste-Marie: Hôtel Dieu; tel: 04 92 74 67 84; www.ville-moustiers-sainte-marie.fr

BELOW LEFT:
Moustiers-Ste-Marie.

Faience

Moustiers-Ste-Marie has been a centre of faience (or tin-glazed earthernware) since the 16th century, when the technique was introduced here by an Italian ceramicist. The industry prospered for the next 200 years, counting Madame de Pompadour among its clients, and the town's population grew to almost four times its present size. Competition from porcelain and English bone china brought about its decline in the 19th century, and the art was not revived until the mid-1920s.

The finest indigenous clays are formed in moulds or turned on a wheel, biscuit-fired, then covered with a white tin glaze and given a second firing, resulting in a hard opaque finish, before the decoration is painted on using pigments made from various metal oxides. The most characteristic motif of the "Moustiers style" (now made throughout Provence as well as in its namesake town) is the early 18th-century *décor à grotesques*. The motif is inspired by the engravings of Jean Berain, which represent fantastic monsters, donkey musicians, monkeys and plumed birds.

The best-known of all the hiking trails is the Sentier Martel, which descends to the bed of the Grand Canyon between the Chalet de la Maline and the Point Sublime. The 15-km (10-mile) trail takes around seven hours and is for experienced walkers only. Invest in a detailed map and walking guide and check on weather conditions before you set off.

BELOW: driving the Corniche Sublime.

Chanier ridges, 19 km (11 miles) from Moustiers, the village of **La Palud-sur-Verdon ❼** is a popular stop-off for hikers, with a few cafés and a sturdy chateau which houses the **Maison des Gorges de Verdon** (open mid-Mar–mid-June and mid-Sept–mid-Nov Wed–Mon 10am–noon, 4–6pm, mid-June–mid-Sept Wed–Mon 10am–1pm, 4–7pm; tel: 04 92 77 32 02; www.lapalud surverdon.com), focusing on the natural history and village life of the region.

For the best views of the canyon, continue east out of La Palud on the D952, then turn right on the D23 – follow the scenic **Route des Crêtes**, which brings you back in a clockwise zigzagging loop, past a series of belvederes, to La Palud. Here you can park your car to admire the views of the gorges below and perhaps spot the impressive griffon vultures that were reintroduced here at the end of the 1990s *(see margin, page 156)*.

Just before you get back to La Palud, the **Chalet de la Maline** (where there's a popular restaurant), marks one of the main routes for serious hikers down to the canyon floor,

starting point for the Sentier Martel *(see left)*. Back on the road to Castellane, a footpath off the D23a side road leads to the aptly named **Point Sublime ❽**, a dizzying belvedere 180 metres (600 ft) above the river.

Castellane

Visitors to the gorges and traffic taking the north–south route along the Route Napoléon (N85) converge at **Castellane ❾**. Another spectacularly situated small town, Castellane, like Moustiers, has its own miracle-rendering Virgin to whom the chapel of **Notre-Dame- du-Roc**, perched on a cliff above the town, is consecrated. Count on a 30-minute walk up to the chapel, past fragments of the old ramparts. The current chapel, filled with ex-votos, dates from the 18th century, but the shrine has been a place of pilgrimage for centuries.

Napoleon paused in the town for lunch at what was then the Mairie, now the **Conservatoire des Arts et Traditions Populaires** (34 rue Nationale; open Easter–Oct Tues–Sat 9am–noon, 3–6pm, plus Sun in July and Aug; admission charge; tel:

04 92 83 71 80), a small museum of local crafts and traditions. Across the street, a fortified gateway-cum-clocktower leads into the attractive pedestrianised old quarter, where the place de l'Eglise is the scene of the annual *Fête des Fêtardiers*. Held on 31 January, it commemorates the lifting of a Huguenot siege in 1586.

Back on the main street below the old quarter, arcaded place Marcel-Sauvaire is home to a lively market on Wednesday and Saturday mornings, as well as the curious **Musée des Sirènes et Fossiles** (open May–Oct Mon and Wed–Sat 9am–noon, 2– 6pm, Sun 9am–noon; admission charge; tel: 04 92 83 19 23). Run by the Geological Reserve of Haute-Provence, it is devoted to Sirenians, a group of herbivorous aquatic vertebrates, ancestors of the sea cow and manatee, that lived 40 million years ago in the nearby Vallée des Sirènes (10 km/6 miles northwest of Castellane on the N85 near the Col de Lèques). The display explains the biology and geology of the fossils, and the mythology that links these creatures to mermaids.

Castellane has plenty of shops selling climbing equipment and organising kayak and rafting trips. For more information, contact the tourist office *(see margin, page 157).*

Bringing prehistory to life

Southwest of Moustiers the gorges are less dramatic; here you cross a sparsely inhabited landscape where little seems to have changed for centuries. One recent arrival, however, is the brilliantly presented **Musée de la Préhistoire des Gorges du Verdon** (open Feb and Mar, Oct-mid–Dec Wed–Mon 10am–6pm, Apr–June and Sept Wed–Mon 10am–7pm, July and Aug daily 10am–8pm; closed mid-Dec–Jan; admission charge; tel 04 92 74 09 59; www.museeprehistoire.com) at **Quinson** ❿, a spectacular, half-buried elliptical building designed by Sir Norman Foster. A ramp leads you back one million years as you work your way through time, past arrowheads, bones, pottery and other archaeological finds from some 60 sites in the region. About 500 metres/550 yds outside the museum, a village has been con-

Map on page 156

TIP

If the Sentier Martel is too daunting or you are with children, the Maison des Gorges du Verdon at Le Palud-sur-Verdon sells a booklet of short waymarked walks that are easily accessible for all the family, such as the Sentiers de la Découverte du Lézard, indicated by a lizard symbol. It also organises guided walks that explore different aspects of the area. www.lapaludsur verdon.com

BELOW: prehistoric museum, Quinson.

Next to the village of Esparron-de-Verdon, the small man-made Lac d'Esparron is used for sailing and canoeing.

BELOW:
view of Valensole across lavender fields.

structed based on archaeological evidence, with dwellings from different epochs of prehistory.

You might well ask why such an ambitious museum has been created in such a tiny hamlet. The answer lies a little further down the River Verdon, where the cave known as the **Grotte de la Baume Bonne** (visits by appointment; telephone the museum for details) was discovered in 1946. First inhabited 500,000 years ago, bones of bouquetin, horses, bison, marmots and even rhinoceros and lions have been excavated here.

From Quinson a choice of roads cross the plateau, either rejoining the Verdon at **Esparron-de-Verdon** ⓫, a small village built around a chateau and next to the pretty **Lac d'Esparron** *(see left)*, or heading north on the D15 to **Allemagne-en-Provence**. The L-shaped **Château** (guided visits Easter–June, mid-Sept–Oct Sat, Sun 4pm, 5pm; July–mid-Sept Tues–Sun, 4pm, 5pm; admission charge; tel: 04 92 77 46 78) reveals both a medieval fortified aspect with its crenellations, and another, Renaissance one. The inte-

riors are noted for their fanciful moulded stucco chimneypieces.

Gréoux-les-Bains

Twelve km (8 miles) west of here, **Gréoux-les-Bains** ⓬ is a spa town dating back to Roman times, later a Templar stronghold. The castle courtyard is used for theatre and concerts in summer, while exhibitions are held in the former guardroom. In the new quarter on the road towards Riez are the baths themselves. The 42°C sulphate- and magnesium-rich water still draws plenty of elderly devotees, though a modern establishment built in the 1970s has replaced the baths frequented by Pauline Bonaparte and the king of Spain in the early 1800s.

On the avenue des Alpes, the **Musée de la Crèche Provençale** (36 avenue des Alpes; open mid-Apr–Oct Tues–Fri 10–noon, 3–5.30pm, plus Sat in July and Aug; tel: 04 92 77 61 08) displays Provençal *santons* (crib figures) in elaborate village settings.

Plateau de Valensole

Sweeping north of the Verdon River, the wide, flat **Plateau de Valensole** ⓭ was dubbed by the writer Giono his "magnificent friend". Today it is France's centre for the production of lavender, but this has not always been the case. The cultivation of lavender is only a 19th-century phenomenon, important both to the fragrance and honey industries (in fact the almond trees that blossom here so spectacularly in early spring are a much more ancient mainstay of the economy). Summer is the time to see the Valensole in all its purple magnificence. On the cusp of July and into August, the dusky violet rows stretch away to the horizon and their intoxicating scent fills the air.

The few villages that huddle on the plain, surviving the winter lashings of wind and hailstorms, are for

the most part unremarkable. The exception is **Riez** , 15 km (10 miles) west of Moustiers on the D952, which is notable for its four Corinthian columns – remains of a Roman temple of Apollo – standing alone in a field just outside the town.

The ancient **Merovingian baptistery** (guided visits only, 15 June–15 Sept Tues, Fri, Sat 6pm; admission charge; tel: 04 92 77 99 09), Riez's other "sight", was built in the 5th century reusing masonry from a Roman baths complex.

The town has an appealingly scruffy old quarter, reached through two fortified gateways. Several fine houses on Grande Rue, notably the Renaissance Hôtel de Mazan, bear witness to its more illustrious past.

East of Castellane

The Verdon River keeps its luminous colour in the northern reaches. In the Vallée du Haut Verdon (Upper Verdon Valley), the **Lac de Castillon** is edged by odd, vertically grooved rock formations that alternate with white sand spits, providing pleasant spots for swimming in summer.

The D955 follows the lake round to the east. At **St-Julien-du-Verdon**, you can branch off towards the delightful little town of **Annot** (see page 169), passing through the dramatic Col de Toutes Aures (Pass of All Winds) which lies in the shadow of the 1,878-m (6,160-ft) high Pic de Chamatte. This richly forested landscape contrasts sharply with the bleak beauty of the canyon region. Here, shaly, precipitous slopes are cloaked with sweeps of dark evergreens. Minuscule villages, such as **Vergons** and **Rouaine**, consist of little more than a handful of drystone houses.

In a valley of orchards and lavender fields, at the head of the lake, sits **St-André-les-Alpes** , a haven for windsurfers, hang-gliders, anglers and other *sportifs*, and a stop on the Train des Pignes line (see page 262). This village has little to recommend it architecturally or historically, but it is redeemed by the genuine hospitality of its people.

North of St-André, the Verdon valley becomes progressively more Alpine as it ascends towards Colmars and its source in the Sestrière. ❏

Map on page 156

Hidden on a garrigue-covered hill southeast of Gréoux-les-Bains, the tiny chapel dedicated to Notre-Dame-des-Oeufs (Our Lady of the Eggs) was long believed to have the power of curing infertility. Women would climb to the church on Easter Monday with an egg in each hand, eating one egg and burying the other. If the buried egg was still intact on a second pilgrimage on 8 September, the woman would be able to have children.

RESTAURANTS

Castellane

Auberge de Teillon
La Garde. Tel: 04 92 83 60 88. Open: L Tues–Sun, D Tues–Sat (July & Aug L Wed–Mon, D daily). Closed: mid-Nov–mid-Mar. €€
Located on the Route Napoléon 6 km (4 miles) outside Castellane, this old-fashioned inn is renowned for its generous helpings of regional cuisine, including mountain lamb, wild mushrooms and autumn game.

La Main à la Pâte
2 rue de la Fontaine. Tel: 04 92 83 61 16. Open: L and D daily. Closed: mid-Dec–mid-Feb. €
Copious salads and pizzas are the speciality at this establishment, which has two cheerful beamed dining rooms and an outdoor terrace.

Moustiers-Ste-Marie

La Bastide de Moustiers
Chemin de Quinson. Tel: 04 92 70 47 47. Open: Apr–Oct L & D daily, Nov–Feb L & D Thur–Sun, Mar L & D Wed–Sun. €€€
www.bastide-moustiers.com
Refined cuisine, using produce from the Bastide's own kitchen garden. Chef Eric Santalucia rustles up an ultra-fine "ravioli" inlaid with herbs, stuffed courgettes and a splendid pigeon.

Les Santons
Place de l'Eglise. Tel: 04 92 74 66 48. Open: L Wed–Mon, D Wed–Sun. €€
www.lessantons.com
This pleasant bistro puts a light touch on Provençal cuisine in tasty dishes such as tomato Tatin and rabbit with rosemary.

La Palud-sur-Verdon

Bar-Restaurant de la Place
Tel: 04 92 77 38 03. €
Expect hearty dishes such as *haricot de mouton* (lamb with beans) or *boudin noir* with potato purée. Popular with the rock-climbing fraternity.

● ● ● ● ● ● ● ● ● ● ● ●
Price includes dinner and a glass of wine, excluding tip.
€€€€ €60 and over,
€€€ €40–60, **€€** €25–40,
€ under €25.

DIGNE AND THE SOUTHERN ALPS

Bordering the Alps, this region shows the wild, rugged face of Provence as the landscape switches from rolling lavender fields to rocky Alpine terrain. The much-vaunted climate is a happy balance between Provençal warmth and crisp Alpine coolness

A t the border between Provence and the Alps, north of the Verdon gorges, the Alpes-de-Haute-Provence is a land of beautiful lakes, bizarre rock formations and inaccessible mountainous terrain. Stark citadels crown many towns, and villages are built to give maximum protection against the elements. Like its architecture, the region's cultural heritage is characterised by its simplicity and austerity. In common with the rest of inland Provence, many villages here were gradually abandoned through the 20th century as locals moved south to work in the wealthier areas along the coast. The Route Napoléon N85, supplemented by the new A51 motorway between Aix-en-Provence and Gap, makes this area a through-route for summer holiday traffic attempting to avoid the Rhône corridor, bringing additional visitors to the area in the process.

Digne-les-Bains

Digne-les-Bains ❶, last stop on the Train des Pignes *(see page 262)*, is a genteel spa town in the sparsely populated Pré-Alpes de Digne. It was here that Victor Hugo set the first chapters of *Les Misérables*. However, Digne is not simply a town of fictional unfortunates, rheumatics and departmental officials. The shady boulevard Gassendi tempts with several pleasant cafés, and in August the town hosts the Corso de la Lavande festival *(see tip on page 165)*.

Digne also has a municipal museum, the **Musée Gassendi** (64 boulevard Gassendi; open Apr–Sept Wed–Mon 11am–7pm, Oct–Mar Wed–Mon 1.30–5.30pm; admission charge; tel: 04 92 31 45 29, www.museegassendi.org), with paintings by old masters and regional artists, and the scientific instruments of the Digne-born astronomer, Pierre Gassendi.

Map on page 164

LEFT: Sisteron viewed from the citadel.
BELOW: Gorge de Dalius.

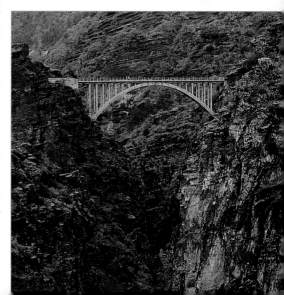

Digne and the Southern Alps

0   10 km
0   10 miles

N

Hautes-Alpes

Alpes-Maritimes

Var

Alpes-de-Haute-Provence

Vaucluse

Drôme

Gorges de Daluis

Gorges du Bachelard

Col d'Allos

Parc National du Mercantour

Col des Champs

Serre Bouréou

la Condamine-Châtelard

Jausiers

Grand Bérard 3048

le Petit Ferrand 2440

Lac de Serre-Ponçon

Esparron 4

la Bréole

St-Vincent-les-Forts

Dormillouse

Montagne de la Blanche

l'Abbaye de Laverq

le Lauzet-Ubaye

les Thuiles

Barcelonnette 18

Faucon

Pra-Loup

le Sauze

Super-Sauze

le Chapeau de Gendarme 2865

la Foux-d'Allos

Allos

Lac d'Allos

Grande Séolane 2909

Cime de Pal 2818

Cime de la Bonette 2802

Ponte Côte de l'Ane 3051

2916

St-Dalmas-le-Selvage

St-Martin-d'Entraunes

Villeneuve-d'Entraunes

Entraunes

Mont Pelat 3051

Guillaumes

le Grand Coyer 2693

Daluis

Grotte du Chat

Sausses

Castellet-lès-Sausses

Braux

Annot

le Ruch 16

2100

Méailles

le Fugeret

Allons

St-André-les-Alpes

Col de Toutes Aures 1124

Vergons

Angles

Entrevaux 14

St-Jean-du-Désert

Pont-St-Roch

Ubraye

Rouaine

Robaudette

Amirat

St-Pierre

Chalvagne

Briançonnet

Gars

Esteron

St-Auban

Estoublon

Demandolx

Soleilhas

Lac de Castillon

St-Julien-du-Verdon

Castellane

Fort de Savoie

Colmars 17

Villars-Colmars

Beauvezer

Thorame-Haute

Thorame-Basse

Peyresq

Laupon 2434

La Bâtie

Lambruisse

Montagne de l'Allier 1789

St-Lions

St-Jacques

la Mûre

Senez

Blieux

Barrême

la Barre

Chaudon-Norante

1620

Majastres

Chiran 1905

Gorges de Trévans

Estoublon

St-Jurs

Bleux

Aillès

Ségriès

Allons 15

Notre Dame

Château-Garnier

Tartonne

Clumanc

St-Lions

Montagne du Cheval Blanc 2961

Sommet du Caduc 2654

Prads

Blégiers

Verdon

Tête de l'Estrop 2961

la Javie

Draix

Archa

le Brusquet

N.D. de Lauzière

la Robine

Digne-les-Bains 1

St-Vincent

St-Michel de Cousson

Châteauredon

Clue de Chabrières

Chaudon

Barrême

Châtelard

St-Jurson

Mézel

Chenerilles

Tête Grosse 2032

l'Oratoire 2071

Crête de Géruen

Auzet

Verdaches

Seyne

Blayeul Sommet 2189

Bès

Bléone

Marcoux

Champtercier

les Sières

Mallemoisson

Mirabeau

Chaffaut-St-Jurson

Mallefougasse

Crête de Liman

Montagne de Gache

St-Geniez

les Monges 2115

Authon

le Castellard

Thoard

Champtercier

Bayons

Turriers

Bellaffaire

Gigors

Reynier

Astoin

Grande Gautière 1825

le Caire

la Motte-du-Caire

Clamensane

Valavoire

Sasse

Montagne de Vaumuse 1435

Entrepierres

Vilhosc

Sélignac

Sisteron 2

Volonne

Château-Arnoux

l'Escale

Peipin

Aubignosc

Montfort

Rochers des Mées 5

les Mées

Puimichel

Paillerol

Bras-d'Asse

St-Julien-d'Asse

Le Brusquet

Chenerilles

Mézel

Pécoule 3

Ribiers

Valernes

Sigoyer

Châteaufort

Thèze

Melve

Claret

Monêtier-Allemont

Upaix

le Poët

Ventavon

Valbelle

Châteauneuf-Val-St-Donat

St-Donat 6

St-Auban

Peyruis

Prieuré de Ganagobie 7

Lurs

Ganagobie

Notre-Dame des Anges 13

Sigonce

Fontienne

St-Étienne-les-Orgues

Cruis

Lardiers

Saumane

Signal de Lure 1826

Montagne de Lure

Notre-Dame de Lure 9

Redortiers 10

Notre-Dame des Anges 11

Banon

Simiane-la-Rotonde 12

Montsalier

Chante Duc 1427

Montfroc

les Omergues

Crête de la Taye 1241

Ballons

Montagne de Chabre

Barret-le-Bas

Salérans

Éourres

le Tréboux 1535

Ongles

Limans

Revest-des-Brousses

Saint-Michel-l'Observatoire

Observatoire de Haute-Provence

Ste-Croix-à-Lauze

Reillanne

Céreste

Oppedette

Dauphin

Mane

Forcalquier

St-Maime

Niozelles

Villeneuve

Volx

Montfuron

Manosque

Laye

Valensole

Brunet

Puimoisson

Roumoules

Riez

Allemagne-en-Provence

Gréoux-les-Bains

Montagne de Lure

Parc Régional du Lubéron

Montagne de la Méouge

Montagne de St-Genis

Barcillonnette

Barcelonnette

Monclus

Montclus

Eyguians

Lazer

Laragne-Montéglin

Antonaves

Châteauneuf-de-Chabre

Montrond

les Bègues

Lagrand

Orpierre

Trescléoux

Chanousse

Montjay

Eaux-Chaudes

Laborel

Eygalayes

Montagne de Gache

Vitrolles

Gap

Lardier-et-Valença

Tallard

Barcillonnette

Curbans

Faucon-du-Caire

Vaumeilh

Chorges

Architecturally, Digne's greatest attraction is the **Cathédrale de Notre-Dame-du-Bourg**, north of boulevard Gassendi on the outskirts of town, built in the Lombardy Romanesque style that continued to be employed in Provence long after northern France was well into the Gothic. Look out for the 13th-century portals in striking blue-and-white limestone, and traces of frescos.

In the later Middle Ages, a second church, the **Cathédrale St-Jérôme**, was built in the Gothic style, though largely rebuilt in the 19th century.

Across the River Bléone, by the Pont des Arches, is the well-ordered **Réserve Géologique** (open Apr–Oct daily, Nov–Mar Mon–Fri; tel: 04 92 36 70 70), described as a "musée-promenade". Two footpaths take you up from the car park through the Parc St-Benoît, past a waterfall and several outdoor works of art, and on to the museum at the top of the tufa knoll, where aquariums and a collection of fossils and prehistoric skeletons await you. Back near the car park, the **Cairn** is a centre for contemporary art exhibitions.

Sisteron

About 40 km (25 miles) further up the Route Napoléon, **Sisteron** ❷ forms a natural gateway to Provence. Sitting on the left bank of the roaring Durance River and looking across to the rugged **Rocher de la Baume**, the setting of this historic town is impressive. A bustling market, some light industry and a steady wave of tourists along the N85 maintain a lively atmosphere.

Napoleon stopped here for lunch on a misty March day in 1815, on his way back from exile on Elba. Still standing in the rue Saunerie is the **Bras d'Or** inn, run at the time by the grandfather of the Sisteron novelist Paul Arène (1843–96). A plaque commemorates the site where the imperial lunch was eaten.

Sisteron's biggest crowd-puller, **La Citadelle** (open Mar–mid-Nov daily, summer 9am–7pm, winter 9am–5.30pm; admission charge; tel: 04 92 61 27 57) dominates the town. It was begun in the 13th century, then redesigned by Henri IV's military engineer Jean Erard during the 16th to double as a fortress and prison.

Map on page 164

TIP

In early August, sleepy Digne asserts its position as the capital of the Alpes-de-Haute-Provence with a boisterous festival called the Corso de la Lavande. Four days of revelry culminate in a grand procession. An array of huge flower-bedecked floats glide down the main boulevard to uproarious applause, preceded by the town's sanitation department trucks, which douse the streets with lavender water.

BELOW: Alpine peaks north of Digne-les-Bains.

Buddhist Retreat

On the outskirts of Digne is the Alexandra David-Néel Foundation (27 avenue Maréchal Juin; guided visits daily 10am, 2pm, 3.30pm; free; tel: 04 92 31 32 38, www.alexandra-david-neel.org). This cultural-centre-cum-museum is named after a Parisian adventurer who spent much of her life travelling in remote parts of Asia. Seduced by the beauty of the Alpes-de-Haute-Provence, which she called a "Himalayas for Lilliputians", she bought a house in Digne in 1927 and named it Samten Dzong (the fortress of meditation). When she died in 1969, aged 101, David-Néel left the house and its contents to the city. The Foundation continues to attract visitors and Buddhist pilgrims.

Sisteron's citadel provides an atmospheric setting for Les Nuits de la Citadelle, one of Provence's oldest arts festivals, founded in 1928. Each year from late July to early August it features top names in contemporary dance, theatre and classical music, who perform in an outdoor theatre cut into the north face of the Citadelle. www.sisteron.com

BELOW:
Rochers des Mées.

Keeps and dungeons, watchtowers, a small chapel and crenellated battlements crowning mighty buttresses rise up on the massive rock that overshadows the town. It's a steep, sticky climb up to the fortress, so take the tourist train that runs from place de l'Eglise.

In 1944 the citadel was bombed by the Allies in an attempt to speed up the retreat of the German occupying army that had taken refuge there. More than 300 people died, and a quarter of Sisteron's fine medieval quarter was destroyed. Fortunately, a good deal still remains of the **Vieille Ville** (old town), huddled at the foot of the fortress rock. Most of the action takes place along rue Saunerie and its continuation, rue Droite, busy with bistros and tourist shops. The numerous little streets and stairways running off to the side and down to the Durance are known here as *andrônes* – from the Latin for "alleyway" or the Greek for "between two houses", depending on whom you ask.

The town bakers sell the local speciality, *fougasse à l'anchois*, a delectable bread smeared with anchovies and sold by the kilo. Butchers display the locally celebrated Sisteron lamb, which is given a fragrant herbal flavour by wild thyme and rosemary that grows in the pastures of the Upper Durance valley.

Northeast of Sisteron, on the D3 in the direction of **St-Geniez**, look out for a rock slab covered with Roman inscriptions. The **Pierre-Ecrite ❸**, carved in the 5th century, records the conversion to Christianity of Claudius Dardanus, prefect of the Gauls.

For many centuries, the Durance was known as one of the "three scourges of Provence" (the mistral and the Parlement at Aix completed the triumvirate). In recent years, the river's unpredictable surges have been harnessed by a series of major dams beginning at **Serre-Ponçon ❹** – on the northernmost border of the *département* – creating the largest artificial lake in Europe. Apple and pear orchards, planted since the 1960s on the newly irrigated alluvial plains, reinvigorated the ailing economy. And hydroelectric power has also helped bring prosperity to the region.

Limestone penitents

As the Durance snakes its way south and meets the Bléone flowing from the east, a sprawling collection of light industrial plants appears. Across the apex of the confluence, south of Château-Arnoux, the village of Les Mées itself does not tempt much, but the staggering "**Pénitents**", or **Rochers des Mées** ❺ do. The curious row of limestone pinnacles, some as high as 100 metres (330 ft), rise out of a stunted forest – some alone, some clustered in groups – until they close ranks to form a single mini-massif, standing eerily over miles of fruit orchards and flat maize fields.

On the opposite bank of the Durance, the ruins of the early Romanesque **Eglise de St-Donat** ❻, reached by the narrow D101, sit isolated in thick oak woods. The retreat of St Donatus, a 6th-century monk, has eight mighty pillars supporting its ancient vaulting. A faded white apse, decorated with pale, terracotta-coloured stars, hint at its former glory.

More obviously impressive is the nearby medieval **Prieuré de**

Ganagobie ❼ (open Tues–Sun 3–5pm; free; www.ndganagobie. com). Its principal attractions, other than the wonderful view of the Durance valley to be had from its grounds, are the magnificent west portal and the 12th-century mosaics that decorate the interior. In red, black and white, they feature lively depictions of knights, dragons and other mythical birds and beasts.

The lure of austerity

The vast and forbidding **Montagne de Lure** is a continuation of lavender-covered Mont Ventoux to the west, and is bordered by the Luberon to the south. Its highest point, the **Signal de Lure** (1,826 metres/5,990 ft) offers sweeping views of the Cévennes and Mont Ventoux. It can be reached from the north by the D946 that winds out of Sisteron, or from the south via the small town of **St-Etienne-les-Orgues** ❽ that lies at its feet. The prosperity of this pretty village was traditionally based on its medicinal remedies concocted from mountain herbs. The Distilleries de Provence in Forcalquier *(see page 168)* keep up the

Map on page 164

A sad legend is connected to the strange rock formations known as the "Pénitents". The story goes that during the Arab invasions in the Middle Ages, a group of monks from the Montagne de Lure were bewitched by the beauty of some Moorish girls, whom they were unable to resist. As the cowled, disgraced figures were banished from the village, St Donatus turned them to stone as punishment for their impropriety.

BELOW LEFT: a welcoming mountain bistro.

Bistrot de Pays

Travel anywhere in France and you'll soon discover how vital a role the café plays as a focus of local life, not just as a place to eat and drink but also as a hub of gossip and social life. The Bistrot de Pays movement aims to help keep open or recreate the village café in small rural communities, where many of the shops and bars have closed, both to serve locals and to act as an ambassador for their area to tourists. The cafés and bistros sign a quality charter promising to provide snacks using local produce (many actually go much further, with full meals and regional specialities), to stay open all year, where possible to provide basic services not found elsewhere in the village, such as selling newspapers, cigarettes, vital groceries, or serving as a bread depot, to provide tourist information and organise at least three cultural events a year, such as literary dinners, storytelling or musical evenings. First created in the sparsely populated area around Forcalquier and the Montagne de Lure, the concept has gradually spread to remote rural districts in many corners of France, including the Haut-Var and Verdon. www.bistrotdepays.com

Made from the milk of goats raised on the Montagne de Lure and the Plateau d'Albion, the small, round banon cheese, an ancient cheese dating back to at least the Middle Ages, is instantly recognisable, wrapped as it is in a dry chestnut leaf tied with raffia.

BELOW:
Simiane-la-Rotonde.

age-old tradition of using local herbs, fruit and wild flowers in its preparations. Founded in 1898, it makes the artisanal Pastis Henri Baudouin as well as a range of plant-based liqueurs and aperitifs (www.distilleries-provence.com).

A road lined with lavender fields leads out of the village. Before long, the lavender gives way to the dense oak-and-fir forest of the mountain. Though seemingly deserted, this route becomes animated in August and September, as locals continue the centuries-old tradition of pilgrimage to the isolated **Chapelle de Notre-Dame-de-Lure** ❾, halfway to the summit. Also founded by the reclusive St Donatus, the chapel has none of the architectural distinction of the Eglise de St-Donat, but its setting is compensation enough.

The wild isolation of the Lure was the inspiration for many of Jean Giono's novels *(see page 94)*. It is widely believed that his fictional Aubignane is based on the ruined village of **Redortiers** ❿, just north of **Banon** ⓫, worth a visit to sample its renowned goat's cheese *(see left)*.

Beautiful and remote, the village of **Simiane-la-Rotonde** ⓬ is dominated by a strange 12th-century rotunda, actually the old castle keep. There are some fine period doorways and an old covered market here. Outside the summer months, however, its closed shutters and deserted streets make it a desolate place.

Rather livelier is **Forcalquier** ⓭, especially on a Monday, the day of its wonderful weekly market, when countless stalls groaning with local produce crowd the spacious **place du Bourguet** and the streets around it.

Forcalquier's main sight is the austere **Ancienne Cathédrale de Notre-Dame**, which has a wide triple nave and impressive organ loft. An aimless wander through the narrow streets of the old town reveals fine stone doorways and arches decorated with chiselled plaques, scrolls and intricate reliefs, and there's a fine Gothic fountain on place St-Michel. Climb rue St-Mary to the grassy mound where the count's fortress once stood, now topped by a neo-Gothic **chapel** ringed by amusing sculptures of angels playing musical instruments.

Frontier fortresses

On the eastern fringes of the *département*, the citadels fortified by Louis XIV's brilliant military architect, Sébastien Le Prestre de Vauban, give an indication of the strategic importance of this region – for a long time at the border between Provence and what was then the Comté de Nice. The area is most easily reached by car from Nice or by the Train des Pignes.

Cross the drawbridge of the **Porte Royale** into the fairy-tale town of **Entrevaux** ⓮. The 17th-century ramparts, turrets, drawbridges and a deep moat formed by the Var River cocoon the town. Cars are firmly relegated to the busy Nice road on the opposite bank.

Like the ramparts, the majority of Entrevaux's tall stone houses date

from the 17th century, as does the former **cathedral**. Its severe façade conceals a Baroque interior with a richly decorated high altar. The tiny main square, **place St-Martin**, has a pleasant café, a clutch of chestnut trees and a butcher who dispenses the local speciality, *secca de boeuf*, a type of dried salt beef best eaten with olive oil and lemon juice. The **citadel** (open daily 24 hours; take coins for entrance token; tel: 04 93 05 46 73) bears testimony to the town's key strategic position *(see right)*.

Back into the modern age, the minuscule **Musée de la Moto** (Motorbike Museum; open May–Sept daily 10am–noon, 2–7pm; free; tel: 04 93 79 12 70) is devoted to the history of the motorbike. Run by two enthusiasts, it houses over 70 vehicles, the oldest dating from 1901.

Annot

West of Entrevaux in the Vaïre valley – and also a stop on the Train des Pignes line – the picturesque town of **Annot** ⑮ is typical of this area's dual aspect: the wrought-iron balconies and stone *lavoirs* are as classically

Provençal as anything found further south; but the majesty of the Alps comes through in the purity of the air and in the steely grey of the many streams that tumble through the town. During the winter months, the town sleeps under a thick blanket of snow.

East of the main square, with its fine esplanade of ancient plane trees, the narrow streets of the picturesque old town climb steeply in medieval formation. Vaulted archways and carved stone lintels decorate the tall houses of the Grande Rue. At the top of the old town, the streets converge on a pretty square with the parish church and surrounding houses painted in a rainbow of pastel hues.

Just outside the town to the south, a group of mammoth rocks known as the **Grès d'Annot** lies scattered over the hillside as if by giants. Locals have built houses directly beside them, often using their sheer faces as an outside wall. To this day, they are the subject of local legends which tell of troglodytes and primitive religions.

Those with stamina and sturdy boots can follow the spectacular

Map on page 164

Entrevaux's citadel is reached by an ascending path of nine zigzag ramps, a remarkable feat of engineering that took 50 years to complete.

BELOW: Entrevaux.

Map on page 164

The ski resorts of Pra-Loup and Super-Sauze are looking to the future. As well as 80 ski runs, Pra-Loup has opened the "Rider Space" for snowboarding and freestyle activities, and provides floodlit night skiing and the chance to snowscoot (a type of snow cycling). Super-Sauze has 65 ski runs and the modern "Snow Park" aimed at daring snowboarders with a love of acrobatics.
www.ubaye.com

BELOW: Villa Morélia, Jausiers, a hotel and prestigious restaurant.

hiking trails into the high-altitude **Val du Coulomp** near by. Alternatively, continuing north up the Vaire valley on the D908 towards Colmars will bring you to the mountain village of **Méailles** , perched high above the river, before rejoining the upper Verdon valley *(see page 155)*.

Colmars

If Entrevaux seems uniquely untouched by its proximity to the Alps, **Colmars** ⑰, 50 km (31 miles) to the north, could hardly be more Alpine. Colmars is crowned by two massive fortresses, and, like Entrevaux, it is a former border post between Provence and Savoy. Inside the well-preserved ramparts of the town, houses have been constructed with tidy wooden balconies known as *solerets* (sun traps), locals sport jaunty alpine caps, and shop windows display Amber bottles of *génépi* liqueur, made from Alpine flowers.

Of the two castles, only the **Fort de Savoie** (open July–Aug daily 2.30–7pm, Sept–June: visits for groups by appointment; admission charge; tel: 04 92 83 41 92), a fine piece of 17th-century military engineering, is open to the public.

A touch of Mexico

In the northwest corner of the Alpes-de-Haute-Provence, just north of the Parc National du Mercantour *(see page 216)*, **Barcelonnette** ⑱ just about squeezes into the glacial valley of the Ubaye, surrounded by towering peaks. It owes its unlikely name to its 12th-century rulers, the counts of Barcelona. The Hispanic connection does not end there. Early in the 19th century, a period of emigration to Mexico began, prompted by the success of three local brothers who opened a textile shop there. Many followed, founding textile factories, department stores and banks. Having made their fortune, some of them later returned to Barcelonnette to build the incongruous, so-called "Mexican" villas for which the town is famous. Set in large gardens in a new district around the edge of the old town, as well as in the nearby village of **Jausiers**, they were shaped by Italian craftsmen or took the forms of the new Art Nouveau style from Nancy. At 10 avenue de la Libération, one such villa, the handsome 1870s Villa La Sapinière, now contains the **Musée de la Vallée** (open mid-July–Aug daily 10am–noon, 2.30– 7pm, rest of year usually Tues,Wed–Sat 2–6pm holidays; admission charge; tel: 04 92 81 27 15, www.barcelonnette.net), which traces the history of this emigration in documents and artefacts.

Today, the "Mexican connection" remains strong with the annual Fêtes Latino-Méxicaines in August, frequent cultural exchanges, shops selling Mexican crafts, and a Mexican restaurant.

From December to April the modern ski resorts of **Super-Sauze** and **Pra-Loup**, just south of Barcelonette, have brought a welcome upturn in local fortunes *(see left)*. ❑

RESTAURANTS AND BARS

Barcelonnette

Villa Morélia

Jausiers. Tel: 04 92 84 67 78.
Closed: Nov–Dec and Apr.
€€€
www.villa-morelia.com
Young and resolutely
modern chef Vincent
Lucas has returned to
Provence after stints in
Monaco, Paris, Oxford
and St-Barthélémy. He
multiplies flavours and
enjoys mixing sweet and
savoury, in artistically
presented dishes like
scallops and crab
velouté, or morels with
red mullet. Located in
one of the famous "Mexi-
can" villas (pictured left).

Château-Arnoux

La Bonne Etape

Chemin du Lac. Tel: 04 92 64
00 09. Open: L & D daily
(Nov–Apr Wed–Sun). Closed:
Jan–mid-Feb. €€€–€€€€
www.bonneetape.com
At this comfortable family-
run Relais et Châteaux,
chef Jany Gleize com-
bines local lavender and
honey with luxury ingredients such as pigeon and
lobster. A second, bistro-
style restaurant, Le Goût
du Jour (open daily, €),
serves up more rustic
dishes – aioli, pieds et
paquets and pumpkin
soup included.

L'Oustaou de la Foun

N85 Route Napoléon. Tel: 04
92 62 65 30. Open: L
Tues–Sun, D Tues–Sat.

Closed: 1–14 July. €€€
A renovated farmhouse is
the showcase for hotly
tipped young chef Gérald
Jourdan. Trained by
Reine Sammut and Alain
Ducasse, he allies tradi-
tion and creativity.

Digne-les-Bains

Le Grand Paris

19 boulevard Thiers. Tel: 04
92 31 11 15. Open: L Fri–Sun,
D daily. Closed: Dec–Feb. €€
www.hotel-grand-paris.com
Noémie Ricaud has taken
over from her father at
this long-established
restaurant housed in a
former monastery. Expect
lavish cooking in the classic mould with some mod-
ern touches.

Forcalquier

Le Lapin Tant Pis

10 avenue St-Promasse. Tel:
04 92 75 38 88. Open: D generally Wed–Sat (reservation
essential, days vary). Closed:
Oct–Mar. No credit cards. €€
This much-loved eatery
has moved to a converted
stable where chef Gérard
Vives presents a set-
choice tasting menu.
Vives also runs the Comp-
toir des Poivres, offering
workshops and classes in
cooking with spices.

La Tourette

20 boulevard Latourette.
Tel: 04 92 75 14 00. Open: L
& D daily. Closed: Wed & D
Sun in low season. €
This relaxed, homely

place on the main street
near the cathedral has an
inexpensive menu of
Provençal staples, with
dishes such as caillettes,
daube, lamb and rabbit.

Lardiers

**Café-Restaurant de la
Lavande**

Place de la Lavande. Tel 04
92 73 31 52. Open: L
Thur–Tues, D Thur–Mon
(Wed–Mon in July & Aug).
Closed: 2 weeks Nov, 2
weeks Feb. €€
Prime example of a
Bistrot de Pays, with its
bar, newspapers, literary
evenings and menu
based on local produce,
such as petits farcis,
truffles, figs and banon
cheese. There is even a
wine list, rare for these
parts. Book ahead.

Sisteron

Grand Hôtel des Cours

Place de l'Eglise. Tel: 04 92
61 00 50. Open: L & D
Wed–Mon (also Tues in July &
Aug). €€
www.hotel-lecours.com
A Sisteron institution for
three generations. A lively
atmosphere prevails,
especially outdoors on
the spacious terrace in
summer. Herby Sisteron
lamb is a speciality.

PRICE CATEGORIES

Prices for a three-course
meal without wine. Note
that many restaurants
have a less expensive
lunch menu.
€ = under €25
€€ = €25–€40
€€€ = €40–€60
€€€€ = more than €60

RIGHT: Mexican flavours come to the Alps.

TOULON AND THE WESTERN VAR

Toulon's reputation as a gritty port town may not entice those in search of Riviera glitz, but this vibrant, historic city deserves a visit. It offers good museums, a great daily market, and ongoing restoration projects are giving run-down quarters a new lease of life

Clustered round a deep natural harbour in the huge bay known as the Rade de Toulon, and enclosed by a crescent of high hills, **Toulon ❶** is home to France's leading naval base – a massive town within the town, covering 268 hectares (662 acres) and employing 12,000 people – that is strictly off limits to the public. Many tourists bypass the city. Its gritty reputation, busy through roads, seedy alleyways, chaotic suburban sprawl and a reputation marred in the 1990s by extreme-right politics offer little obvious enticement to the casual visitor. However, along with all the low-life trappings of a major seaport, Toulon has its own share of grand buildings, chic boutiques, lively markets and a cosmopolitan energy that is matched in Provence only by Marseille.

But Toulon is also changing. Much of the town centre has been renovated, as have several once seedy hotels. Part of the motorway has been funnelled underground, a new coast path has been created and, as with many of France's larger cities, there are plans for a tramway to link its disparate *quartiers*.

Central Toulon divides broadly into two districts: the Haute Ville, laid out in the late 19th century with expansive Hausmannian squares

and avenues, and the Basse Ville leading towards the port, which incorporates the narrow medieval alleys of the old town.

Haute Ville

Centrepiece of the Haute Ville is the **boulevard de Strasbourg**, which bisects the grid of tall apartment blocks, department stores and imposing administrative buildings that make up 19th-century Toulon. Admire the elaborate **Opéra de Toulon**, with its splendid gold-and-

Map on page 174

LEFT: aircraft carrier in Toulon harbour.
BELOW: on the waterfront, Toulon.

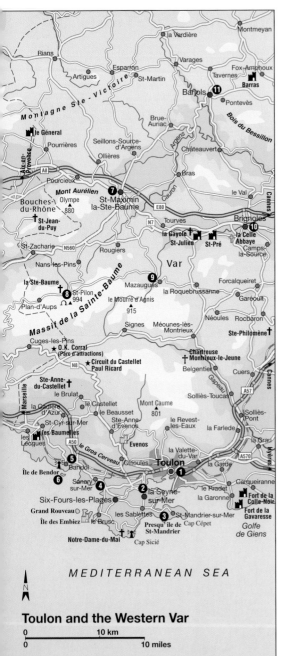

Toulon and the Western Var

0   10 km

0   10 miles

red interior, still used to stage dance, theatre and opera productions, and spacious **place de la Liberté**, with its palm trees and the ornate façade of the **Grand Hôtel**.

The neo-Renaissance **Musée d'Art** (113 boulevard du Maréchal Leclerc; open Tues–Sun noon–6pm; free; tel: 04 94 36 81 00) has paintings by the Provençal school and a collection of contemporary art. In the same building, the **Muséum d'Histoire Naturelle** (open Mon–Fri 9am–6pm, Sat–Sun 11am–6pm; free; www.museum-toulon.org) has all the usual stuffed birds and animals, and a display about the dinosaurs that once roamed the Var.

Just down the road a fine 19th-century villa houses the **Hôtel des Arts** (236 boulevard du Maréchal Leclerc; open Tues–Sun 11am–6pm, closed between exhibitions; free; tel: 04 94 91 69 18), which puts on contemporary art exhibitions, often with a Mediterranean emphasis.

Basse Ville

South of the Opéra lies the warren of narrow streets of the Basse Ville (Lower Town). Insalubrious bars rub shoulders with dingy restaurants. Scruffy kids play football in the shadow of peeling tenements, and locals watch the world go by.

The Basse Ville isn't all sleaze, however, and is undergoing major restoration. The attractive place Puget, with its pavement cafés, plane trees and fountain, draws elegant locals. Superb fish, vegetable and flower markets characterise mornings (Tues–Sun) in the **cours Lafayette**. Here you'll also find the **Musée du Vieux Toulon** (69 cours Lafayette; open Mon–Sat 2–5.45pm; free; tel: 04 94 62 11 07), which evokes Toulon's history.

Near by is Toulon's **Cathédrale Ste-Marie des Seds**, worth a look for the Baroque altar sculpted by Pierre Puget's nephew and pupil

Map on page 174

Christophe Veyrier. From here, the patchwork of streets leads towards Toulon's *raison d'être*: the port.

The port

Much of the Basse Ville's bad press comes from the avenue de la République, a grubby roadway lined by one long concrete post-war housing block. Go through one of the archways, however, and the vision changes totally as you find yourself beside Toulon's lively marina and its quayside cafés, such as the ever-fashionable **Grand Café de la Rade** and the designer **Soleil Café**, which are popular with locals for an early evening aperitif.

Boats leave from here for trips around the bay *(see page 176)*, across the bay to La Seyne-sur-Mer, Tamaris and Les Sablettes, and to the Iles d'Hyères (in season).

The original gateway to the arsenal, a rare relic of the old port, now forms the entrance to the **Musée de la Marine** (Place Monsenergue; open Feb–Dec Wed–Mon 10am– 6pm; admission charge; tel: 04 94 02 02 01; www.musee-marine.fr), housing historic ships' figureheads, model ships and marine paintings.

Mont Faron

For a terrific bird's-eye view of the city and some respite from the crowds, take a ride up to Mont Faron, the white limestone mountain which frames the city. You can reach it by car via a long and winding road, but the best way up is on the **Téléphérique** (open Feb–Nov Tues–Sun, daily in July and Aug, times vary, doesn't run in high winds; admission charge; tel: 04 94 92 68 25), which leaves from the Gare Inférieure on boulevard Amiral-Vence. Views from the cable car as you climb are stunning. At the top, amid a rocky landscape of parasol pines, evergreen oaks and maquis scrub, lie miles of footpaths, picnic areas, children's play areas, restaurants and the **Zoo du Mont Faron** (closed on rainy days; tel: 04 94 88 07 89), which specialises in breeding tigers, panthers, snow leopards and other wild cats.

Not far from the Téléphérique station is the Tour Beaumont, a 19th-

Grand Hôtel on Toulon's spacious place de la Liberté.

BELOW: bird's-eye view of Toulon.

TIP

For a glimpse of
Toulon's impressive but
out-of-bounds naval
docks and military
arsenal, the best bet is
a boat tour of the Rade,
Toulon's huge natural
harbour. Several com-
panies run trips from
quai Cronstadt, which
go past the arsenal,
navy battleships and
the numerous forts that
encircle the bay. Trips
last about an hour.

century surveillance tower housing the **Mémorial du Débarquement** (open summer daily 10am–noon, 2–5.30pm, closed Mon in winter; admission charge; tel: 04 94 88 08 09), a museum dedicated to the Liberation of Provence in August 1944.

Forts and Beaches

East of the city centre, the **Plages de Mourrillon** have a distinctly urban feel, drawing a local city population rather than tourists to their long stretch of sand, restaurants, lawns and playgrounds in the shelter of the Fort St-Louis. The corniche continues through Toulon's more upmarket suburbs to **Cap Brun**, where a coastal path leads to a series of little creeks, and the tranquil Anse de Méjean with its fishermen's shacks.

Rounding the bay west of Toulon, the first impression of **La Seyne-sur-Mer** ❷ is one of industrial dereliction. But this once important shipbuilding town hides some unusual gems. Built into the seashore, the 17th-century Fort Balaguier now contains the **Musée Naval** (924 corniche Bonaparte; open Tues–Sun

10am–noon, 2–6pm, July and Aug Tues–Sun 10am–noon, 3–7pm; admission charge; tel: 04 94 94 84 72), which commemorates Napoleon's capture of Toulon and also has a display about the notorious penal colony, La Bagne.

Up on the Caire hill, the **Fort Napoléon** (Chemin Marc Sangnier; tel: 04 94 87 83 43), built by Napoleon after his victory over the English, is today used for a summer jazz festival and other cultural events. But most fascinating of all here are the remains of **Tamaris**, an early seaside resort built in the 1890s by wealthy sailor and marine adventurer Michel Pacha, who made his fortune as director of lighthouses of the Ottoman Empire. Extravagant villas, hotels and a casino were built, most of them in a neo-Moresque style, as was his own vast chateau. Tamaris never quite made it big, and by the 1920s it had gone out of fashion. But it was bypassed rather than destroyed, and a number of buildings remain intact, including the classical-style **Villa Tamaris** (avenue de la Grande Maison; open Tues–Sun

BELOW RIGHT: Plages
de Mourrillon.

The Naval Port

Though the city was a base for the royal navy as early as 1487, Toulon's era of major expansion occured in the 17th century. During the reign of Louis XIV, Toulon became the lynchpin of royal naval strategy against the Anglo-Spanish alliance (while Marseille was favoured for commerce): the arsenal was expanded and the city's fortifications enlarged by the king's brilliant military engineer Vauban, who added the *darse neuve* (new dock), new forts and a set of star-shaped ramparts. Over 20 new forts and towers, constructed both on the coast and on the surrounding hills, protected the port.

A century later, the city took the side of the English against the Revolutionary government and was promptly brought to heel by a young Napoleon Bonaparte. The English fleet was defeated in 1793, ensuring that the general's name would never be forgotten. During World War II the French sabotaged their own fleet in 1942 to blockade the harbour and try and prevent the Nazis from taking the city, and in 1944 much of the town was razed by retreating Germans and advancing Allied troops.

2–6pm; free; tel: 04 94 06 84 00), on the hill, now used for contemporary art shows, and the palatial Ottoman-style Institut Michel Pacha, a marine research institute on the sea front.

The **Baie de Lazaret** is used for mussel production, and is filled with mussel beds and picturesque mussel farmers' cabins on stilts (long known as *moules de Toulon*, you'll now find the mussels on many menus referred to as *moules de Tamaris*). Sea bream and sea bass are also farmed in the bay.

From Tamaris you can cross a little isthmus to the **Presqu'île de St-Mandrier** ❸, which has an attractive little fishing port with numerous restaurants, or continue around the Six Fours peninsula to the sandy beaches of **Les Sablettes**, **Mar Vivo** and **Fabregas**.

At Cap Sicié, the southern point of the peninsula, the **Chapelle de Notre-Dame-du-Mai** sits on a high clifftop that drops sharply towards the sea. The Fôret de Six-Fours is a protected natural habitat with a wide variety of pines, oaks, eucalyptus and aromatic plants. Its beauty is in sharp contrast to the downmarket hotels of sprawling Six-Fours-les-Plages down on the coast, whose beaches are popular with windsurfers.

Calm resorts

Continuing westwards along the coast, the pretty pink-and-white resort of **Sanary-sur-Mer** ❹ benefits from a sheltered position supplied by a rocky outcrop known as the Gros Cerveau (big brain). Family oriented and low key, with its pastel façades, palm trees along the promenade and a handful of wooden fishing boats in the harbour, Sanary has a sort of timeless charm lacking in more fashionable resorts.

Artists and writers began to flock to Sanary in the early 1930s, inspired by the presence of Aldous Huxley (1894–1963), who wrote *Brave New World* at his villa on Cap de la Gorguette in 1931. They were soon joined by a group of German intellectuals, headed by Nobel Prize-winning writer Thomas Mann (1875–1955) and his novelist brother Heinrich (1871–1950), who fled here after Hitler's rise to power in 1933.

TIP

A medieval watch-tower in Sanary-sur-Mer is home to the Musée Frédéric Dumas (open July–Aug daily 10am–12.30pm, 4–7.30pm, Sept–June Sat, Sun and school hols 10am–12.30pm, 3–6.30pm), a small museum devoted to underwater diving.

BELOW:
Sanary-sur-Mer.

Despite a battle-worn façade, the interior of the basilica in St-Maximin-la-Ste-Baume has a magnificent tall, vaulted nave, a Baroque altarpiece and ornately carved walnut choirstalls.

Screened from the ravages of the mistral by an arc of wooded hills, **Bandol**  has attracted numerous visitors to its sandy coves and pleasant promenades since the arrival of the railway at the beginning of the 20th century. Among its more famous visitors were the New Zealand author Katherine Mansfield (1888–1923), who wrote *Prelude* in the quayside Villa Pauline in 1916.

Most modern-day visitors come for the town's sandy beaches, lively harbour and sophisticated boutiques. Another plus is Bandol's vineyards, spread over 1,000 hectares (2,500 acres) between the Ste-Baume Massif and the coast, around pretty medieval villages such as **La Cadière d'Azur** and fortified **Le Castellet**, which produce wines (particularly reds) that are rated among the best in Provence.

About 2 km (1 mile) off the coast of Bandol lies the tiny island of **Bendor** ❻, which was enterprisingly transformed into a holiday village in the 1950s by the pastis magnate Paul Ricard. On the island is a hotel, a clutch of rather expensive cafés, and a re-creation of a Provençal fishing village. Though the island has an air of artificiality, its shady paths, lined with mimosa and eucalyptus, and tiny sandy beach are reason enough for a visit. Boats leave regularly from the *embarcadère* on Bandol harbour for the seven-minute crossing (information from Bandol tourist office, tel: 04 94 29 41 35).

St-Maximin

On the western edge of the Var lies **St-Maximin-la-Ste-Baume** ❼. Pilgrims have poured into this town since the 5th century to view one of the greatest Christian relics – the presumed bones of Mary Magdalene, which had been discovered here in an ancient crypt. After the Boat of Bethany *(see page 23)* landed at Stes-Maries-de-la-Mer in the Camargue, its saintly crew dispersed to preach the word of God throughout Provence. Mary Magdalene is said to have made her way to the Massif de la Ste-Baume, where she lived in a cave for more than 30 years. She died in St-Maximin, where her remains were jealously guarded by the Cassianites.

In 1295 work began on the **Eglise Ste-Marie-Madeleine** (Place des Prêcheurs; tel: 04 42 38 01 78), founded by Charles II, king of Sicily and count of Provence, as a suitably magnificent receptacle for the relics. The result is the finest Gothic church in Provence *(see opposite)*. The well-preserved abbey buildings adjoining the church have been converted into a charming hotel, with a restaurant in the chapter house and cloister.

The 19th-century writer Prosper Mérimée, in his role as inspector of monuments, dismissed St-Maximin as a dreary place, and, excluding the basilica, it's tempting to share his view. But the **Vieille Ville** (old town) does have some notable medieval arcades in rue Colbert.

The Ste-Baume Massif

To the south of St-Maximin, in the heavily forested limestone mountain range of Ste-Baume, is the evocative, dank cave where Mary Magdalene is said to have spent her last years. From the village of **Nans-le-Pins**, the GR9 long-distance footpath follows the chemin des Rois, the pilgrimage path taken by popes and sovereigns for centuries. Reaching the cave's entrance involves a strenuous climb through towering beach trees and lush undergrowth (around 40 minutes from the Hôtellerie de la Baume, above the village of **Le Plan d'Aups-Ste-Baume**). Some 150 stone steps lead up to the cliffside cave. Inside, the dark, dripping recess is filled with altars and saintly effigies. A final effort will bring you to **St-Pilon** ❽, which is almost the highest point of the massif. Mary Magdalene was said to have been lifted up to this peak by angels seven times a day during her years of cave-dwelling.

Inhabited for thousands of years, the massif was used for sheep rearing, as well as a number of small industries including charcoal, slake lime and ice production. The main centre of ice production was the village of **Mazaugues** ❾ on the eastern side of the massif, which for centuries produced ice for Marseille and Toulon through a complex system of underground freezing reservoirs and ice stores. There's a small museum (Hameau du Château; open June–Sept Tues–Sun 9am–noon, 2–6pm, Oct–May Sun 9am–noon, 2–5pm; admission charge; tel: 04 94 86 39 24; http://museedelaglace.free.fr), and you can visit the restored **Glacière de Pivaut**, an impressive 23-metre (75-ft) high stone cylinder, 7 km (4 miles) from Mazaugues towards Le Plan.

The old quarter of Barjols (see page 180).

Brignoles and La Provence Verte

Brignoles ❿, once a mining centre for bauxite, is the administrative centre for the Var region. The medieval quarter preserves bits of ramparts and the former residence of the counts of Provence, which now contains the small **Musée du**

BELOW: the Ste-Baume Massif.

Map on page 174

Held on the weekend nearest to 16 January, Barjols' Fête de St Marcel marks the town's victory over nearby Aups in securing the relics of St Marcel for its chapel. The day the relics arrived, in 1349, coincided with the pagan practice of sacrificing an ox for a village feast. Every four years (next in 2010) an ox, decorated with garlands, is roasted on the place de la Roquière to be shared out among the hungry revellers.

BELOW: one of Barjols' 28 fountains.

Pays Brignolais (open summer Wed–Sat 9am–noon, 2–6pm, Sun 9am–noon, 3–6pm; winter Wed–Sat 10am–noon, 2–5pm, Sun 10am–noon, 3–5pm; admission charge; tel: 04 94 69 45 18). This delightful museum is devoted to local history, with an eclectic collection of assorted paintings, fossils and an early Christian sarcophagus.

Brignoles sits at the heart of what is known as La Provence Verte (Green Provence), because of its verdant landscape watered by several rivers and underground springs. It is a popular area for walking, cycling and canoeing. But the green tag has taken on a double meaning because of the significant amount of organic produce now farmed in the area, notably at Correns.

Twenty km (12 miles) north of Brignoles along the D554 is **Barjols** ⓫, dubbed the "Tivoli of Provence" – a small industrious town filled with streams, fountains and masses of peeling plane trees. What is reputedly the largest plane tree in France, measuring an impressive 12 metres (40 ft) in circumference,

casts its shadow over the most celebrated of Barjols's 25 fountains, the vast moss-covered "Champignon" (mushroom) fountain, next to the Hôtel de Ville in the tiny place Capitaine Vincens.

Though the Tivoli tag attracts a good number of summer visitors, Barjols is in reality more of a workaday town than a successful tourist trap. Its prosperity was originally based on its tanneries, the last of which closed in 1986. Barjols is still, however, known for the manufacture of the traditional Provençal instruments, the *galoubet* (a three-holed flute) and *tambourin* (a narrow drum), which are played simultaneously by a single musician.

Barjols' old quarter, known as "**Réal**", is being extensively renovated. Ancient cobwebbed hovels alternate with low medieval archways in the dusty alleyways around the church of **Notre-Dame-de-l'Assomption**. An undistinguished square close to the church conceals one of Barjols's best treasures, the magnificent entrance to the Renaissance **Maison des Postevès**. ❑

RESTAURANTS AND BARS

Bandol

Le Clocher

1 rue de la Paroissel. Tel: 04 94 32 47 65. Open: L Thur–Sun, D daily. Closed: Wed in winter. €€
Revised Provençal specialities in an attractive setting on a pedestrianised street near the church.

Les Oliviers

Hôtel L'Ile Rousse, 25 boulevard Louis Lumièrel. Tel: 04 94 29 33 00. Open: L & D daily. €€€
www.ile-rousse.com
Elegant Mediterranean dining in a seaside hotel with two private beaches.

Brignoles

Hostellerie de l'Abbaye de la Celle

Place du Général de Gaulle. Tel: 04 98 05 14 14. Open: L & D daily (Thur–Mon in winter). €€€
www.abbaye-celle.com
Foodies head for Alain Ducasse's elegant country inn and restaurant, 4 km (2½ miles) southwest of Brignoles. The 18th-century *auberge* adjoining a medieval abbey has a sophisticated restaurant run in partnership with truffle king Bruno Clémént. Ducasse disciple Benoît Witz puts a refined spin on regional dishes, much of it using produce from the kitchen garden. Note that the Romanesque abbey church, which is currently being restored, is open for guided visits (daily; ring ahead for times on 04 94 59 19 05), along with the cloister and wine cellars.

La Cadière d'Azur

Hostellerie Bérard

Avenue Gabriel Pér. Tel: 04 94 90 11 43. Open: L & D daily. €€€€
www.hotel-berard.com
Chef René Bérard and his son Jean-François marry classic and contemporary touches in a stylish dining room looking out over the Bandol vineyards. The inn consists of a number of houses in a medieval hill village.

St-Maximin-la-Ste-Baume

Hôtellerie le Couvent Royal

Tel: 04 94 86 55 66. Open: L daily, D Mon–Sat. €€
www.hotelfp-saintmaximin.com
Attractively presented classic French cuisine and regional wines are served in the lovely Gothic chapter house or out under the arcades of the cloister of this beautiful royal abbey.

Sanary-sur-Mer

Hôtel-Restaurant de la Tour

Port de Sanary. Tel: 04 94 74 10 10. Open: L & D Thur–Mon. Closed: Dec. €€
www.sanary-hoteldelatour.com
Sanary's most pleasant hotel also has an excellent restaurant with a terrace overlooking the port. The speciality is in fresh fish and shellfish, perhaps baked in a salt crust or simmered in a bouillabaisse.

Toulon

Le Nautique

Carré du Port, Quai Constadt. Tel: 04 94 93 49 88. €
An inexpensive café-brasserie by the port where you can watch the boats go by over a beer, a salad or a *plat du jour*.

Au Sourd

10 rue Molière. Tel: 04 94 92 28 52. Open: L & D Tues–Sat. €€
Toulon's oldest restaurant was opened in a 1862 by a soldier who had returned deaf *(sourd)* from the Crimean war. Today it serves high-quality fish straight from the local catch.

PRICE CATEGORIES

Prices for a three-course meal without wine. Note that many restaurants have a less expensive lunch menu.
€ = under €25
€€ = €25–€40
€€€ = €40–€60
€€€€ = more than €60

RIGHT: mussels are a menu staple in this coastal region.

INLAND VAR HILL VILLAGES

North of the coast-hugging Maures and Estérel Massifs,
the interior of the Var is made up of densely forested
hills, vine-covered valleys and restored villages
built into the soft tufa rock. This is good
walking and wine-tasting country

orth of the A8 *autoroute*, the
landscape of the inland Var
progresses upwards in a series
of tiers. The vineyards on the plain
and lower valleys (this is one of the
main areas for Côtes de Provence
wines) rise to olive groves. These
give way to densely forested hills –
prowled by game-hunters, truffle-
seekers and walkers – which open
onto the sparse expanses of the
Grand Plan de Canjuers, a high
mountain plateau, most of which
belongs to the French army.
Although some restored hill villages, such as Fox-Amphoux and
Tourtour, have taken on a gentrified
sheen, authentic Var villages and
wilderness can still be found.

The central Var

Le Luc ❶ is a small market town
which lies at the intersection of the
A8 and N7 motorways, in the heart
of the central Var region. Like many
of its neighbours, it suffers from the
sheer volume of through traffic
which it was not designed to cope
with. Its centrepiece is a 27-metre
(90-foot) high hexagonal tower, built
in the 16th century. Le Luc's rich history as a Roman spa town and
Protestant refuge can be traced in the
local museum, the **Musée His-
torique du Centre Var** (open 15
June–15 Oct Mon–Sat 3–6pm, rest of

year by appointment; tel: 04 94 60 70
20; admission charge), housed in the
17th-century Chapelle de Ste-Anne.

Squeezed between the *autoroute*
and the Maures, just north of Le Luc,
the wine-producing commune of **Le
Cannet-des-Maures** has two distinct halves. Clustered around an
11th-century church, **Le Vieux Cannet ❷** – old Cannet – is one of the
region's prettiest hill villages. Down
on the plain the modern town developed with the arrival of the railway in the 1860s. Remnants of the

Map
on page
184

LEFT: the waterfall,
Sillans-la-Cascade.
BELOW: vineyard
near Draguignan.

Two summer music festivals are held in the lovely setting of the Abbaye du Thoronet. The first, in late July, focuses on medieval music. The Musique et Esprit festival in mid-August features classical and choral music. Information from the Office de Tourisme, tel: 04 94 60 10 94.

Roman settlement of Forum Voconi, a halt on the Via Aurelian, have recently been excavated here.

North of Le Cannet, in the thick of the Darboussière forest, stands one of the most imposing sights in Provence: the 12th-century **Abbaye du Thoronet** ❸ (open Apr–Sept Mon–Sat 10am–6.30pm, Sun 10am–noon, 2–6.30pm, Oct–Mar Mon–Sat 10am–1pm, 2–5pm, Sun 10am–noon, 2–5pm; admission charge; tel: 04 94 60 43 90; www.monum.fr). Thoronet is the finest of the Provençal trio of "Cistercian sisters", which includes the abbeys of Sénanque *(see page 92)* and Silvacane *(see page 86)*. All were built during the 12th century to the ascetic precepts of the Cistercian Order. Only the play of light and shadow decorates the finely proportioned, simply designed chapel, cloisters and chapter house.

Les-Arcs-sur-Argens ❹ is at the heart of the Var's wine industry, and

its **Maison des Vins** (tel: 04 94 99 50 20; www.caveaucp.fr) is a useful place to embark on a wine trail. Its cellars contain around 500 Côtes de Provence wines and they provide information on touring the vineyards. The town has an attractive old quarter, known as Le Parage, and the remains of a feudal castle destroyed after the Revolution. The 19th-century St-Jean-Batiste church contains an early 16th-century polyptych.

Just east of Les Arcs, the **Château Ste-Roseline** (open daily; tel: 04 94 99 50 30; www.sainte-roseline.com), a former Carthusian nunnery, is now one of Provence's best-known vineyards. You can visit the **Chapelle Ste-Roseline** (open Tues–Sun 2.30–6pm), a Romanesque chapel with an extravagant gilded Baroque retable. An ornate reliquary contains the "living" eyes of local saint, Roseline. More recent artworks include a celebrated mosaic by Chagall and church furnishings by Giacometti.

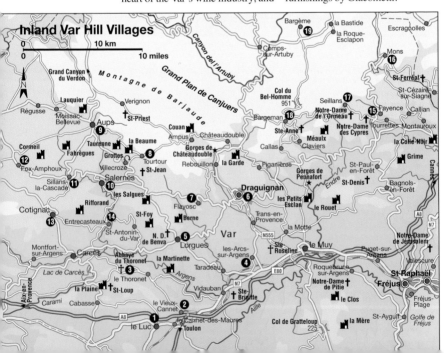

Northwest of here, **Lorgues ❺**, a busy town with some grand 18th-century buildings and tiny medieval alleyways, draws foodies to the restaurant of truffle king Bruno Clément *(see page 189).*

Draguignan and the Upper Var

Draguignan ❻, the main town in inland Var and home to a large garrison, is not a major tourist attraction, but its very ordinariness has a certain appeal for those after a taste of everyday French provincial life. Within a grid of 19th-century boulevards, there is a compact but appealing old town. A superb market sets up on place du Marché every Wednesday and Saturday morning.

Housed in an old monastery, the **Musée des Arts et Traditions Populaires** (15 rue Joseph Roumanille; open Tues–Sat 9am–noon, 2–6pm, Sun 2–6pm; admission charge) is worth seeing. The social and cultural history of the community is relayed through a series of reconstructed scenes, using costumes, tools, furniture and household items.

At the top of the hill stand the recently restored 12th-century Chapelle St-Sauveur and the Tour de l'Horloge, an impressive fortified clock tower built in 1663 topped by a wrought-iron campanile. There's a good view from the top. Near by, on rue de la Juiverie stand the remains of a synagogue façade, a relic of the sizeable Jewish community that thrived here in the Middle Ages.

On the eastern edge of town is an American military cemetery, the legacy of a bloody battle fought here in August 1944, while just northwest on the D955 is the mysterious dolmen known as the Pierre de la Fée ("fairy stone"), a vast slab of Neolithic rock on three mighty stone legs, dating from 2500 to 2000 BC.

Five km (3 miles) west of Draguignan, the pretty village of **Flayosc ❼** huddles around an 11th-century church. It is known for its excellent olive oil, and just north of here, in the hamlet of Flayosquet, there's an old working olive oil mill (Moulin du Flayosquet; tel: 04 94 70 41 45).

A little further on you'll come to the **Gorges de Châteaudouble**. Cut

Map on page 184

The town of Draguignan is named after a dragon which was said to have terrorised the town in the 5th century, until vanquished by Hermentaire, bishop of Antibes. This mythical creature can be seen in stone crests on many of the old town's medieval gateways and houses.

BELOW: Draguignan's market square.

TIP

The Route des Ambassadeurs des Crus Classés takes in 13 Côtes de Provence wine chateaux with the prestigious *cru classé* status; most are located along the Var coast or around Les Arcs in the central Var. www.cruclasse provence.com

BELOW: Aups.

through by the River Nartuby, the ravine was the habitat of the Draguignan dragon *(see page 185)*. Perched on a rocky spur is the village of **Châteaudouble** and, upstream, **Ampus** is another picturesque village which has been restored.

More commercial, but more spectacular, is gentrified **Tourtour** ❽, "the village in the sky", where medieval vaulted passageways open onto breathtaking views. People congregate on the café terraces of place des Ormeaux, the main square. Sadly, the *ormeaux* – two elms planted to commemorate the birth of Louis XIV – fell prey to disease and were replaced by olive trees.

Mullioned Renaissance windows peer out of the red cliff face at neighbouring **Villecroze** from troglodyte dwellings carved into the soft tufa rock. Below, the unusual Jardin de la Cascade was laid out in the 19th century, with pools and basins fed by water that cascades down the cliff.

High up on the plateau, **Aups** ❾ is an access point for the Grand Canyon du Verdon *(see page 155)* and a busy market town, particularly famed for its truffle market on Thursday mornings in winter. The town is crowned by a fine 16th-century clocktower adorned with a sundial. Aups, and the northern part of the Var in general, has a strong tradition of republican resistance, and it was the scene of many popular uprisings during the mid-19th century. The portal of the town's Eglise de St-Pancrace bears the republican inscription: *Liberté, Egalité, Fraternité.*

Housed in an old Ursuline chapel, the **Musée Municipal Simon Segal** (open 15 June–15 Sept daily 10am–noon, 4–7pm; admission charge; tel: 04 94 70 01 95) has a collection of works by the Russian-born painter and other artists associated with the Ecole de Paris in the 1920s, as well as works by Provençal artists.

Outside town, the **Musée de Faykod** (open July–Aug Wed–Mon 10am–noon, 3–7pm, Sept–June Wed–Mon 2–6pm, closed Nov; admission charge; tel: 04 94 70 03 94; www.musee-de-faykod.com) is a sculpture garden of romantic white Carrara marble sculptures by Maria de Faykod, a Hungarian-born sculp-

tor who carried out commissions for several public sculptures and religious works in France.

Salernes ⑩ – the tile-making capital of Provence – is larger and more sprawling than Aups. It has one of the best markets in the area, held on Wednesday and Sunday mornings on the big central square.

A few kilometres west of Salernes, **Sillans-la-Cascade** ⑪ still has several remnants of its fortified town wall. Below the village a footpath leads to an impressive waterfall which tumbles 42 metres (140 ft) down a cliff into a deep pool. Minuscule **Fox-Amphoux** ⑫ crouches on a hill to the west, its pretty streets clustered round a Romanesque church.

The animated village of **Cotignac** ⑬ is set against the dramatic backdrop of a tall red cliff crowned with the remains of two fortified towers. It is popular with tourists, as the antique and gift shops testify, but it retains a workaday charm. Stately plane trees line the central cours Gambetta, providing dappled shade for the cafés and restaurants.

The D50 snakes east to **Entre-casteaux** ⑭, a delightful village overlooking the River Bresque, dominated by an elegant classical **chateau** (guided visit usually Sun–Fri 4pm, ring for extra times in summer; tel: 04 94 04 43 95; admission charge), dating from the 16th to 18th centuries. In 1974, the chateau was bought by painter, soldier and adventurer Ian McGarvie-Munn, a larger-than-life Scotsman who set about the castle's restoration, despite considerable local hostility. Although very long, most of it is only one room wide. The formal gardens (open daily) were designed by André Le Nôtre, the landscape gardener of Louis XIV's gardens at Versailles.

The eastern Var

Fayence ⑮, the largest town in the eastern Var and a big hang-gliding centre, has little overt charm, but its satellite villages are among the prettiest in Provence. On the edge of town towards Seillans the **Ecomusée de Fayence** (open Tues–Sun 2–6pm; admission charge; tel: 04 94 84 77 60) displays vine- and olive-growing

Map on page 184

TIP

Lac de St-Cassien, a large man-made lake surrounded by wooded hills south of Montauroux, is a popular spot for picnicking, swimming, birdwatching, fishing and watersports.

BELOW: Draguignan's belltower.

Campaniles

Originally the bell that served as a warning in times of danger, either on the town hall or the church tower, campaniles soon became far more than mere functional structures. With their fancy curlicues and finials, the elaborate wrought-ironwork became a way of proclaiming the village's identity and showing off the craftsman's skill, especially in the 18th century, when they were often added to much earlier structures. Countless campaniles can be found throughout Provence, but there are some particularly fine examples in the hill villages of the Var, including the clock tower gateway at Aups, the village churches at Flayosc and le Vieux Cannet and the town belfry at Lorgues.

Map on page 184

The ruins of a medieval fortress in the village of Bargème.

BELOW: Seillans.

equipment, wine presses and other traditional agriculture implements.

To the east of Fayence is **Mont-auroux**, a scenic village with a medieval church and 18th-century houses, where Christian Dior bought an extravagant villa, the Château de la Colle Noir, at the end of the 1950s.

North of Fayence, at an altitude of 814 metres (2,670 ft), **Mons** ⓰ has all the ingredients of a perfect Provençal village: steep cobbled stairways, a fine 13th-century church (visits daily 2.30pm, 4pm) and superb views from the café-filled place St-Sébastien.

The Surrealist painter Max Ernst (1891–1976) spent the last 11 years of his life in **Seillans** ⓱, an atmospheric pink and ochre village which spills down a steep hillside. A bronze cast of his *Génie de la République* stands on place de la République, and more of his work can be seen at the Office de Tourisme (place du Valat; open Tues–Sat 2.30–5.30pm; admission charge; tel: 04 94 76 85 91). Seillans' boundaries are marked by the chateau at the top of the hill and the place du Thouron at the bottom.

The **Chapelle Notre-Dame-de-l'Ormeau** (open Thur 11am–12.30pm), just down the road, has a stunning colourful altarpiece, carved from wood by an unknown 16th-century Italian artist. The countryside around Seillans is also known for its *bories (see page 92)*, low igloo-shaped drystone structures.

The Var was a major battlefield during the liberation of Provence in August 1944. The **Musée du Souvenir** (route de Draguignan, Broves-en-Seillans; open Feb–Sept daily 2–6pm; admission charge; tel: 04 94 84 77 93) commemorates its key role in a private collection of American military vehicles, ambulances and other memorabilia.

Bargemon ⓲, west of Seillans, with ramparts dating back to the 11th century, has medieval streets to wander and a good Thursday market. From here you can head south to **Callas** and the stunning landscapes of the **Gorges de Pennafort** or head 17 km (10 miles) north, climbing in steep hairpin bends over the Col du Bel Homme pass, to **Bargème** ⓳, the highest village in the Var. ❑

RESTAURANTS AND BARS

Ampus

La Fontaine d'Ampus
Place de la Mairie. Tel: 04 94 70 98 08. Open: L & D Thur–Sun (July–Aug L daily, D Mon–Sat). €€€
A well-respected place in the centre of the village, with a menu featuring local figs, ceps and truffles when available.

Les Arcs-sur-Argens

Le Relais des Moines
Route Ste-Roseline. Tel: 04 94 47 40 93. Open: L Tues–Sun, D Tues–Sat (and Sun July–Aug). €€€
www.lerelaisdesmoines.com
In a historic stone farmhouse, *cuisine de terroir* is revisited with finesse by a young chef. There's an excellent wine list, too.

Cotignac

La Table de la Fontaine
27 cours Gambetta. Tel: 04 94 04 79 13. Open: L & D Tues–Sun. Closed: Dec–Feb. €
This good-value little bistro with a terrace on Cotignac's main street is a popular place for lunch after the Tuesday market or dinner in summer.

Le Clos des Vignes
Route de Montfort. Tel: 04 94 04 72 19. Open: L & D Wed–Sun. €€
Outside town with a view over vineyards. Classic French cuisine (foie gras, game) with some specialities from the chef's native Alsace.

Flayosc

L'Oustaou
5 place Brémond. Tel: 04 94 70 42 69. Open: summer L Thur, Sat, Sun, D Tues–Sun, winter L Thur–Sat, D Tues, Thur–Sat. €€
A well-regarded restaurant. Watch the world go by from the terrace.

Lorgues

Chez Bruno
Route de Vidauban. Tel: 04 94 85 93 93. Open: L & D daily (winter closed Sun D & Mon). €€€€
www.restaurantbruno.com
Expect extremely rich menus based around truffles and foie gras at this beautifully situated country *mas*, where larger-than-life character Bruno Clément, the truffle king, draws the sort of clientele who helicopter in for dinner.

Montauroux

Les Fontaines d'Aragon
Quartier Narbonne. Tel: 04 94 47 71 65. Open: L & D Wed–Sun. €€€€
www.fontaines-daragon.com
A rising name on the French culinary scene, owner-chef Eric Maio is another fan of the truffle, which even appears in the ice cream.

Salernes

Tout en Passant
Chez Gilles
20 avenue Victor Hugo.

Tel: 04 94 70 72 80. Open: L Fri–Sun, D Tues–Sun. €
A tiny, animated bistro, where friendly chef Gilles makes the most of the Var's organic produce.

Tourtour

La Bastide de Tourtour
Montée St-Denis. Tel: 04 98 10 54 20. Open: L Sat–Sun, D daily; July–Aug L & D daily. €€€
www.verdon.net/tourtour
Modern classical French cuisine served in the elegant dining room of this tufa-stone hotel. Stunning views of the Haut Var.

Les Chênes Verts
Route de Villecroze. Tel: 04 94 70 55 06. Open: L Wed–Mon, D Mon, Wed–Sat. Closed: June. €€€€
Reservations are essential at this highly rated country restaurant where chef Paul Balade presents the best of seasonal Provençal dishes.

La Farigoulette
Place des Ormeaux. Tel: 04 94 70 57 37. Open: L & D daily. €
This is a local favourite with a terrace on the main square. The traditional menu includes a delicious *daube de boeuf*.

PRICE CATEGORIES

Prices for a three-course meal without wine. Note that many restaurants have a less expensive lunch menu.
€ = under €25
€€ = €25–€40
€€€ = €40–€60
€€€€ = more than €60

RIGHT: La Bastide de Tourtour.

ST-TROPEZ, THE MAURES AND THE ESTÉREL

Glitzy St-Tropez, the star of the Var coast, is as fashionable as ever, but just beyond its boundaries is the surprisingly wild hinterland of the Massif des Maures and the Massif de l'Estérel. Sun-worshippers and nature-lovers are both well catered for here

Nice
Marseille

Between Hyères and la Napoule, the Var has one of the most spectacular and best-preserved coastlines in the south, with glorious sandy beaches set against fine mountain backdrops. The glamour of St-Tropez and busy resorts like Fréjus and St-Raphaël contrast starkly with the rugged, forested expanses of the Massif des Maures and the Estérel. Vineyards, fruit production and the steep terrain means that this area has been spared the worst of the concrete developments of the Alpes-Maritimes further east.

relegated Hyères, sitting above the coast rather than down by the shore, to a distinctly unfashionable position.

In many ways, the town's lack of chic and air of faded gentility is now one of its most attractive qualities. Hyères plays host to several sporting and cultural events, including heats of the world windsurfing championships, a fashion photography festival and summer jazz festival, and has a thriving agricultural economy, mainly cultivating peaches, strawberries, cut flowers and palm trees.

Map on page 192

LEFT: view across the rooftops of the Vieux-Port of St-Tropez.
BELOW: traditional fishing boat.

Hyères-les-Palmiers

Grandmother of the Riviera towns, **Hyères ❶** was the first resort to be established on the Côte d'Azur, setting a trend that spread rapidly east from the late 18th century onwards. The list of famous consumptives and pleasure-seekers drawn to its balmy winter climate reads like an international *Who's Who*: Queen Victoria, Tolstoy, Pauline Bonaparte, Aubrey Beardsley, Edith Wharton. Robert Louis Stevenson, though very ill during his stay, wrote: "I was only happy once – that was at Hyères."

By the 1920s, however, medical opinion had switched its allegiance to the curative properties of mountain – rather than sea – air. This and the arrival of the summer season soon

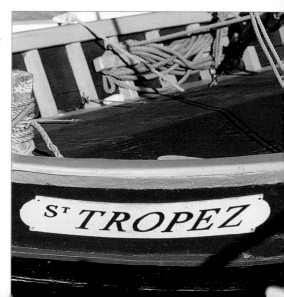

ST TROPEZ

Villa Noailles, a 1920s Cubist house visited regularly by members of the Dada and Surrealist movements.

Amid all the modern sprawl and a complicated one-way system lies the compact medieval **Vieille Ville** (old town), with ancient houses and steep, narrow streets. It is best entered through the **Porte Mabillon**, a fragment of the old city fortifications. From here rue Mabillon, busy with food shops, leads to the lively, café-filled place Mabillon where the square **Tour des Templiers** (open Wed–Sun 10am–noon, 2–5.30pm, July and Aug 10am–12.30pm, 3–7pm; tel: 04 94 35 22 36), the remains of a Templar *commanderie*, is now used for temporary

exhibitions. Steep steps next to the tower lead up to the **Collégiale St-Paul**, a large, mainly Gothic church most notable for the array of naive ex-voto paintings on the walls.

Hyères' chief tourist attraction is the **Villa Noailles** (open during exhibitions, winter Wed–Sun, summer Wed–Mon, hours vary; tel: 04 98 08 01 98; www.villanoailles-hyeres.com), further up the hill below the castle ruins. This masterpiece of early Modernist Cubist architecture, built in the 1920s by Robert Mallet-Stevens, was in its heyday the ultimate expression of modern living

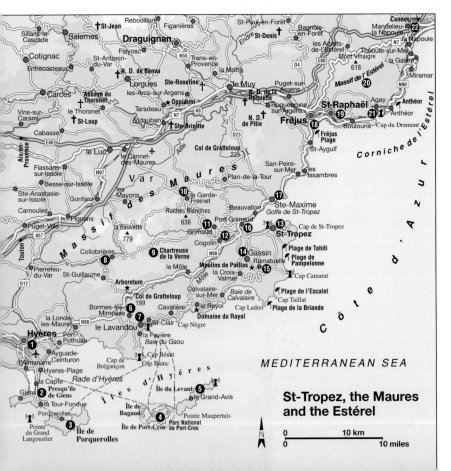

St-Tropez, the Maures and the Estérel

MEDITERRANEAN SEA

0   10 km
0   10 miles

and aesthetics. Buñuel, Giacometti, Stravinsky, Man Ray and other arty guests lounged on its sun terraces. Restored in the 1990s, the villa is now used for exhibitions.

Above the villa, the road continues to the ruins of a 14th-century castle and the 19th-century Castel Ste-Claire, home from 1927 to 1937 of American novelist Edith Wharton, who planted the surrounding **Parc Ste-Claire** with numerous species from South America and Australia.

The modern town retains some of its 19th-century elegance in the white stucco villas of avenue Joseph Clotis and the renovated **Casino des Palmiers**. Around the exotic **Jardins Olbius Riquier** on avenue Amboise Thomas are some notable examples of neo-Moorish architecture, dating from the 1870s.

Lower down, towards Le Capte, lies the **Site Archéologique d'Olbia** (open Apr–Sept 9.30am–12.30pm, 3–7pm; admission charge; tel: 04 94 57 98 28; www.monum.fr), the remains of the maritime trading post of Olbia founded by the Greeks in the 4th century BC.

Jutting out into the sea, south of Hyères-Plage is the **Presqu'île de Giens ❷**; on the sheltered eastern side of the peninsula, the beach road of La Capte is lined with cheap hotels and campsites, while the road along the western side runs between the abandoned salt marshes of Les Pesquiers, now a nature reserve, and the long windy Plage de l'Almanarre, a favourite with windsurfers.

The Iles d'Hyères

The main reason for taking this uninspiring route is to catch a boat from la Tour-Fondue – the remains of a fortress built by Richelieu at the tip of the isthmus – to the beautiful and densely vegetated Iles d'Hyères, also known as the Iles d'Or, because of the mica or "fool's gold" which sparkles in the sand and rocks of the islands. (Boats also sail from Hyères, Le Lavandou and Cavalaire.)

Unless you're a naturist or a botanist, **Porquerolles ❸**, the largest island and said to be the inspiration for Robert Louis Stevenson's *Treasure Island*, is probably the best choice for a visit. Its village, estab-

Ile de Porquerolles, one of the unspoilt Iles d'Hyères off the Var coast. Boats to the islands are frequent in July and August, but limited the rest of the year (see tip, page 194).

BELOW: sunset over Porquerolles island.

TIP

TLV (tel: 04 94 58 21
81; www.tlv-tvm)
operates ferries from
Hyères to Port-Cros (1
hour) and Ile de Levant
(1½ hours), and from
La Tour-Fondue on the
Presqu'île de Giens to
Porquerolles (30 mins).
Vedettes Iles d'Or
(tel: 04 94 71 01 02;
www.vedettesilesdor.fr)
runs ferries from Le
Lavandou to the Ile de
Levant (35 mins; 1
hour via Port-Cros),
and to Porquerolles in
summber, as well as
boats from La Croix-
Valmer and Cavalaire.

BELOW: beach volley-
ball, Le Lavandou.

lished as a small military base in the
19th century, is more colonial than
Provençal in character, with a large
parade ground-like square surrounded by eucalyptus trees and several cafés. From here, you can hire
bicycles to tour the island – note that
cars are not allowed and that some
parts of the island may be out of
bounds due to fire risk in summer.
Major beauty spots include the lighthouse at the Cap d'Arme and the
Plage d'Argent and Plage de la Cour-
tade on either side of the village.

Rugged, mountainous **Port-Cros**
❹ (www.portcrosparcnational.fr) is
a national park, and strict rules
against smoking and fires must be
observed. A small tourist centre, open
in summer, provides maps and
advice. Perhaps the most rewarding
walk (around two hours for the round
trip) takes you along the Vallon de la
Solitude, which cuts across the
southern end of the island. Divers can
follow an underwater "path" to see
the marine flora and fauna.

The third island, **Levant** ❺, is
inhabited by the French military and
mostly out of bounds, except for the

dramatic western tip which is occupied by Héliopolis, a nudist colony
founded in the 1930s.

Bormes-les-Mimosas and the corniche des Maures

West of Hyères a number of towns
line the coast road that leads to St-
Tropez. The first of these is **Bormes-
les-Mimosas** ❻, a chocolate-box
pretty hill village with coral-coloured
houses and steeply sloping streets
overflowing with bougainvillea,
mimosa and other exotic plants, and
lovely views of the Iles d'Hyères.
Place Gambetta is the hub of Bormes
life; from here rue Carnot winds
through the old village with stepped
streets and covered alleyways leading off to either side. Look out for the
painted sundial on the Eglise St-
Trophime and the small **Musée
d'Art et d'Histoire de Bormes** (103
rue Carnot; open summer Tues–Sun
10am–noon, 3.30–6.30pm, winter
Tues–Sat 10am–noon, 2.30–5pm,
Sun 10am–noon; tel: 04 94 71 56
60), in a fine 17th-century house, that
contains some terracottas by Rodin
and neo-Impressionist paintings.

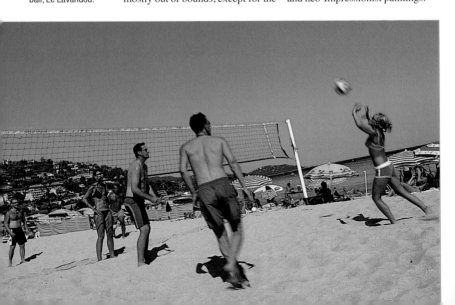

On the edge of the old village is the 16th-century **Chapelle St-Vincent de Paule**. Above the town, a road leads up to the remains of the Château des Seigneurs de Fos (private), offering magnficent views.

South of Bormes, linked to the exclusive promontory of Cap Bénat by a dyke, the Fort de Brégançon, summer residence of the French president, sits proudly on its own peninsula. The fort cannot be visited, but the Cap itself, planted with vineyards and pine woods, has some lovely unspoilt beaches, such as the Plage de Cabasson (parking fee), the beautiful Plage de l'Estagnol (open Easter–Oct; parking fee) and the long Plage de Pellégrin (open Easter–Oct; parking fee), with its pines and sand dunes.

Bormes' own modern beach suburb of La Favière, to the north of Cap Bénat, has a sandy beach, a marina, watersports facilities and numerous restaurants. Almost adjoining it is the popular resort of **Le Lavandou** ❼. Glitzy bars and discos make this a lively place by night, although there are also a few relics of the old fishing town behind the port, and a huge general market behind the promenade on Thursday morning. (This is also the best place for boats to Port-Cros and the Ile de Levant.)

A worthwhile detour east on the D559 coast road is a visit to the wonderful gardens of the **Domaine du Rayol** (open daily 9.30am–5.30pm, until 7.30pm in summer; admission charge; tel: 04 98 04 44 00; www. domainedurayol. org; *see page 204*).

The Massif des Maures

One of the most surprising aspects of the Var coast is that only a couple of miles from the jet-set beaches of St-Tropez, you find yourself in the steep, densely forested mountains of the Maures – the name comes from old Provençal *mauro*, meaning dark – an ancient massif made up of deep grey schist shot through with glittering mica and serpentine. Sadly, the area has often been ravaged by forest fires, sparked either by human carelessness or by arsonists. Many of the footpaths may be closed off in high summer, especially on windy days.

Few roads cross the mountains, and those that do are mostly narrow and extremely twisty. Far better to take one of the long-distance footpaths, such as the GR51, GR9 and GR90, indicated by red-and-white striped markings. To access the area take the D41 from Bormes-les-Mimosas over the Col de Gratteloup and Col de Babaou passes, offering sea views in one direction and dense wooded mountain the other, descending through magnificent chestnut trees towards Collobrières.

The Office National de Forêts (ONF) organises a variety of guided walks in the Maures to discover flora and fauna, prehistoric remains or hidden chapels (Bormes-les-Mimosas tourist office; tel: 04 94 01 38 38; www.bormeslesmimosas. com).

Collobrières ❽ is a refreshingly workaday place, dedicated to the

Map on page 192

TIP

Rather than the long and crowded main beach of Le Lavandou, take the corniche des Maures (D559) road which winds round the coast to one of the satellite villages, such as St-Clair, framed by a bowl of mountains, or Cavalière, with a fine beach amid pine trees and views of the Iles de Hyères, or secluded Cap Nègre.

BELOW: Grimaud.

TIP

A small museum at Confiserie Azuréenne, Collobrières, explains the process of making marrons glacés; chestnuts are harvested in October and November, peeled and cooked before being soaked in syrup for seven days, then given a coat of icing sugar, dried in the oven and individually wrapped. There's a shop and a café, in summer, serving delicious chestnut-based ice cream sundaes. Confiserie Azuréenne, tel: 04 94 48 07 20.

BELOW: red rooftops of La Garde-Freinet.

timber trade and the cultivation and transformation of chestnuts – marrons glacés and crème de marrons are local specialities (see left) – with a pleasant low-key old town. The chestnut harvest is celebrated with the Fête de la Chataigne on the last three Sundays in October.

Further east along the D14 towards Grimaud, turn off along the D214 to the **Chartreuse de la Verne** ❾ (open Wed–Mon summer 11am–6pm, winter 11am–5pm, closed Jan; admission charge; tel: 04 94 43 45 41; http://la.verne.free.fr), an atmospheric monastery hidden on the hillside at the end of a remote valley. Built out of local schist edged with green serpentine, the Carthusian monastery was founded in 1170.

Amid cork oaks, chestnut trees, pines and occasional olive groves is **La Garde-Freinet** ❿, an ancient Arab stronghold, and much later a centre of cork production. By 1846, the town produced more than 75 percent of France's bottle corks but, like many of the traditional industries, decline set in after the 1950s. Since the early 1980s, however, the industry has diversified into other uses of cork, and neatly stripped trunks of cork oaks line the massif's winding roads and tracks. In the town, the only obvious evidence of cork production are the cork bowls and ornaments on sale to tourists in the pricey boutiques of the rue St-Jacques. The village still has some down-to-earth local cafés and stores among more fashionable restaurants and gift shops. North of the village, a walk to the ruins of the Arab fortress is rewarded with great views of the massif and the sea.

The roller-coaster road heading south from La Garde-Freinet cuts through the centre of the Maures to the St-Tropez peninsula. En route is the picturesque hilltop village of **Grimaud** ⓫, a maze of pretty streets draped here and there in bougainvillea and oleander. Wander along the rue des Templiers for its medieval arcades, then head up to the ruined castle.

Cogolin ⓬, 3 km (1½ miles) to the south, is a small but lively town known for the manufacture of briar pipes and carpets. It is also an important producer of good-quality wines. Visits can be made to the pipe and carpet factories.

St-Tropez

Once on the peninsula, you won't be able to resist the pull of **St-Tropez** ⓭, enduringly connected with the French sex symbol Brigitte Bardot and the bikini. What had been a simple fishing village "discovered" by Guy de Maupassant, Paul Signac and the neo-Impressionists in the 19th century and by the writer Colette in the early 20th century was confirmed as the playground of the rich and famous. Although it's lost its exclusivity, "St-Trop" still features the most celebrities per capita of any spot on the Riviera.

First port of call is inevitably the **Vieux-Port**, lined with tall houses and cafés from which to ogle the

swanky yachts lined up along the quay. On the west side the **Musée de l'Annonciade** (place Gramont; open Sept–June Wed–Mon 10am–noon, 2–6pm, July–Aug daily 10am–1pm, 3–7pm; admission charge; tel: 04 94 17 84 10) is a superb collection of modern art displayed in a deconsecrated chapel, featuring the work of many of the artists who visited St-Tropez at the beginning of the 20th century, including Signac, Bonnard, Marquet, Maillol and Dufy.

One of the best places to see the real St-Tropez is on the **place des Lices**, where there is a colourful market on Tuesday and Saturday mornings, offering all the best produce of Provence. At other times, the shaded square serves as a terrain for boules (*pétanque*); you can even hire a set of boules from the famous Le Café. On one of the streets, a small village house contains the **Maison des Papillons** (9 rue Etienne Berny; open Apr–Oct and Christmas hols Mon–Sat 2.30–6pm; admission charge; tel: 04 94 97 63 45), a display of over 4,500 colourful butterflies from around the world collected by painter Dany Lartigue, son of the famous 1920s society photographer.

Just off the port beyond Café Sennequier, the **Château Suffren** is a relic of the old castle; from here rue Portlet leads to another remnant of fortifications and the little cove of the Glaye, starting point of a coast path that winds its way round the waterside houses and tiny coves and the old Port des Pêcheurs. Up above the old town the 16th-century **Citadelle** (Montée de la Citadelle; open daily summer 10am–6pm, winter 10am–noon, 2–6pm; tel: 04 94 97 59 43) boasts an impressive set of ramparts and bastions. The hexagonal keep houses the **Musée Naval de la Citadelle** (due to reopen after renovation in summer 2007), containing souvenirs of local hero Admiral de Suffren (who took his fleet on an odyssey around the Cape of Good Hope in 1781), model ships and diving equipment.

The main attraction of St-Tropez, however, is its glorious beaches, fringed with restaurants, and packed with sun-bronzed bodies all summer long. Those nearest to town are the

It was the film And God Created Woman, made in 1956 by Brigitte Bardot's then husband, Roger Vadim, that rocketed the overtly sexy actress to stardom and put St-Tropez, where it was filmed, on the tourist map.

BELOW: the Vieux-Port, St-Tropez.

BELOW:
Pampelonne bay.

Plage de la Bouillabaisse on the road in from Ste-Maxime and the Plage des Graniers and Plage des Salins to the east of town, but it is the fashionable **Plage de Pampelonne** that is the main upholder of Saint-Tropez's sun, sea and sex image *(see below)*.

Many of St-Tropez's more glamorous residents actually hide out in discreet villas hidden among the vineyards of the St-Tropez peninsula. Perched up above are two gorgeous hill villages, **Gassin** ⓮ and **Ramatuelle** ⓯. Both have stunning views over the Golfe de St-Tropez and numerous tiny streets, some no more than an arm's length across. Ramatuelle is well known for its summer jazz and theatre festivals. Between the two villages, on the highest point of the peninsula, are a group of ancient windmills, the Moulins de Paillas, and a superb panorama.

Port Grimaud and Ste-Maxime

Heading west along the Golfe de St-Tropez, Another chic getaway is **Port Grimaud** ⓰, a modern resort designed in the 1960s by the architect François Spoerry around a network of canals to resemble a contemporary Venice, with plenty of space for boats to tie up right outside the houses.

Ste-Maxime ⓱ is a low-key resort, offering an old-fashioned taste of the Côte with its palm trees, restaurant-lined promenade and golden beaches. The stone **Tour Carrée** (place de l'Eglise; open Wed–Sun 10am–noon, 3–6pm; admission charge; tel: 04 94 96 70 30) built in 1520 as a refuge against pirates, is now a small folk museum, after having served variously as barn, town hall and prison. A covered market is held here every morning (except Monday in winter).

When quayside strutting and café lounging loses its appeal, seek out the **Musée du Phonographe et de la Musique Mécanique** (Museum of Sound and Mechanical Instruments; open Easter–Sept Wed–Sun 10am–noon, 3–6pm; admission charge; tel: 04 94 96 50 52), in the Parc de St-Donat to the north of the town. It houses a wonderful collection of old phonographs and bizarre music boxes.

Plage de Pampelonne

The Plage de Pampelonne is a 5-km (3-mile) stretch of sand between Cap Pinet and Cap Camaret, bordered by bamboos, pines and vineyards. Much of the bay is taken up by "private" beach clubs, ranging from the boho bamboo shack with its beach restaurant and sun loungers to designer haunts offering cosmopolitan menus, cocktail bars, DJs and spas. Trendy spots include the veteran showbiz haunt Tahiti, the Millesim, venerable Club 55, Kon Tiki, the Nikki Beach, Voile Rouge, Nioulargo, Key West, the simpler Tropicana and fish restaurant Chez Camille. But there are also free public stretches where you can park your parasol – and the shorefront is accessible to anyone.

Fréjus and St-Raphaël

Squeezed between the massifs of the Maures and Estérel, the next main resort heading east is **Fréjus ⑱**, which is scattered with Roman remains. Located on the Via Aurelia, it was founded as a port in 49 BC by Julius Caesar. It was developed into a naval base by Emperor Augustus – an alternative to unruly Marseille. The **Lanterne d'Auguste**, one of two towers that originally guarded the harbour, still survives. The Roman harbour has long since silted up. In its place there's a modern marina and apartment complex known as **Port-Fréjus**.

Fréjus' most impressive Roman remains are the 2nd-century **Arènes** (rue Henri Vardon; open Tues–Sun 9.30am–12.30pm, 2–6pm, Nov–Apr until 5pm; tel: 04 94 51 34 31) which could once accommodate 10,000 spectators. Although substantially damaged, the amphitheatre is still used for rock concerts and bullfights. Also of note is a tower in the **Porte des Gaules**, which formed part of the Roman ramparts and marked one end of a 40-km (25-mile) long aqueduct.

In the centre of town stands the medieval **Cathédrale St-Léonce**, begun in the 10th century and bordered by a fine 12th-century cloister that features a fantastical wooden ceiling decorated with animals and chimeras. Within the cathedral complex is an unmissable 5th-century baptistery (Cité Episcopale, 48 rue Fleury; open Oct–May Tues–Sun 9am–noon, 2–5pm, June–Sept daily 9am–6.30pm; admission charge; tel: 04 94 51 26 30), one of the most ancient in France, reached from an entrance on place Formigé.

Near by on place Calvini, the **Musée Archéologique** (open May–Sept Tues–Sun 9.30am–12.30pm, 2–6pm, Oct–Apr Tues–Sun 9.30am–12.30pm, 2–5pm; tel: 04 94 32 15 98) has a fine collection of Roman and early Ligurian tiles, mosaics and sculptures, including the two-faced bust of Hermes that has become the symbol of the town.

In addition to Fréjus's Roman and medieval attractions, there are a couple of very un-Gallic curiosities nearby. A Buddhist pagoda sitting in

TIP

Unless you've got a yacht, reaching St-Tropez can be a nightmare in summer. Avoid the worst of the traffic jams by arming yourself with a good map and using back roads (fire restrictions permitting) from Ramatuelle. The western route along the corniche des Maures from Le Lavandou is usually less busy than the eastern route from Ste-Maxime. Or else leave your car at Ste-Maxime and take a ferry.

BELOW: Port Grimaud.

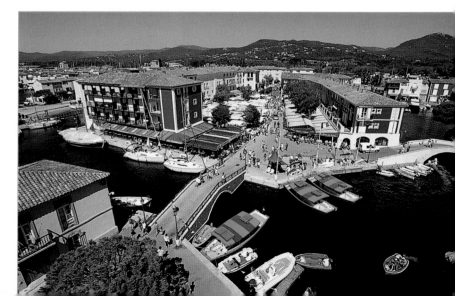

Vineyard near St-Tropez, one of many producers of the Côtes de Provence wines made in the warm coastal hinterland.

an oriental garden, just off the N7 to Cannes, commemorates the death of 5,000 Vietnamese soldiers in World War I. And a replica of the Missir Mosque in Mali lies unprepossessingly in the middle of an army camp off the D4 to Bagnols.

Merging into Fréjus to the east is the lively resort of **St-Raphaël** ⑲, which started life as a holiday resort for the Roman legionaries of Fréjus. The town, which has a population of around 30,000, has a turbulent history involving the Romans, plundering Arabs, 10th-century Lérins monks and, from the 13th century, the Knights Templar. In the 19th century, Napoleon landed in St-Raphaël on his return from Egypt, and this was also his departing point 14 years later when he was banished to Elba.

St-Raphaël's status as a fashionable resort is largely down to Alphonse Karr, chief editor of *Le Figaro* in the 19th century. Karr lived in Nice until he discovered St-Raphaël and encouraged his friends to follow him down the coast. Those that did included Alexandre Dumas, Guy de Maupassant, Hector Berlioz

and Charles Gounod. Now, though less trendy and marred by some huge apartment blocks, St-Raphaël has no lack of visitors, even if they're just here to lose a few euros at the rather hideous casino on the palm-lined seafront.

More fun is the daily fish market in the old port, where as well as a small fishing fleet you can take boats in summer to St-Tropez, Port Grimaud and the Ile de Port-Cros. Behind here is the small, rather unkempt old town, with a good covered market on place Victor-Hugo. The **Musée Archéologique** (place de la Vieille Eglise; open Tues–Sat 9am–noon, 2–6pm; admission charge; tel: 04 94 19 25 75), in the presbytery of the 12th-century Romanesque church of St-Pierre-des-Templiers, contains Roman amphorae and a display of underwater equipment.

The Massif de l'Estérel

The red porphyry rock of the Estérel tumbles down to the sea in a dramatic sweep of hills and ravines. Highwaymen and sundry criminal types ruled the impenetrable reaches of the **Massif de l'Estérel** ⑳ for many centuries, the most notorious of them Gaspard de Bresse *(see page 201)*, who hung out at the picturesque village of Les Adrets de l'Estérel. Forested with pines, cork oak, juniper, rosemary and arquebousiers (strawberry trees), in winter the hills turn yellow with mimosa.

The corniche d'Or coast road is one of the least crowded sections of the Côte, though the familiar pattern of private villas, hotels and apartments "de grand standing" blocking views and access to the sea can be very frustrating even here. East of St-Raphaël, the forested **Cap du Dramont** has some lovely stretches of coast path. The Plage du Dramont was one of the main landing beaches for Allied forces in the liberation of

Provence: 20,000 America GIs, commemorated in a marble monument, landed here in less than 10 hours on 15 August 1944.

Nearby **Agay** ㉑ has a sheltered bay with three sandy beaches that are wonderful for swimming. Inland, those with an eye for a panorama should head for **Mont Vinaigre** (at 618 metres/2,027 ft, the highest point of the massif); for great sea views make for the Pic de l'Ours.

Further east is the resort of **Théoule-sur-Mer**, its westward extension Miramar and the tiny port and sandy beach of La Figueirette, a good starting point for several footpaths into the Estérel. Follow the signs to **Notre-Dame d'Afrique**. Placed here in 2002, the 12-metre (39-ft) high statue facing across the Mediterranean is a copy of the black statue of the Virgin at Notre-Dame d'Afrique in Algiers and is a place of pilgrimage for the French *pieds noirs* returned from Algeria, with a blessing ceremony each May.

Another curiosity to look out for high above the corniche is the **Palais Bulles** built in 1968 by experimen-

tal Finnish-born architect Antti Lovag for couturier Pierre Cardin. Lovag rejected straight lines and angles: everything here is globular curves. The outside amphitheatre is the setting for an eclectic summer music festival.

Sitting on the seafront at **Mandelieu-la Napoule** ㉒, just west of Cannes, is the fantastical **Château de la Napoule** (open mid-Feb–mid-Nov daily 10am–6pm, mid-Nov–mid-Feb Sat, Sun and school hols 10am–6pm, Mon–Fri 2–6pm; admission charge; www.chateau-lanapoule.com). Originally a fortress belonging to the powerful Villeneuve family, later a glass factory, it was acquired by eccentric American artist Henry Clews in 1918, son of a wealthy banking family. He and his wife gave the place a complete medieval makeover with turrets, crenellations and gargoyles, adding Clews' own weird sculptures and topiaried gardens. The couple who liked to dress in medieval attire are buried in a mausoleum in the garden. Today the castle is an arts foundation offering residences to writers and artists. ❏

Map on page 192

Gaspard de Bresse, the Robin Hood of the Estérel, was the most notorious of the brigands operating in the Estérel in the 18th century. He targetted tax officers and wealthy voyagers, always giving a portion of his proceeds to the poor. A gentleman thief who robbed without bloodshed, a prankster and a dandy, he won over several of his female victims. He was arrested for good at an inn in La Valette du Var and executed in 1781.

BELOW:
Côte de l'Estérel.

RESTAURANTS, BARS AND CAFÉS

Bormes-les-Mimosas

Lou Portaou

1 rue Cubert des Poètes.
Tel: 04 94 64 86 37. Open:
D daily in summer, D Wed–
Sun in winter. Closed: mid-
Nov–mid-Dec. €€
Located in a fortified
medieval tower in the
village. Provençal dishes
with an original touch.

Restaurant de l'Estagnol

Parc de l'Estagnol. Open: L
and D in summer. €€
Alfresco eating under the
pines just back from the
beach at l'Estagnol. The
speciality is fresh fish
and langoustines grilled
on an open wood fire.

La Tonnelle

Place Gambetta. Tel: 04 94
71 34 84. Open: L Fri–Tues,
D Thur–Tues. Closed: mid-
Nov to mid-Dec. €€
www.la-tonnelle-bormes.com

In a pleasant, airy dining
room on the square, Gil
Renard's attractively presented modern Mediter-
ranean cooking includes
such dishes as tuna
tartare with artichokes
or land-sea combinations
like lamb with anchovies.
Home-made bread and
fruit-based desserts.

Cogolin

Grain de Sel

6 rue du 11 novembre. Tel:
04 94 54 46 86. Open: L & D
Tues–Sat. €€
Fresh seasonal bistro
cooking, such as stuffed
vegetables, roast lamb
and fruit tarts, prepared
in an open kitchen by an
young haute cuisine-
trained chef.

Collobrières

Hôtel-Restaurant des Maures

19 boulevard Lazare Carnot.
Tel: 04 94 48 07 10. €
A popular, unpretentious
family-run restaurant
with tables on the ter-
race spanning the Réal
Collobrier River. Sustain-
ing rustic fare includes a
fine wild boar stew.

Gassin

Villa Belrose

Boulevard des Crêtes la
Grande Bastide. Tel: 04 94
55 97 97. Open: L & D daily
(D only July–Aug). Closed:
Nov–Easter. €€€€
www.villabelrose.com
A luxurious hotel-
restaurant with a superb
terrace overlooking the
bay of St-Tropez.

Grimaud

Le Coteau Fleuri

Place des Pénitants. Tel: 04
94 43 20 17. Open: L & D
Wed–Mon. Closed: Nov–
Dec. €€€
www.coteaufleuri.fr
In an 18th-century
house, quietly situated in
the old village.
Renowned locally for its
gastronomic take on
regional cuisine by Jean-
Claude Paillard.

Hyères

Les Jardins de Bacchus

32 avenue Gambetta.
Tel: 04 94 65 77 63. Open: L
Tues–Fri, Sun; D Tues–Sat.
€€
www.les-jardins-de-bacchus.com
On the main street lead-
ing up to the old town,
chef Jean-Claude San-
tioni prepares classic
southern cuisine with
cosmopolitan touches.

Le Lavandou

Les Roches

Hôtel des Roches, 1 avenue
des Trois-Dauphins, Aigue-
belle. Tel: 04 94 71 05 07.
Open: L & D. €€€€
www.hotellesroches.com
The Dandine brothers
from L'Escoundudo at
Bormes-les-Mimosas
have recently taken over
the restaurant at this
luxury waterside hotel,
with a chic new contem-
porary decor for Mathieu
Dandine's modern
interpretation of
Provençal cuisine.

Les Tamaris "Chez Raymond"

Plage de St-Clair. Tel: 04 94
71 02 70.
The most upmarket of
the fish restaurants
along the Plage de St-
Clair is renowned for its
bourride and the excel-
lent daily catch.

Ramatuelle

Chez Camille

Route de la Bonne Terrasse.
Tel: 04 98 12 68 98. Open: L
& D Wed–Sun (D daily in July
& Aug). Closed: Oct–Easter.
€€€
Right at the Cap Camarat
end of the Plage de Pam-
pelonne, this ancient
fisherman's shack draws
"le tout St-Trop" for its
bouillabaisse, fish soup,
lobster and grilled fish.

La Farigoulette

Rue Victor Léon. Tel: 04 94
79 20 49. Open: L & D daily
(D only July & Aug). Closed:
Oct–Mar.
A simple, informal bistro
on the old rampart climb,
serving grilled meats, an
intense herby daube de
boeuf, anchoïade and
pasta dishes.

La Forge

Rue Victor Léon. Tel: 04 94
79 25 56. Open: L & D daily
(Wed–Mon in low season).
Closed: mid-Nov to mid-Feb.
A quietly dressy place
in a former forge for
chef Pierre Fanzio's
accomplished bistro
cooking.

Rayol-Canadel

Maurin des Maures
Boulevard du TCF. Tel: 04 94
05 60 11. Open: L and D
daily. €€
www.maurin-des-maures.com
This noisy, animated
institution has lots of
atmosphere, combining
popular restaurant where
you are packed elbow to
elbow down long tables,
and local bar with its pin-
ball and table football.
Come for fish dishes and
Provençal classics like
daube de boeuf and rab-
bit. Reserve ahead.

St-Raphaël

L'Arbousier
9 l'angle de la rue Marius
Allongue. Tel: 04 94 95 25
00. Open: L and D Wed–Sun.
€€. www.arbousier.com
Using seasonal produce
and regional recipes,
this cosy Provençal
restaurant has become a
local favourite for the
generously served cook-
ing of Philippe Troncy.
Magnolia-shaded terrace
in warm weather.

St-Tropez

La Bouillabaisse
Quartier la Bouillabaisse.
Tel: 04 94 97 54 00. Open:
L and D daily May–Sept,
weekends only Mar–Apr,
Oct–Nov. €€
In an old fisherman's
cottage serving excellent
fresh fish from the ter-
race right by the beach.

Le Café
Place des Lices. Tel: 04 94
97 44 69. Open: L and D
daily. €€

Traditional bistro with
hearty fare on the site of
the Café des Arts, the
original hang-out of the
Places des Lices boules
players. €

Le Girelier
Quai Jean Jaurès. Tel: 04 94
97 03 87. Closed: Nov to
mid-Mar. €€
Highly reputed fish cook-
ing in the midst of the
portside buzz.

Joseph
1 place de l'Hôtel de Ville.
Tel: 04 94 97 01 66. Open: L
& D daily. Closed: mid-Nov
to mid-Dec and Tues in low
season. €€€
A trendy contemporary
restaurant with two
chefs and two styles of
cuisine, one Provençal,
the other Thai.

Leï Mouscardins
Tour du Portalet. Tel: 04 94 97
29 00. Closed: Oct–Nov and
Wed in low season. €€€€
Considered by many to
be St-Tropez's best
restaurant, chef Laurent
Tarridec serves light,
innovative southern
cooking.

Spoon Byblos
Hôtel Byblos, avenue
Maréchal Foch. Tel: 04 94 56
68 20. Closed: Nov–Mar.
€€€
www.byblos.com
Alain Ducasse's mix-and-
match world food concept
allows you to put together
different sauces and
accompaniments to go
with your lacquered beef,
seared tuna or scallop
kebab, with a more
Mediterranean emphasis
than in the Paris original.

It's within the ultra-
fashionable Byblos Hotel.

St-Tropez Bars

A St-Tropez evening
might well start with a
drink on the Vieux-Port,
observing the fauna
from the red directors'
chairs at **Sénéquier**
(quai Jean Jaurès), the
eternal **Gorille** (1 quai
Suffren), the retro chic
Bar du Port (7 quai
Suffren) with its cock-
tails and DJs, or from
the balcony vantage
point of **Le Sube** at the
heart of the port.
   Clubbers congregate
at **Le Café** on place
des Lices (see above),
nibble on tapas at
Baroque-style lounge
bar **Chez Maggy** (rue
Sibille) or sink into the
low chairs at the
Octave Café, a stylish
piano bar (place de la
Garonne).

Théoule-sur-Mer

L'Etoile des Mers
Miramar Beach Hôtel, 47
avenue de Miramar. Tel: 04
93 75 05 05. Open: L and
D daily. €€€.
www.mbhriviera.com
The panoramic dining
room is popular with
locals as well as hotel
guests. The creative cooking can fall down when
too complicated, but is
excellent when doing an
update of classics, like
the grand aioli, with filo-
wrapped cod, whelks and
seasonal vegetables.

PRICE CATEGORIES

Prices for a three-course
meal without wine. Note
that many restaurants
have a less expensive
lunch menu.
€ = under €25
€€ = €25–€40
€€€ = €40–€60
€€€€ = more than €60

LEFT: style and colour. **RIGHT:** a selection of cheeses.

TROPICAL GARDENS

The Riviera's mild climate and abundant sunlight have made it a paradise for a remarkable range of flora

All sorts of tropical and subtropical plants have been naturalised in the Riviera region – not just cultivated in gardens and public parks, but also growing wild, like the mimosa trees that thrive in the Estérel hills, and the eucalyptus in the Maures forests.

The Belle Epoque was the golden age of Riviera gardens. Most of these exotic edens were created between the 1890s and the 1920s, many of them by the foreigners who came to winter in the region. Almost as varied as the plants they contained were the people who created them: English aristocrats and colonels, American writers, Russian princesses, landscape designers, architects and artists, explorers, botanists and other scientists. Some gardens were created for scientific purposes, others as luxuriant backdrops to go with their exuberant *palazzi* and avant-garde villas.

These green-fingered eccentrics introduced countless new species to the native Mediterranean flora of herbs, parasol pines, olive trees and cork oaks, ranging from the agaves and date palms of desert regions to the dank ferns, banana trees and purple bougainvillea of the tropics. Against the formal restraint of traditional French gardens, with their gravel paths and neatly trimmed hedges, these places were often flamboyantly exotic creations bursting with colour.

LEFT: the Serre de la Madone, Menton. The romantic gardens of the Serre de la Madone were designed in the 1920s by Lawrence Johnston, creator of the garden at Hidcote Manor in England. Water is a big feature in this garden, laid out with geometrical pools and Italianate terraces, fountains and classical statues that create different and perspectives and environments for irises, acanthus, camellias, water plants, toxic daturas and other flora from all over the globe.

LEFT: Jardin Exotique, Eze. A prickly feast of cacti and strangely shaped succulents sprout up among the sun-baked ruins of Eze's castle mound, laid out in stone terraces, with spectacular views to the sea hundreds of metres below, and dotted by terracotta nudes by sculptor Jean-Philippe Richard.

BELOW: Domaine du Rayol, Le Rayol-Canadel. Perched on the clifftop, these fabulous gardens were originally planted in 1910 by Paris banker Alfred Courmes, who packed the grounds with exotic plants from all over the world. The grounds are arranged in climatic zones, ranging from arid desert to tropical jungle. Gullies, bowers and secret paths are dotted about this jungle, punctuated by dramatic vistas and seaside drops. There's even an underwater garden, which can be visited with snorkel and flippers.

GARDEN TRAILS

1. The Route des Parcs et Jardins du Var (www.tourismevar.com) follows a 325-km (200-mile) loop between Saint-Zacharie in the Ste-Baume Massif to Hyères, taking in tiny hill village gardens, herb and scent gardens, historic chateau gardens and the arty gardens of Hyères, as well as addresses of some of the *département's* best nurseries.
2. The Route du Jardins de la Riviera follows the Alpes-Maritimes coast between Mandelieu-la Napoule and Menton, visiting gardens, villas and grand hotels of the Belle Epoque, including the famous Villa Ephrussi and the gardens of Menton, and smaller treasures, such as Villa Eilen Roc in Antibes and the garden of actor-playwright Sacha Guitry at Cap d'Ail.
3. The Route du Mimosa (www.bormeslesmimosas.com) traces the fragrant yellow puffballs *(main picture)* across the Var and Alpes-Maritimes *départements*, between Bormes-les-Mimosas and the perfumeries of Grasse. At its best during the flowering season (December to March), the route suggests gardens and nurseries to visit, including the national collection of mimosa at Pepinière Gérard Cavatone in Bormes and the Massif de Tannéron near Mandelieu, where wild and cultivated trees make up the largest mimosa forest in Europe.
4. Undisputed garden capital of the coast is Menton, famed for its lemons *(see top right)* and reputed to have the mildest climate of all. As well as the Jardin des Agrumes, the Jardins du Val Rahmeh, the Serre de la Madone and the olive groves of the Parc du Pian, other gardens can be visited through the Maison du Patrimoine de Menton (tel: 04 92 10 97 10).

ABOVE: Jardins d'Ephrussi Rothschild, St-Jean-Cap Ferrat. A succession of themed gardens created by Béatrice Ephrussi, daughter of Baron Alphonse de Rothschild and wife of wealthy banker Maurice Ephrussi, on the crest of Cap Ferrat. At the top is a small classical gazebo, the Temple d'Amour, from where she could watch her 30 gardeners as they worked, dressed in berets with red pompons. Around a central formal French garden with a pool and musical gardens, the seven themed gardens evoke not just different climates and vegetation but different historic eras and moods, from the melancholy of Gothic ruins, poetry of Italian Renaissance terraces and Spanish grottoes to the calm of Japanese shinto shrines.

BELOW: The Jardin Botanique Exotique Val Rahmeh, Menton. Over 700 species grow in profusion on a hilly site around a 1920s villa. A winding trail leads between medicinal plants, towering palms, dank tropical ferns, forests of bamboo and exotic cocoa, avocado, banana, guava and citrus trees, tea bushes and spice trees.

ST-PAUL, VENCE AND THE GORGES DU LOUP

Picture-postcard St-Paul-de-Vence has the finest art
museum in the region, while Vence is best-known for
Matisse's extraordinary Chapelle du Rosaire. Around
the Gorges du Loup are some classic *villages perchés*,
and fragrant Grasse is centre of perfume production

West of the River Var, the ancient city of Vence and historic hill towns such as St-Paul-de-Vence and Tourrettes-sur-Loup rest against an impressive mountain backdrop. This part of the Alpes-Maritimes remained a part of Provence, and later France, even when the eastern territory of the Comté de Nice was under Piedmontese-Sardinian sovereignty – hence some impressive fortifications put up by the French monarchy anxious to control the border. Less crowded and less built-up than the coastal strip, the hinterland nonetheless has an artistic and architectural heritage ranging from medieval chateaux to modern masterpieces, while the gentle climate favourable to the cultivation of flowers has made Grasse a world centre for the perfume industry.

St-Paul-de-Vence

Sitting within picture-perfect ramparts on top of a hill, **St-Paul-de-Vence ❶** epitomises all that is best and worst about Provence: while undeniably picturesque, the village itself is easily overrun with tourists and any semblance of everyday life has been glossed over by arts-and-crafts galleries and souvenir shops. Thankfully, far more illustrious than the art touted in the old village are the works on show at the **Fondation**

Maeght *(see page 209)*, outside the village. One of the finest collections of modern art in the world, it is a wonderful example of the integration of art with architecture and nature.

The village gained its reputation as a centre for art in the 1920s. The **Auberge de la Colombe d'Or**, situated just outside the ramparts, became a meeting place for a bevy of artists – including Picasso, Utrillo, Bonnard, Chagall, Modigliani and Soutine – who, as the tale goes, left their canvases behind, sometimes to settle

Map on page 208

LEFT: Vence façade.
BELOW:
the Colombe d'Or.

For centuries, St-Paul served as a fortress guarding the border between France and the Comté de Nice. When King François I built the ramparts of the village in the 16th century, he uprooted all the inhabitants and packed them off to live in nearby La Colle-sur-Loup. Over 100 years later, new residents arrived: the monks of the Ordre des Pénitents Blancs.

BELOW:
a splash of colour
in St-Paul-de-Vence.

long-running accounts. Whatever the truth, the Colombe d'Or has now assembled its own priceless collection of paintings and a ceramic mural by Léger. You must dine or stay here, however, a delightful if pricey experience, in order to see the collection.

Lesser mortals can at least take a seat opposite the Colombe d'Or at the **Café de la Place** – which looks like it served as the model for the French café of countless Hollywood productions – and observe the residents of the smart villas that abound here pretending to be Provençals as they play *pétanque* on the sandy pitch outside.

Bissecting the area within the town walls and its hub is rue Grande, lined with art galleries and craft shops. It runs from the 14th-century Porte Nord (or Porte Royale) to the Porte Sud (or Porte de Nice), the south gate outside the cemetery in which the painter Marc Chagall is buried.

About halfway along rue Grande, at the place de la Grande Fontaine, a

street climbs to a small square at the high point of the village. Here you'll find the **Eglise Collégiale**, in which is a painting attributed to Tintoretto; the **Chapelle des Pénitents Blancs**; the Mairie (town hall), housed within the remains of the castle keep; and a small museum where costumed figures of François 1er illustrate key moments in St-Paul's history. You can also follow the path along the western ramparts, which provides fine views over vineyards and luxury villas to the coast.

Vence

Modern-art pilgrims should make for **Vence ❷**, just 4 km (2½ miles) further north, and its **Chapelle du Rosaire** (468 avenue Henri Matisse; open Mon, Wed, Sat 2–5.30pm, Tues, Thur 10–11.30am, 2–5.30pm; admission charge; tel: 04 93 58 03 26), on the edge of town on the route de Ste-Jeannet. It was designed between 1948 and 1951 by the then elderly

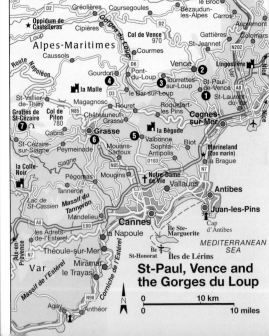

St-Paul, Vence and
the Gorges du Loup

Henri Matisse (1869–1954), who had moved to the Villa le Rêve in Vence during World War II, encouraged by the young Dominican nun Sister Jacques-Marie.

In design, the chapel is typically Provençal in its simplicity. Overall, it is strikingly pure and bright: the roof in glazed blue-and-white tiles, and the only colour in its white interior contributed by the stained-glass windows and the dappled reflections they create over the walls. The figurative tiles on three of the walls capture Matisse's fluid mastery of line in the single stroke of his drawings. On the simple stone altar is an equally simple and moving tiny bronze crucifix. In an adjacent room you can see Matisse's preparatory sketches and the priest's copes which he also designed.

A spiritual testament by the aged artist, Matisse called the chapel his most satisfying work. And he was not the only artist attracted to Vence: Chagall also lived here, and the writer D.H. Lawrence came here after having been diagnosed with tuberculosis.

Within the city walls

Today, Vence is a large, lively city of some 17,000 inhabitants. The 15th-century walls of the Vieille Ville (old town) betray its former feudal vocation: Ligurians, Lombards, Romans, countless Christians and Saracens, plus the Germans and Italians of World War II, all passed through here.

Begun in the 4th century and by then already a bishopric, the **Ancienne Cathédrale**, located in place Clémenceau on the site of a Roman temple, reflects the town's battle-torn past. The building is a patchwork of styles and eras, with its simple Baroque façade, some Byzantine stonework, Gothic windows, Roman tombs, fine 15th-century carved choir stalls and a 1979 mosaic of the saving of Moses by Chagall in the baptistery.

From here, narrow streets lead to place du Peyra with its pretty fountain. Abutting a medieval tower on one side of the square is the **Château de Villeneuve-Fondation Emile Hugues** (open Tues–Sun 10am– 12.30pm, 2–6pm, closed between exhibitions; tel: 04 93 58 15 78; www.museedevence.com), a 17th-

Map on page 208

TIP

The Villa le Rêve in Vence, where Matisse lived from 1943 to 1949, is now used for painting courses and artists' residences. Half- or one-day visits can be arranged by appointment: 261 avenue Henri Matisse, tel: 04 93 58 82 68.

BELOW:
Giacometti sculpture, Fondation Maeght.

Fondation Maeght

The Fondation Maeght (Montée des Trious, St-Paul-de-Vence; open daily July–Sept 10am–7pm, Oct–June 10am–12.30pm, 2.30–6pm; admission charge; tel: 04 93 32 81 63; www.fondation-maeght.com) is arguably the most interesting of all the museums on the Côte d'Azur, inaugurated in 1964 to house the fabulous modern-art collection put together by Paris art dealer Aimé Maeght and his wife Marguerite. The brick-and-white-concrete building was designed by the Spanish architect José-Luis Sert, and is beautifully integrated with both landscape and artworks, inside and out. A series of pools, terraces and sculptures include funky, colourful ceramic fountains by Miró and tiled designs by Braque. Other sculptures, among them works by Giacometti and Calder, are dotted around the pine-shaded garden. All the structural features were devised to promote an understanding of 20th-century art, and the architect worked directly with some of the artists, principally Miró and Chagall, to achieve this. A few of the holdings are sometimes on outside loan and the collection is rehung for themed exhibitions each summer, but with reserves this large there is always something to see.

century baronial residence of the powerful Villeneuve family, now used for high-quality temporary exhibitions of modern and contemporary art. Through the Porte du Peyra, the place du Frêne contains a venerable ash tree supposedly planted by François I in 1538.

The Gorges du Loup

Six km (4 miles) west of Vence, the hilltop village of **Tourrettes-sur-Loup ❸**, dubbed the "city of violets" *(see left)*, overlooks the southeastern end of the Gorges du Loup through olive trees and, in spring, fields of violets.

Although home to the requisite Provençal clan of potters, painters and woodcarvers, attractive Tourrettes lives peacefully in the shadow of its more illustrious neighbours. A Roman and subsequently Saracen stronghold, the only evocations of war today come from the 15th-century chateau, once marking the entrance to the village, now at its centre and occupied by the Mairie (town hall). A belfry crowns the archway leading through to the cobbled,

hilly streets of the old quarter. And in the main square, the church conceals a triptych by the Bréa school.

The road from Tourrettes descends through woodland into the river valley at **Pont-du-Loup** – home to the much publicised **Confiserie Florian** (tel: 04 93 59 32 91), an old-fashioned sweet manufacturer open to visitors. Here you can decide to head southwards towards Le Bar-sur-Loup or upstream on the D6 along the imposing Gorges du Loup.

The Loup valley is one of the most spectacular in the region, the torrential river scything its way through a gorge of grey rock and lush vegetation. It is punctuated by some impressive waterfalls, notably the **Cascade de Courmes** which plunges down about 50 metres (160 ft) halfway along the Gorges; the smaller **Cascade des Desmoiselles** near by; and, further up, **Saut du Loup** (Wolf's Leap). Signs advise on sudden rises in the water level, dependent on the hydro-electric station upstream.

In the other direction, **Le Bar-sur-Loup** is a relatively ungentrified village whose church (currently

closed for restoration) contains a fascinating if macabre painting of the dance of death.

Gourdon

If the term *village perché* needed a perfect example, **Gourdon** ❹ would be it. One whole side of the village teeters on the edge of a rocky cliff, providing perfect sightlines to allied villages and obviating the need for any fortress walls to repel invaders.

A brief walk up through the village's main street – cars are not allowed here – brings you to the feudal **Château de Gourdon** (medieval museum open Wed–Mon 2–6pm, July–Aug also 11am–1pm; art-deco museum open July–Aug Wed–Mon 11am–1pm, 2–6pm; rest of year by appointment; children under 12 not admitted; tel: 04 93 09 68 02; www. chateau-gourdon.com).

Recently transformed from a museum of weaponry into the **Musée des Arts Décoratifs et de la Modernité**, it contains superb examples of furniture and lighting by avant-garde designers and architects such as Eileen Gray and Chareau.

From Gourdon the D3 zigzags down to Grasse. On your way you might choose to take a detour to **Valbonne** ❺. Valbonne immediately stands out from its neighbours as it was laid out in the 16th century on a strict rectangular grid plan by monks from the Abbaye de Chaalis, itself on the southern edge of the town.

Another very different planned city lies east of here on the Plateau de Valbonne. Founded in the early 1970s, **Sophia-Antipolis** is southern France's answer to Silicon Valley, a brave new world of high-tech companies, research institutes and a branch of the university of Nice.

Grasse, the perfume capital

Literature fans may recognise **Grasse** ❻ as the 18th-century setting for Patrick Süskind's novel, *Perfume*. France's sprawling perfume capital is not one of Provence's most attractive towns, and the hilly geography and boulevards that wind round the ancient quarters make finding your bearings difficult. But the municipality is at last making an effort to revive the rather run-down

West of Valbonne, and running into the southern edge of Grasse, is Mouans-Sartoux, whose main appeal is the Espace de l'Art Concret (open Sept–June Tues–Sun 11am–6pm, July–Aug daily 11am–7pm; admission charge; tel: 04 93 75 71 50; http://art. concret.free.fr) at the Château de Mouans. The gallery was founded by artist Gottfried Honegger and the widow of Josef Albers in 1990 to exhibit their collection of abstract art.

BELOW: Gourdon.

Perfumes of Provence

The perfume industry in Grasse originated with an immigrant group of Italian glove-makers in the 16th century. They discovered the wonderful scents of the flowers in the area and began perfuming their soft leather gloves, a fashion introduced by Catherine de'Medici and a favourite way to use perfume (along with pomanders and scented handkerchiefs) at a time when the odour of the general populace definitely required masking.

Demand for the floral perfumes steadily grew in the 18th and 19th centuries, and Grasse prospered as a perfume mecca. Local production of the raw material declined, however, after World War II. Competition from countries such as Turkey, Egypt and Bulgaria, where labour costs were much lower than in France, proved decisive; on top of which, the gentle climate attracted many wealthy people to the area, pushing land prices sky-high and causing acres to be sold off as building plots.

Today, Grasse is better-known for improving raw materials imported from other countries. Nonetheless, each morning you can still see vast mountains of rose petals, vats

of mimosa or jonquils and spadefuls of violets and orange blossom just picked and waiting to be processed.

The flowers must be picked early in the day, when the oil is most concentrated, and delivered immediately. It takes vast quantities of blooms to produce the tiniest amounts of "absolute" (concentrated) perfume: around 750 kg (1,650 lbs) of roses for just 1 kg (2.2 lbs) of rose absolute and about 4,000 kg (8,800 lbs) for 1kg of essential oil.

Various methods are used to create the absolutes and essential oils that the perfumer mixes to create a fragrance. The oldest method is steam distillation, now used mainly for orange blossom. Water and flowers are boiled in a still, and the essential oils are extracted by steam.

Another ancient, though expensive, method is *enfleurage*. The flowers are layered with a semi-solid mixture of lard, spread over glass sheets and stacked in wooden tiers. When the fat is fully impregnated with perfume, the scent is separated out by washing the *axonge* (fat) with alcohol. A more modern method is extraction by volatile solvents, leaving a final dose of concentrated essence.

The highly trained perfumers or "noses" of Grasse can identify and classify hundreds of fragrances. In creating a fragrance, a perfumer is rather like a musician, blending different "chords" of scent to create a harmony. The desired result is a complex perfume that will radiate around the body in a slow process of diffusion – what the French call *sillage*. A good perfume may include hundreds of different ingredients to achieve the right balance. Nowadays, many of the raw ingredients are imported, with the exception of jasmine and may rose; others, such as musk and amber-grey, formerly made from animals, are chemically synthesised. But the perfumiers' know-how still keeps Grasse at the forefront of the industry, not just with perfumes for the great fashion houses but with the fragrances used in household cleaning products and food-industry flavourings. ❑

LEFT: visiting the Perfumerie Fragonard factory.

town centre through a programme of restoration and pedestrianisation.

Grasse is a town with a distinguished history. Between 1138 and 1227 it was a free city, allied to Pisa and Genoa, and governed by a consulate, like the Italian republics, before being annexed by the counts of Provence. When Provence was united with France in 1482, Grasse continued to trade with Italy, importing animal skins and selling linen and leather goods. Grasse leather was of high quality, typified by the greenish hue caused by treating it with myrtle leaves. In the 16th century, the fashion for perfumed gloves encouraged the perfume industry in Grasse, but it was not until the 18th century that tanning and perfumery began to develop as separate trades.

Perfume museum

On a still day, Grasse lives up to its reputation as a scent capital: a sweet aroma lingers in the air. Huge hoardings everywhere announce the factory visits to the three big perfumiers – Fragonard, Molinard and Galimard – all actually located some way out-side the town centre. The **Musée International de la Parfumerie** (8 place du cours Honoré Cresp; due to reopen Jan 2008; tel: 04 93 36 80 20; www.museesdegrasse.com) is currently closed for expansion and modernisation, but some of its huge collection of perfume bottles can be seen at the **Musée de l'Histoire de Provence** (2 rue Mirabeau; open June–Sept daily 10am–7pm, Oct, Dec–May Wed–Mon 10am–1.30pm, 2–5.30pm; admission charge). Once owned by the Marquise de Cabris, the splendid late 18th-century neoclassical mansion set in formal gardens shows how the people of Provence used to live, with rooms furnished in fine period style.

The Fragonard connection

On boulevard Fragonard in an 18th-century building is the perfume factory of **Parfumerie Fragonard**, with a shop and a collection of antique perfume stills. Also here is the **Musée Provençal du Costume et du Bijou** (2 rue Jean Ossola; open daily 10am–1pm, 2–6pm; Nov–Jan Mon–Sat; tel: 04 93 36 44 65), with a col-

Map on page 208

TIP

The Moulin de la Brague at Opio has been run by the Michel family for over 150 years. Although water power has now been replaced by electricity, traditional methods are still used to make high-quality olive oil from the tiny purple *caillette* or "olive de Nice". Open Mon–Sat except 15–30 Oct; tel: 04 93 77 23 03; www.moulin-opio.com.

BELOW: gathering jasmine, Grasse.

Map
on page
208

Carved statue representing the perfumier's art outside the Perfumerie Fragonard, one of Grasse's oldest perfume-making establishments.

BELOW: cradle vaulting of Grasse cathedral.

lection of 18th- and 19th-century costumes and jewellery, and the **Musée de la Marine**, commemorating the life of Admiral de Grasse.

Painter Jean-Honoré Fragonard (1732–1806) was born in Grasse, a connection the town makes the most of. He spent most of his career in Paris or on the Grand Tour of Italy with aristocratic patrons, and it was only after the French Revolution that he returned to Grasse. He stayed in the house of a wealthy cousin, now the **Villa-Musée Fragonard** (23 boulevard Fragonard; open June–Sept daily 10am–7pm, Oct, Dec–May Wed–Mon 10am– 1.30pm, 2–5.30pm;www.museesdegrasse.com). The most remarkable aspect of the house is its stairwell, decorated with grisaille frescos by Fragonard's son when he was only 13 years old.

You can see one of Fragonard's rare religious subjects, *The Washing of the Feet*, in the sober **Cathédrale Notre-Dame-de-Puy**, a much altered Romanesque structure on place du Petit-Puy, in the heart of the medieval town. It also contains three paintings by Rubens: *The Crown of Thorns*, *The Crucifixion* and *St Helen in Exaltation of the Holy Cross*.

Grottes de St-Cézaire

Napoleon passed by Grasse after escaping from Elba and landing on the coast at Golfe Juan *(see page 239)* in March 1815. The N85 road, known as the Route Napoléon, roughly follows the route he took through Provence and the Alps on his return to Paris for the Hundred Days. From Grasse, the route zigzags up through more mountainous country, climbing over the Col du Pilon pass before reaching the hamlet of St-Vallier-de-Thiey, sitting on a rocky plateau.

From here you can continue to Castellane *(see page 158)* or turn off on the D5 to the **Grottes de St-Cézaire ❼**, a cave complex with stalactites in extraordinary shades of dark red and pink. St-Cézaire itself is a quiet, pretty town with a Romanesque chapel. From here you can return to Grasse via the village of **Cabris** (6 km/4 miles from Grasse on the D4 road), which commands an impressive view from its old chateau ruins. ❏

Restaurants and Bars

Le Bar-sur-Loup

L'Hostellerie du Château
6–8 place Francis Paulet.
Tel: 04 93 42 41 10. Open:
L & D Tues–Sun (Wed–Sun in
winter). Closed: Feb. €€
www.lhostellerieduchateau.com
In the former castle of
the counts of Grasse,
artistically presented
modern southern cook-
ing is served in a pared-
down dining room with
panoramic views over
the Loup valley. In sum-
mer, you also have the
choice of a simpler café
opening onto the village
square.

Cabris

**Auberge du Vieux
Château**
Place du Panorama. Tel: 04
93 60 50 12. Open: L
Wed–Sun, D Tues–Sun. €€
www.aubergeduvieuxchateau.
com
This place is very popular
among Grasse's anglo-
phone expats, with its
terrace views and a
frequently changing,
market-inspired Mediter-
ranean menu.

Grasse

La Bastide St-Antoine
48 avenue Henri Dunant.
Tel: 04 93 70 94 94. €€€€
www.jacques-chibois.com
Difficult to find but well
worth the search, this
restaurant set in an old
olive grove outside
Grasse is fashionable for

the gourmet cuisine of
Jacques Chibois. In
season, truffles and wild
mushrooms are both
house specialities.

St-Paul-de-Vence

La Colombe d'Or
1 place du Général de Gaulle.
Tel: 04 93 32 80 02. Closed:
Nov–Christmas. €€€€
www.la-colombe-dor.com
Once frequented by pen-
niless artists who per-
suaded the original
owner to accept their
paintings in payment for
meals and board, this
legendary hotel and
restaurant now displays
works by Miró, Picasso,
Modigliani, Matisse and
Chagall for its jet-set
clientele. Classic cuisine
and arguably the most
beautiful terrace in the
region.

Tourrettes-sur-Loup

Chez Grand'Mère
Place Maximilien Escalier.
Tel: 04 93 59 33 34. Open:
L Sun–Tues, Thur, Fri,
D Thur–Tues. €
www.chezgrandmere.com
Popular for its North
African and Provençal
dishes, and meats grilled
over an open fire. Good
food at good prices.
Reservations recom-
mended.

Valbonne

**Lou Cigalon – Alain
Parodi**

4 boulevard Carnot. Tel: 04 93
12 27 07. Open: L & D
Tues–Sat. €€€
Self-taught chef Alain
Parodi conjures up a well-
balanced interpretation of
regional cuisine from his
tiny kitchen. The superb-
value weekday lunch
menu introduces dishes
such as lentil soup with
foie gras and truffles.

Vence

La Farigoulette
15 rue Henri Isnard. Tel: 04 93
58 01 27. Open: L Thur–Mon,
D Mon, Thur–Sat. Closed:
winter school hols. €€
Haute cuisine-trained
Patrick Bruot puts his
own adventurous spin
on Provençal cooking at
this attractive restaur-
ant, which has a pleas-
ant outside terrace in
summer.

**La Table d'Amis Jacques
Maximin**
689 chemin de la Gaude.
Tel: 04 93 58 90 75. Open: L
Sun in July & Aug,
D Wed–Sun, daily in July and
Aug. Closed: mid-Nov to
mid-Dec. €€€
www.tabledamis.com
Nouvelle cuisine person-
ality Jacques Maximin
now presides over his
own, more relaxed,
restaurant set in lovely
gardens.

Price Categories

Prices for a three-course
meal without wine. Note
that many restaurants
have a less expensive
lunch menu.
€ = under €25
€€ = €25–€40
€€€ = €40–€60
€€€€ = more than €60

RIGHT: spectacularly situated restaurant, Gourdon.

MERCANTOUR NATIONAL PARK AND THE EASTERN VALLEYS

Away from the coast, the eastern side of the Alpes-Maritimes is characterised by wild mountains, plunging gorges, clear sparkling rivers and Italianate villages with frescoed churches

Map on page 218

The rugged, sparsely populated Mercantour Massif provides a startling contrast to the busy, built-up coast. Ice and fast mountain torrents have cut deep gorges through the rock, flowing roughly north to south: the River Cians with its red schist gorges, the Tinée and Vésubie, which all empty into the River Var, and further east the Bévéra and Roya Rivers. The scenery ranges from olive groves grown on the lower slopes to pines and edelweiss, mountain lakes and bare Alpine peaks, many of them over 2,000 metres (6,560 ft). The area is a paradise for hikers and mountaineers, and offers respite from the crowds and heat of the coast in summer or for skiers in winter.

In addition to its spectacular scenery, this Alpine region by the Italian border also has a little-known architectural and artistic heritage that reflects a period when it was more populated than it is today, largely because of the active trade routes linking the Comté de Nice, Piedmont and Liguria. Chapels, often decorated with ornate frescos, were put up as protection against the frequent outbreaks of plague that swept the area; and during the Counter-Reformation, fine Baroque churches were constructed as the Catholic Church sought to reassert its authority against the Protestant Reformation.

Parc National du Mercantour

Covering a large swathe of this region is the **Parc National du Mercantour** (www.parc-mercantour.com) ❶, a huge national park created in 1979 which joins up with the Parco Naturale Alpi Marittime around the Argentera Massif in Italy. It consists of two zones: the highly protected, largely uninhabited central zone, and the peripheral zone where the villages are situated.

BELOW: ibex roam the Mercantour Massif.

Botanists now believe that more than half of the 4,000 or so species of wild flowers found in France grow in the Mercantour, including 63 varieties of orchid. Wildlife includes ibex, chamois, the ptarmigan, black grouse, golden eagle and rare species of owl. More controversial are the wolves that have returned to the area after crossing the border from Italy, now a source of heated argument between environmentalists and the shepherds who claim that the wolves are killing their sheep.

Vallée des Merveilles

At the heart of the national park lies the mysterious **Vallée des Merveilles** ❷, where the rugged mountains shelter a remarkable display of over 40,000 prehistoric rock engravings.

Located just west of the Lac des Mèsches, the **Minière de Vallaure** is an abandoned mine quarried for copper, zinc, iron and lead from pre-Roman times until the 1930s. Early Bronze Age settlers carved mysterious symbols on the polished rock, smoothed by glaciation. First recorded in the 17th century, these carvings are similar to ones found in the Camerino valley near Bergamo in Italy. The French carvings are exceptional, though, in that they depict a race of shepherds rather than hunters: the scarcity of wild game in the region forced the Bronze Age tribes to turn to agriculture and cattle-raising. These primitive inscriptions served as territorial markers for the tribes in the area.

However, the drawings are also open to some less earthbound interpretations. Anthropomorphic figures represent domestic animals and chief tribesmen but also dancers, devils, sorcerers and gods. Such magical totems are in keeping with Mt-Bégo's *(see page 218)* reputation as a sacred spot. Given the bleakness of the terrain, it is hardly surprising that the early shepherds looked heavenwards for help. Nowadays, as then, flocks of cows, sheep and goats graze by the lower lakes, especially at Fontanalbe. However, the abandoned stone farms and shepherds' outhouses attest to the unprofitable nature of mountain farming.

Thousands of Bronze Age drawings can be seen in the Vallée des Merveilles.

BELOW: Alpine flowers.

Some demanding hiking

There are two main points of access into the Vallée des Merveilles: from **St-Dalmas-de-Tende** in the Roya valley on the eastern side, and from **Madone de Fenestre** in the Vésubie valley to the west. The valley is accessible only in summer and only on foot (although a few all-terrain vehicles are permitted), and is really only suitable for those hikers with limbs and lungs strong enough to endure a day or two of solid walking and with a stock of hiking gear to match. If an overnight stay is necessary, try one of the simple mountain refuges administered by the Club Alpin Français (www.cafnice.org). Often, there aren't even any paths, let alone signposts to look at if you lose your way.

For the less experienced hiker, a mountain guide is essential, and the tourist office in **Tende** (*see right*) should be able to help. Hardened hikers can probably make do with a large-scale map – arm yourself with

the IGN 1:25,000 map and a Topoguide. The valley is only accessible between June and October (and occasionally in May).

The area between **Mt-Bégo** and the 2,934-metre (9,626-ft) **Mont du Grand Capelet** makes for a good, if tough, hike, with several lakes on the way. There are mountain refuges either end of the 60-km (40-mile) valley. If a thunderstorm strikes, don't panic: for the shepherds working in the valleys below more than 3,000 years ago, Mt-Bégo was like a temple, a place where sheep were sacrificed in an attempt to appease terrifying storms. In contemporary and less superstitious times, the mountain is simply seen as an effective lightning conductor.

Tende

The main base for excursions into the Mercantour, especially for walkers heading for the Vallée des Merveilles, is **Tende** ❸ (tourist office tel: 04 93

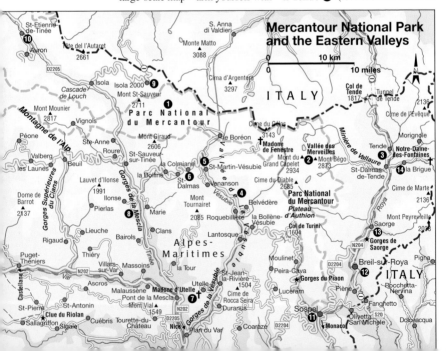

04 73 71). When the rest of the Comté de Nice rejoined France in 1860, this upper part of the Roya valley, the favourite hunting ground of king Vittorio Emanuele II, was granted to Italy, only joining France in 1947. The stacked houses, many of them dating from the 15th century, are built with a local green-hued schist and have balconies and overhanging roofs. The 15th-century **Eglise Collégiale Notre-Dame de l'Assomption** (open summer daily 9am–6pm; winter daily 9am–5pm) has a belfry shaped like two stacked barrels and a Baroque interior with 17th-century organ loft.

The **Musée des Merveilles** (open May–mid-Oct Wed–Mon 10am–6.30pm, daily in July and Aug, mid-Oct–Apr Wed–Mon 10am–5pm; admission charge; tel: 04 93 04 32 50; www.museedesmerveilles.com), in a striking modern building, has an exhibition devoted to the prehistory of the park, including original fragments from the rock drawings and mouldings of the most famous motifs. The museum also gives useful information about walks in the Vallée.

Vallée de la Vésubie

Within easy reach of Nice and the coast, the glorious **Vallée de la Vésubie** ❹ leads you away from a Mediterranean landscape to the fresher Alpine scenery of tall, dark-green pines, waterfalls near Le Boréon and green pastures at Roquebillière. The main town of the region is **St-Martin-Vésubie** ❺, which offers cool respite as a mountaineering centre in the summer. This is a sleepy and unpretentious place, disturbed only by the rush of water down a 1-metre (3-ft) wide canal. The twin torrents of le Boréon and the Madone de la Fenestre converge in the town to form the River Vésubie.

The town's native inhabitants seem to have the thick skin that goes with decades spent in the mountains, yet they are unmistakably Mediterranean by dint of their robust, olive complexions. In summer, they sit and watch the hikers leave the Bureau des Guides de la Haute-Vésubie, generally on trips into the nearby Mercantour. Summer for a Vésubian starts on 2 July, when a procession wends its way out of St-Martin carrying an

Map on page 218

TIP

Several companies based in Tende and nearby villages offer guided 4WD excursions to the archaeological sites of the Vallée des Merveilles. You should still allow for about three hours walking. www.tende merveilles.com

BELOW: the national park is dotted with refuges for hikers.

800-year-old wooden statue of Notre-Dame-de-Fenestre 12 km (7 miles) to the sanctuary at **Madone de Fenestre** (open daily). Winter begins when the procession makes the return journey in the third week of September.

Situated a few kilometres to the west of St-Martin-Vésubie is a small skiing resort at **La Colmiane** , complete with a few old chalets. Visitors like to call the area "Little Switzerland", which produces a quizzical look on the face of many of the locals – if only because the translation, "*Petit Suisse*", is the brand name for a type of cream cheese. The nickname is, in fact, a very apt reminder that for several centuries the region north of Nice belonged to the kingdom of Savoy, which covered what is now a part of western Switzerland.

The **Gorges de la Vésubie** begin at St-Jean-la-Rivière; there is a spectacular panorama from above the fortified village of **Utelle**, at **Madone d'Utelle** ➐. The sanctuary here (open daily; tel: 04 93 03 19 44; http://madone.utelle.free.fr), at

1,180 metres (3,870 ft), is on the site of an ancient shrine to a statue of the Virgin, destroyed in the French Revolution. The new church, consecrated in 1806, is still a place of pilgrimage, with simple accommodation, a restaurant and a café.

Tinée valley

The Gorges de la Vésubie end at the Plan du Var. Leaving the N202 at the Pont de la Mescla, the D2205 heads up the Tinée valley through the **Gorges de la Mescla** ➑, where spectacular slabs of rock overhang both road and river. Further up, the old village of **Isola** is today largely a doorway to the modern ski resort of **Isola 2000** ➒ (*see box below*), but it does have several of the chapels indicative of the once fervent religious life of these valleys, three *lavoirs* (wash-houses) and a communal bread oven in use until 1950.

Further up the valley, rural **St-Etienne-de-Tinée** ➓ has an important religious heritage. The walls and vault of the **Chapelle St-Sébastien** (contact tourist office for visits: St-Etienne tel: 04 93 02 41 96, Auron tel:

The "Route du Baroque Nisso-Ligure" (www.guide riviera.com) promotes the Baroque heritage of the Alpes-Maritimes and neighbouring Liguria. The richly decorated churches were the visible symbol of the Counter-Reformation, as the Catholic Church asserted its power against the Protestant Reformation. Many of them are in the Mercantour along the route Royale between Nice and Turin.

BELOW: restored mill by the Roya River.

Winter Sports in the Alpes-Maritimes

In winter, the 85 percent of the population of the Alpes-Maritimes resident near the coast suddenly seems to acquire a taste for the backcountry. The right bank of the Var becomes a fashionable artery as the Niçois head to the skiing resorts: Auron and Isola 2000 for the *sportif* in search of a conversation piece; Valberg and Beuil for the less pretentious or those more inclined to cross-country skiing. **Valberg** (www.valberg.com) is a family-oriented resort with good facilities for children, and a snowboarding park. Its *domaine* is now linked to **Beuil** (www.beuil.com), an ancient village which was once the seat of the Grimaldis. **Auron** (www.auron.com), founded in the 1930s, lines up a full range of slopes and trails for the inveterate skier, as well as a modern snowpark for snowboarders. The modern chalets, flats and ski lifts dotting the pastures are the inland equivalent of the concrete structures on the coast. However, you can also stay in some of the more charming villages in the area. Inaugurated in 1971, **Isola 2000** (www.isola2000.com) has space-age architecture, and its 120 km (75 miles) of pistes have been joined by high-thrill snowboarding and heli-skiing. Its altitude guarantees a good supply of both snow and sun.

04 93 23 02 66, generally Mon and Thur 4pm in summer) are covered with lively paintings telling the life of the martyr saint, attributed to Jean Canavesio and Jean Baleisoni, and dating from 1492. Even the nearby ski resort of **Auron** *(see box opposite)* contains the ancient **Chapelle St-Erige**, unlikely survivor amid the modern apartment blocks.

Sospel

On the southeastern edge of the Parc National is the charming Italianate town of **Sospel ⑪**. It's popular with the Mentonnais for a day out, for walking (the GR52 long-distance footpath runs through here) or for hunting in autumn. Successively under the rule of the counts of Ventimiglia, Provence and Nice, it was the second-most important town in the Comté de Nice in the Middle Ages, when it had a flourishing religious life, and in the early 18th century it was known for its literary circle. The Bévéra, a tributary of the Roya, runs through it, leaving a series of islets around the **Vieux Pont** (old bridge). The bridge is an

oddity, with a toll gate in the middle for levying tax on the salt route. Today it contains the tourist office.

North of the bridge is the oldest part of the town, a cluster of buildings with wooden balconies overlooking the river. By the river, a sheltered *lavoir* filled with water even at the height of summer still survives. On the southern side of the bridge, houses come in weathered shades of orange, yellow, ochre or red stucco, and the early 18th-century Baroque **Cathédrale St-Michel** lords it over an attractive cobbled square. Inside is an altarpiece by Francesco Brea, a member of the celebrated Niçois dynasty of painters.

You can also visit the reinforced concrete **Fort St-Roch** (open Apr, May, Oct Sat, Sun 2–6pm; June–Sept Tues–Sun 2–6pm; admission charge; tel: 04 93 04 00 70), built as part of the Maginot Line (there's another one at Ste-Agnès, further south near Menton), the defensive system of partially underground fortresses built along the eastern border of France in the 1930s.

Map on page 218

TIP

Each August, the Festival International des Orgues Historiques gives the chance to hear the historic organs housed in many of the churches of the Roya and Bévéra valleys. Tel: 04 93 04 92 05; www.royabevera.com

BELOW: road to Sospel.

Northwest of Sospel, the D2566 climbs through deep pine forests to the **Col de Turini**, with a small ski resort and a good starting point for some relatively gentle walks.

The nearby **Plateau d'Authion** was a battlefield on more than one occasion; you'll find the **Cabanes Vieilles** there, ruins of Napoleonic barracks, destroyed during combat with retreating German troops at the end of World War II.

Roya Valley and Saorge

Northeast of Sospel, the D2204 takes you over the Col de Brouis (Brouis pass) to join the Roya valley just north of **Breil-sur-Roya** ⓬. On a flat expanse of valley, the wide Roya has here been turned into an artificial lake that lies along the edge of town. Breil produces olive oil and is the centre for a type of olive that is only found in the Alpes-Maritimes, the *cailletier*.

The **Vallée de la Roya** was retained by the Italians until October 1947, because it was the only link with the Mercantour and the hunting grounds of the king of Italy.

The town of Breil makes for a restful stop. Beyond here the road, which shares the valley with the railway, gets more dramatic, passing through some steep gorges on the way to the spectacularly situated town of **Saorge** ⓭, which still has the appearance of a mountain stronghold. Packed into a cliff face, it takes a trek on foot to reach the centre, through some of the steepest cobbled alleyways imaginable. Tall, narrow houses tower over dark streets. Some people do still live here, but the young tend to be quick to move out to search for employment elsewhere. The contemporary exodus contrasts with ancient times, when it seemed like everyone was trying to invade the fortified village – unsuccessfully. Such was its reputation for impregnability that the town's would-be invaders eventually gave up trying.

The steepness does not rule out the existence of a fine Renaissance church, **St-Sauveur**, with an imposing altar of red and gold. The finely carved church organ was made in Genoa in the 19th century. Its instal-

Breil is well-worn hiking country; signed walks lead to medieval watchtowers, such as La Cruella, or to isolated chapels to the west of the village. Longer hikes lead to Sospel or La Vésubie further west.

BELOW: Saorge.

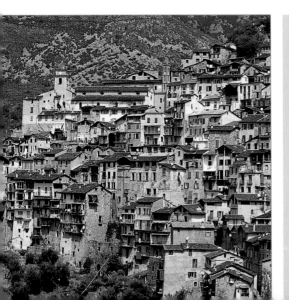

Mountain Trains

Three railway lines run into the interior of the Alpes-Maritimes. The SNCF-run Nice–Cuneo line follows the Peillon, Bévéra and Royal valleys through long tunnels and over numerous viaducts, stopping at Peillon, Sospel, Breil-sur-Roya, Saorge, La Brigue and Tende. In summer, a special tourist train, dubbed the "Train des Merveilles", leaves Nice at 9am, arriving at Tende at 10.46am, complete with tourist commentary and slowing down for photo opportunities. In winter the "train des neiges" is a special service for skiers with shuttle from Tende to Castérino. Another line joins this one from Ventimiglia in Italy to Breil-sur-Roya.

lation, and even the building of the church, would not actually have been possible without the strength and agility of the mules used to carry materials up the hill. Saorge has not forgotten the contribution the animals made (and still make) to life in the village: one of the village festivals is dedicated to St Eloi, patron saint of mules.

Monastery of Saorge

Visitors may complain about the steep alleyways but, for the Franciscan monks that live in the monastery, this all helps maintain a tranquil and serene atmosphere. The **Monastère de Saorge** (open Wed–Mon 10am–noon, 2–6pm, until 5pm in winter; admission charge; tel: 04 93 04 55 56; www.monum.fr) nestles in a small square at the top of the village, among a cluster of olive trees. A fine example of the local Baroque style, the church has an elaborate master altar with barley-sugar columns surrounding a statue of the Virgin. The whitewashed two-storey cloister is painted with several ornate sundials.

The valley here apparently has a good echo, a feature that allowed 20th-century soldiers to communicate from the ruined castle above with a nearby chateau.

Sistine Chapel of the Alps

At St-Dalmas-de-Tende, side roads lead off in one direction towards the Vallée des Merveilles, and in the other to **La Brigue ⑭**, another of those mountain villages clearly once more populated and prosperous than it is today. It has some finely carved lintels, Baroque churches, arcaded medieval houses and the ruins of the 14th-century Château Lascaris, which is floodlit at night.

However, the main reason to pause here lies 4 km (2½ miles) further east, where the simple exterior of the isolated **Chapelle de Notre-Dame-des-Fontaines** (call tourist office for visits, tel: 04 93 79 09 34) does little to prepare you for the extraordinary wealth of frescos within. Attributed to Jean Baleison and Jean Canavesi, the 15th-century cycle of the Virgin has earned it the nickname "the Sistine Chapel of the southern Alps". ❏

The chapel of Notre-Dame-des-Fontaines, near La Brigue, is a local place of pilgrimage, renowned for its vivid frescos, painted in 1492 by Canavesi of the Niçoise school.

Breil-sur-Roya

Castel du Roy
146 route de l'Aigara. Tel: 04 93 04 43 66. Open: D only. Closed: mid-Oct–Easter. €€
www.castelduroy.com
A lovely riverside hotel restaurant, with tranquil, tree-shaded terrace, serving specialities of the region.

La Brigue

Le Mirval
Rue Vincent Ferrier. Tel: 04 93 04 63 71. Open: L Sat–Thur, D daily. Closed:

Dec–Mar. €
www.lemirval.com
Delightful riverside restaurant, just outside the village. Try Italian and Niçois dishes like trout, spinach ravioli and game.

St-Martin-Vésubie

Le Boreon
Quartier La Cascade.
Open: L & D daily (weekend only Jan). Closed: mid-Nov–Dec. €
A pretty mountain chalet in the heart of the Mercantou, where hearty

cooking includes game stews and duck fillet with honey.

Sospel

Restaurant Bel Aqua
Hôtel des Etrangers, 7 boulevard de Verdun. Tel: 04 93 04 00 09. Open: L Thur–Mon, D Wed–Mon. Closed: Nov–Feb. €€
This restaurant is a favourite with locals and Mentonnais. Specialities include the local trout.

Tende

Le Prieuré
Rue Jean Médecin. Tel: 04 93 04 75 70. Open: L & D

daily. €. www.leprieure.org
This hotel and restaurant with lovely views, the starting point for the Vallée des Merveilles, is linked to an employment scheme for the disabled. The chef finds inspiration in the local mountains, producing *tourte brigasque*, terrines, mountain ham and home-made pasta with gorgonzola sauce. Summer terrace.

● ● ● ● ● ● ● ● ● ● ● ●
Prices for a three-course meal without wine. €€€€ more than €60, €€€ €40–60, €€ €25–40, € under €25.

NICE

Queen of the Riviera, capital of the Côte d'Azur, Nice is a gem of a city, with a wealth of museums, lively old town markets, and enough gardens, fountains and palm trees to raise life alfresco to an art form

With a population of around 350,000, **Nice** is a vibrant, important city, France's fifth-largest, with its second-busiest airport, an opera house and excellent philharmonic orchestra, a university, several good museums, numerous shops, and hotels and restaurants to rival the world's best.

Founded around 350 BC by the Greeks, Nikaea was built on the hill by the waterfront. Later, the Roman settlement of Cemenelum developed further inland on the Cimiez hill. When Provence was incorporated into France in 1486, Nice remained an independent *comté* and was often a pawn between the rival ambitions of the French crown and the Holy Roman Empire. After the Revolution, Nice briefly became part of France again under Napoleon, before falling under the thrall of the kingdom of Sardinia. In 1860, the population voted to become French.

Nice's Italianate legacy can still be seen in the city's culinary specialities, such as ravioli, and in the Genoan-style painted façades in the old town. But Nice was first embraced as a fashionable winter resort by English and Russian aristocrats in the 1830s. Railways, hotels, villas and gardens were all built to serve the needs of the Riviera royalty that followed in their wake. The fashion for sun and sea-bathing came in the 1920s, bringing artists and writers to the city.

Each *quartier* has its character, illustrating Nice's long and colourful history: Roman remains at Les Arènes, pastel-coloured Italianate buildings in the old town, Belle Epoque mansions overlooking the sea and startling modern architecture.

Today, the city's traditional mellow lifestyle goes hand in hand with an increasing awareness of its business potential. It is France's second-largest convention city after Paris,

Maps:
City 226
Area 234

LEFT: Baie des Anges.
BELOW: the Monday flea market on cours Saleya.

*The Museum of
Modern and
Contemporary Art
(MAMAC) has an
important collection
of French and
American Art from
the 1960s on. Le
Relève (16 bis rue
Delille) is a bar and
restaurant conve-
niently located for
the museum, with
good music and art
exhibitions.*

and the high-tech industry is growing rapidly, rivalling tourism as the
city's main revenue generator. This
technology boom has resulted in
improved services, chic new hotels
and a new tramway.

Nice divides up neatly into old and
new parts, with the tightly packed
medieval streets of Vieux Nice to the
east, in the shadow of Le Château
(not a castle but a headland), and the
broad avenues and squares of the
new town stretching out behind the
promenade des Anglais. Laid out in
the late 19th century, the new town
comprises broad avenues and
squares, and further up the hill the
elegant residential districts of Coste-
belle and Cimiez.

Vieux Nice

Dating from the 1700s, Vieux Nice
is a maze of lively, narrow streets
and pastel façades, where tiny grocers, butchers and bakers rub shoulders with nightclubs, art galleries

and internet cafés. The best place to
start exploring is the **cours Saleya**
Ⓐ, lined with cafés, brasseries, a
vibrant flower market (Tues–Sat
6am–5.30pm, Sun until 1pm) and a
fruit and vegetable market every
morning except Monday, when
there's a flea market instead. Early
risers can also hit the fish market on
place St-François.

On the south side, along the
seafront, are **Les Ponchettes**, a row
of low white buildings once used by
fishermen, now mostly galleries and
restaurants. To the north is the former
palace of the Sardinian kings, now
housing the Préfecture. On the western side is the Opéra de Nice, a feast
of Second Empire opulence.

Wander through the narrow lanes,
many filled with bars and shops selling souvenirs; take side streets to discover quiet corners; keep an eye out
for façades adorned with *trompe l'œil*
and frescos, and look up at the lintels,
some of which are inscribed.

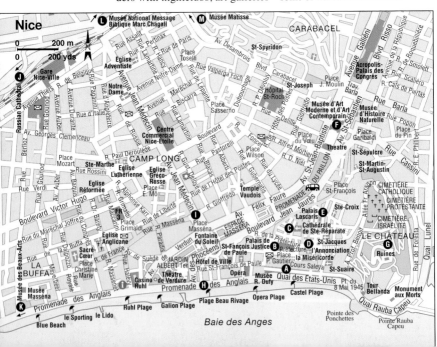

On the place du Palais de Justice is Nice's imposing law court, the **Palais de Justice** (open to the public when in session), which was inaugurated in 1892. The pavement cafés opposite are an ideal spot to enjoy this newly renovated square, and on Saturdays there's a market here selling pottery and books.

At the heart of Vieux Nice is the Baroque **Cathédrale de Ste-Réparate** (place Rossetti; open daily; free; tel: 04 93 62 34 40), named after the patron saint of the city, a young virgin brought here in the 4th century from Israel in a boat decked out with flowers and pulled by angels. Her landing place is now known as the Baie des Anges (Angels' Bay). The cathedral has a fine dome of glazed tiles and an 18th-century bell tower. The square itself is a great spot for coffee or ice cream. Another notable Baroque church, the gilt-decorated **Chapelle de l'Annonciation** , is near by, at 1 rue de la Poissonnerie.

At 15 rue Droite is the **Palais Lascaris** (open Wed–Mon 10am–6pm; free; tel: 04 93 62 05 54), a grand 17th-century mansion reflecting the city's Genoese past, with a splendid balustraded staircase, salons with painted mythological scenes and a notable decorative arts collection, including faience, tapestries and Baroque furniture; there's an 18th-century pharmacy by the entrance.

The elegant 18th-century arcaded **place Garibaldi**, at the northeastern corner of Vieux Nice, is named after the popular hero of Italian unification, who was born in the city and is buried in the cemetery on Le Château.

Outside the old town, on the promenade des Arts, is the **Musée d'Art Moderne et d'Art Contemporain** (MAMAC; tel: 04 97 13 42 01; www.mamac-nice.org; open Tues–Sun 10am–6pm; admission charge). In a striking building of octagonal marble towers joined by glass walkways, the focus here is on French and American art from the 1960s to the present, including some iconic Pop Art pieces by Andy Warhol and Roy Lichtenstein, a room devoted to local hero Yves Klein, and a large collection of Nikki de Saint-Phalle's colourful papier-mâché figures.

Map on page 226

TIP

The place to try the Niçois speciality *socca*, a kind of chick-pea pancake, is Chez René Socca on rue Miralheti (northern end of Vieux Nice, near place Garibaldi). Here you'll find all kinds of local delicacies at very low prices.

BELOW: promenade des Anglais and the pink dome of the Negresco.

Matisse lived in many locations in Nice before settling in Cimiez. One of his homes was in the big yellow house at the end of cours Saleya (1 place Charles Félix). Here, Matisse painted odalisques, drawing inspiration from the views of the sea and the flower market below.

BELOW:
the Russian Cathedral.

Sparkling views

The old town's eastern extremity is flanked by **Le Château** , the site of a pleasant park on a hill – the 12th-century castle was demolished by Louis XIV in 1706. There are a couple of rides for kids, an artificial waterfall and a splendidly Baroque cemetery, but most people make the climb for the marvellous panoramic views of the city from the top; if you don't want to walk, you can take the lift (at the end of quai des Etats-Unis).

Promenade des Anglais

The **promenade des Anglais** , funded in the 1920s by Nice's English colony, is a palm tree-lined walkway running along the seafront of the sweeping Baie des Anges. Despite being next to a busy main road running 5 km (3 miles) along the beach, the 'prom' is still *the* place for a stroll and a spot of people-watching: glamorous Italians, retired Niçois, young lovers, not to mention joggers, rollerbladers and cyclists, all come here to enjoy the sea views and soak up the sun and atmosphere. Nice's grand Belle Epoque hotels look on;

at No. 37 is the magnificent **Hôtel Negresco**, built in 1912, where F. Scott Fitzgerald stayed. The infamous American dancer Isadora Duncan spent her last months at the Hôtel Negresco in 1927. It was outside the hotel that she had her fatal accident, when her scarf caught in the wheels of her Bugatti and broke her neck.

A little further on, the **Palais de la Méditerranée** is a modern casino and luxury hotel with a striking art-deco façade. Behind the Negresco, the **Musée d'Art et d'Histoire Palais Masséna** (65 rue de France and 35 promenade des Anglais; tel: 04 93 88 11 34; due to reopen mid-2007), in a lavish villa built in 1898, is being refurbished as a museum of Nice's art and history.

New town

Behind the promenade des Anglais lies the new town, which developed in the late 19th and early 20th centuries, laid out with garden squares, fanciful villas and Belle Epoque and art-deco buildings. This is the commercial area, and **Avenue Jean Médecin**, a wide thoroughfare lined with plane trees, is the main business and shopping street. **Place Masséna** , at its southern end, is the heart of the city, well placed for Vieux Nice, the promenade des Anglais and the shopping district; it's a fine square lined with 19th-century neoclassical buildings painted in shades of ochre and red. With the **Jardin Albert Ier** to the west and **Espace Masséna** to the east, this is a refreshing oasis of fountains and ornamental gardens.

Cathedrals and museums

A couple of blocks west of the station, on avenue Nicolas II, the **Russian Cathedral** (open daily 9am–noon, 2.30–5pm, June–Sept until 6pm) is a startling reminder of Nice's once thriving Russian colony. Complete with five onion domes, precious

icons and an ornate gilded iconostasis, this is more 17th-century Moscow than Belle Epoque France.

At the western end of the beach, a grand Belle Epoque villa built for Russian royalty houses the **Musée des Beaux-Arts Jules Cheret** (33 Avenue des Baumettes; tel: 04 92 15 28 28; open Tues–Sun 10am–6pm; admission charge). Here you can see European fine arts from the 17th to 20th centuries, with highlights from Brueghel, Dufy, Bonnard, Sisley and Rodin.

Continuing west along the promenade, almost at Nice airport, you'll come to the exotic, flower-filled **Parc Phoenix**. Set by a lake on the edge of the park, the **Musée des Arts Asiatiques** (tel: 04 92 29 37 00; open Wed–Mon 10am–5pm, May–mid-Oct until 6pm; www.arts-asiatiques. com), in a spectacular circular building designed by Japanese architect Kenzo Tange, has a fine collection of Asian artefacts. You can participate in a tea ceremony in the tea pavilion (tel: 04 92 29 37 02; Sun 3pm and 4pm, not 1st Sun of month; reservations necessary).

Another museum well worth a visit is the **Musée National Message Biblique Marc Chagall** (tel: 04 93 53 87 20; avenue du Docteur Ménard; www.musee-chagall. fr; open Wed–Mon 10am–5pm, July–Sept until 6pm; admission charge). This is a phenomenal collection of Chagall's works, showing his vast, exuberant canvases illustrating stories from the Old Testament (hence *Message Biblique*).

Cimiez

The fashionable residential area of Cimiez developed on the hills overlooking town in the late 19th century; here you'll find palm-filled gardens, extravagant Belle Epoque villas and pastel-painted hotels, with the crowning jewel being the Hôtel Excelsior Régina (71 avenue Régina), built in 1895. A statue of Queen Victoria in front commemorates her frequent visits here. It was later converted into apartments, one of which Matisse lived in during World War II.

Cimiez is also the site of Roman Nice. Set amid olive groves in a park known locally as Les Arènes, the

Roman ruins in Cimiez, part of the archaeological park known as Les Arènes.

BELOW: costume parade at the Nice carnival.

Carnaval de Nice

Nice celebrates Mardi Gras with the largest pre-Lent carnival in France (www.nicecarnaval.com), culminating in a spectacular explosion of fireworks above the Baie des Anges. For two weeks around Shrove Tuesday huge papier-mâché floats proceed through the town amid confetti battles, bands and throngs of spectators. Highlights include the *bataille des fleurs*, when thousands and thousands of fresh flowers are tossed into the crowds, and the ceremonial burning of *Sa Majesté Carnaval*, the carnival king, on the promenade des Anglais at the end of the festival. If you want to join in the spectacle, make sure you book your accommodation well in advance.

Map on page 226

Maps:
City 226
Area 234

Heading west out of Nice, along the route de Bellet, the terraced vineyards on the hills of Bellet soon come into view. This is the tiny and rather fashionable wine district of Bellet, one of the smallest appellations in France. Bellet wine is very hard to find outside Nice.

BELOW: the perched village of Peille.

Musée Archéologique (tel: 04 93 81 59 57; open Wed–Mon 10am–6pm; admission charge) includes Roman baths and an amphitheatre – the site of Nice's jazz festival in July.

Henri Matisse

Also in the park is the **Musée Matisse** (164 avenue des Arènes de Cimiez; tel: 04 93 81 08 08; open Wed–Mon 10am–5pm, Apr–Sept until 6pm; admission charge), set in a red-ochre 17th-century Genoese villa and its modern underground extension. Matisse *(see page 40)* loved Nice and its "clear, crystalline, precise, limpid" light; before his death in 1954 he bequeathed many works to the city, which form the core of this fabulous collection.

Matisse and Raoul Dufy are buried in the cemetery of the **Notre-Dame monastery** (tel: 04 93 81 00 04); the adjoining church has three medieval masterpieces by Louis Bréa and a monumental Baroque altar; the monastery's gardens are in a beautiful setting, with cypress trees, climbing roses, and a sweeping panorama of the Baie des Anges.

To the west of Cimiez is the 18th-century **Villa Arson** (20 avenue Stephen Liegeard; tel: 04 92 07 73 73; open Wed–Mon 2–6pm, June–Sept until 7pm; free), home to the Centre National d'Art Contemporain and the hub of the city's avant-garde scene.

The Arrière-Pays Niçois

The hinterland of Nice is studded with medieval hilltop villages, built for protection during the war-torn Middle Ages. After years of neglect and depopulation, they are attracting a new generation of artists, craftspeople and holidaymakers.

Peillon ❷, 15 km (9 miles) east of Nice, clings like an eagle's eyrie onto a jagged ridge above the river. Vaulted alleys and steep stairways are lined with 16th-century houses, and the whole village is remarkably unspoilt. In the Chapelle des Pénitents Blancs on the edge of the village are dramatic 15th-century frescos of the Passion of Christ.

Further along steep narrow roads and hairpin bends stands the perched village of **Peille** ❸, with some lovely Renaissance and Gothic fountains, doorways and stonework amid the cobbled alleyways.

Coaraze ❹, another delightful village balancing at an altitude of 650 metres (2,100 ft), calls itself *le village du soleil*. Wander through the narrow cobbled streets and look out for the sundials, which have been a feature here since Jean Cocteau decorated the town hall with one. Next to the lizard mosaic on place Félix-Giordan is a poem relating the local legend of how the villagers caught the devil, who cut off his tail to escape. (Coaraze derives from the Provençal words 'coa raza' meaning 'cut tail'.)

On the edge of the village is the **Chapelle Bleue**, named after the blue murals created by Ponce de Léon in 1965. Here in all its intensity is the azure blue for which the region is famous. ❑

RESTAURANTS AND BARS

Nice

L'Ane Rouge
7 quai des Deux Emmanuel.
Tel: 04 93 89 49 63. Open: L
& D Fri–Tues, D only Thur.
€€€. www.anerougenice.com
The best of the restaurants on the Vieux Port.
The speciality is fish,
although you will also
find some meat dishes.

Café des Fleurs
13 cours Saleya. Tel 04 93
62 31 33. Open: L daily. €
Traditional bar with zinc
counter and wooden
tables inside, terrace
outside for coffee, tea
and selection of beers.

La Cantine de Lulu
26 rue Alberti. Tel: 04 93 62
15 33. Open: Mon–Fri.
Closed Mon pm & Aug. €
Friendly, unpretentious
café serving Niçois classics like courgette-flower
fritters, mesclun salad
and daube de boeuf.

Chez René Socca
2 rue Miralheti
Tel: 04 9392 05 73. Open: L
& D Tues–Sun. Closed three
weeks in Jan. €
Popular local place for
socca; self-service with
basic wooden tables.

Le Comptoir
20 rue St-François de Paule.
Tel: 04 93 92 08 80. Open:
L & D daily Jun–Sept;
Mon–Sat Oct–May. €€
A 1930s-style art-deco bar
and restaurant perfect
for late-night dining.

Fenocchio
2 place Rosetti. Tel: 04 93 80
72 52. Open daily. Closed
Nov–Feb. €

Wonderful outside café
on a square that's
perfect for people-watching, famous for the
best selection of Italian
ice cream in Nice.

Grand Café de Turin
5 place Garibaldi. Open:
daily all day. €€
www.cafedeturin.com
This classic seafood
brasserie is a local institution, though staff can be
grumpy and regulars
claim it has lost some of
its charm since a recent
expansion. A good place
to people-watch.

Jouni Atelier du Goût
10 rue Lascaris. Tel: 04 97
08 14 80. Open: L & D daily.
€€€. www.jouni.fr
Scandinavian chef Journi
Tourmanen, one of
Nice's most inventive
new talents, works wonders with traditional
Mediterranean ingredients in this little bistro.

La Maison de Marie
5 rue Masséna. Tel : 04 93
82 15 93. Open: L & D daily.
€€
www.lamaisondemarie.com
Dine in an attractive
courtyard or a sleek dining room just off rue
Masséna. Mod Med and
French classics. Look out
for some good Corsican
bottles on the wine list.

La Merenda
4 rue Terasse. No phone.
Open: L & D Mon–Fri. €€
This tiny bistro in the old
town is considered by
many to serve the best
traditional Niçois cuisine

in the city, although the
lack of phone (stop by
ahead to bag a table) and
weekend closing makes
eating here difficult.

La Petite Maison
11 rue St-Francois de Paule.
Tel: 04 93 85 71 53.
Open: L & D Mon–Sat. €€
A former grocer's shop,
this restaurant serves
traditional Niçoise specialities and is extremely
popular with the locals.

Restaurant du Gésu
1 place du Gésu. Tel: 04 93
62 26 46. Open: L & D
Mon–Sat. Closed mid-Dec–mid-Jan. €
Petits farcis, grilled red
peppers and pizzas are
among the rustic fare
served at this budget joint
in Vieux Nice, though you
come here for the raucous atmosphere more
than the food. The ceiling
draped with football
scarves from all over the
world matches the young
international clientele.

Le Safari
1 cours Saleya. Tel: 04 93 80
18 44. Open: L & D Daily. €€
www.restaurantsafari.com
This atmospheric
brasserie overlooking the
flower market draws an
eclectic mix of locals and
visitors. Niçois specialities include marinated
peppers, bagna cauda
and courgette-flower fritters. Wood-fired pizzas,
too. Serves all afternoon.

Le Zucca Magica
4 bis quai Papacino. tel: 04
93 56 25 27. Open: L & D

Tues–Sat. €
www.lazuccamagica.com
The magic pumpkin is
that rare thing in France: a
vegetarian restaurant
and, what's more, one
with culinary ambition.
The principle is a daily
changing menu going
from soup to dessert via
pastas and gratins. Busy.

The Hinterland

Auberge de Bellet
St-Roman de Bellet. Tel: 04
93 37 92 51.Open: L & D
Tues–Sun. €€
Vintage wines and delicacies like lobster, pigeon
and garlic stew, in Nice's
most famous vineyard.

Auberge de la Madone
3 place Auguste Arnulf, Peillon Village. Tel: 04 93 79 91
17. Open: L & D Thur–Tues.
Closed Nov to Jan, except
Christmas hols. €€€
Father and son duo
Christian and Thomas
Millo produce an
imaginative gastronomic
version of regional cuisine
in this perched village 17
km (10½ miles) north of
Nice, much of it using
local produce.

PRICE CATEGORIES

Prices for a three-course
meal without wine. Note
that many restaurants
have a less expensive
lunch menu.
€ = under €25
€€ = €25–€40
€€€ = €40–€60
€€€€ = more than €60

THE RIVIERA FROM CANNES TO CAGNES

More than a century after France's azure coast
established itself as a tourist hotspot, it remains a
fashionable holiday destination. Lovely (if crowded)
beaches, a balmy climate, a great artistic legacy and
an unspoilt hinterland are key components of its allure

Originally a winter destination favoured by the British and Russians, the stretch of coast from Cannes to the Italian border was dubbed the French Riviera by the Italians and the Côte d'Azur by the French – the latter term coined in 1887 by French writer Stephen Liegeard, who was inspired by the deep blue of its sea.

In 1923, the Hôtel du Cap stayed open over the summer for the first time, heralding the birth of the summer season and a new era in tourism, kick-started by glamorous American visitors. Scott Fitzgerald, Ernest Hemingway and Dorothy Parker were joined by artists and writers, Colette and Picasso among them, who migrated to the area, drawn by the quality of the light and cheap rents. They all helped build the Riviera myth with its jazz-age images of a hedonistic lifestyle centred on the new pastime of sunbathing and cocktail parties.

An even greater revolution came with the advent of paid holidays, introduced by France's first socialist government in 1936, and the continued democratisation of holiday-taking after World War II. Consequently, the coast oscillates between two extremes: the Côte d'Azur of the very rich – a privileged world of yachts, villas and beautiful people –

versus the campsites and cheap hotels catering for backpackers and budget travellers in search of their own slice of Mediterranean paradise.

Map on pages 234–5

Cannes

Long an insignificant fishing village, **Cannes ❺** was first put on the map in 1834 when the British Lord High Chancellor, Lord Brougham, was forced to winter here due to an outbreak of cholera in Nice. Brougham was so taken with Cannes that he had a villa built here, thus starting a

LEFT: Cannes' crowded beach and La Croisette. **BELOW:** one man and his dog.

One theory has it that Cannes takes its name from the Provençal cano, for the reeds in the marshes that used to surround the town. Another more probable explanation comes from the Ligurian word for high ground or peak – the original fortified settlement was on Le Suquet hill where the castle still stands.

The Belle Epoque Hotel Carlton, a Cannes landmark.

trend for wintering in the town. Within three years, 30 new villas had been built and, the following year, the harbourside avenue now called La Croisette was laid.

Cannes's international status was cemented with the establishment of the town's film festival *(see pages 242–3)*, inaugurated in 1946. For ten days each May, the town becomes the centre of the film universe, thronged by movie magnates, film stars and fans. However, for all its glamour, Cannes qualifies as a real town. Year-round trade fairs and conferences give it a permanent population and an economy not entirely reliant on tourism. Film stars may stock up on designer wear along rue d'Antibes and La Croisette, but out of the festival season, the town has a pleasantly lived-in feel.

La Croisette

Sweeping east along the seafront is **La Croisette**, a long promenade lined with plush hotels and apartments on one side, manicured beaches and smart beach clubs on the other. At No. 1 La Croisette is the **Palais des Festivals et des Congrès**, which since 1983 has been home to the Film Fes-

tival (tours Wed afternoons by appointment only; tourist office tel: 04 93 39 24 53). On the ground outside this brutalist block of concrete, nicknamed the "Bunker", film stars have left a trail of hand prints.

La Croisette's hotels, among the grandest in Cannes, pay homage to the resort's glamorous history. The oldest and most elaborate of these is the **Carlton** at No. 58, with a wedding-cake façade that has barely changed since it was built in 1912. The pepper-pot cupolas at each end are said to be modelled on the breasts of la Belle Otero, a celebrated dancer and courtesan of the art-deco period. At No. 14, the **Majestic** is another piece of Belle Epoque finery and host to the Villa des Lys, one of the best restaurants on the coast. Further down the drag, at No. 73, is the art-deco **Hôtel Martinez**, the largest hotel in France when it opened in 1929.

Virtually swamped by the **Noga Hilton Hotel**, a concrete eyesore built in 1992, is **La Malmaison**, the only surviving part of the original Grand Hotel – 19th-century forerunner of today's seafront giants, since replaced by a 1970s high-rise. The elegant building houses temporary art exhib-

itions (open Wed–Mon; admission charge; tel: 04 93 99 04 04).

The harbour and Le Suquet

West of the Palais des Festivals sits Cannes' old harbour. Behind the quay's brasseries and cafés lies pedestrianised rue Meynardier and the excellent covered market, **Marché Forville** (food market mornings daily in summer, Tues–Sun in winter; flea-market all day Mon). Cannes' oldest neighbourhood, **Le Suquet**, still with its secret alleyways and half-hidden *auberges* and bistros, climbs up the hill to **place de la Castre** and commanding views of the shoreline.

The square's 19th-century church, **Notre-Dame d'Espérance**, backs onto a castle and tower built by Lérins monks in the 11th century to guard against Saracen attack. The castle, together with the 12th-century Romanesque Chapelle Ste-Anne, house the **Musée de la Castre** (tel: 04 93 38 55 26; open Apr–June & Sept Tues–Sun 10am–1pm, 2–6pm, July–Aug daily 10am–7pm, Oct–Mar Tues–Sun 10am–1pm, 2–5pm; admission charge), which deals with ethnology, archaeology, the art of the region and musical instruments.

Le Cannet

A short bus ride away from Cannes is **Le Cannet ⑥**, once a separate village now more or less engulfed by its bigger neighbour. Le Cannet is notable as the former home of the painter Pierre Bonnard, who lived in the Villa du Bosquet from 1939 until his death in 1947. However, it's also worth visiting for its good-value restaurants, quirky narrow streets and musical evenings in summer.

Iles de Lérins

If you want to escape the crowds on the Côte, take a boat from quai Laubeuf, in Cannes' old harbour, and head for the delightful **Iles de Lérins**.

At a mere 400 metres (1,300 ft) in width, **Ile St-Honorat ⑦**, mainly covered by parasol pines, eucalyptus and cypresses, is the smaller of the two Lérins islands. Although it may seem like a quiet backwater today, the island has an impressive ecclesiastical history, dating back to a monastery founded by St Honorat in the 5th century *(see right)*. For centuries it was a religious centre where many important bishops – including Ireland's St Patrick – trained. It was so powerful that it

Map on pages 234–5

Most of the monastic buildings on Ile St-Honorat date from the 11th and 12th centuries. However, the abbey church (open daily, closed for Sun services;www.abbaye delerins.com) was built in the late 19th century by the Cistercian monks who bought the island in 1869. There's also a small museum and a shop where the monks sell a herb-based liqueur called Lérina.

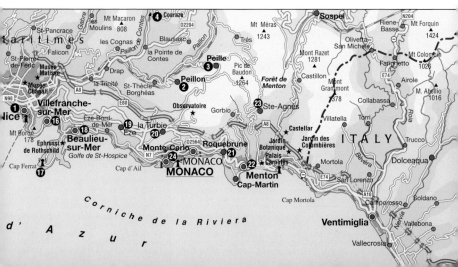

BELOW RIGHT:
Picasso in 1948.

owned much of the land along the Mediterranean coast, including Cannes. Note there are no restaurants on the island, so bring a picnic.

Named after Honorat's possibly non-existent sister, **Ste-Marguerite ❽**, the larger island, is home to the fortress that featured in Alexandre Dumas's *Man in the Iron Mask*, the 17th-century **Fort Royal**. Inside, the **Musée de la Mer** (open Tues–Sun 10.30am–1.15pm, 2.15–5.45pm, Oct–Mar until 4.45pm; admission charge) displays artefacts salvaged from nearby wrecks, including a 1st-century AD Roman ship. If you're looking for real seclusion, veer away from the crowded port and you'll find quiet paths through the woods and rocky inlets for bathing.

Mougins

Just 5 km (2½ miles) inland from Cannes, **Mougins ❾**, which over-shadowed the former during the Middle Ages, has guarded its image as a pristine southern hill village. Its steep, narrow streets, terraces trailing flowers and concealed mansions, as well as some of the best restaurants on the

Côte, make it a chic place for Cannes conference-goers to hang out.

In the 1920s and 1930s, when it became the done thing to holiday on the Côte d'Azur, Picabia built his eccentric Château de Mai here, and other artists, such as Cocteau and Man Ray, also arrived, enticed by the location and the excellent quality of the light. Picasso lived here from 1961 until his death in 1973. The town's artistic connections are now-adays reflected in its numerous art and craft galleries. For photography-lovers there is the **Musée de la Photographie** (67 rue de l'Eglise; open July–Aug daily, Sept–Oct and Dec–June Wed–Sun pm only, closed Nov; admission charge; tel: 04 93 75 85 67), which has numerous photographs of Picasso, as well as works by master snapper Robert Doisneau.

Vallauris

Another town with strong links to Picasso is **Vallauris ❿**, the next main stop south east of Mougins, hidden in a valley of its own barely 3 km (2 miles) from the sea. Ceramics have been the mainstay of Vallauris for

Picasso's Pots

In 1946, Picasso discovered Vallauris when he visited a pottery exhibition and the Madoura workshop of Suzanne and Georges Ramié. In 1948, he settled in the town with his companion Françoise Gilot. Although he had experimented with ceramics in Paris in the 1920s, this was the start of a true fascination with clay and a burst of creativity that saw the production of some 4,000 pieces of pottery before his death in 1973. To begin with, Picasso did not make the plates and jugs himself but worked in close collaboration with the Ramiés and their craftsmen, painting the pots with wonderfully free, swift designs of faces, fish or bullfighting scenes that often show him at his most joyful. If some items were merely series decorated by the artist (and he also licensed Madoura to produce some of his designs in limited editions), he was later to mould and pummel the damp clay to create new forms in zoomorphic vessels. His heads, owls or birds and tanagra-shaped vases are true sculptural one-offs. Long dismissed by art critics as "not proper Picasso" and by art potters as "not proper pottery", Picasso's pots are now seen as a true aspect of the artist's oeuvre and a contribution to the vitality of modern ceramics.

more than four centuries, and unfortunately the main shopping street is now clogged with tacky shops of that ilk. Uphill, however, visitors can experience the more highbrow side to Vallauris in the shape of the town's three museums, all housed in the largely Renaissance chateau.

In the chateau chapel, the **Musée National Picasso La Guerre et la Paix** (Château de Vallauris; open Wed–Mon 10am–noon, 2–6pm, 5pm in winter; admission charge; tel: 04 93 64 71 83; www.musee-picasso-vallauris.fr) contains Picasso's ode to peace, completed in 1952, with its two massive panels *War* and *Peace*, and a third panel depicting figures of the four continents around a dove of peace. Some of the pottery made by Picasso during the six years when he had his Fournas atelier (now 95 avenue Pablo Picasso), is exhibited in the **Musée de la Céramique** (same hours), also in the chateau. The collection traces the pottery heritage of Vallauris: from early domestic wares, via some spectacular Art Nouveau forms by the Massier dynasty, to modern art pottery. A third museum,

the **Musée Magnelli** (same hours) contains paintings by abstract painter Alberto Magnelli. Just outside the chateau stands Picasso's bronze of a man holding a sheep, which he presented to the town in 1949.

The **Madoura Pottery** (avenue Suzanne et Georges Ramié; open Mon–Fri), set a few yards away from the main avenue Clemenceau, still retains the copyright to Picasso's ceramics. Today, on top of its numerous pottery workshops, Vallauris keeps the pottery tradition alive with the Biennale de la Céramique every even numbered year.

Antibes

Back on the coast, the historic port of **Antibes** contrasts with the luxurious villas and tropical vegetation of the Cap d'Antibes and the indulgent party town of **Juan-les-Pins**, renowned for its clubs, expensive boutiques and casinos. Founded by the Phoenician Greeks, who named it Antipolis, Antibes was a keystone in French naval strategy. Having been sacked twice by Emperor Charles V in the 16th century, Kings Henri II

Map on pages 234–5

TIP

The Musée Peynet in Vieux Antibes (place Nationale; open Tues–Sun 10am–noon, 2–6pm) presents comic drawings by cartoonist Raymond Peynet (creator of "les Amoureux", the lovers) and other drawings by newspaper cartoonists.

BELOW: Plage de la Garoupe, Cap d'Antibes.

Held each July in the Pinède Gould, Jazz à Juan is one of the world's leading jazz festivals and the place to catch first-rate names of American jazz, blues and fusion, such as B.B. King, Dizzy Gillespie, Wayne Shorter and Keith Jarrett, in a stunning setting againt the Mediterranean Sea. Recently established Jazz Révélations is a smaller festival in April seeking out new acts. www. antibes-juanlespins.com

BELOW: relaxing among the fishing boats in Juan-les-Pins; Golfe Juan.

and Henri III added fortifications; and in 1680 Louis XIV brought in his brilliant military engineer Vauban to give it the impressive star-shaped ramparts and bastions that line the shore.

Antibes has a splendid cobble-stoned **Vieille Ville** (old town) with an excellent covered market on cours Masséna (open Tues–Sun), the largest yachting marina in Europe, and a big expat English community who dominate its bars and pubs. During the 1940s, Picasso lived for six months in the **Château Grimaldi**. The chateau now houses the **Musée Picasso** (tel: 04 92 90 54 20; closed until end 2007 for renovation), which features his celebrated work *Joie de Vivre* (the joy of life), as well as sculptures by Germaine Richier on the terrace. Looking over the port is the **Fort Carré** (guided visits every 30 mins Tues–Sun 10am–6pm, 4.30pm in winter; admission charge).

Juan-les-Pins

On the western side of the promontory, **Juan-les-Pins'**  reputation for hedonism is well established: self-indulgent visitors, including the F.

Scott Fitzgeralds and other wealthy American socialites, were swinging here as early as the 1920s. The adjoining **Cap d'Antibes** features the jet-setters' favourite, Hôtel du Cap – Eden Roc, the hotel that set the trend for the summer season, and Bacon, a top fish restaurant. La Garoupe, the long sandy beach there, is still the place to enjoy the sun, and there are some public stretches between the snooty private beach concessions.

The **Villa Eilen Roc** (open Sept–June house Wed 9am–noon, 1.30–5pm; gardens Tues–Wed 9.30am–5pm), designed by Charles Garnier of Paris and Monte Carlo opera houses fame, has palm tree-filled gardens where the Musiques au Cœur classical music festival is staged every July. Above the beach, the **Jardin de la Villa Thuret** (41 boulevard du Cap; open Mon–Fri, summer 8am–6pm, winter 8.30am– 5.30pm), with its jungle-like tangle of plants, was created in 1857, and is one of the oldest botanic gardens on the Riviera.

Heading east from Antibes, **Marineland** (www.marineland.fr; open Feb–Dec daily 10am–7pm;

admission charge) is a huge marine theme park with afternoon whale and dolphin shows. On the same site are Aquasplash (open June–Sept; admission charge), an aquatic fun park; crazy golf; and the cowboy-themed farm, La Petite Ferme du Far West (open daily; admission charge).

Biot

The artist Fernand Léger (1881–1955) adopted **Biot** ⑬, another medieval perched village about 3 km (2 miles) from the sea, as his outpost. The **Musée National Fernand Léger** (tel: 04 92 91 50 30; open Wed–Sun 10am–noon, 2–6pm, Sept–June until 5pm; admission charge) has a vast ceramic mosaic on its exterior, and is the permanent home of nearly 400 of the artist's paintings, tapestries, stained glass and ceramics, surrounded by a garden with giant versions of some of his sculptures.

Like Vallauris, Biot was long known for its potteries – the speciality here being sturdy clay storage jars. Since 1956, however, it has been more associated with glass and the beautiful creations of the **Verrerie de Biot**, famed for its bubble glass. You can watch the master glass-blowers at work in the factory, which is located at the foot of the village; adjoining it are a shop and showroom, a small glass museum and the Galerie Internationale du Verre, exhibiting the work of international art glassmakers.

Villeneuve-Loubet

The resort of **Villeneuve-Loubet** ⑭ is often associated with the gigantic pyramidal forms of the **Marina Baie des Anges** development (contact tourist office for visits; tel: 04 92 02 66 16). Built in the 1970s, it was long decried as one of the monstrosities of coastal over-construction. Today it has become a part of the landscape, its clever system of stepped-back

terraces and roof gardens seeming positively restrained compared to the urban sprawl that surrounds it.

Villeneuve-Loubet also has its old medieval hill town, located 3 km (2 miles) inland up the Loup valley. Above the village, which is characterised by steep, narrow lanes and ancient buildings that resist gentrification, is the imposing medieval **castle** where French king François I stayed for three weeks in 1538 for the signature of the Treaty of Nice. Although the castle is still privately owned, it is now open for guided visits (open July–Aug Wed, Sun; Sept–June two Sundays a month; reserve with tourist office, tel: 04 92 02 66 16). The path round the castle walls has good views out to the Baie des Anges.

Lower down the hill, the **Musée Escoffier de l'Art Culinaire** (open Dec–Oct Sun–Fri 2–6pm, 7pm in summer; www.fondation-escoffier. org) preserves the memory of Auguste Escoffier, "king of chefs and chef of kings", in the house where he was born in 1846. Exhibits include Escoffier's handwritten recipe book

Map on pages 234–5

TIP

Napoleon's landing on the beach at Golfe-Juan on 1 May 1815 following his escape from the island of Elba is re-enacted in period costume each year on the first weekend in March. Visit http://napoleon.golfe. juan.free.fr or www. vallauris-golfe-juan.fr

BELOW: bubble glass *(verre à bulles)* of Biot.

Map on pages 234–5

On the ground floor of the Château-Musée-Grimaldi, a small museum pays homage to the olive tree, while upstairs are paintings of the Montparnasse cabaret singer Susy Solidor by artists such as Cocteau.

BELOW:
Musée Renoir, Cagnes.

and photographs of Australian soprano Dame Nelly Melba, for whom he invented the Peach Melba.

Cagnes-sur-Mer

Cagnes-sur-Mer ⑮ splits into three parts. At the lower end, Cros-de-Cagnes is a rather downmarket modern seaside resort, with the Hippodrome de la Côte d'Azur racetrack and a pebbly beach backing onto the road and railway line, and the added disadvantage of frequent aircraft noise. Cagnes-sur-Mer, with its public park and a good covered market (mornings only) occupies the middle ground. And rising up above the both of them is the medieval town of **Haut-de-Cagnes**, a maze of narrow stepped streets crowned by the crenellated tower of the **Château-Musée Grimaldi** (open May–Sept Wed–Mon 10am–noon, 2–6pm, Oct–Apr Wed–Mon 10am–noon, 2–5pm, closed 2 weeks Nov; admission charge).

Originally a simple watchtower belonging to the Grimaldi family, in the Renaissance it was transformed into a comfortable residence by Jean-Henri Grimaldi, with rooms leading off an arcaded galleried courtyard. The highlight is the grand ceremonial room on the first floor. Its ceiling painted by Italian artist Giulio Benso Pietra is a vertiginous feat, with *trompe l'œil* vaulting around a depiction of Phaethon falling out of the sky with his chariot and horses.

Cagnes was also where the elderly Renoir lived from 1906 to 1919. Set in an ancient olive grove above terraced orange trees, the house which he built at Les Collettes, just east of Cagnes-sur-Mer, is now the **Musée Renoir** (open May–Sept Wed–Mon 10am–noon, 2–6pm, Oct–Apr Wed–Mon 10am–noon, 2–5pm, closed 2 weeks Nov; admission charge). It remains much as it was when the artist lived here. Paintings of his garden, of his granddaughter Coco, and a version of his *Large Bathers* reflect the high tonality of his late works painted under the burning southern sun. There are also several of the bronze sculptures Renoir increasingly turned to at the end of his life, crafted in collaboration with his assistant Richard Guino. ❑

RESTAURANTS AND BARS

Antibes/Juan-les-Pins

Bacon
Boulevard de Bacon, Cap
d'Antibes. Tel: 04 93 61 50
02. Open: L Wed–Sun, D
Tues–Sun. Closed: Nov–Feb.
€€€€
www.restaurantdebacon.com
A legendary luxury fish
restaurant founded in
1950 with views across
the bay to old Antibes.
Go for the catch of the
day or splurge on the
renowned bouillabaisse.

Les Pêcheurs
10 Boulevard Maréchal Juin,
Cap d'Antibes, Juan-les-Pins.
Tel: 04 92 93 13 30. Open:
July–Aug D Wed–Mon;
Sept–June L & D Thur–Mon.
€€€€
www.lespecheurs-lecap.com
Under the same owner-
ship as the Juana hotel,
this new waterside
restaurant complex with
private sandy beach has
rejuvenated the local
scene with its stylish
contemporary decor in
teak and brushed
aluminium and the
acclaimed modern cook-
ing of Francis Chauveau.

Taverne du Safranier
1 place du Safranier, Antibes.
Tel: 04 93 34 80 50. €€
Animated bistro in Vieux
Antibes, popular with arty
locals. Specialities
include marinated sar-
dines, ravioli and a gigantic lemon meringue tart.

Les Vieux Murs
25 promenade Amiral de
Grasse, Antibes. Tel: 04 93 34
06 73. Open: L Wed–Sun, D
Tues–Sun. €€€
www.lesvieuxmurs.com
This long-standing estab-
lishment with vaulted
rooms looking out over
the ramparts has
recently changed hands,
gaining a cocktail bar.
Chef Thierry Grattorola
keeps up the culinary
kudos with solid south-
ern dishes such as hare
with gnocchi.

Biot

Galerie des Arcades
16 place des Arcades. Tel: 04
93 65 01 04. Open: L
Tues–Sun, D Tues–Sat.
Closed: Nov. €€
This popular village inn on
Biot's main square
doubles as an art gallery.
Provençal cuisine is
served indoors or under
the medieval arcades.

Cagnes-sur-Mer

Le Cagnard
Rue de Pontis-Long, Haut-de-
Cagnes. Tel: 04 93 20 73 21.
Open: L Fri–Wed, D daily.
Closed: mid-Nov to mid-Dec.
€€€€
www.le-cagnard.com
In an ancient fortified
building, chef Jean-Yves
Johany presents elegant,
southern-inflected clas-
sic cooking, such as foie
gras pigeon and sea
bream with artichokes.

Cannes

Astoux et Brun
27 rue Félix Faure. Tel: 04 93
39 21 87. Food served all day
daily. €€. www.astouxbrun.com
At this brasserie over-
looking the old port, it's
not the decor that counts
but the huge platters of
excellent shellfish.

Aux Bons Enfants
80 rue Meynardier. No phone.
Open: L & D Mon–Sat. Cash
only. €
Opened in 1935 and still
run by the same family,
this bistro is popular for
its generous home cook-
ing. Expect starters like
caponata or grilled
sardines, followed by beef
daube or grilled lamb.

Les 3 Portes
16 rue des Frères Pradignac.
Tel: 04 93 38 91 70. Open: L
Tues–Fri; D Tues–Sat (D only
in summer). €€€
www.3portes.com
Fashionable food for the
fashionable set:
minimalist decor and
light dishes with an
exotic touch.

Villa de Lys
Hôtel Majestic, 10 La
Croisette. Tel: 04 92 98
77 00. Open: D Tues–Sat.
Closed: mid-Nov–Dec. €€€€
www.lucienbarriere.com
Chef Bruno Oger has
made this one of Cannes'
top restaurants with his
balance of creativity and
grand tradition, and his
use of superb ingredients.

Mougins

Alain Llorca Moulin
de Mougins
Avenue Notre-Dame de Vie.
Tel: 04 93 75 78 24. Open: L
& D Tues–Sun. €€€€
www.moulin-mougins.com
In this legendary
restaurant, hotly tipped
chef Alain Llorca presents
his "deconstructed" take
on Provence and the Med.
Try the weekly changing
déjeuner de soleil lunch
menu, with inventions
such as cocoa beans with
chorizo and mussels; or
put the whole table in
Llorca's hands for the
ronde de tapas menu.

Brasserie de la
Mediterranée
Place de la Mairie. Tel: 04 93
90 03 47. Open: L daily, D
Mon–Sat. €€
www.restaurantlamediterranee.
com
A casual-chic restaurant
with trad brasserie decor
and an appealing choice
of southern favourites.

Le Mas Candille
Boulevard Clément Rebuffel.
Tel: 04 92 28 43 43. Open: L
and D daily. Closed: Jan. €€€€
www.lemascandille.com
Despite the rather stuffy
tented decor, the modern
Provençal cooking at this
luxury hotel is excellent.
There's also an informal
poolside restaurant in July
and August.

PRICE CATEGORIES

Prices for a three-course
meal without wine. Note
that many restaurants
have a less expensive
lunch menu.
€ = under €25
€€ = €25–€40
€€€ = €40–€60
€€€€ = more than €60

The Cannes Film Festival

Artistic event, commercial circus or celebrity-spotters' paradise? Cannes Festival is all these things and more.

The Festival de Cannes (it has recently dropped film from its title, after all *everyone* knows it's a film festival) was conceived by the French government in the 1930s to provide an alternative to the Venice Film Festival, where only those films meeting the approval of Mussolini's censors were shown. Cannes was elected for its "sunny and enchanting location". The first festival was scheduled for 1939, with film pioneeer Louis Lumière presiding over the jury. Plans were scuppered, however, by the onset of World War II, and it was not until 20 September 1946 that reels were rolled and glasses raised at the belated inaugural festival.

The 10-day event, which since 1951 has occupied its current slot in the spring calendar, is held in the Palais des Festivals et des Congrès, a massive architectural eyesore that dominates the seafront. The original Palais, where the Noga Hilton now stands, was replaced by the present modern structure – nicknamed "the bunker" by locals – in 1983.

The judging

Each year the festival's board of directors chooses a 10-member international jury: nine artists and a president, who is almost exclusively a leading figure in the film world. Past presidents range from Jean Cocteau (1953 and 1954) to the first woman president of the board, Olivia de Havilland (1965) and, in more recent years, Martin Scorsese (1998), David Cronenberg (1999), Luc Besson (2000) and Chinese director Wong Kar Wai (2006).

The jury's job is to award the prestigious "Palme d'Or" (golden palm) for Best Film, as well as prizes including Best Actor, Best Actress, Best Director and Best Screenplay for feature films that have been made in the year leading up to the festival. (To qualify, entries must not have been shown outside their country of origin nor entered for any other competition.) Alongside the "Official Selection", which often includes some more blockbuster-style movies screened outside the competition (*The Da Vinci Code* was the 2006 opener) are a series of parallel selections and prizes seen as a springboard to later inclusion in the Official Selection, awards for short films and for the best three films presented by the Cinéfondation, Cannes' champion for productions from film schools.

The Semaine Internationale de la Critique (international critics' week) was founded in 1962 to promote the work of new film-makers in their first or second films (Bertolucci, Loach and Ozon are among those first distinguished here) and the Quinzaine des Réalisateurs (directors' fortnight) was launched in 1969 to promote the freedom of international cinema in the aftermath of the May '68 student riots in Paris. More recent side selections include screenings of vintage movies and the Cinemas of the World, presenting films from minor film-making countries from Romania to Iran.

For all the endless debate as to artistic merit or controversy over who gets the Palme d'Or, the films screened at Cannes remain phenomenally international.

Money talks

Critical cinematic appreciation and highbrow prize-giving are not the sole concerns of the Cannes Festival, however. It's also a major venue for the hard-nosed buying and selling of film rights, for industry schmoozing and boozing. Much of this wheeler-dealing goes on in the basement of the Palais, at the Marché du Film. However, this aspect of the festival is often criticised, accused of being a marathon homage to bad taste and conspicuous consumption, a big excuse to take advantage of swollen expense accounts at Cannes' luxury palace hotels such as the Carlton, Martinez or Majestic. It could be argued that the invisible hand of capitalism – the driving force behind the Marché du Film – is why over 30,000 film producers, directors, distributors and actors from around 80 countries, more than 4,000 journalists and countless hangers-on come to Cannes for two weeks every year.

Glamour and glitz

Officialdom and cynicism aside, however, much of the hullabaloo surrounding Cannes is without doubt due to the pull of the stars. Ever since the festival's glitzy heyday during the 1950s and 1960s the paparazzi have travelled to the southern French shores in May to snap gorgeous stars in glamorous evening attire as they climb the red carpeted steps of the Palais des Festivals and – more popularly – scantily-clad, wannabe cinema-lovelies on the beach at Cannes.

Brigitte Bardot made the biggest splash of them all in 1953, when she attended her first Cannes Festival – then unknown, Bardot went on to be a screen sensation, most notably in films by her then husband, Roger Vadim.

Other eternal Riviera beauties include the American actress Grace Kelly, for whom romance was in the air in 1955, when she visited the Monagasque royals during her fortnight at Cannes. The film star married her prince, and the Grimaldis have been a source of celebrity gossip ever since.

Success stories

Although winning the Palme d'Or at Cannes does not guarantee box-office success – some past winners have received little or no attention outside the festival – this is not the absolute rule. Enduring past winners include Carol Reed's *The Third Man* (1949), Federico Fellini's *La Dolce Vita* (1960), Martin Scorsese's *Taxi Driver* (1976), Steven Sonderbergh's *Sex, Lies and Videotape* (1989), David Lynch's *Wild at Heart* (1990) and Quentin Tarentino's 1994 trigger-happy *Pulp Fiction*. Emir Kursturica (1985 and 1995) and the Dardenne brothers (1999 and 2005) have both won the Palme d'Or twice.

Invitations

The festival is supposed to be for industry insiders only, with tickets to screenings and other evening events notoriously difficult to come by. However, if you're determined to get in to see the stars, you have a talent at charming bodyguards and local gendarmes, and your holiday budget stretches to the extortionate prices charged at the luxury hotels on the Cannes waterfront (around €16 a pop for an alcoholic drink), you may yet get to take part in the action.

The public can get to see some films – since 2002, the festival has organised the outdoor Cinéma de la Plage, screenings on the beach for the general public of classic movies and non-competition films from the official selection (pick up invitations at the tourist office). ❏

LEFT: 1953 festival: Dany Robin, Kirk Douglas, Olivia de Havilland and Edward G. Robinson.
RIGHT: Julianne Moore posing, 2006.

THE RIVIERA FROM VILLEFRANCHE TO MENTON

This stretch of the Côte d'Azur bordering Italy has some of its most appealing spots: pretty, unpretentious Villefranche-sur-Mer, exclusive Cap Ferrat, the perched medieval villages of Eze and La Turbie, and Italianate Menton with its balmy climate and lemon festival

Map on pages 234–5

BELOW:
Villefranche-sur-Mer.

Three corniche roads snake along the coast eastwards from Nice towards the Italian border. The Basse Corniche (N98), or Corniche Inférieure, hugs the coast, winding between villas and apartment blocks and providing an overview of how heavily built-up it has become – though still interspersed by old ports and exclusive headlands.

The Moyenne Corniche (N7) is the shortest and probably the most stylish of the three routes. Alfred Hitchcock caught a bus here, as an extra in his 1955 film *To Catch a Thief.* In that same movie, who could forget Grace Kelly – Hollywood star and the epitome of elegance, who was having a real-life romance at the time of filming with Prince Rainier of Monaco – as she swooped along the curves of the Moyenne Corniche in her roadster? She died tragically following a car accident on that same corniche in 1982.

The Grande Corniche (D2564), roughly in the trace of the Roman Via Aurelia, is the highest of the three cor-

niches, passing through a sparsely vegetated limestone landscape. It is also the longest route from Monaco to Nice, though not necessarily the slowest, since heavy traffic often clogs the coast road. For those in a hurry, the A8 *autoroute* runs parallel to it, a little bit further inland.

Villefranche-sur-Mer

The Basse Corniche leaves the Vieux-Port of Nice climbing up round the fantastical villas of Mont Boron. First stop to the east, the town of **Ville-franche-sur-Mer** ⑯ was established in the 14th century as a customs-free port by Charles II d'Anjou. In the 16th century, Philibert of Savoy built the **citadelle** to protect the port. British and American ships still use this sheltered harbour, which is one of the deepest in the world, as do cruise ships and a small fishing fleet.

The town is well restored but not bijou, with tall painted stucco houses and lively fish restaurants lining the quayside. Here you'll also find the **Chapelle St-Pierre** (1 quai Courbet; open Tues–Sun summer 10am–noon, 4–8pm, winter 10am–noon, 2–6pm;

admission charge), one of the most extraordinary works by Surrealist writer, artist and film-maker Jean Cocteau. He restored the medieval chapel dedicated to St Peter, patron saint of fishermen, painting it with quirky fishing scenes and episodes from the saint's life.

Cap Ferrat

Continuing east along the bay from Villefranche, a side road leads to **Cap Ferrat** ⑰. Hideout of the seriously rich and famous, this is one of the few areas of the coast that guards its aura of exclusivity. Much of it lurks behind security fences and guard-dog warnings, but the Plage Passable is a pleasant little beach, not far from the former villa of King Leopold II of Belgium, from where you can join the coastal path round the Cap.

The **Fondation Ephrussi de Rothschild** (open Feb–Oct daily 10am–6pm, July–Aug until 7pm, Nov–Jan Mon–Fri 2–6pm, Sat, Sun and school hols 10am–6pm; admission charge; www.culture-espaces. com) gives a hint of the champagne lifestyle: 7 hectares (17 acres) of

TIP

The main attraction of the Fondation Ephrussi de Rothschild is its nine themed gardens. A meandering promenade takes you past exotic cacti, Provençal flora, roses, and through a French formal garden with musical fountains, a Japanese garden with gravel and little shrines, an Italian Renaissance garden, and the romantic lapidary garden with its fragments of Gothic architecture and medieval statuary.

BELOW: cruise liner in Villefranche harbour.

TIP

For beach restaurants, try fashionable **Plage Restaurant La Paloma** (tel: 04 93 01 64 71) on Paloma Beach at Cap Ferrat; it's casual for grilled fish and salads at lunchtime, more romantic (and expensive) for candlelit dinners. At Cap d'Ail, laidback **L'Eden** (tel: 04 93 78 17 06) serves good-value traditional French cooking amid a Bali-style tropical decor on the idyllic Plage Mala. It can be reached by boat or on foot down steps from the coast path.

BELOW:
Eze village, with Cap Ferrat in the distance.

exotic gardens are spread along the crest of the Cap with gorgeous views on all sides. The pink-and-white Belle Epoque villa was built to house the art collection of Baroness Ephrussi de Rothschild (1864–1934). Around a Venetian Gothic-style central courtyard are panelled rooms laden with her collection of 18th-century French furniture, a ceiling painted by Tiepolo, and precious Sèvres and Vincennes porcelain.

Not far away, the **Zooparc du Cap Ferrat** (open daily 9.30am–7pm, 5.30pm in winter; tel: 04 93 76 07 60; www.zoocapferrat.com) is like a lushly planted garden itself, where crocodiles, zebras, lemurs, gibbons and wild cats live amid its pools, palm trees, islands and waterfalls. Recent additions include a panther canyon and a nocturnal environment for rats and bats. Further round the Cap, **St-Jean-Cap Ferrat** has a chic harbour frequented by the yachting fraternity.

Across the bay from the Villa Ephrussi you can spot another glamorous mansion. On the water's edge at **Beaulieu-sur-Mer**, the **Villa Kerylos** (open Feb–Oct daily 10am–6pm, July–Aug until 7pm, Nov–Jan Mon–Fri 2–6pm, Sat, Sun and school hols 10am–6pm; admission charge; tel: 04 93 01 01 44; www.villa-kerylos.com) is a 1902–08 reconstruction of an ancient Greek villa by wealthy German scholar Theodor Reinach. Together with architect Emmanuel Pontremoli he created what is not so much a replica villa as an idealised version, with marble columns and cool courtyards open to the sea and sky, and housing a large collection of mosaics, frescos and furniture.

Beaulieu-sur-Mer ⓲ itself is a genteel retirement town with a Belle Epoque casino, luxury hotels and elegant rest homes reclining in the sheltered climate. From here the Basse Corniche passes through the sprawling resort of Eze-Bord-de-Mer and Cap d'Ail before reaching Monaco.

Eze and La Turbie

East of Beaulieu, impaled on a rocky spike some 400 metres (1,300 ft) above the sea is the picturesque village of **Eze** ⓳, with its cluster of pantiled medieval houses and Baroque church. Access is from the Moyenne

Corniche or by donkey track from the coast, and its entrance – through a small, hidden archway – comes after a short winding climb from the main road. Few other *villages perchés* command the popularity of Eze, and pushing through the narrow streets at the height of summer can be trying. However, the village's current prosperity belies its troubled past, mostly as a charred ruin: razed successively over several centuries, enslaved by Arabs, its citizens regularly tortured and burnt.

These days, one undoubtedly flourishing aspect is the **Jardin Exotique** (open Mar–Aug daily; closed Sept–Feb; admission charge), a fine collection of cacti and succulents, interspersed with terracotta sculptures. This garden was planted in 1950 around the ruins of the chateau, which had been dismantled in 1706.

High up on the Grande Corniche beyond Eze, the white marble columns of the ruined Roman monument at **La Turbie** 🈀 stand out against the sky. The village derives its name from the Latin *tropaea*, meaning trophy, after the vast monument, la **Trophée des Alpes** (18 avenue Albert I; open daily Apr–June 9am–6pm, July–Sept 9am–7pm, Oct–Mar 9.30am–5pm; admission charge; tel: 04 93 41 20 84; www.monum.fr), erected here in 6 BC. Inscribed inside are tributes to Augustus and a list of the 44 conquered tribes *(see margin)*, in all the longest surviving intact Roman inscription.

The Trophy dominates the narrow streets of the medieval village, which still has its fortified gateways. The **Eglise St-Michel** is an 18th-century Baroque offering. Inside, the red marble is extensive, bordering on the gaudy, insolent style that might befit a film star's villa in St-Tropez.

Roquebrune Cap-Martin

Between Monaco *(see page 253)* and Menton lies **Roquebrune Cap-**

Martin 🈀, an exclusive millionaire's haunt: Empress Eugénie and Winston Churchill stayed here, as did some less desirable characters, Emperor Bokassa among them. Much of it is off-limits, although you can walk round the Sentier du Littoral, which hugs the sea edge, with opportunities for bathing from the rocks. Just west of the Cap itself, within easy reach of Roquebrune Cap-Martin station, the pleasant beach of Cabbé sits under the gardens of the elegant Villa Mangano. It is largely pebble, but has some sand at low tide, unlike the shingle beach of more downmarket suburb, Carnolès (on the Menton side).

Up on the coast path sits the **Cabanon** (visits Tues and Fri 10am; reserve at least one day ahead with tourist office, tel: 04 93 35 62 87; admission charge), the tiny log cabin constructed by Le Corbusier in 1951–2. It's not the only avant-garde building here: Eileen Gray's groundbreaking Villa E-1027 was designed by the Irish-born decorator and architect in 1929. Long empty, there are plans to restore it.

Map on pages 234–5

The Trophée des Alpes was built by the Roman Senate as a reward to Emperor Augustus for his successful campaign against the remaining 44 rebellious Alpine tribes.

BELOW: Cap-Martin.

TIP

The attractive town of Ventimiglia just across the Italian border from Menton is a popular hop for locals thanks to its vast food and general goods market, every Friday. Beware the fake designer handbags sold here: people are regularly stopped at the border customs post and may incur large fines for smuggling.

BELOW: Menton, beach and old town.

Perched high up above Carnolès is old **Roquebrune Village**, a picturesque tangle of alleys and houses built into the rock. Its **Château** (open daily 10am–12.30pm, 2–6pm, July–Aug until 7.30pm, Nov–Jan until 5pm; admission charge; tel: 04 93 35 07 22) dates back to the 10th century when Conrad I, count of Ventimiglia, built it to keep out the Saracens. In the cemetery next to the village, Le Corbusier, who drowned while swimming in the sea in 1965, is buried alongside his wife in a tomb of his own design.

Roquebrune's other popular landmark, along the steep footpath that runs down to the lower town, is the wonderfully gnarled **Olivier Millénaire**, an ancient olive tree that is probably even older than its name (1,000-year old olive tree) claims.

Menton: lemon capital

Sheltered by mountains, **Menton** ㉒ basks in an enchanted setting with 300 days of sun a year and a climate at least two degrees warmer than that of Nice. Mexican and North African vegetation, as well as citrus fruit, flourish in this subtropical greenhouse.

In the second half of the 19th century, Menton was renowned as a winter sanatorium, one of the first health resorts to benefit from the start of grand tourism thanks to a Dr Bennet. The English doctor promoted Menton's mild climate as perfect for invalids, and as a result British and Germans flocked here in wintertime, as did Russians, who added another of the Riviera's Russian Orthodox churches to the town. Royal visitors such as Queen Victoria helped the town acquire a reputation as the most aristocratic and anglophile of all the resorts on the Riviera. And along the seafront and in the hills surrounding the Italianate old town, grand hotels and romantic villas were built.

Nowadays, most of the grand hotels have been demolished or converted into apartments, and the mild climate has given Menton the reputation of a cosy retirement home. However, the town has been rejuvenated since 1993 when Menton and Ventimiglia together became the European Union's first joint urban community,

combining frontier posts and municipal and business activities.

The Italianate old town

Surrealism fans will be interested to learn that the room used to conduct marriage ceremonies in Menton's **Hôtel de Ville** (town hall), the *salle des mariages*, was decorated with murals by Jean Cocteau in the 1950s. In fact, a tiny fort on Quai Monléon, by the harbour, contains the **Musée Jean Cocteau** (open Wed–Mon 10am–noon, 2–6pm; admission charge), with the artist's ceramics, tapestries, mosaics and pastels.

Next to the **place aux Herbes** is the excellent **covered market** and the place du Marché with its flower stalls. Running behind them, pedestrianised rue St-Michel and avenue Félix-Faure hum with shops and restaurants. The Italianate old town occupies the hill, all narrow shady streets stacked with houses. Flights of steps decorated with black-and-white pebble mosaics lead up from Quai Bonaparte to Baroque **Eglise St-Michel Archange**, which has a pink-and-orange campanile and sculptures on its façade. A second Baroque church stands across the square, the **Chapelle de la Conception**.

Built in tiers where the castle once stood, the **Cimetière du Vieux-Château**, at the top of the hill, has the tombs of many of the Russian and British families who settled here from the end of the 19th century, including those of illustrator Aubrey Beardsley and William Webb Ellis, creator of the modern game of rugby.

At the western end of the town is the 18th-century pink-and-white **Palais Carnolès**, the former summer residence of the Monaco royal family, still with its fine staircase and some of its original panelling and painted ceilings. Today it contains the **Musée des Beaux Arts** (3 avenue de la Madone; open Wed–Mon 10am–noon, 2–6pm; free; tel: 04 93 35 49 71), including a Madonna by Louis Bréa, Flemish and Dutch paintings, and works by Suzanne Valadon, Raoul Dufy and Graham Sutherland. Surrounding it, the **Jardin des Agrumes**, run by INRA (the state agricultural research institute), has many different species of citrus tree.

Map on pages 234–5

Menton hosts an impressive array of cultural events: concerts, exhibitions, a theatre season from November to April, flower festivals, a circle of poets, the literary Katherine Mansfield Prize and the lemon festival. For two weeks every February, lemons and oranges are piled high into incredible sculptures, and on the Sundays, floats and bands parade along the seafront. For details, contact: www.feteducitron.com

BELOW: view of Castellar *(see page 250)* and the mountains beyond.

Walking the Caps

Although the Riviera's exclusive headlands can seem like the preserve of the rich and famous, everyone has the right to walk along the French seashore, a right increasingly enforced by the local authorities as they maintain and improve the signposting on the Sentier du Littoral (coastal path). The path takes you around three of the region's most beautiful headlands: Cap Ferrat (footpath from Plage Passable to Port St-Jean), Cap d'Ail (footpath from Plage Mala to Plage Marquet), and Cap Martin (along the Sentier Corbusier, between the Plage du Cabbé and Carnolès). At times the path hugs the water or crosses beaches, with opportunities for bathing from the rocks or in surprisingly wild coves, inaccessible from the road and surrounded by Mediterranean vegetation and azure seas – or with surreal views of Monaco's tower blocks. At other times, steps climb up the cliffs and the path skirts the rear of private grounds, offering glimpses of Belle Epoque villas, tropical gardens and the lifestyle of the privileged few. The Conseil Général des Alpes Maritimes publishes a Randoxygène guide, *Rando Pays Côtier*, available from tourist offices. Try also: www.randoxygene.org

Map on pages 234–5

The Jardin Botanique Exotique Val Rahmeh is one of the institutions cultivating the sophoro toromiro tree in the hope of introducing it back into the wild. Once endemic on Easter Island, the species died out, leaving just one specimen – now long gone – growing inside a volcano crater. Thankfully, explorer Thor Heyerdahl was able to take some seed pods back to Sweden with him in 1956, hence the trees now growing in Menton.

BELOW: the Serre de la Madone garden.

A horticulturalist's paradise

Menton boasts a remarkable number of exotic gardens – two of these are easily accessible to the public. The **Jardin Botanique Exotique Val Rahmeh** (avenue St-Jacques; open Oct–Mar Wed–Mon 10am–12.30pm, 2–5pm, Apr–Sept 10am–12.30pm, 3.30–6.30pm; admission charge; tel: 04 93 35 86 72; www.mnhn.fr), arranged around a 1920s villa, proves that everything can indeed grow in Menton. A winding trail leads between magical and medicinal plants, dry and wet environments, towering palms, dank tropical ferns, forests of bamboo and exotic cocoa, avocado, banana, guava and citrus fruits, tea bushes and spice trees. Run by the Muséum National d'Histoire Naturel in Paris, there's always something to see here.

The **Serre de la Madone** (route de Gorbio; open Tues–Sun 10am–6pm, Dec–Mar until 5pm, closed Nov; admission charge; tel: 04 93 57 73 90; www.serredelamadone.com) is a romantic garden designed in the 1920s by Lawrence Johnson, creator of the garden at Hidcote Manor in England. It is laid out with geometrical pools, terraces, fountains and classical statues that create different perspectives and environments for irises, acanthus, camellias, water plants, toxic daturas and flora from all over the globe.

Interesting gardens that can only be visited on tours organised by the Service du Patrimoine (tel: 04 92 10 33 66) include the Jardin des Colombières (July–mid-Aug only, by appointment), inspired by Greek and Roman mythology, the Jardin de la Fontana Rosa (Fri 10am), which has ceramic motifs paying tribute to Don Quixote, and the palm-filled grounds of Villa de la Maria Serena (Tues 10am).

Hillside retreats

You might prefer to head away from the coastal sprawl and explore the hill villages of **Gorbio**, often shrouded in morning mist, medieval **Castellar** and **Ste-Agnès ㉓**, the highest perched village on the coast. Just north of these villages, you can take refuge in the simplicity and quietness of the backcountry. ❑

RESTAURANTS AND BARS

Eze

Château de la Chèvre d'Or
Rue du Barri. Tel: 04 92 10 66 61. Open: L and D daily. Closed: mid-Nov–Feb. €€€
www.chevredor.com
Luxurious dining with spectacular views. Chef Philippe Labbé prepares elaborate concoctions combining fine ingredients with the local touches of herbs, *blettes* and rare tomatoes.

Loumiri
Avenue du Jardin Exotique. Tel: 04 93 41 16 42. Open: L and D daily (Thur–Tues in winter). €
The affordable option is this simple stone bistro at the entrance to the village. Salads, *plats du jour* and regional dishes like *petits farcis*.

Menton

A Braijade Meridounale
66 rue Longue. Tel: 04 93 35 65 65. Open: Sept–June L and D Thur–Tues; July and Aug D only. €€
www.abraijade.com
Regional cooking served in a beamed dining room in the old town. Specialities include vegetable fritters, grilled skewered meats and fish and *bagna caouda* (anchoïade).

Le Nautic
27 quai de Mauléon. Tel: 04 93 35 78 74. Open: L and D daily. €€
A good fish restaurant

with friendly Italian owners. Try generously served fried squid, john dory with courgettes or sea bass cooked in a salt crust, and the strawberry *sabayon* for dessert.

Roquebrune Cap-Martin

Les Deux Frères
Place des Deux Frères. Tel: 04 93 28 99 00. Open: summer L Wed–Sun, D Tues–Sun; winter L Tues–Sun, D Tues–Sat. Closed: mid-Nov–mid-Dec. €€€. www.lesdeuxfreres.com
The old village school is now a pleasant small hotel and restaurant. Attractive southern dishes might include artichoke salad or red mullet in a herb crust.

Au Grand Inquisiteur
15 rue du Château. Tel: 04 93 35 08 37. Open: summer L and D Tues–Sun; winter Wed–Sun. €€
This old stone sheepfold by the castle (no car access) has long been a local favourite for its good traditional cooking with some imaginative touches.

St-Jean-Cap Ferrat

Le Provençal
2 avenue Denis-Semeria. Tel: 04 93 76 03 97. Open: summer L and D daily; winter L daily, D Fri–Sun. Closed: November. €€€€
Jean-Jacques Jouteaux

offers a brilliant repertoire of Provence-inspired dishes. The lunchtime menu is less expensive.

La Turbie

Café de la Fontaine
4 avenue du Général de Gaulle. Tel: 04 93 28 52 79. Open: L & D daily. €
A superb-value blackboard menu of homely specials, such as lentil salad, marinated sardines, rack of pork and home-made fruit tarts. Open for breakfast too.

Hostellerie Jérôme
20 rue Comte de Cessole. Tel: 04 93 41 51 51. Open: L & D Wed–Sun (daily in July & Aug). €€€€
Chef Bruno Cirino, whose CV includes the Royal Monceau in Paris, is passionate about fresh

produce, stocking up at markets in Nice and Ventimiglia or from fishermen in the Ligurian ports.

Villefranche-sur-Mer

La Mère Germaine
9 quai Courbet. Tel: 04 93 01 71 39. Open: L and D daily. Closed: mid-Nov–Christmas. €€€ www.meregermaine.com
The most famous of the restaurants along the harbour (Cocteau was a regular) is reputed for its fine-quality fish and shellfish, including bouillabaisse.

PRICE CATEGORIES

Prices for a three-course meal without wine.

€ = under €25
€€ = €25–€40
€€€ = €40–€60
€€€€ = more than €60

MONACO

Monaco is Europe's second-smallest independent country after the Vatican, with a huge concentration of wealth and sky-high property prices to match. This mini-state has a plethora of museums, a busy cultural and sporting season, and a legendary casino

Seen from across the bay, **Monaco** ❷④ is a surreal sight with its cluster of glitzy skyscrapers crammed in behind a backdrop of mountains, like Hong Kong on the Mediterranean. Indeed, comparisons with Hong Kong are not unjustified: a tiny, densely populated state squeezed between coast and mountains, a mix of modernity and Belle Epoque splendour and an important banking centre.

Of the 32,000 residents, only 7,000 are Monégasque citizens, and of the 40,000 people who actually work in Monaco to serve all its tax exiles, gamblers and holidaymakers, many don't actually live in the state itself but commute in from more affordable lodgings in surrounding towns. High property prices are due not only to all the rich residents and high-income tourists, but also because Monaco is bursting at the seams. One of the quandaries for the royal oligarchy is how to extend the city, not just building upwards but through continued projects of land reclamation over the sea or, indeed, through colonisation of neighbouring France: the swanky Monte-Carlo Country Club at the far end of avenue Princesse Grace is actually in Roquebrune-Cap Martin, while the Monte-Carlo Golf Club is at La Turbie.

A new Grimaldi

In 2005 Prince Albert II acceded to the throne *(see box page 254)*, on the death of his father, Prince Rainier III, in April 2005 after 56 years as head of state. In theory Monaco is a constitutional monarchy, with a Minister of State who heads a cabinet of four ministers and a legislature of 24 elected by Monégasque citizens, but in practice the Prince remains enormously powerful. The Minister of State is chosen by the prince and approved by the French government.

Maps:
Area 234
City 255

LEFT: the skyscrapers of Monaco. **BELOW:** changing of the guard.

Princess Grace, formerly American film star Grace Kelly, who married Prince Rainier in 1956 and died in a car crash in 1982, is buried in the cathedral cemetery, along with numerous other members of the Rainier dynasty.

BELOW: Prince Albert II at his coronation.

Life on the Rock

Monaco is split into seven districts: medieval Monaco-Ville or the old town, La Condamine port area just below it, glamorous Monte-Carlo with the Casino and Opera, the Larvotto beach district further east, La Fontvieille on reclaimed land west of the Rocher, and the Monaghetti residential district on the hill behind.

Monaco-Ville, the historic centre of Monaco, is often referred to as "Le Rocher" (the Rock), since it sits on a sheer-sided block of land, which juts around 800 metres (2,600 ft) into the sea between the old Port de Monaco and the modern port of Fontvieille. Le Rocher is crowned by the pink royal palace, the **Palais Princier ⓐ** (place du Palais; open June–Sept daily 9.30am–6pm, Oct 10am–5pm; admission charge; tel: +377-93 25 18 31; www.palais.mc), with its Cour d'Honneur and sumptuous 17th- and 18th-century state apartments, including the Salon Louis XV and the Throne Room. If you visit in late morning you can also watch the changing of the guard that takes place on the square out-

side each day at 11.55am. Also on the square is the **Musée des Souvenirs Napoléoniens** (open June–Sept daily 9.30am–6pm, Oct–11 Nov daily 10am–5pm, mid-Dec–May Tues–Sun 10.30am–noon, 2–4.30pm; admission charge; tel: +377-93 25 18 31), a collection of memorabilia from the French Second Empire, as well an exhibition of documents from Monaco's history.

A lighter take on Monaco history can be found amid the narrow alleyways of the rather too pristine Vieille Ville at the **Historial des Princes de Monaco** (27 rue Basses; open Mar–Sept daily 10am–6pm, Oct–Feb 11am–5pm; admission charge; tel: +377-93 30 39 05), a wax museum with scenes featuring the Grimaldis since the 13th century.

Also in the old town is Monaco's neo-Byzantine **Cathédrale ⓑ** (4 rue Colonel Bellando del Caste; open daily), which was built in white stone from La Turbie during the 19th century. Near by, the **Musée de la Chapelle de la Visitation** (place de la Visitation; open Tues–Sun 10am–4pm; admission charge; tel:

Albert II

The year 2005 saw the arrival of a new head of Europe's second-smallest but richest state with the coronation of Albert II, hitherto best known for his sporting achievements (a member of Monaco's Olympic bobsleigh team) and succession of glamorous female companions, including Claudia Schiffer, Naomi Campbell and Brooke Shields. Will it be a new style of monarchy? Prince Rainier III had done much to transform the Monaco economy in his 56-year reign but was increasingly surrounded by octogenarian councillors. Forty-eight-year-old Prince Albert II has already begun bringing in a younger team of ministers and advisers, is actively engaged against climate change and for sustainable development – and one year on female staff are being allowed to wear trousers for the first time. As to the important question of an heir to the throne, Albert remains a bachelor with no direct heir (although he has now recognised not one but two illegitimate children, ending years of speculation that he might be gay), and his sister Princess Caroline, married to Prince Ernst of Hanover, is currently second in line.

+377-93 50 07 00) houses a collection of Baroque paintings, including works by Rubens and Ribera.

On the edge of the rock towering over the sea is the majestic **Musée Océanographique** (avenue St-Martin; open daily Oct–Mar 10am–6pm, Apr–June and Sept 9.30am–7pm, July and Aug until 7.30pm; admission charge; tel: +377-93 15 36) with more than 90 tanks of tropical fish and crustaceans, a shark lagoon and coral reef.

Climbing perilously up the cliffside in the Moneghetti district behind Le Rocher, the **Jardin Exotique** (boulevard du Jardin Exotique; open daily 15 May–15 Sept 9am–7pm, 16 Sept–14 May 9am–6pm or dusk; admission charge; tel: +377-93 30 33 65) is a feast of prickly cacti and succulents from deserts and other dry zones. At the foot of the garden, you can visit the **Grotte de l'Observatoire**, a cave complex with strange stalactites and stalagmites.

The harbours

La Condamine district is Monaco's old harbour area and the site of a daily food market as well as numerous other shops. This area is particularly popular with artists, who have set up studios in some of the old warehouses along the port. In 2002, the Port de Monaco or Port Hercule was expanded with a huge new semi-floating jetty towed in across the Mediterranean from Algeciras in Spain, and further work began in 2006 on a new quay to enable large yachts and cruise ships to dock here.

On the western side of town, **Fontvieille** was an entirely new district created on reclaimed land in the 1980s around a modern marina. Just back from the port on the Terrasses de Fontvieille is a cluster of museums: the **Collection de Voitures Anciennes** (open daily 10am–6pm; admission charge; tel: +377-92 05 28 56), the late Prince Rainier's collection of vintage cars and carriages, the

TIP

Monaco has a different dialling code to France. If you're calling Monaco from abroad – including the surrounding Côte d'Azur – you'll need to use the international dialling code (00 377); to call France from Monaco, dial 00 33 and leave off the 0 at the start of French phone numbers.

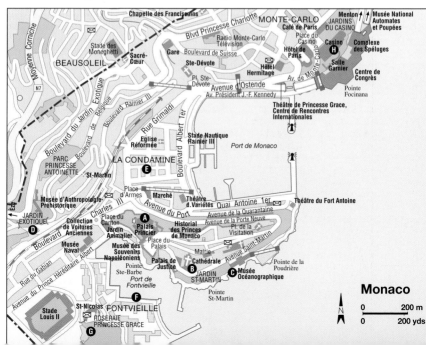

Michael Schumacher in action in the 2006 Monaco Grand Prix. Book months ahead for grandstand places at the Grand Prix, at the end of May, when Formula 1 racing cars tear around the Principality's hairpin bends. Tel: +377-93 15 26 00; www.acm.mc

BELOW: the Casino.

...e des Timbres et des Mon-... (Stamp and Coin Museum; ...Oct–June daily 10am–5pm, ...ept daily 10am–6pm; admis-...arge; tel: +377-93 15 41 50); ...sée Naval (open daily 10am–...mission charge; tel: +377-92 ... 28 48; www.musee-naval.mc), and the **Jardin Animalier** (open daily Oct–Feb 10am–noon, 2–5pm, Mar–May 10am–noon, 2–6pm, June–Sept 9am–noon, 2–7pm; admission charge; tel: +377-93 25 18 31; www.palais.mc), a small zoo.

In Fontveille you'll also find the **Roseraie Princesse Grace** ⑤ (Princess Grace Rose Garden), laid out with 4,000 rose bushes planted amid Mediterranean pine and olive trees, palms, a lake and a collection of modern sculpture.

Monte-Carlo

For most people the district that really epitomises Monaco is Monte-Carlo – or more particularly the ensemble of the Casino, Café de Paris and the Hôtel de Paris with its ornate Second Empire architecture, formal gardens, luxury boutiques and swarms of Fer-

raris and Rolls-Royces. Here, you can visit the chocolate-box **Casino** ⓗ (place du Casino; open to over 18s only, ID required; Mon–Fri 2pm until late, Sat, Sun noon until late; admission charge; tel: +377-92 16 20 00), built in the late 19th century and a wash of pastel colours, gilt, cherubs and other neo-rococo trimmings. Opera and ballet are performed in the overtly decorative **Salle Garnier** in the Casino. Reeopened in 2005 after two years of painstaking restoration work, it is a feast of coloured marble, mosaics and glittering chandeliers.

Next door the domed pavilion of the Café de Paris – where great chef Auguste Escoffier once held sway – also has a casino, decorated with a Grand Prix theme, while its brasserie terrace offers perfect opportunities to watch the clientele coming in and out of the palatial Hôtel de Paris across the square. If you really want to blow your budget, visit überchef Alain Ducasse's Louis XV Restaurant on the ground floor of the hotel or go shopping on the avenue des Beaux-Arts at such luxury boutiques as Cartier, Bulgari and Ribolzi.

Along the seafront below the Casino, accessible by a series of lifts, is the **Musée National Automates et Poupées** (Museum of Dolls and Automata; 17 avenue Princesse Grace; open Easter–Sept 10am–6.30pm, Oct–Easter 10am–12.15pm, 2.30–6.30pm; admission charge; tel: +377-93 30 91 26), housed in a pretty stucco villa. The museum is home to over 400 dolls, an impressive collection of 18th- and 19th-century dolls' houses and various automata.

Almost opposite is a modern **Japanese garden** with its symbolic landscape and shinto shrines and the angular, glass-sided **Grimaldi Forum** (10 avenue Princesse Grace; tel: +377-99 99 20 00; www.grimaldiforum.com), used for congresses, art exhibitions, concerts and dance. ❏

RESTAURANTS AND BARS

Bar et Boeuf
Le Sporting Monte-Carlo, Avenue Princesse Grace, Monte-Carlo. Tel: +377-98 06 71 71. Open: mid-May–late Sept. €€€€
Ducasse's fashionable summer restaurant overlooks Jimmy'z and the sea at the très chic Sporting Club. The concept is centred on just two ingredients: bar (sea bass) and boeuf (beef), and interpretations that vary from sea bass with a Provençal-style vegetable *tian* to carpaccios and Asian wok cooking.

Le Café de Paris
Place du Casino, Monte-Carlo. Tel: +377-92 16 20 20. Open: daily noon–2am. €€
Completely renovated in 1920s style, the place where the crêpe Suzette was supposedly invented by accident for Edward VII (and named after one of his mistresses) deserves to be visited as one of the sights of Monte-Carlo. Classic brasserie food and great people-watching from the terrace.

Joël Robuchon Monte-Carlo
Hôtel Metropole, 4 avenue de la Madone, Monte Carlo. Tel: +977-93 15 15 15. Open: L & D daily. €€€€
www.metropole.com
After Paris, Robuchon has brought his contemporary global tapas concept to Monte-Carlo in the

hands of chef Christophe Cusset, with a succession of inventive little dishes and sometimes daring combinations of flavours, although there is also a more conventional rotisserie menu.

Le Louis XV
Hôtel de Paris, Place du Casino, Monte-Carlo. Tel: +377-98 06 88 64. Open: L & D Thur–Mon (plus Wed D in summer). Closed: Dec & 2 weeks in Mar. €€€€
www.alain-ducasse.com
The flagship of the Ducasse empire, in the hands of Franck Cerruti, a native of Nice, serves lavish seasonal Mediterranean cuisine in the palatial dining room of the Hôtel de Paris. Smart dress required.

Maya Bay
Roccabella, 24 avenue Princesse Grace. Tel: +377-97 70 74 67. Open: L & D Tues–Sat. €€€
A slick modern restaurant and lounge bar with an Asiatic decor (Buddha statue, exotic woods) and fusion food. Popular with regulars and tourists alike.

Polpetta
2 rue Paradis, Monte-Carlo. Tel: +377-93 50 67 84. €€
Once frequented by Frank Sinatra, this bistro offers hearty Italian food, and is among the best value for money in Monaco.

St-Benoît
10 ter avenue de la Costa. Tel: +377-93 25 02 34. Open: L Tues–Sun, D Tues–Sat. €€€
A favourite with locals, with views over the marina and the Espace Grimaldi. The emphasis is on fish and shellfish.

Tip Top
11 avenue des Spélugues, Monte-Carlo. Tel: +377-93 95 50 69 13. Open: L & D Mon–Sat noon–dawn; Sun 7pm–dawn. €€
A busy convivial bistro and café frequented by an enormously eclectic crowd, ranging from local office workers to Albert II and scores of Formula 1 drivers, as photos on the walls reveal. The speciality is steak with matchstick chips, but they'll

also do you a pizza in the dead of night.

Zebra Square
10 avenue Princesse Grace, Monte-Carlo. Tel: +377-99 99 25 50. €€€
www.zebrasquare.com
A very fashionable brasserie and lounge bar with a stylish rooftop terrace in the Grimaldi Forum conference and exhibition centre. DJs at night.

PRICE CATEGORIES

Prices for a three-course meal without wine. Note that many restaurants have a less expensive lunch menu.

€ = under €25
€€ = €25–€40
€€€ = €40–€60
€€€€ = more than €60

RIGHT: Le Louis XV, the swankiest restaurant in Monaco.

TRANSPORT

GETTING THERE AND GETTING AROUND

GETTING THERE

By Air

From the UK

There is a good variety of low-cost flights to the region. **British Airways** operate flights to Marseille from Gatwick, and to Nice from Heathrow, Gatwick and Birmingham. **Jet2** flies from Leeds and Manchester to Nice; **Bmibaby** flies East Midlands and Heathrow to Nice. **Bmi** flies Heathrow and Leeds to Nice. **EasyJet** operates flights to Nice from Belfast, Newcastle, Liverpool, Luton, Stansted and Gatwick. **Ryanair** flies to Nîmes from Liverpool, East Midlands and Luton and from Stansted to Toulon. **Flyglobespan** flies from Edinburgh to Nice. **Flybe** goes from Southampton to Nice and Avignon. **Aer Lingus** also flies from Dublin direct to Marseille and Nice, and from Cork to Nice.

From the US

Delta has a daily flight from JFK-New York to Nice. Otherwise flights from the US go via Paris. To reach Provence from Paris, **Air France** flies from Paris to Nice, Marseille, Avignon and Toulon.

Internet Booking

The Internet is an excellent place to look for attractive air fares. Some of the better-known ticketing sites include www.travelocity.com and www.expedia.com (UK and US sites), www.cheapflights.com (UK) and www.cheaptickets.com (US). www.lastminute.fr and www.anyway.com are two popular French sites; www.opodo.com has sites for both France and the UK.

Specialist travel agencies cater to students and travellers under 26. Look for CTS Travel in the UK (www.ctstravel.co.uk),

AIRLINE COMPANIES

National Carriers

Air France: tel: 0845 0845 111 (UK); 800 237 2747 (US); 08 20 82 08 20 (France); www.airfrance.com
American Airlines: tel: 08457 789 789 (UK); 800 433 7300 (US); 08 10 87 28 72 (France); www.aa.com
British Airways: tel: 0870 850 9850 (UK); 800 247 9297 (US); 08 25 82 54 00 (France); www.britishairways.com
British Midland: tel: 0870 607 0222 (UK); 800 788 0555 (US); 01 41 91 87 04 (France);
www.britishmidland.com
Delta: tel: 0800 414 767 (UK); 800 241 4141 (US); 08 11 64 00 05 (France); www.delta.com
United Airlines: tel: 0845 8444 777 (UK); 800 241 6522 (US); 08 10 72 72 72 (France); www.united.com

Budget Airlines

Aer Lingus: tel: 0870 876 5000 (UK); tel: 0818 365 000 (Ireland), tel: 01 70 20 00 72 (France); www.aerlingus.com
Bmibaby.com: tel: 0871 224 0224 (UK); 800 788 0555 (US); 08 90 71 00 81 (France); www.bmibaby.com
easyJet: tel: 0870 6000 000 (UK); 08 99 70 00 41 (France); www.easyjet.com
Flyglobespan: tel: 0870 556 1522 (UK); www.flyglobespan.com
Flybe: tel: 0871 700 0535 (UK), from abroad tel: 00 44 139 226 8529; www.flybe.com
Ryanair: tel: 0906 270 5656 (UK); 1530 787 787 (Ireland); 08 92 23 23 75 (France); www.ryanair.com

TRANSPORT

USIT (www.usitnow.com) in Ireland, and STA Travel (www.statravel.com) and Student Universe (www.student universe.com) in the US.

By Train

The TGV high-speed track has now reached Marseille, reducing the journey time from Paris Gare de Lyon to only around 3 hours. There are between 10 and 12 TGVS per day from Paris to Marseille, 9 per day to Nice (journey time approx. 5 hours 30 minutes) and 15 a day to Avignon (approx. 3 hours). All these stations connect with the local train network (see Getting Around, page 262).

International trains connect with Spain, Italy, Switzerland, Germany and the Benelux countries. From the UK, Eurostar trains run to Lille and Paris Gare du Nord.

Sleepers

A comfortable way to get to the south is by overnight sleeper. The cheapest alternative is the couchette, which has six beds per carriage. The voiture-lit – a carriage for up to two people – is more private. You can travel first and second class in both types of carriage. Reservations must be made well in advance.

Tickets

In the UK, tickets for journeys in France can be booked at the Rail Europe Travel Centre (178 Piccadilly, London W1, tel: 0870 837 1371), or book online at www.raileurope.co.uk.

In the US, call Rail Europe at 888 382 7245 or book online at www.raileurope.com.

In France, buy tickets in any SNCF train station or by phone on 3635 (In France only), open 7am–10pm daily. You can also book, pay and find web discounts on the Internet site: www.voyages-sncf.com. Journeys on the TGV must always be booked in advance.

Remember that before you get on the train you have to

ABOVE: the TGV on the corniche d'Estérel.

date-stamp your ticket in the composteur machine at the station, which will be marked "compostez votre billet".

Discounts and Passes

A variety of passes and discounts are available for travel to and within France, many of which can be purchased at Rail Europe (www.raileurope.com). For travel exclusively within France, visit the website of the national railway, the SNCF (www.voyages-sncf.com).

A **Eurodomino pass** (only for EU citizens) allows unlimited travel on France's rail network for 3–8 days' duration within one month, but this must be bought before travelling to France. Discounted rates are available to children aged 4–11, or young people aged 12–25.

European and North African citizens are eligible for the **InterRail Pass** (www.interrail.com), which permits unlimited second-class travel in up to 28 European and North African countries.

Non-Europeans and non-North Africans can buy a **Eurailpass** (www.eurail.com). It allows unlimited first- or second-class travel throughout France and 18 other participating countries. Eurail also offers Flexi and Select passes for more limited travel. These must be purchased before your arrival in Europe.

You can save on train fares by purchasing special discount

cards in France. The **Carte 12/25** gives 12- to 25-year-olds a 25–50 percent reduction. Pensioners benefit from similar terms with a **Carte Senior**. A **Carte Enfant +** entitles a child under 12 and up to four accompanying adults to travel at a 25–50 percent reduction.

There are also discounts for weekend round trips (**Découverte Séjour**) as well as for a round trip for two people (**Découverte à 2**). Ask when making reservations or consult the SNCF website for more information on **Découverte** discounts.

The SNCF website also posts special offers.

By Ferry

Since the Channel Tunnel opened, ferry services have become increasingly competitive, so it's worth shopping around for discounts and special offers. The following companies operate across the English Channel to various ports, and all of these firms carry cars as well as foot passengers.

Brittany Ferries

This company offers sailings from Portsmouth to Caen, Cherbourg or St-Malo; from Plymouth and Cork to Roscoff; and, May–Oct only, from Poole to Cherbourg: The Brittany Centre, Wharf Road, Portsmouth PO2 8RU;

ACCOMMODATION

ACTIVITIES

A – Z

LANGUAGE

UK tel: 0870 366 5333;
France tel: 08 25 82 88 28,
www.brittany-ferries.com

Norfolkline Ferries

Norfolkline sails from Dover to
Dunkerque in 1 hour 45 min-
utes: Norfolk House, Eastern
Docks, Dover, CT16 1JA, Kent;
UK tel: 0870 870 1020;
France tel: 03 28 28 95 50;
www.norfolkline-ferries.com

P&O Ferries

P&O sails from Dover to Calais
in 90 minutes: Channel House,
Channel View Road, Dover CT17
9TJ; UK tel: 0870 598 0333;
France tel: 08 25 12 01 56,
www.poferries.com

Transmanche Ferries

This line runs from Newhaven to
Dieppe: UK tel: 0800 917 1201;
France tel: 08 00 65 01 00;
www.transmancheferries.com

By Bus

The cheapest way to get to
Provence is by bus, although
this does entail a long journey.
Eurolines (UK tel: 0870 580
8080; France tel: 08 92 89 90
91; Marseille tel: 04 91 50 57
55; Nice tel: 04 93 80 08 70;
www.eurolines.com) run regular
services from London to Avignon,
Marseille, and Nice.

*For local bus information see
Getting Around, page 261.*

By Car

If you don't mind a long drive,
and want to have a car to tour
when you get to Provence, then
driving from the UK is a good
option. However, note that in July
and August – particularly around
15 August, which is the main
national holiday of the summer –
the roads get very busy. Look for
the small green **BIS** (Bison Futé)
signs, which indicate scenic diver-
sionary routes. Traffic bulletins
on Radio Traffic (107.7FM) are
useful, with hourly bulletins in
English in summer.

Road distances to the South
are as follows:

• Calais–Nice:
  1,167 km (725 miles)
• Caen–Nice:
  1,161 km (721 miles)
• Dieppe–Avignon:
  854 km (531 miles)
• Calais–Avignon:
  965 km (600 miles)

The fastest route to Provence is
from Calais via Paris and the A6
Autoroute du Soleil to Lyon and
the Rhône valley. Alternatively
you could go via the *autoroute*
through the Massif Central,
the A10–A71–A75 via Bourges
and Clermont-Ferrand, which
offers spectacular scenery. All

FRENCH ROADS

Motorways *(autoroutes)* are
designated "A" roads,
National Highways *(routes
nationales)* "N" or "RN"
roads. Local roads are known
as "D" routes.

autoroutes have *péage* toll
booths, where payment may be
made in cash or by credit card.
Tolls can work out fairly expensive on long journeys; a trip from
Calais to Nice, for example,
would cost around €100.
www.autoroutes.fr

Another option is to drive to
Paris and then put you and
your car on the train. The SNCF
has "Auto/Train" service from
Paris to Marseille, Toulon and
Fréjus/Saint-Raphaël. You travel
in a comfortable TGV compart-
ment while your car rides
behind in a special wagon. Visit
www.voyages-sncf.com/autotrain for
information and schedules.

Eurotunnel

Eurotunnel carries cars and their
passengers from Folkestone to
Calais on a simple drive-on-drive-
off system (journey time 35 minutes). Payment is made at toll
booths (which accept cash,
cheques or credit cards). It is
best to book ahead, particularly
during peak periods; you will pay
less and save time. If you haven't
reserved, you can turn up half an
hour before and wait for the next
available service. Eurotunnel runs
24 hours a day, all year round,
with a service about three times
per hour during the day, and every
two hours from midnight to 8am.

Information and bookings from
Eurotunnel, Customer Relations,
PO Box 2000, Folkestone, Kent
CT18 8XY; tel: 0870 535 3535;
www.eurotunnel.com. In France, tel:
08 10 63 03 04.

Car Hire

Car hire is very expensive in
France, mainly due to high VAT
(TVA) rates. Sometimes fly-drive

BELOW: motorway above Menton.

packages, or arranging car hire in advance, can work out slightly cheaper than hiring once you arrive. Fly-drive packages are available from most airlines, and the SNCF offers substantial discounts with train-plus-car rental packages under its "Voyage Alacarte" scheme (www.voyages-sncf.com).

To hire a car you need to be at least 21 years old and must have held a driving licence for at least a year. Some hire companies will not rent out to people under 26 or over 60. Check in advance that you know what to do in case of an accident or breakdown.

The bigger hire companies offer the best deals for weekly car hire – expect to pay about €245 a week for a small car with insurance and 1,700 km (1,056 miles) included. You can sometimes find good weekend deals, usually from Friday evening to Monday morning. Watch out for cheaper companies that may balance a low hire cost with high charges in the event of damage to the vehicle.

Avis, tel: 08 20 05 05 05
www.avis.com
Budget, tel: 08 25 00 35 64
www.budget.com
Europcar, tel: 08 25 358 358
www.europcar.com
Hertz, tel: 01 39 38 38 38
www.hertz.com
Rent-a-Car, tel: 08 91 700 200
www.rentacar.fr
Thrifty, tel: 01 34 29 86 76
www.thrifty.com

Bicycles

Most long-distance trains have special areas designated for bicycle transport. You must reserve in advance and pay a small fee. Alternatively, if you partially dismantle your bicycle and put it in a carrier (available at most bicycle shops) you can carry it on as luggage for no extra fee. Most regional trains also make provisions for bicycles, as does the Eurostar. Ask about bicycle transport when you book your ticket.

GETTING AROUND

Although it is possible to get around Provence by train and bus, a car (or, if you're energetic, a bicycle) is essential if you want to explore the region independently. Bus and train services are adequate between towns and cities, but there may only be one bus a day – and sometimes no buses at all – to small villages. There is a good train service along the coast, and a number of small mountain train services.

It is pleasant to drive inland, but traffic on the coast can be highly congested in summer. It's worth remembering that the hallowed French lunch break is still widely observed, so this is a good time to travel. French school holidays last through July and August, and the roads are at their worst around 15 August, a major national holiday.

From the Airports

The main gateway to the south of France is the **Nice-Côte d'Azur Airport** (www.nice.aeroport.fr). The 20-minute taxi ride to the centre of town can be expensive (€20–30); the bus is a better option. The express bus (No. 98) from Terminal 2 takes 20 to 30 minutes to get to the town centre and costs only €4. If the next leg of your travel is by train, take Bus No. 99 direct to the Gare SNCF.

If your flight arrives in **Marseille** (Marseille Provence Airport, www.marseille.aeroport. fr), an express bus to Marseille Gare St-Charles train station takes 25 minutes and costs €8.50. The only other alternative is a taxi, which runs to €40–50.

Toulon (Toulon-Hyères Airport, www.toulon-hyeres.aeroport.fr) is another convenient arrival point, particularly for St-Tropez. Bus line No. 102 takes 40 minutes from the airport to the main bus station and costs only €1.40, but there are only 5 per day; consult the

website for a schedule at www.reseaumistral.com. Otherwise, a taxi to the centre of town takes around 25 minutes and costs €45 during the day and €55 at night.

Montpellier (www.montpellier. aeroport.fr; tel: 04 67 20 85) is just 10 minutes by taxi from the town centre and costs around €25. Alternatively, the shuttle bus can be taken from outside the tramway station Léon Blum; a single ticket costs €4.80. The hours vary depending on flights, tel: 04 67 92 01.

Avignon (www.avignon.aeroport.fr; tel: 04 90 81 51 51). The only option is to take a taxi from the city centre, which costs around €22 and takes about 15 minutes.

Nîmes (www.nimes.cci.fr; tel: 04 66 70 49 49) A shuttle bus to the airport can be caught just opposite the train station in the city centre, and costs €5 for a one-way ticket. The hours depend upon flight times, tel: 04 66 29 27 29. For a taxi prepare to pay around €25.

Public Transport

Public transport within larger towns and cities in Provence is fairly efficient and avoids the problem of finding a parking space. If you are going to be staying in one or two different towns on your trip, a car is not really necessary, as there are trains and buses to get you from one place to another. On the other hand, if you will be touring, or you are planning to stay out in the country, a car is essential.

By Bus

Details of routes and timetables are generally available free of charge from tourist offices and bus stations (gares routières). Both places also give details of coach tours and sightseeing excursions. When boarding, tickets should be punched in the machine next to the driver, and passes should be shown.

Between towns and cities: visit the site www.vaucluse.fr for

BUS STATIONS

Below are telephone numbers for the main bus station *(gare routière)* of the larger towns.
Aix-en-Provence: 08 91 02 40 25
Avignon: 04 90 82 07 35
Cannes: 04 93 45 20 08
Grasse: 04 93 36 37 37
Marseille: 04 91 50 57 55
Menton: 04 93 35 93 60
Monaco: +377-97 70 22 22
Nice: 08 92 70 12 06

information on bus companies in the Vaucluse *département*, and www.cg13.fr if travelling from Marseille, Salon-de-Provence, Arles, Ciotat or Aix-en-Provence.

For travel for the area between Cagnes and Menton (including Nice and the surrounding area) contact **Ligne d'Azur**, Le Grand Hôtel, 10 Avenue Félix-Faure, Nice, tel: 08 10 06 10 06; www.lignedazur.com.

Between Toulon and Hyères, **Réseaumistral** rules the roads (720 Avenue Colonel Picot, Toulon, tel: 04 94 03 87 03, www.reseaumistral.com).

For bus travel in the Var region (including St-Tropez and St-Raphaël), contact the departmental office, tel: 08 25 00 06 50, or visit www.transports.var.fr, which has hours and itineraries for all the bus lines in the *département*.

For bus services and timetables in the Alpes-Maritimes visit www.cg06.fr/tam-html. Here again, local tourist offices can be very helpful, or contact the bus stations directly *(see box above)*.

By Train

There is a reasonably good SNCF rail network in the south of France, especially in the Val du Rhône and along the coast. You can pick up free local timetables from railway stations *(gares SNCF)* or visit www.voyages-sncf.fr. Services range from the high-speed TGV lines, which stop only at main stations, to the local TER services, which run along the Côte

d'Azur, stopping at all stations between Marseille and Ventimiglia. Out-of-town stations usually (but not always) have a connecting *navette* (shuttle bus) to the town centre. Sometimes the SNCF runs a connecting bus service (indicated as "Autocar" in timetables) to stations where the train no longer stops or along disused lines; rail tickets and passes are valid on these routes. Children under 4 years old travel free, those from 4 to 12 may travel for half-fare. Before boarding the train remember to validate your ticket at one of the machines in the station. These are marked "compostez votre billet".

Two scenic mountain lines depart from Nice. The **Roya Valley line** (www.ter-sncf.com/paca) runs from Nice to Tende through the Paillon and Roya-Bévéra valleys. And the privately operated **Train des Pignes** (www.trainprovence.com; tel: 04 92 31 01 58) has four return journeys from Nice that run up the Var valley to Digne-les-Bains. Vintage steam trains run on Sundays in summer.

By Car

Within cities: driving in towns is best avoided, especially in high season. Larger towns are well served by public transportation.
Between cities: roads to and around the main resorts get completely choked up during July and August, and you can spend as much time getting to the beach as you spend on it. Try to avoid weekends, mid- to late mornings (when everyone's going to the beach), and late afternoons (when everyone's going home from the beach). Lunchtime is usually a good bet, as is taking the *autoroutes* for longer distances.

Parking in the main resorts is costly; once again, time is of the essence because the cheaper spots on the street get snapped up early. Parking meters have been replaced by *horodateurs*, pay-and-display machines, which take coins and/or special parking

cards that can be bought at any tobacconist *(tabac)*.

British, US, Canadian and Australian licences are all valid in France. You should always carry your vehicle's registration document and valid insurance. Additional insurance cover, in some cases including a "home-return" service, is offered by a number of organisations, including the British Automobile Association (www.theaa.com, tel: 0800 107 0567) and Europ-Assistance (www.europ-assistance.co.uk; tel: 0870 737 5720).

Another useful address is FFAC (Fédération Français des Automobiles Club et des Usagers de la Route), 14, avenue de la Grande Armée, 75017 Paris; www.automobileclub.org; tel: 01 40 55 43 00. This group assists with breakdowns and liaises with non-French automobile clubs.

Speed Limits

Speed limits are as follows, unless otherwise indicated: 130 kph (80 mph) on motorways; 110 kph (68 mph) on dual carriageways; 90 kph (56 mph) on other roads, except in towns where the limit is 50 kph (30 mph). There is a minimum limit of 80 kph (50 mph) on the outside lane of motorways in daylight with good visibility and on level ground. Speed limits are 20 kph (12 mph) less on motorways in wet weather. On-the-spot fines can be levied for speeding; on toll roads, the time is printed on the ticket you take at your entry point and can thus be checked and a fine imposed on exit.

Rules of the Road

Drivers should follow the rules of the road. Heavy on-the-spot fines are given for traffic offences such as speeding, and drivers can be stopped and breathalysed during spot checks. Note the following:
• Drive on the right.
• The minimum age for driving in France is 18. Foreigners may not drive on a provisional licence.
• Full or dipped headlights must be used in poor visibility and at

night; sidelights are not sufficient unless the car is stationary. Beams must be adjusted for right-hand-drive vehicles, but yellow tints are not compulsory.

• The use of seat belts (front and rear) is compulsory.

• Children under 10 are not allowed to ride in the front seat unless the car has a rear-facing safety seat.

• Carry a red warning triangle to place 50 metres (165 ft) behind the car in case of a breakdown or accident. In an accident or emergency, call the police (dial 17) or use the free emergency telephones (every 2 km/1 mile) on motorways. If another driver is involved, lock your car and go together to call the police. It is useful to carry a European Accident Statement Form (obtainable from your insurance company), which will simplify matters in the event of an accident.

Traffic on major roads has priority, with traffic being halted on minor approach roads by means of one of the following signs. *Cédez le passage* – give way *Vous n'avez pas la priorité* – you do not have right of way *Passage protégé* – no right of way. However, care should be taken in smaller towns and in rural areas where there may not

BELOW: motoring the Alps in style.

be road markings, in which case you will be expected to give way to traffic coming from the right.

If an oncoming driver flashes their headlights it is to indicate that he or she has priority – not the other way around. A yellow diamond sign indicates that you have priority; the diamond sign with a diagonal black line means you do not have priority.

Fuel

Unleaded petrol *(essence sans plomb)* and diesel are widely available in France. A map showing the location of filling stations is available from main tourist offices. Petrol is generally cheapest at hypermarkets and most expensive on motorways.

Motorcycles and Mopeds

Rules of the road are largely the same for two-wheeled riders as for car drivers. The minimum age for driving machines over 80cc is 18. Nationality plates (eg GB stickers) must be shown, and it is compulsory to wear crash helmets. Dipped headlights must be used at all times, and children under 14 may not be carried as passengers.

Hitch-hiking

Hitch-hiking *(faire l'autostop)* is more common in France than in the UK. The safest way to arrange a lift is through a hitch-hiking agency, such as **Allô-Stop** (30 rue Pierre Sémard, 75009 Paris; tel: 01 53 20 42 42; www.allostop.net). You pay an agency fee and then a small fee per kilometre, which goes directly to the driver. Contact the agency well in advance to arrange a convenient lift. Avignon, Marseille and Nice are all popular destinations.

By Bicycle

Bicycles are readily available for hire: contact tourist offices for rental listings. Bicycles are car-

ried free of charge on buses and some trains; on other, faster services you will have to pay. Travelling by a combination of bicycle and bus or train can be an excellent way of touring the region.

On Foot

France has a network of footpaths, called *Grandes Randonnées*, which are well signposted and offer good facilities for walkers en route. The paths are classified with a "GR" number. The IGN Blue Series maps at a scale of 1:25,000 are very good for walkers.

For information on walking holidays, see page 282.

Taxis

Taxis are normally available at railway stations and official taxi ranks in city centres. Outside the cities check telephone directories. Between cities is a very expensive option. If possible consider alternatives.
Aix tel: 04 42 27 71 11
Antibes tel: 04 93 67 67 67
Avignon tel: 04 90 82 20 20
Marseille:
Eurotaxi, tel: 04 91 05 31 98.
There are eight ranks in Marseille, and you can hail taxis in the street.
Menton tel: 04 92 10 47 00
Monaco tel: 377 93 15 02 02
Nice:
Centrale de Taxi, tel: 04 93 13 78 78. There are 29 taxi ranks in the city but you can also hail them in the street. Pay by the kilometre.

In the Air

Tourist flights in helicopters are offered by:
Héli Sécurité (St-Tropez), tel: 04 94 555 999; www.helicopter-saint-tropez.com
Héli Air Monaco, tel: 00 377-92 05 00 50; www.heliairmonaco.com.
Héli Riviera (Cannes), tel: 04 93 90 53 00; www.heliriviera.com

ACCOMMODATION

WHERE TO STAY

Hotels

All hotels in France conform to national standards and carry star ratings, which are set down by the Ministry of Tourism, according to their degree of comfort and amenities. Prices, which are charged per room not per person, range from as little as €35 for a double room in an unclassified hotel (ie its standards are not sufficient to warrant a single star, but it is likely to be clean, cheap and cheerful), to around €200 for the cheapest double room in a four-star luxury hotel.

Hotels are required by law to display their menus outside, and details of room prices should be visible either outside or in the reception, as well as on the back of bedroom doors. Note that it is possible for a hotel to have a one-star rating, with a two-star restaurant. Don't rely too heavily on the star system – the ratings are more about facilities (size of rooms, presence of hairdryers, etc) than quality.

When booking a room you should normally be shown it before you agree to take it, so don't hesitate to ask to do so. Supplements may be charged for an additional bed or a cot (lit bébé). You may be asked when booking if you wish to dine, particularly if the hotel is busy – and

you should confirm that the hotel's restaurant is open (many are closed out of season on Sunday or Monday evenings).

Lists of hotels can be obtained from the French government tourist office in your country or from regional or local tourist offices in France. If you just want an overnight stop to break a journey, you may find clean, modern, basic chains such as Première Classe and Ibis handy.

Bed and Breakfasts

Bed and breakfast (chambre d'hôte) accommodation is fairly widely available in private houses, often on working farms, whose owners are members of the **Fédération Nationale des Gîtes Ruraux de France**. Bookings can be made for an overnight stop or a longer stay. Breakfast is included in the price, and evening meals, which are usually made with local produce and very good value, are often also available.

Gîtes de France has very strict standards for its members, and you can generally count on cleanliness and quality. Contact Gîtes de France, 59 Rue St-Lazare, 75439 Paris Cedex 09; tel: 01 49 70 75 75; fax: 01 42 81 28 53; www.gites-de-france.fr.

Bed and Breakfast in France lists B&Bs, including chateaux.

UK booking service, tel: 0871 781 0834; www.bedbreak.com

If you don't wish to book in advance, you can always just look out for signs along the road (usually most common in the country) offering chambres d'hôte. You shouldn't have too many difficulties finding a bed out of season, and you may be surprised by the good value of the simple farm food and accommodation on offer.

Gîtes

Rural gîtes (vacation cottages) are a good way to holiday in the south, though most will be found in rural areas away from the coast. Accommodation ranges from converted barns to grand chateaux. There are several national networks of gîtes, the largest of which is Gîtes de France (see left), whose members are regularly inspected by the Relais Départemental (the regional office of the national federation) and rated; the number of "épis" (ears of corn) indicates the level of quality.

Other networks include **Clévacances** (www.clevacances.com), which has furnished apartments, cottages, and B&Bs, and **Fleurs de Soleil** (www.fleurs-soleil.tm.fr), which offers B&Bs only.

Gîtes are self-catering, and you should check exactly what you need to supply. They are often in remote locations and you will need your own transport. *Gîte* owners will be able to advise about shopping, local sights and activities, bicycle hire, and so on. Some *gîtes* are equipped for wheelchair users; check the descriptions on the websites or contact the network office for details.

Brittany Ferries are UK agents for Gîtes de France, and bookings can be made through The Brittany Centre, Wharf Road, Portsmouth PO2 8RU; tel: 0870 536 0360, www.brittany-ferries.co.uk. The list of *gîtes* in the Brittany Ferries brochure is only a selection of those available.

Various UK-based tour operators also offer a range of self-catering accommodation as part of a package holiday. Try: **Chez Nous**, tel: 0870 191 7740; http://cheznous.com **French Life**, tel: 0870 444 8877; www.frenchlife.co.uk **Individual Travellers**, tel: 08700 780 189; www.indiv-travellers.com

Gîtes d'Etape

Gîtes d'Étape offer very basic accommodation for walkers or cyclists, often in remote mountain areas; expect communal accommodation, bunk beds, shared bathrooms, etc. You will need to make reservations, especially in busy periods. *Gîte de neige*, *gîte de pêche* and *gîte équestre* offer similar facilities.

Mountain refuges *(refuges)* offer similar accommodation and some also provide food. Many refuges are open from June to September only, and they should always be booked in advance. Prices vary from €8 to €15 per person. Lists of refuges are available from local tourist offices.

Youth Hostels

To stay in most youth hostels *(auberges de jeunesse)* you need to be a member of the International Youth Hostel Association (YHA) or the Fédération Unie des Auberges de Jeunesse, which is affiliated to the International Youth Hostel Federation. For more information, contact: **Fédération Unie des Auberges de Jeunesse** (FUAJ), 27 rue Pajol, 75018 Paris; tel: 01 44 89 87 27; fax: 01 44 89 87 49; www.fuaj.org **Hostelling International USA**, 8401 Colesville Road, Suite 600, Silver Springs, MD 20910, tel: 301 495 1240; fax: 301 495 6697; www.hiusa.org **International Youth Hostel Federation**, 2nd Floor, Gate House, Fretherne Road, Welwyn Garden City, Herts AL8 6RD; tel: 01707 324 170; fax: 01707 323 980; www.hihostels.com

Camping

French campsites *(campings)*, many of which are run by local councils, can often be remarkably comfortable and well appointed. Prices range from around €15–30 per night for two people with a car, caravan or tent. On the coast during high season the campsites can be extremely crowded. Although camping rough *(camping sauvage)* is generally not permitted, it may be worth asking the owner of the land for permission if there is nowhere official to pitch up near by. Fire is an ever-present risk in the region, so be particularly careful when cooking.

Campsites are graded from one-star (minimal comfort, water points, showers and sinks) to four-star luxury sites, which allow more space for each pitch and offer above-average facilities. The majority of sites are two-star. Sites that are designated *Aire naturelle de camping* and *Camping à la ferme* tend to be cheaper and have fewer services than standard sites.

The *Guide Officiel* of the **French Federation of Camping and Caravanning** (FFCC), available from French Government Tourist Offices as well as the FFCC website (www.ffcc.fr), lists 11,000 sites nationwide, and indicates those that have facilities for disabled campers. The FFCC also runs another site, www.campingfrance.com, with an extensive listing of French campsites. The *Michelin Guide: Camping France* is also very informative.

Reservation Services

Avis Car Away (camping cars; France), tel: 01 47 49 80 40; www.aviscaraway.com **Canvas Holidays** (UK), tel: 0870 192 1154; www.canvasholidays.co.uk **Select Site Reservations** (UK), tel: 01873 859 876; www.select-site.com **Vancansoleil**, tel: 0870 077 8779, www.vacansoleil.co.uk

Hotel guides

Various guides can be obtained from the French Tourist Office. These include *Châteaux & Hotels de France* (mid- to high-end hotels, restaurants and stays in private chateaux; tel: 08 92 23 00 75; www.chateauxhotels.com) and *Relais du Silence* (mid- to high-end hotels "de charme", often in chateaux or grand houses, that are in particularly peaceful settings; 01 44 49 90 00; www.silencehotel.com).

Logis de France is France's biggest hotel federation, with over 3,000 private hotels all over France. Most of these hotels are in the budget to mid-range category, and they vary greatly in facilities, atmosphere and levels of service. Contact the **Fédération Nationale des Logis et Auberges de France**, 83 avenue d'Italie, 75013 Paris; tel: 01 45 84 70 00; www.logis-de-france.fr, or the French Government Tourist Office for a Logis de France handbook. They also offer a listing of hotels that are accessible for disabled travellers.

Hotel Listings

Hotels are listed according to the chapters in this book, and thereafter by place, then hotel name, in alphabetical order.

TRANSPORT
ACCOMMODATION
ACTIVITIES
A – Z
LANGUAGE

AVIGNON

Avignon

Auberge de Cassagne
450 allée de Cassagne
Le Pontet-Avignon
Tel: 04 90 31 04 18
www.hotelprestige-provence.com
This extremely upmarket hotel is located around 8 km (5 miles) from the centre of Avignon, providing a refuge from the buzz of the city. Facilities include a sauna, exercise room and a lovely pool, set among exotic vegetation. There's a top-quality, if expensive, restaurant. €€€

Hôtel Cloître St-Louis
20 rue du Portail Boquier
Tel: 04 90 27 55 55
www.cloitre-saint-louis.com
Set around a pleasant cloister, the comfortable Cloître St-Louis combines a wing of a former monastery with a dramatic modern steel-and-glass wing, designed by Jean Nouvel, complete with swimming pool on top. €€

Hôtel de Blauvac
11 rue de la Bancasse
Tel: 04 90 86 34 11
www.hotel-blauvac.com
A lovely budget option on a narrow side street

just off rue de la République. The 17th-century former residence of the Marquis de Blauvac is simple but alluring with its elegant staircase and exposed stone walls. €–€€

Hôtel de la Mirande
4 place de la Mirande
Tel: 04 90 85 93 93
www.la-mirande.fr
The faultlessly decorated Mirande offers 20 personalised rooms in the 17th-century Hôtel de Vervins. The salons and glazed-in courtyard still have the feel of a private house and, as a bonus, you can take cookery courses in the old kitchens. €€€€

Hôtel d'Europe
12 place Crillon
Tel: 04 90 14 76 76
www.heurope.com
Set behind a lovely courtyard, in an antique-filled 16th-century mansion, this building has been a hotel for over 200 years and has seen everyone from Napoleon, Lamartine, Victor Hugo and John Stuart Mill to more recent politicians and actors. It is conveniently situated, quiet, elegant and comfortable. €€€

Hôtel Mignon
12 rue Joseph Vernet
Tel: 04 90 82 17 30
www.hotel-mignon.com
This sweet little hotel with 15 rooms is surprisingly adequate for its category and price. It's not luxurious, but the location is central and the bathrooms sparkle. €€

Hôtel Saint-Georges
12 traverse de l'Etoile
Tel: 04 90 88 54 34
www.hotel-saint-george.com
This clean, good-value hotel is located outside the ramparts on the road to Marseille. Friendly staff. €

La Ferme
Chemin des Bois
Ile de la Barthelasse
Tel: 04 90 82 57 53
www.hotel-laferme.com
A beautiful farm in a peaceful spot on an island yet within easy reach of the city centre. Pleasant rooms, a pool and fresh, simple cuisine. €€

Mercure Cité des Papes
1 rue Jean Vilar
Tel: 04 90 80 93 00
www.accor.com
If you are determined to stay next door to the

lovely Palais in Avignon, consider the 73-roomed Cité des Papes. Be sure to request one of the quiet back rooms with palatial views. €€

Villeneuve-lès-Avignon

Hôtel-Restaurant La Magnaneraie
37 rue Camp de Bataille
Tel: 04 90 15 92 00
www.hotellerie-la-magnaneraie.com
If you're having trouble finding somewhere to stay in Avignon (sometimes a problem during the summer festival), you could stay in Villeneuve. This hotel is housed in a 15th-century building in a garden with ponds, palms and ancient oaks. More contemporary facilities include a swimming pool and tennis courts; you can also hire bicycles from here. €€€

ORANGE AND THE MONT VENTOUX

Carpentras

Le Fiacre
153 rue Vigne
Tel: 04 90 63 03 15
www.hotel-du-fiacre.com
An interesting old town house and an excellent choice if you want to stay somewhere central. €–€€

Châteauneuf-du-Pape

La Sommellerie
Route de Roquemaure
Tel: 04 90 83 50 00
www.la-sommellerie.com
In the heart of the famous vineyards, 4 km (2½ miles) from the village centre, this restored 17th-century farm build-

ing has pleasant rooms with rustic furnishings. Provençal-style dining room serves regional cuisine. Pool. €€

Orange

Château de Massillan
Chemin Hauteville
Tel: 04 90 40 64 51
www.chateau-de-massillan.com

If money is no object, this luxury hotel-restaurant just a few kilometres northeast of Orange is the place to stay. The historic chateau has been given an ultra-modern interior by Babylon Design in London. The 12 bedrooms are due to be extended to 20 in 2007. Extensive grounds.**€€€€**

Glacier
46 cours Aristide-Briand
Tel: 04 90 34 02 01
www.le-glacier.com
A straightforward hotel in a good location on the edge of the old town. Very friendly staff. No restaurant. **€€**

Hôtel Arène
Place des Langes
Tel: 04 90 11 40 40
www.hotel-arene.com
A great central hotel on a tranquil square. Good restaurant. **€€**

Sault

Hostellerie du Val de Sault
Ancien chemin de Sault
Tel: 04 90 64 01 41
www. valdesault.com
This is an elevated modern hotel with gardens and a swimming pool looking out onto Mont

Ventoux. There are rooms with terraces, and the cuisine served is typical of the region and tasty. **€€€**

Vaison-la-Romaine

Hostellerie le Beffroi
Rue de l'Evêché
Tel: 04 90 36 04 71
www.le-beffroi.com
Le Beffroi is a delightful 16th-century hostelry with period decor and a restaurant offering good cuisine. The views from here are excellent. **€€**

THE LUBERON

Bonnieux

Bastide de Capelongue
Tel: 04 90 75 89 78
www.capelongue.com
Beautiful modern *mas* in the midst of the *garrigue* plateau above the village. Now in the hands of top chef Edouard Loubet.
€€€–€€€€

Le Prieuré
Tel: 04 90 75 80 78
www.hotelprieure.com
Vaulted ceilings, sculpted niches, gigantic fireplaces and a chapel remain from this ancient building's past as a religious charity hospital built into the ramparts of the medieval town. There's an attractive dining room and walled garden. **€€–€€€**

Gordes

La Bastide de Gordes
Route de Combe
Tel: 04 90 72 12 12
www.bastide-de-gordes.com
A fine Renaissance

building on the ramparts with elegant rooms, wonderful views and many modern facilities, including a solarium and sauna. Visits to local vineyards can be arranged. 29 rooms and 2 suites. **€€€€**

L'Isle sur la Sorgue

Mas de Cure Bourse
Tel: 04 90 38 16 58
www.masdecurebourse.com
Set in orchards 3 km (2 miles) from the town, this former 18th-century coaching inn has pleasant, traditionally decorated rooms, a large garden and swimming pool. **€€**

Lourmarin

Le Mas de Guilles
Route de Vaugines
Tel: 04 90 68 30 55
www.guilles.com
Quiet and relaxing *mas*, set amid vineyards at the end of a long avenue of olive trees, just outside

Lourmarin. Rooms are spacious and attractive with big old Provençal wardrobes and colourful kelims. Swimming pool and tennis courts in the grounds. **€€**

Manosque

Francois 1er
18 rue Guilhempierre
Tel: 04 92 72 07 99
hotel-francois1er@wanadoo.fr
A quiet, friendly two-star hotel. **€€**

St-Saturnin-sur-Apt

Domaine des Andéols
Tel: 04 90 75 50 63
www.domainedesandeols.com
This painstakingly restored hamlet has brought conceptual design to deepest Provence. A world away from the clichés of Provençal prints, the nine achingly hip "houses" are furnished with modern design classics and contemporary artworks. There's

an equally immaculate garden and a restaurant run by Alain Ducasse. Closed Nov–Mar. **€€€€**

Vaugines

Hostellerie du Luberon
Tel: 04 90 77 27 19
www.hotellerieduluberon.com
A simple, Provençal *mas* with a friendly, family-run atmosphere. The restaurant looks out onto the pretty gardens and a pool. **€€**

PRICE CATEGORIES

Price categories are for an average double room in high season:
€ = under €80
€€ = €80–150
€€€ = €150–250
€€€€ = more than €250

MARSEILLE AND THE CALANQUES

Marseille

Hôtel Alizé
35 quai des Belges
Tel: 04 91 33 66 97
www.alize-hotel.com
A functional Provençal-style hotel. The rooms at the front have almost the same view of the port for a fraction of the price. €€

Hôtel Le Corbusier
280 boulevard Michelet
Tel: 04 91 16 78 00
www.hotellecorbusier.com
Architecture fans might like to check in at this hotel on the 7th floor of Le Corbusier's Cité Radieuse. Basic but iconic. €–€€

Le Petit Nice
Anse de Maldormé, corniche de J.F. Kennedy
Tel: 04 91 59 25 92
www.passedat.fr
A luxurious Belle Epoque villa sitting on its own promontory with stunning sea views. A top-class restaurant. €€€

Mercure Grand Hôtel Beauvau
4 rue Beauvau
Tel: 04 91 54 91 00
www.mercure.com
Occupying a prime site on the Vieux-Port, this grand hotel has welcomed such luminaries as George Sand, Chopin and Alfred de Musset.

Recently refurbished to a level of luxury 4-star comfort, many of the rooms overlook the Vieux-Port. €€€

Résidence du Vieux-Port
18 quai du Port
Tel: 04 91 91 91 22
www.hotelmarseille.com
A comfortable 1950s hotel with smartly redecorated Provençal-style rooms, some with balconies overlooking the port. No restaurant. €€€

Cassis

Les Jardins de Cassis
Avenue Auguste Favier

Tel: 04 42 01 84 85
www.lesjardinsdecassis.com
A lovely Provençal-style hotel situated on the hillside above the town centre of Cassis, sitting in a palm tree-filled garden. The rooms are clean and well maintained, some with private terraces opening onto the garden. Pool. €€

AIX-EN-PROVENCE

Grand Hôtel Nègre Coste
33 cours Mirabeau
Tel: 04 42 27 74 22
www.hotelnegrecoste.com
Set on Aix's elegant main street, this hotel may not be as grand as it once was (its original reception rooms have lost out to a pizzeria), but the reasonably sized bedrooms offer lovely views of the cours Mirabeau and over pantiled rooftops to the cathedral. Good value considering its location. €€

PRICE CATEGORIES

Price categories are for an average double room in high season:
€ = under €80
€€ = €80–150
€€€ = €150–250
€€€€ = more than €250

Hôtel Cardinal
24 rue Cardinal
Tel: 04 42 38 32 30
Fax: 04 42 26 39 05
A charming 18th-century building cluttered with antique furniture houses this budget hotel neighbouring the Musée Granet. €€

Hôtel Cézanne
40 avenue Victor Hugo
Tel: 04 42 91 11 11
www.hotelaix.com
Located between the Quartier Mazarin and the station, the Cézanne is a rare case of a chain hotel (a former Mercure) returning to private ownership. It is now a lovely boutique hotel with a relaxing downstairs bar with neo-Baroque armchairs, individually decorated rooms and new king-size beds. Very helpful staff. €€€

Hôtel des Augustins
3 rue de la Masse
Tel: 04 42 27 28 59
www.hotel-augustins.com
The Hôtel des Augustins is housed in a building that was an Augustine convent until the French Revolution of 1789. It became a hotel in the 1890s. Conveniently located near the cours Mirabeau, this place has comfortable rooms and a very imposing reception area. €€

Hôtel des Quatre Dauphins
54 rue Roux Alphéran
Tel: 04 42 38 16 39
Overlooking the dolphin fountain, this small hotel has lots of fans, and with good reason. It is inexpensive but not without character and comfort. There is no hotel restaurant, but

that is hardly a problem in this central part of town. €€

Le Pigonnet
5 avenue du Pigonnet
Tel: 04 42 59 02 90
www.hotelpigonnet.com
This is a luxurious and tranquil retreat (with prices to match), just a short walk from the city centre. It has an up-market restaurant, swimming pool and shady garden in which Cézanne, who is closely associated with Aix (*see page 120*), once painted a view of the Mont Ste-Victoire. €€€€

TRANSPORT

ST-RÉMY AND LES ALPILLES

Fontvieille

Hôtel Peireiro
36 avenue des Baux
Tel: 04 90 54 76 10
www.hotel-peireiro.com
Good value hotel with
43 rooms, a lovely
veranda, pool, sauna
and mini-golf. €€

Les Baux-de-Provence

L'Oustau de Baumaniere
Route d'Arles
Tel: 04 90 54 33 07
www.oustaudebaumaniere.com
This is a superbly
renovated 16th-
century farmhouse
near Les Baux, with a
magnificent view and

celebrated restaurant
with two Michelin stars.
€€€€

St-Rémy-de-Provence

Hôtel Château des Alpilles
D31, St-Rémy de Provence
Tel: 04 90 92 03 33
www.chateaudesalpilles.com
Sophisticated 19th-
century chateau in its
own park includes
accommodation in
restored farm and
chapel, with pool, and
restaurant serving
excellent regional
dishes. €€€
Hôtel du Cheval-Blanc
6 avenue Fauconnet
Tel: 04 90 92 09 28

www.hotelcheval-blanc.com
A simple and slightly
eccentric hotel, but the
reasonably sized rooms
and bargain prices, plus
a centre-town location,
make this a long-
standing budget
favourite. The owners
do insist you pay
upfront. Closed Nov to
early Mar. €
Hôtel les Ateliers de l'Image
36 boulevard Victor Hugo
Tel: 04 90 92 51 50
www.hotelphoto.com
Occupying a former
music hall, this is a very
stylish hotel. Particu-
larly lovely is the Japan-
ese-inspired garden
with its pools and path-
ways. It also offers a

modern restaurant,
sushi bar, photography
courses and exhibi-
tions. €€€
Le Sommeil des Fées
4 rue du 8 mai 1945
Tel: 04 90 92 17 66
www.alpilles-delices.com
Beautifully renovated
and decorated in
Provençal style, this five-
room guest house is in
the middle of town, with
rooms overlooking a
pretty patio and garden.

ACCOMMODATION

ARLES AND THE CAMARGUE

Arles

Grand Hôtel Nord-Pinus
Place du Forum
Tel: 04 90 93 44 44
www.nord-pinus.com
This luxury hotel with its
fashionable bar and art-
deco brasserie is an
Arles institution. The
stairway decorated with
feria bullfighting posters
and Peter Beard photos
shows the town's
double orientation. €€€
Hôtel Calendal
22 Place Pomme
Tel: 04 90 96 11 89
www.lecalendal.com
Homely Provençal-style
rooms in a cluster of old
houses set around a
pretty courtyard. Good
location behind the
Arena; some rooms
have views of the
Théâtre Antique. €€

Hôtel d'Arlatan
26 rue du Sauvage
Tel: 04 90 93 56 66
www.hotel-arlatan.fr
A very popular hotel. It
has a pool, an enclosed
garden and a scattering
of Roman archaeologi-
cal remains. 34 rooms
and 7 suites. €€–€€€
Hôtel du Cloître
16 rue du Cloître
Tel: 04 90 96 29 50
www.hotelcloitre.com
Conveniently located,
pleasantly run and well-
priced hotel with trad-
itional Provençal decor.
Good location on a nar-
row street near the
Roman Théâtre Antique.
€€
Hôtel du Forum
Place du Forum
Tel: 04 90 93 48 95
www.hotelduforum.com
The Forum lacks the

style of the Grand Hôtel
Nord-Pinus (*see left*),
but it is still comfort-
able and has the advan-
tage of a swimming pool
in a secluded courtyard.
€€
Hôtel du Musée
11 rue du Grand Prieuré
Tel: 04 90 93 88 88
www.hoteldumusee.com
A 17th-century mansion
tucked away on a
winding street, with a
pretty courtyard for
breakfast. €

Le Sambuc

Le Mas de Peint
Tel: 04 90 97 20 62
www.masdepeint.com
This elegant *mas* (coun-
try house) offers the full
rural Camargue experi-
ence, including deli-
cious Provençal meals *à*

la table d'hôte (by reservation only) and bulls
and horses outside.
Swimming pool. €€€

Stes-Maries-de-la-Mer

Hotel Camille
13 avenue de la Plage
Tel: 04 90 97 80 26
www.hotel-camille.camargue.fr
This hotel offers very
reasonable rates for the
Camargue, especially
for somewhere with
views of the sea. No
frills but friendly. €–€€

ACTIVITIES

A – Z

LANGUAGE

NÎMES AND THE PONT DU GARD

Nîmes

Hôtel Amphithéâtre
4 rue des Arènes
Tel: 04 66 67 28 51
Just behind the Arena on a little side street, this is an excellent budget hotel. Attractive rooms with antique furniture. **€**

Hôtel Imperator
Quai de la Fontaine
Tel: 04 66 21 90 30
www.hotel-imperator.com
The low-key façade

hides comfortable, traditional rooms, a good restaurant, a vintage lift and a luxuriantly planted garden. This is where toreadors have traditionally stayed – and, of course, bullfighting buff Ernest Hemingway. **€€€**

New Hôtel La Baume
21 rue Nationale
Tel: 04 66 76 28 42
www.new-hotel.com
Occupies a fine 17th-century *hôtel particulier*

with a magnificent galleried interior courtyard. The spacious rooms are comfortable and decorated with richly coloured furnishings. **€€€**

Royal Hôtel
3 boulevard Alphonse Daudet
Tel: 04 66 58 28 27
www.royalhotel-nimes.fr
The Royal Hôtel is a cult address with its artfully casual boho decor, worn leather armchairs, wood floors, modern art and

friendly staff. Most rooms overlook the place d'Assas, where its trendy tapas bar, La Bodeguita, has tables out on the pavement. **€€**

THE GORGES DU VERDON

Castellane

Auberge du Teillon
La Garde, Route Napoleon
Tel: 04 92 83 60 88
www.auberge-teillon.com
Six km (4 miles) outside Castellane. Basic rooms but excellent cuisine (booking essential). **€**

Nouvel Hôtel de Commerce
18 place de l'Eglise

Tel: 04 92 83 61 00
www.hotel-fradet.com
Reasonably priced rooms and an excellent restaurant, managed by a former student of Alain Ducasse. **€€**

Moustiers-Ste-Marie

Chemin de Quinson
Tel: 04 92 70 47 47

Fax: 04 92 70 47 48
www.bastide-moustiers.com
This ancient, beautifully restored *bastide* is the first of Alain Ducasse's country *auberges*, where luxury and rural calm are the key features. Swimming pool and helicopter pad. **€€€**

La Bonne Auberge
Le Village
Tel: 04 92 74 6618

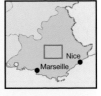

A reasonable, mid-range hotel. Rustic restaurant serving regional dishes, and pool. **€€**

DIGNE AND THE SOUTHERN ALPS

Digne-les-Bains

Château de Trigance
Trigance
Tel: 04 94 76 91 18
www.chateau-de-trigance.fr
A member of the Châteaux et Hôtels de France group, this 10th-century castle is a lovely place to stay in the hilltop village of Digne. Good restaurant (booking advised). **€€€**

Hôtel Coin Fleuri
9 boulevard Victor Hugo
Tel: 04 92 31 04 51
Fax: 04 92 32 55 75

Visitors on a modest budget will find Digne's 13-roomed Coin Fleuri a pleasant option, with bright, practical rooms. **€**

Hôtel le Grand Paris
19 boulevard Thiers
Tel: 04 92 31 11 15
www.chateauxhotels.com
Le Grand Paris, a 17th-century former convent with an old-fashioned ambience, is the place to stay in Digne if you have both discerning taste and a large wallet. The restaurant is excellent, and there's a

stylish health centre. 16 rooms and 3 suites. **€€–€€€**

Sauze

Hôtel Pyjama
Super-Sauze
Tel: 04 92 81 12 00
www.lepyjama.com
Ski buffs should make for this homely winter-sports hotel. Geared for the snow-seeker, it is also open in summer (20 Dec–20 May and mid-June–mid-Sept). Some rooms have mez-

zanines to accommodate families. There is no restaurant, but breakfast can be taken in your room, in front of the log fire in winter, or outside on the terrace in summer. 10 rooms and 4 studios. **€€**

TOULON AND THE WESTERN VAR

Bandol

Hostellerie Bérard
Avenue G. Péri
Tel: 04 94 90 11 43
www.hotel-berard.com
Rooms and restaurant in an atmospheric old convent in the middle of the village. €€
L'Ile Rousse
25 boulevard Louis-Lumière
Tel: 04 94 29 33 00
www.thalazur.com
Provençal-style hotel with a spectacular view of the sea. Thalasso-therapy centre, pool and refined cuisine served in the restaurant. €€€

Ile de Porquerolles

Mas du Langoustier
Tel: 04 94 58 30 09
www.langoustier.com
A warm Provençal *mas* that is luxurious if a bit precious, surrounded by exotic gardens. Fabulous restaurant. Free transport from the port to the hotel. €€€

Ile de Port Cros

Le Manoir
Tel: 04 94 05 90 52
Fax: 04 94 05 90 89
The only hotel on the no-smoking, no-car island of Port Cros. Rooms in the colonial-style 19th-century building are cosy and some have balconies. Large garden. €€€

Saint-Maximin-la-Sainte-Baume

Hôtellerie Le Couvent Royal
Place Jean Salusse
Tel: 04 94 86 55 66
www.hotelfp-saintmaximin.com
Occupies a royal monastery founded in 1295 adjoining the finest Gothic church in Provence. The former monks' cells have been converted with simpli-

city and good taste into 67 bedrooms. Meals are served in the vaulted chapter house or in the cloister. €€

Sanary-sur-Mer

Hôtel de la Tour
24 quai General de Gaulle
Tel: 04 94 74 10 10
www.sanary-hoteldelatour.com
Located right next to the Saracen tower with most rooms overlooking the port. 24 rooms. €€

Toulon

Le Grand Hôtel Dauphinée
10 rue Berthelot
Tel: 04 94 92 20 28
www.grandhoteldauphine.com
For a hotel in such a central location in the old town, this place offers good value. Friendly staff. €€
New Hôtel Tour Blanche
Boulevard Amiral Vence

Tel: 04 94 24 41 57
www.new-hotel.com
An amusing 1960s hotel built on stilts into the hillside next to the Mont Faron cable-car route. Rooms have kept their original curvy modular furniture; those at the front have stunning panoramic views of the bay. Swimming pool and restaurant. Parking. €€

Villecroze

Auberge des Lavandes
Place Général de Gaulle
Tel: 04 94 70 76 00
A small, good-value *auberge* in this picturesque village, with a good restaurant. €–€€

ST-TROPEZ AND THE MAURES

Bormes-les-Mimosas

Hôtel Bellevue
14 place Gambetta
Tel: 04 94 71 15 15
www.bellevuebormes.fr.st
An amber-coloured hotel-restaurant set on the lively main square of the old village with views down to the coast and a busy restaurant. Most rooms newly decorated with Provençal print fabrics. Closed mid-Nov to mid-Jan. 12 rooms. €

Fréjus

Aréna
145 boulevard Général de Gaulle
Tel: 04 94 17 09 40
www.arena-hotel.com
Situated in the old town with a pool, a nice garden and an excellent regional restaurant. €€

Grimaud

Hostellerie du Coteau Fleuri
Place des Pénitents
Tel: 04 94 43 20 17

www.coteaufleuri.fr
A welcoming 1930s inn on the outskirts of town with views over the vineyards. The restaurant serves traditional Provençal cuisine. €€
La Boulangerie
Route de Collobrières
Tel: 04 94 43 23 16
A small but comfortable and friendly hotel situated in the quiet of the Massif des Maures. The hotel's amenities include a pool and tennis courts. €€

PRICE CATEGORIES

Price categories are for an average double room in high season:
€ = under €80
€€ = €80–150
€€€ = €150–250
€€€€ = more than €250

La Croix-Valmer

La Pinède Plage
Tel: 04 94 55 16 16
www.pinedeplage.com
Comfortable neo-Provençal hotel set amid parasol pines on the Plage de Gigaro. Great for sporting types: you can pretty much step straight outside onto the sand, where there are free kayaks, pedalos and windsurfers, and the possiblity of jet-skiing and water-skiing. €€€€

Le Lavandou

Beau Soleil
Tel: 04 94 05 84 55
www.beausoleil-alcyons.com
Reasonably priced hotel where the rooms have balconies and you can dine beneath the plane trees. €€
Les Roches
1 avenue des trois Dauphins
Tel: 04 94 71 05 07
www.hotellesroches.com
Set on the cliffs with fabulous sea views, a luxurious modern hotel, tastefully decorated and furnished. Private beach, freshwater swimming pool. Closed in winter. €€€

Le Rayol-Canadel

Le Bailli de Suffren
Tel: 04 98 04 47 00
www.lebaillidesuffren.com
Set on the beach below the beautiful gardens of the Domaine de Rayol. The curved 1960s building – all rooms with balconies or terraces and sea views – has been pleasantly refurbished in calm, modern-Provençal chic, with pool, private beach, bar, restaurant and hire boats to explore the St-Tropez peninsula without the traffic jams. €€€€

Plan-de-la-Tour

Mas des Brugassières
1.5 km (1 mile) south of the village
Tel: 04 94 55 50 55
www.masdesbrugassieres.com
Away from the coast in the Maures hills, 10 km (6 miles) from Ste-Maxime, this intimate hotel was modelled on a Provençal *mas*, or farmhouse. The large garden includes a small pool; many rooms open on a semi-private terrace. Closed mid-Oct–Mar. 14 rooms. €€

Ramatuelle

La Ferme d'Augustin
Plage de Tahiti
Tel: 04 94 55 97 00
www.fermeaugustin.com
Set in vineyards next to Tahiti Beach, this lovely old farmhouse is surrounded by greenery. The bedrooms overlook the gardens, and many have balconies and sea views. Heated pool. Secured parking. Closed Oct–Mar. 46 rooms. €€€
Le Baou
Avenue Gustave Etienne
Tel: 04 98 12 94 20
www.alpazurhotels.com
Upmarket hotel with good-sized modern rooms with balconies and delightful views. €€€–€€€€

St-Tropez

Benkirai
11 chemin du Pinet
Tel: 04 94 97 04 37
www.hotel-benkirai.com
At last, a totally contemporary hotel in St-Tropez, courtesy of star French designer Patrick Jouin. Sleek modern finishes in leather, metal and concrete, and all-blue bathrooms contrast with warm Moroccan reds. All rooms have balconies or terraces around the pool. Excellent Thai restaurant. €€€€
Hotel Sube
Port de St-Tropez
Tel: 04 94 97 30 04
www.hotel-sube.com
A long-established hotel right on the port where all the action is (though that means it can be noisy). Best rooms have views of the port. The hotel bar is a favourite

meeting place for yachtie types. €€–€€€
La Bastide Rouge
Chemin du Pinet
Tel: 04 94 97 41 24
www.la-bastide-rouge.com
A pleasant mid-range *bastide* with tropical gardens, pool and tasteful rooms. €€€
La Maison Blanche
Place des Lices
Tel: 04 94 97 52 66
www.hotellamaisonblanche.com
Beautifully decorated in calm creams and whites, this small hotel in the heart of town has the feel of a private house. €€€€
La Ponche
3 rue des Remparts
Tel: 04 94 97 02 53
www.laponche.com
Discreet, exclusive retreat conjured out of a group of old fishermen's cottages next to the Port des Pêcheurs. Bedrooms are stylish, some with private roof terraces and sea views. Good regional cooking in the restaurant. Private garage. Closed Nov–mid-Feb. €€€
Le Yaca
1 boulevard d'Aumale
Tel: 04 94 55 81 00
Fax: 04 94 97 58 50
www.hotel-le-yaca.com
An attractive old Provençal residence that has been tastefully refurbished. Accommodation is built around a pool and gardens. €€€
Lou Cagnard
18 avenue P. Roussel
Tel: 04 94 97 04 24
www.hotel-lou-cagnard.com
A friendly, simple, family-run hotel in an old village house with a pretty courtyard. Near the port and very reasonably priced. Closed Nov–Dec. €€

INLAND VAR HILL VILLAGES

Draguignan

Hôtel du Parc
21 boulevard de la Liberté
Tel: 04 98 10 14 50
www.hotel-duparc.fr
An ordinary but reliable 20-roomed hotel outside the old town. €

Fayence

Moulin de la Camandoule
Chemin de Notre-Dame des Cyprès
Tel: 04 94 76 00 84
www.camandoule.com
This ancient olive mill in the valley below Fayence has been elegantly converted into a small, peaceful hotel with a good restaurant serving traditional

Provençal fare. Swimming pool. Nine bedrooms and two duplex-suites. €€

Les-Arcs-sur-Argens

Logis du Guetteur
Place du Château
Tel: 04 94 99 51 10
www.logisduguetteur.com
Pleasant, atmospheric hotel occupying part of an 11th-century castle overlooking the village and the beautiful Argens valley. Good restaurant and swimming pool. €€–€€€

Seillans

Hôtel des Deux Rocs
Place Font d'Amont

Tel: 04 94 76 87 32
www.hoteldeuxrocs.com
This converted 18th-century manor house is set in a lovely spot above the town and is complete with a good restaurant, lovely terrace and outdoor fountain. With 14 rooms. €€

Tourtour

Bastide de Tourtour
Route de Flayosc
Tel: 04 98 10 54 20
www.bastidedetourtour.com
Palatial 24-room hotel, set in a park with fabulous views over the Var and beyond. The facilities include a heated pool, jacuzzi and billiard room. €€€

L'Auberge St-Pierre
Route d'Ampus
Tel: 04 94 50 00 50
www.guideprovence.com/hotel/saint-pierre
Lovely converted 16th-century farmhouse just outside the village of Tourtour. Fresh produce from the working farm takes pride of place on the restaurant menu. There are 16 rooms in all, with wonderful views. Closed Nov–Mar. €–€€

PARC DU MERCANTOUR AND ALPINE VALLEYS

Breil-sur-Roya

Hôtel Le Roya
place Bianchéri
Tel: 04 93 04 48 10
A simple hotel next to the village car park (market here on Tues-

days) offering B&B for those on a budget. €€

Lantosque

Hostellerie de l'Ancienne Gendarmerie
Quartier du Rivet
Tel: 04 93 03 00 65
www.hotel-lantosque.com
Hotel in the former *gendarmerie* with a rustic but elegant interior. Eight brightly decorated bedrooms. The restaurant looks out onto the swimming pool and the valley. Friendly welcome. €€

Sospel

Hôtel des Etrangers
9 boulevard de Verdun
Tel: 04 93 04 00 09
www.sospel.net
This hotel has a pool on

site, English is spoken, and the proprietor is an expert on local history. €€

Tende

Le Chamois d'Or
Hameau de Casterino
Tel: 04 93 04 66 66
www.hotelchamoisdor.net
A traditional mountain chalet on the threshold of the Vallée des Merveilles. The large rooms are furnished in a contemporary *montagnard* style. Regional cuisine served in the wood-panelled restaurant. 22 rooms. €€
Le Prieuré
St-Dalmas-sur-Tende
Tel: 04 93 04 75 70
Fax: 04 93 04 71 58
www.leprieure.org

Three-star hotel with a good restaurant, set in a lovely valley. Has a policy of employing people with disabilities. Organises summer trips to the Vallée des Merveilles. €

PRICE CATEGORIES

Price categories are for an average double room in high season:
€ = under €80
€€ = €80–150
€€€ = €150–250
€€€€ = more than €250

ST-PAUL, VENCE AND GRASSE

Biot

Hôtel des Arcades
16 place des Arcades
Tel: 04 93 65 01 04
Fax: 04 93 65 01 05
Quirky, antique-filled hotel in a 15th-century mansion. The restaurant is also an art gallery. A good budget choice. €€

Grasse

Hôtel des Parfums (Odalys)
Rue Eugène Charabot
Tel: 04 92 42 35 35
www.hoteldesparfums.com
Basic, moderately priced rooms with gorgeous views. Facilities include a jacuzzi, hammam, pool and fitness room. €€
La Bastide Saint-Antoine
48 avenue Henri Dunant
Tel: 04 93 70 94 94
www.jacques-chibois.com
This 18th-century *bastide* has stark but chic, modern rooms and

offers wonderful views of the mountains and sea. It has a pool, olive grove and organises regular art exhibitions. It's best known for its gastronomic restaurant. €€€€

St-Paul-de-Vence

Hostellerie des Remparts
72 rue Grande
Tel: 04 93 32 09 88
www.hotel-les-remparts.net
A cheap, slightly eccentric option right in the heart of the old village. Friendly staff and a restaurant. €
La Colombe d'Or
Place des Ormeaux
Tel: 04 93 32 80 02
www.la-colombe-dor.com
The 16-roomed Colombe d'Or was once frequented by unknown, penniless artists who persuaded the original owner, Paul Roux, to accept their paintings in payment for meals and board. Works by Miró,

Picasso, Modigliani, Matisse and Chagall can now be viewed by guests of the hotel and restaurant. €€€€
Mas d'Artigny
Route de la Colle
Tel: 04 93 32 84 54
www.mas-artigny.com
Sprawling hotel in the woods between St-Paul and La Colle. Splendid views of the sea and the mountains. Spa and tennis courts. 43 rooms, plus 21 apartments, each with its own private garden and pool. €€€

Vence

Château du Domaine St-Martin
Route de Coursegoules
Tel: 04 93 58 02 02
www.chateau-st-martin.com
True luxury set on the hills above Vence, with a magnificent view of the coast. Extensive grounds and a swimming pool. A member of the Relais et Châteaux group. €€€€

Miramar
167 avenue Bougearel
Tel: 04 93 58 01 32
www.hotel-miramar-vence.com
Charming 1920s building with a pink façade overlooking the valley from the Plateau St-Michel. No restaurant, but you can have breakfast or early evening drinks on the panoramic terrace. Pool. €€
La Villa Roseraie
14 avenue Henri Giraud
Tel: 04 93 58 02 20
www.villaroseraie.com
This pretty Belle Epoque villa has a lovely garden, pool and 14 rooms (some small) decorated with Provençal fabrics. A five-minute walk from the old town of Vence. No restaurant. €€

NICE

Grimaldi
15 rue Grimaldi
Tel: 04 93 16 00 24
www.le-grimaldi.com
A lovely little bed and breakfast, with prettily furnished rooms. Good value and conveniently located. €€
Hi-hotel
avenue des Fleurs
Tel: 04 97 07 26 26
www.hi-hotel.net
Nice's latest hotel with "concept" bedrooms for music-lovers, computer freaks or movie fans –

there is even one with a rock pool. Postmodern design and casual, chatty service. No restaurant, but DIY bar on each floor. There's a garden courtyard, DJ bar and rooftop sundeck with minuscule swimming pool. €€€
Hôtel Aria
15 avenue Auber
Tel: 04 93 88 30 69
www.aria-nice.com
This recently renovated 19th-century hotel overlooks an attractive

garden square amid the Belle Epoque and art deco buildings of the new town. Rooms are light and high-ceilinged in sunny colours. Good value. 30 rooms. €€
Hôtel Beau Rivage
24 rue St Francois-de-Paule
Tel: 04 92 47 82 82
www.nicebeaurivage.com
The 118-room Beau Rivage – handily located in the old town – is a modernised 1930s hotel with a private

beach. Matisse had an apartment here, and Nietzsche and Chekhov were also guests. Its recent refurbishment by architect Jean-Michel Wilmotte is suavely minimalist. Internet access and plasma TVs in rooms. Private beach. €€€€

Hôtel Negresco
37 promenade des Anglais
Tel: 04 93 16 64 00
www.hotel-negresco.com
This flamboyant Belle Epoque hotel (pictured right) is the last vestige of Nice's golden era. Its dome is a prominent landmark on the Baie des Anges. The 150 rooms and apartments are magnificently furnished with antiques, priceless paintings and tapestries. The celebrated Chantecler restaurant is acknow-

ledged as one of the best tables of the region. Fabulous. €€€€

La Pérouse
11 quai Rauba-Capéu
Tel: 04 93 62 34 63
www.hotel-la-perouse.com
Perched on a cliff at the east end of the promenade des Anglais, this remarkable hotel offers stunning views over the Baie des Anges and is conveniently situated between the old town and the port. Access is via two lifts from the quayside. Restaurant specialising in alfresco grills (open mid-April to mid-Sept). Pool. €€€

Hôtel Windsor
11 rue Dalpozzo
Tel: 04 93 88 59 35
www.hotelwindsornice.com
From the outside it looks like a 19th-century hotel, but inside this boho arty hotel boasts a hammam, aviary, exotic garden,

and rooms commissioned by different contemporary artists, including joined-up ramblings by Ben, a sunbeam by François Morellet and cheerful designs by flower-happy Lily van der Stokker. €€

THE RIVIERA

Antibes

Bleu Marine
4 rue des Chemins
Tel: 04 93 74 84 84
www.bleumarineantibes.com
Modern, budget hotel 500 metres from the beach. Most bedrooms have sea views and balconies. Lift and parking. No restaurant. €

Relais du Postillon
8 rue Championnet
Tel: 04 93 34 20 77
www.relaisdupostillon.com
It's hard to find a bargain in high season on the Côte d'Azur, but the 15-roomed Relais du Postillon in the old town of Antibes comes pretty close. It's pleasant enough and has a good restaurant. The only drawback is that it's not right by the sea. €€

Beaulieu-sur-Mer

La Réserve de Beaulieu
5 boulevard Leclerc
Tel: 04 93 01 00 01

www.reservebeaulieu.com
A luxurious late 19th-century villa, situated in a lovely spot on the coast. Facilities include a private beach and harbour and a swimming-pool in the garden. €€€€

Le Métropole
15 boulevard du Général Leclerc
Tel: 04 93 01 00 08
www.lemetropole.com
This grand yet intimate hotel has welcomed royalty and heads of state since the late 19th century. Rooms are spacious and comfortable, many with balconies overlooking the sea. There's a pool in the garden, sun terrace and private jetty. 40 bedrooms and suites. €€€€

Cagnes-sur-Mer

Hôtel Beau Rivage
39 boulevard de la Plage
Tel: 04 93 20 16 09
www.beaurivage.biz

The Beau Rivage is a down-to-earth choice for those on a budget in this overpriced area. On the seafront. Some rooms have balconies and seaviews. €

Cannes

3.14 Hotel
5 rue François Einesy
Tel: 04 92 99 72 00
www.3-14hotel.com
A gloriously over-the-top creation of the sort that you could only get away with in Cannes, and a comfortable contemporary alternative to the famous Croisette palaces. Five floors of bedrooms are each themed according to a continent, all laid out on feng shui principles. A glass fountain, lovebirds at reception, bar, restaurant and lounge are on the ground-floor "earth" and a pool on the rooftop "sky". €€€€

Carlton Intercontinental
58 boulevard de la Croisette
Tel: 04 93 06 40 06
www.intercontinental.com
Cannes's world-famous waterfront luxury hotel (pictured overleaf) is still a magnet for the rich and famous. The rooms have been completely renovated and are now more splendid than ever. Top-floor health centre and casino. €€€€

PRICE CATEGORIES

Price categories are for an average double room in high season:
€ = under €80
€€ = €80–150
€€€ = €150–250
€€€€ = more than €250

Hôtel de Provence
9 Rue Molière
Tel: 04 93 38 44 35
www.hotel-de-provence.com
Comfortable, quaint
lodgings 100 metres
from La Croisette. The
small balconies on the
front-facing rooms look
out over a lush garden
(and the back of the
Noga Hilton). Closed
Dec. 30 rooms. €€

Hôtel Splendid
4–6 rue Félix-Faure
Tel: 04 97 06 22 22
www.splendid-hotel-cannes.fr
A sparkling white Belle
Epoque edifice in the
heart of the action, near
the port and almost
opposite the Palais des
Festivals. Rooms have
been comfortably
updated while retaining
period flourishes; break-
fast is served on a large
sunny terrace. 62
rooms. €€–€€€

Le Cavendish
11 boulevard Carnot
Tel: 04 97 06 26 00
www.cavendish-cannes.com
Attractive Belle Epoque

building on the big
boulevard that leads
towards La Croisette.
Decorated in comfort-
able period-town-house
style, with some won-
derful circular rooms in
the corner turret. €€€

Martinez
73 boulevard de la Croisette
Tel: 04 92 98 73 00
www.hotel-martinez.com
The ultimate art-deco
extravaganza. When it
opened, it was France's
largest hotel, boasting
476 spacious master
bedrooms and 56 bed-
rooms for clients' per-
sonal staff. Its
construction happily
coincided with the tran-
sition of the French Riv-
iera from winter to
summer season in the
early 1930s, and with
the arrival of the Cannes
Film Festival in 1946 its
future was assured. A
major facelift in 2003
saw the creation of two
vast rooftop suites and
a luxurious Givenchy
spa, and renovation of
the splendid façade,
grand staircase and
hall. €€€€

Cap d'Antibes

**Grand Hôtel du Cap-
Eden Roc**
Boulevard Kennedy
Tel: 04 93 61 39 01
www.edenroc-hotel.fr
High-profile hotel set on
the water's edge in
wooded grounds, this is
the ultimate in Riviera
glamour and luxury. A
serious splurge. €€€€

La Jabotte
13 avenue de Max Maurey
Tel: 04 93 61 45 89
www.jabotte.com
Adorable – and afford-
able – lodgings with
bright and cheerful
decor in a residential

neighbourhood a few
minutes from the beach.
The original artwork in
the rooms is the work
of one of the owners.
Closed Nov and Christ-
mas week. 10 rooms.
€€–€€€

Eze

**Château de la
Chèvre d'Or**
Rue de Barri
Tel: 04 92 10 66 66
www.chevredor.com
Staying here is an un-
forgettable experience.
The 28-room hotel com-
bines a warm provincial
elegance with Riviera
élan, and the four-star
restaurant has magnifi-
cent views of the coast.
€€€€

Château Eza
Rue de la Pise
Tel: 04 93 41 12 24
www.chateaueza.com
Perched high above the
Mediterranean, this has
to be one of the most
romantic hotels on the
Riviera. In a medieval
building in the ramparts
of Eze, bedrooms have
pretty *toile de Jouy*
fabrics, many have
exposed stone walls
and stone fireplaces,
some have terraces.
There's a sleek bar, and
the gastronomic restaur-
ant has a new chef,
Pierre Daret, at the
helm. No access to vehi-
cles. Closed November.
8 rooms. €€€€

Juan-Les-Pins

Belles Rives
Boulevard Edouard-Baudoin
Tel: 04 93 61 02 79
www.bellesrives.com
Close enough to town to
enjoy the lively atmos-
phere, yet sufficiently
far away from the noise

and crowds. The Belles
Rives has retained all
the attraction of the
stylish art-deco period,
when it was the home of
Zelda and F. Scott
Fitzgerald. €€€€

Garden Beach Hotel
15–17 boulevard Baudoin
Tel: 04 92 93 57 57
www.juanlespins.lemeridien.com
Located on the site of
the former casino, in
the heart of town. A
terrace overlooks the
bay. €€€

Hôtel des Mimosas
rue Pauline
Tel: 04 93 61 04
www.hotelmimosas.com
A large, early 20th-
century house set in
quiet gardens just a
5-minute walk from the
beach. Attractive bed-
rooms, swimming pool.
No restaurant. Closed
Oct–Apr. 34 rooms. €€

La Turbie

Hostellerie Jérôme
20 rue du Comte de Cessole
Tel: 04 92 41 51 51
www.hostelleriejerome.com
Primarily known for its
Michelin two-star res-
taurant, this tiny hotel
offers elegant rooms
with furniture *à l'anci-
enne*, some of which
have splendid views of
the sea. Closed
Dec–Jan. 5 rooms. €€

Menton

**Grand Hôtel des
Ambassadeurs**
3 rue Partouneaux
Tel: 04 93 28 75 75
www.ambassadeurs-menton.com
Even genteel Menton
has gained a designer
boutique hotel following
the make-over of the
venerable Ambas-
sadeurs in an extrava-
gantly Baroque style,

with different floors dedicated to painting, literature, music and cinema. Champagne bar and restaurant. 32 rooms. Entirely non-smoking. €€€€

Hôtel Royal Westminster
Tel: 04 93 28 69 69
www.vacancesbleues.com
A classic seafront hotel evoking Menton's dignified past, opening onto the town centre or a garden that runs down to the seaside promenade. 92 rooms and spacious salons with restaurant, piano bar and billiard room. €€

Mougins

Manoir de l'Etang
Bois de Font-Merle (route d'Antibes)
Tel: 04 92 28 36 00
www.manoir-de-letang.com
A fine old house in a wooded park with lake just outside Mougins. Pool. €€€

Le Mas Candille
Boulevard Clément Rebouffel
Tel: 04 92 28 43 43
www.lemascandille.com
A luxurious hotel on the

edge of the old village. Choose the rooms in the main *mas*, decorated with light Provençal colours and antique furniture, rather than the rather dark Asian-themed rooms in the modern *bastide* annexe. Spacious gardens, a lovely pool and a salubrious Shiseido spa. Good modern Provençal cooking in the restaurant. €€€€

Le Moulin de Mougins
Notre-Dame de Vie
Tel: 04 93 75 78 24
www.moulindesmougins.com
A beautifully restored old mill with three rooms, and four suites overlooking the garden. Chef Alain Llorca prepares exquisite dishes in the gourmet restaurant. €€€

Peillon

Auberge de la Madone
Tel: 04 93 79 91 17
www.auberge-madone-peillon.com
Located at the gates of the hilltop village of Peillon, this *auberge* offers a flowery terrace

with a wonderful view, a one-star Michelin restaurant and gorgeous rooms fitted with antiques. €€€

Roquebrune-Cap-Martin

Les Deux Frères
Roquebrune village
Tel: 04 93 28 99 00
www.lesdeuxfreres.com
The only hotel in Roquebrune village with a good restaurant. Ten rooms, all different, range from veiled bridal room to Moorish-inspired. €–€€

Vista Palace Hotel
1551 route de la Grande Corniche
Tel: 04 92 10 40 00
www.vistapalace.com
A modern luxury hotel high above Monaco with wonderful views. Spacious rooms, pool and fitness centre. Closed Feb–mid-Mar. 68 rooms. €€€–€€€€

St-Jean-Cap Ferrat

Brise Marine
58 avenue Jean Mermoz

Tel: 04 93 76 04 36
www.hotel-brisemarine.com
A small hotel in an attractive terraced garden. Some of the rooms overlook the sea. Closed Nov–Jan. €€€

Grand Hôtel du Cap Ferrat
71 boulevard Général de Gaulle
Tel: 04 93 76 50 50
www.grand-hotel-cap-ferrat.com
This is a magnificently situated, luxurious palace with a park, flowery gardens, a sea-side swimming pool and a private funicular to the beach. Closed Jan–Feb. 44 rooms and 9 suites. €€€€

La Voile d'Or
Yachting Harbour
Tel: 04 93 01 13 13
www.lavoiledor.fr
An Italian villa situated in a lovely garden overlooking the yachting harbour. Rooms of all sizes are available and all are attractively decorated. Amenities include a seawater swimming pool and private beach. Closed Nov–Apr. €€€

MONACO

Columbus Hotel
23 avenue des Papalins
Fontvieille
Tel: 00 377-92 05 90 00
www.columbushotels.com
Set a little way out of the centre, in the Fontvieille area of Monaco, this is nonetheless a comfortable modern hotel. It overlooks the new harbour and has lovely views. €€€€

Hôtel de France
6 rue de la Turbie

Tel: 00 377-93 30 24 64
www.monte-carlo.mc/france
Clean but unremarkable hotel near the train station for those with slimmer purses. Conveniently located just ten minutes from the palace and casino. Breakfast is included. 26 rooms. €

Hôtel de Paris
Place du Casino
Monte-Carlo
Tel: 00 377-98 06 30 16
www.montecarloresort.com

The celebrated Hôtel de Paris, located by the Casino and which boasts Alain Ducasses's three-star restaurant, the Louis XV. It is the most magnificent and glamorous place to stay in Monaco. Past celebrity visitors are far too numerous to name. €€€€

Hôtel Hermitage
Square Beaumarchais
Tel: 00 377-98 06 48 12
www.montecarloresort.com

Beautiful Edwardian architecture, spacious, comfortable rooms. Facilities include a swimming pool and fitness centre and pink-marbled restaurant. €€€€

A CTIVITIES

THE ARTS, FESTIVALS, NIGHTLIFE, OUTDOOR ACTIVITIES, CHILDREN AND SHOPPING

THE ARTS

Provence is now an established cultural destination, especially in the summer, when world-class festivals of music, theatre and dance are staged here. Avignon is famous for its theatre festival, Cannes is world-renowned for film, and there are also the jazz festivals of Nice and Juan-les-Pins, plus the opera festival of Orange. Traditional festivals abound, where everything from bullfights and flowers to garlic and lemons is celebrated.

Provence has a magnificent legacy of art, and there are many major art museums in the region. There are also many smaller museums and galleries offering a variety of art and crafts. In larger towns such as Marseille, Nice, Avignon, Aix, Arles, Cannes or Monte-Carlo you will find opera, theatre and cinema venues.

Most museums charge an entrance fee, but look out for discounts for families, or off-peak periods. As a rule, national museums are closed on Tuesday, while municipal museums shut on Monday. Opening times vary. Most museums close from noon to 2 or 2.30pm, although major sites are often open continuously, especially in summer.

Venues

Aix-en-Provence

Cité du Livre, 8–10 rue des Allumettes; tel: 04 42 93 54 19; www.citedulivre-aix.com. Multi-disciplinary arts centre with annual literary festival.
Théâtre des Ateliers, 29 place Miollis; tel: 04 42 38 10 45; www.theatre-des-ateliers-aix.com. Contemporary theatre.

Arles

Les Arènes d'Arles, tel: 04 90 96 64 31/08 91 70 03 70; www.arenes-arles.com. Bullfights, concerts and films.
Théâtre de la Calade, Le Grenier à Sel, 49 quai de la Roquette; tel: 04 90 93 05 23. Arles's main theatre company.
Cargo de Nuit, 7 avenue Sadi-Carnot; tel: 04 90 49 55 99. Venue for world music and jazz concerts.

Avignon

Théâtre Municipal, 20 place de l'Horloge; tel: 04 90 85 02 32. The main permanent theatre in Avignon. Stages official festival productions in July.
Théâtre des Carmes, 6 place des Carmes; tel: 04 90 82 20 47. Avignon's oldest theatre company, based in a restored Gothic cloister.

Cannes

Théâtre Alexandre III, 19 boulevard Alexandre; tel: 04 93 94 33 44. A former cinema, this theatre stages plays, including classics and modern interpretations.
Palais des Festivals et des Congrès, 1 boulevard de la Croisette; tel: 04 93 39 01 01. This is the venue for the annual Festival du Film, and serves as a venue for plays, ballets and concerts.

Marseille

Cité de la Musique, 4 rue Bernard du Bois; tel: 04 91 39 28 28. Variety of musical concerts.
Théâtre du Gymnase, 4 rue du Théâtre-Français; tel: 04 91 24 35 35/08 20 00 04 22. Restored theatre that puts on innovative theatre.
Opéra Municipal, 2 rue Molière; tel: 04 91 55 14 99. Opera and classical music.

Monte-Carlo

Théâtre de Princesse Grace, 12 avenue d'Ostende; tel: 00 377-93 50 03 45. Concerts, spectacles and classic theatre on the programme.

Nice

Opéra de Nice, 4 Rue St-François-de-Paule; tel: 04 92 17 40 40. Classic venue for

symphony, ballet and opera.
Théâtre de Nice, promenade des Arts; tel: 04 93 13 90 90. French and foreign classics and contemporary work.

FESTIVALS

January

Antibes: Festival of Sacred Art (Jan & Feb).
Isola 2000: *Trophy Andros*, car-racing tournament on ice.
Monaco: Monte-Carlo Rally; International Circus Festival.

February

Isola 2000: Snow Carnival.
Menton: Lemon Festival.
Nice: Carnival and Battle of Flowers.

March

Antibes: Festival of Magic.
Arles: Easter Festival.
Menton: *Salon des Orchidées*.
Vallauris: *Fête Napoléon*. Local people dress in period costume to commemorate the landing of Napoleon at Golfe Juan.

April

Cannes: MIP-TV (TV festival).
Monte-Carlo: Biennial *Les Printemps des Arts* (odd-numbered years, until end Sept); Monte-Carlo Tennis Open.
Roquebrune-Cap-Martin: Procession to the castle on Good Friday.

May

Cannes: Film Festival.
Cavaillon: Ascension Day Parade.
Fréjus: *Bravade St-François*. Festival in honour of the patron saint of Fréjus.
Grasse: *Expo Roses*. Rose show.
Monaco: Grand Prix.
Nice: May Festival and International Youth Folk Festival.
St-Tropez: *Bravades* festival, with lively costume parades.

Stes-Maries-de-la-Mer: *Pèlerinage de Mai*. France's biggest gypsy festival.
Vaucluse: *Fête de la Vigne et du Vin*.

June

Antibes: International Young Soloist Festival.
Monte-Carlo: St-Jean Folk Festival.
Nice: Sacred Music Festival.
Nîmes: *Feria de Pentecôte*, bull-fighting, music and festivities.
Tarascon: *Fête de la Tarasque*. Celebrating the legend of the monster that terrorised the town.
Uzès: *Foire à l'Ail*. Garlic fair.

July

Aix-en-Provence: *Festival d'Art Lyrique*. Opera festival.
Antibes: International Jazz Festival.
Arles: *Rencontres Internationales de la Photographie*. Prestigious photography festival with exhibitions until Sept.
Suds à Arles. World-music festival (until mid-Aug).
Avignon: *Festival d'Avignon*. Theatre festival (until mid-Aug).
Beaulieu-sur-Mer: Venetian Fête.
France: Bastille Day (14 July).
Fréjus: Feria; Forum des Arts et de la Musique: concerts, dance, theatre.
L'Isle-sur-la-Sorgue: *Festival de la Sorgue*.
Monte-Carlo: Season of con-

certs in the courtyard of the Palais du Prince; Fireworks Festival and the Monaco Carnival.
Nice: International Folk Festival; *Grande Parade du Jazz*.
Orange: *Les Chorégies*. Lyric opera (until mid-Aug).
Roquebrune-Cap-Martin: Theatre Festival.
Uzès: *Nuits Musicales d'Uzès*.
Vallauris: *Biennale de Céramique* (Pottery Festival, until Oct).
Vence: Classical concerts in the cathedral and open-air.

August

Brignoles: *Festival de Jazz*.
Fréjus: *Fête du Raisin*. Wine-tasting and feasting.
Golfe Juan: Jean Marais Festival (theatre and music).

WHAT'S ON AND TICKETS

César, a weekly listings magazine, is distributed free in the Gard, Vaucluse and Bouches-du-Rhône *départements*.

Friday editions of newspapers are a good source of information on the local nightlife: see *La Provence* and *La Marseillaise*. Also visit www.nicematin.fr and www.laprovence-presse.fr

For details of exhibitions and concerts, contact local tourist offices *(see page 292)* or visit:

www.provencemagazine.info, and www.cotedazur-en-fetes.com.

Tourist offices may also have tickets for local music, theatre or cultural events. Many theatre and opera box offices accept credit card telephone bookings. In major cities, FNAC (www.fnac.com) and Virgin stores are ticket agents for local gigs. Tickets can also be bought via **France Billet** (tel: 08 92 69 21 92; www.francebillet.com).

Grasse: Festival of Jasmine.
Menton: International Chamber Music Festival.
Orange: *Les Chorégies*. Lyric opera (until mid-Aug).
Roquebrune-Cap-Martin: Theatre Festival; costumed procession to the castle.
St-Rémy: *Feria Provençale*.

September

Arles: *Fêtes des Prémices du Riz*. Rice festival.
Cannes: *Régates Royales*. Sailing regatta.
Cavalaire-sur-Mer: *Grand Prix de France*. Jet-skiing.
France: *Journées du Patrimoine*: third weekend in September, throughout France, when historic monuments and official buildings are open to the public for free.
Grasse: *Bio-Grasse Foire*. Organic produce fair.
Nice: *Fête de San Bertoumieu*. Craft and "produits de terrroir" fair.
St-Tropez: *Les Voiles de St-Tropez*. Sailing regatta.

October

Collobrières: Chestnut Fair.
Roquebrune-sur-Argens: *Fête de Miel* (honey).

November

Arles: *Salon International des Santonniers* (until mid-Jan). Provençal craftsmen exhibit *santons* (small clay figures of saints used for nativity scenes); *Marché de Noël*.
Monte-Carlo: 19 November, National Holiday: parades, ceremonies and spectacles (fireworks the previous evening).

December

Bandol: *Fêtes des Vins*.
Fréjus: *Foire aux Santons* (see *Salon International des Santonniers*, above).
Le Val: *Noël en Provence*. Christmas fair.

NIGHTLIFE

In smaller towns and villages in Provence there is usually little going on at night unless a festival is taking place. In most places, however, cafés and bars stay open all day, often until the early hours of the morning, so there is usually somewhere to go for a drink in the evening. If festivities are happening, however, these will probably continue late into the night, so don't expect to get a good night's sleep if you are staying in a town-centre hotel.

In the larger cities there is likely to be a variety of bars and clubs. The Côte d'Azur is famed for its nightlife, in particular the legendary casinos, which nowadays often also incorporate nightclubs, cabarets and restaurants. The following is a selection of recommended venues in the major towns in the region.

For details of particular events, see Festivals *(page 147)*, or enquire at local tourist offices, and check local papers and magazines for listings.

Aix-en-Provence

Cinéma Renoir, 7 rue Villars; tel: 04 42 91 33 32. Three auditoriums, one with a big screen. Shows art-house and box-office films in their original language.
Hot Brass, route d'Eguilles; tel: 04 42 63 37 30. Live jazz.
Le Scat Club, 11 rue de la Verrerie; tel: 04 42 23 00 23. Bar-club with dance floor and live music (pop, funk, R'n'B) nightly.

Antibes

La Siesta, pont de la Brague; tel: 04 93 33 31 31. Restaurant, bar, casino and club.

Avignon

Le Bokao's, 9 bis quai St-Lazare; tel: 04 90 82 47 95. Big trendy dance club.

Café In et Off, 5 place du Palais; tel: 04 90 85 48 95. Favourite festival meeting place with terrace tables offering a good view of the Palais des Papes.
L'Esclave, 12 rue du Limas; tel: 04 90 85 14 91. Predominantly gay clientele. Popular during the summer theatre festival.
L'Hélicon, 23 rue Bancasse; tel: 04 90 16 03 99. Traditional French *chanson* performed by guest stars or the owner himself at the piano, plus good-value menus.
Le Rouge Gorge, 10 bis rue de la Peyrolerie; tel: 04 90 14 02 54. Restaurant-cabaret with diverse entertainment including café-theatre and live concerts.
Utopia, 4 rue des Escaliers Ste-Anne; tel: 04 90 82 65 36. Avignon's main *'VO'* or *version-originale* (original-language) cinema, with a lovely bohemian bistro and café.

Cannes

Cinéma Les Arcades, 77 rue Felix-Faure; tel: 08 92 68 00 39. Mainstream cinema showing films in their original language.
Les Coulisses, 29 rue du Commandant André; tel: 04 92 99 17 17. Fashionable nightclub, especially popular during the film festival.
Jimmy's, Palais des Festivals; tel: 04 92 98 78 00. Fashionable disco.
Le J's, avenue Georges Galice, Juan-les-Pins; tel: 04 93 67 22 74. Nightclub.

TOURS

Information on guided tours is available at tourist offices. Choose from themed tours such as *La Route de Mimosa*, between Bormes-les-Mimosas and Grasse, *Routes de Vins* in the Var, *Route de Miel* (honey), *Route des Fleurs* around Toulon, *Route de l'Olivier* from Bandol to Draguignan, and the *Route du Baroque*.

Le Loft, 13 rue Dr Monod; tel: 04 93 39 40 39. Disco popular with the young and fashionable.

Le Milk, avenue Georges Galice; tel: 04 93 67 22 74. Club with excellent DJ and a clientele that enjoys dancing around the tables.

Palm Beach Casino, 57 boulevard F. Roosevelt; tel: 04 97 06 36 90. Casino, restaurant and piano bar (11pm–5am).

Whisky à Gogo, La Pinède; tel: 04 93 61 26 40. Nightclub.

Zanzibar, 85 rue Félix-Faure; tel: 04 93 39 30 75. Established gay bar and club.

Marseille

Cinéma Le César, 4 place Castellane; tel: 08 92 68 05 97. Recent films in their original language.

L'Intermediaire, 63 place Jean-Jaurès; tel: 04 91 47 01 25. Jazz, blues and rock as well as traditional southern French music.

Le Pelle Mêle, place aux Huiles; tel: 04 92 54 85 26. Some of France's greatest jazz musicians have played in this atmospheric jazz club near the Vieux-Port.

Le Trolleybus, 24 quai de Rive Neuve; tel: 04 91 54 30 45. Huge club offering techno, salsa and jazz.

The New Cancan, 3 rue Sénac-de-Meilhan; tel: 04 91 48 59 76. The most popular gay club in Marseille.

Monte-Carlo

Casino de Monte-Carlo, place du Casino; tel: 00 377-92 16 23 00. The original and still the most famous casino on the Côte d'Azur. Formal dress is required. Open all year: main salon from noon, private rooms from 3pm. Has a separate cabaret and several restaurants. Over 18s only.

Le Cabaret du Casino, place du Casino; tel: 00 377-98 06 24 30. Classic French cabaret.

La Rascasse, quai Antoine; tel: 00 377-93 25 56 90. All-night pub with an outdoor terrace and a restaurant. Plays jazz and rock.

Le Sporting Club, avenue Princesse Grace; tel: 00 377-92 16 22 77. Fashionable Euro-trash rendezvous. Open during summer season only.

Nice

Le Bar aux Oiseaux, Vieux Nice, 5 rue St-Vincent; tel: 04 93 80 27 33. Mainly jazz and flamenco in a typical Niçoise ambience.

Baroque Bar, Vieux Nice, 25 rue de la Croix; tel: 04 93 80 08 74. Excellent Baroque concerts on Saturday nights.

Cinémathèque de Nice, 3 esplanade J.F. Kennedy; tel: 04 92 04 06 66. Recent films in their original language with subtitles.

St-Tropez

Les Caves du Roy, Hôtel Byblos, place des Lices; tel: 04 94 97 16 02. Legendary club in Hôtel Byblos.

Le Papagayo, Résidence du Port; tel: 04 94 79 29 50. Still the place to spot famous faces.

Le VIP Room, Résidences du Nouveau Port; tel: 04 94 97 14 70. St-Tropez's most fashionable club and restaurant.

OUTDOOR ACTIVITIES

Provence has a huge range of sports and activites to choose from. The mountains and river valleys offer walking, riding, cycling and climbing, river-rafting and canoeing, and, in the winter months, skiing. Golf is very popular, as is tennis, and even quite small villages often have tennis courts, though you may have to become a temporary member to use them. (Enquire at the local tourist office or mairie, the town hall, which will also provide details of all other local sporting activities.)

Antibes and Cannes are major watersports centres, and the Iles de Lérins, the Iles d'Hyères and the Calanques offer some of the

best diving in the Mediterranean. For detailed listings pick up the Watersports Côte d'Azur brochure from main tourist offices or go to www.france-nautisme.com

Most private beaches have a good range of equipment for hire: dinghies, catamarans, surfing and water-skiing equipment, etc. To hire a boat, or a yacht, for a day or longer, all you need really do is stroll around the pleasure ports of the resorts and ask. Another source of information is the local syndicat d'initiative or tourist office (see page 292).

General information on sports and activities can be picked up at local tourist offices, or national organisations. Many UK travel firms offer holidays tailored to specific activities (see page 292).

Swimming

Although it is not necessary to be a millionaire and member of the most fashionable yacht club to enjoy the pleasures of the sea, if you wish to hire a luxury yacht for a week's cruise, being a millionaire might just help. You certainly need some money to enjoy several of the Côte's most exclusive beaches. In fact, only 70 percent of the beaches along the Côte d'Azur are open to the public; the rest – nearly 150 beaches – are privately owned (usually by hotels), and an entrance fee is charged to access them.

The sea is usually warm enough to swim in from June to September, and almost every town will have a municipal pool, though it may only be open during school holidays.

Scuba Diving

Fédération Française d'Etudes et de Sports Sous-Marins, 24 quai de Rive Neuve, Marseille; tel; 04 91 33 99 31; fax: 04 91 54 77 43; www.ffessm.fr

Sailing and Windsurfing

Comité Régional de Voile Côte d'Azur, Espace Antibes, 2208 route de Grasse, Antibes; tel: 04 93 74 77 05; www.ffvoile.org
Station Voile, 9 Rue Esprit Violet, Cannes; tel: 04 92 18 88 88.

Canoeing and Kayaking

Fédération Française de Canoë-Kayak et des Sports Associés en Eau-Vive, 87 quai de la Marne, Joinville-le-Pont; tel: 01 45 11 08 50; fax: 01 48 86 13 25; www.ffck.org

Climbing

Provence offers many opportunities for climbers. You can find guides for day outings or clubs that will organise beginners' courses. For further information contact: **Club Alpin Français,** 14 avenue Mirabeau, Nice; tel: 04 93 62 59 99; www.cafnice.org

Cycling

Cycling is a wonderful way to enjoy Provence *(see page 261 for advice on transporting your own bike).* If you don't have a bike, you can rent cycles locally, from bike shops or youth hostels *(see page 265).* You could consider a package cycling holiday, with accommodation

booked in advance and your luggage transported for you.

The IGN (Institut Géographique National) 906 Cycling France map gives details of routes, clubs and places to stay. Information is also available from the Touring Department of the **Cyclists Touring Club** (tel: 0870 873 0060; www.ctc.org.uk). Its service to members includes competitive cycle and travel insurance, free detailed touring itineraries and general information sheets about France, whilst its tours brochure lists trips to the region, organised by members.

The club's French counterpart is **Fédération Française de Cyclotourisme,** tel: 01 56 20 88 87; www.ffct.org. Regional contact: **Ligue de la Côte d'Azur de Cyclotourisme et de VTT,** Toulon; tel: 04 94 40 96 06; www.ffct.org

The **Adventure Cycling Association** in Montana, USA, offers a similar service to its members (tel: 800 755 2453 toll-free; www.adv-cycling.org).

Fishing

Here you have a choice of sea- or freshwater fishing. The season opens around the second Saturday in March. For freshwater fishing you will need to be affiliated to an association. For general information and addresses of local fishing associations contact local tourist offices. **Union Nationale pour la Pêche,** tel: 01 48 24 96 00; www.unpf.fr

Golf

Provence has many excellent golf courses, and the good weather in the region means golf can be played all year round. Most clubs offer lessons.
Fédération Française de Golf, 68 rue Anatole France, Levallois; tel: 01 41 49 77 00; fax: 01 41 49 77 01; www.ffgolf.org.
Ligue de Golf de Provence-Alpes, Vitrolles; tel: 04 42 76 35 22.

Hiking

Local tourist offices or ramblers' organisations may put on guided walks of local sights, plants or wildlife. The **Comité Départemental de Randonnée Pédestre Alpes-Maritimes** (tel: 04 93 20 74 93; www.cdrp06.org) organises a variety of activities throughout the year: guided walks taking a day, a weekend or more, as well as themed walks.

For local information contact the relevant tourist office, or **Fédération Française de la Randonnée Pédestre,** 14 rue Riquet, Paris; tel: 01 44 89 93 90; fax: 01 40 35 85 48; www.ffrandonnee.fr. You could also contact the

CHILDREN'S ACTIVITIES

• Bandol and Fréjus zoos.
• Butterfly park at St-Tropez.
• Glass-blowing workshop at Biot.
• Marineland at Antibes (www.marineland.fr) – themed water park.
• Musée des Santons at Brignoles.
• Musée des Merveilles at Tende.
• Musée Océanographique at Monaco (www.oceano.mc).

Comité Départemental de la Randonnée Pédestre, 4 avenue de Verdun, Cagnes-sur-Mer; tel/fax: 04 93 20 74 73.

Ensure you are suitably equipped with water, warm clothing and good boots. There is an excellent network of signposted long-distance footpaths (sentiers de grande randonnée) in the region, but make sure that you also have a good map (see above).

Walking holidays are an increasingly popular way to enjoy Provence, especially in the mountains. Various walking holidays with accommodation either in hotels or under canvas are available. Some are organised through package operators in the UK, others are bookable through French organisations such as **Terres d'Aventure**, which specialises in walking holidays (tel: 08 25 84 78 00; www.terdav.com).

Horse-riding

Horse-riding and pony-trekking are popular activities in Provence, with centres equestres (equestrian centres) all over the region, in rural areas, the mountains, less inhabited parts of the coast, and especially in the Camargue. For further information, contact: **Ligue Régionale de Provence de Sports Equestres**, 298 avenue du club Hippique, Aix-en-Provence, tel: 04 42 20 88 02. **Féderation Française d'équitation**, tel: 04 92 97 46 77; www.ffe.com

Skiing

The Maritime Alps are very popular for skiing, and there are several large resorts in that area, such as Auron, Valberg and Isola 2000. They are only a few hours from the coast, and at certain times of the year you can combine the beach and skiing in one day. For details, contact: **Fédération Française de Ski**, 50 avenue des Marquisats, Annecy; tel: 04 50 51 40 34; www.ffs.fr

MAPS AND WALKING GUIDES

The French Ramblers' Association, **Fédération Française de la Randonnée Pédestre**, FFRP (www.ffrandonee.fr) in Paris publishes **Topo-guides** (guide books in French incorporating IGN 1:50,000 scale maps) to all France's footpaths. These are available from map retailers (high-street stores or online) and from all good bookshops in the region.

There is a series of guidebooks in English published by Robertson-McCarta called **Footpaths of Europe** which are based on the French Topoguides, with IGN maps, and include information about accommodation along the way. Titles appropriate to the region are: Walking the GR5: Larche to Nice, Walks in Provence and Walking the GR5: Modane to Larche.

IGN Blue series (Série Bleue) maps at a scale of 1:25,000 are ideal for walkers; IGN also publish maps of the national parks and produce walking maps on CD-ROM under the **IGN Rando** logo – the Série Bleue and the Top 25 are for walkers.

Club Alpin Français, 14 rue Mirabeau, Nice; tel: 04 93 62 59 99.

Downhill Skiing
Auron: Office du Tourisme Tel: 04 93 23 02 66.
Isola 2000: Office du Tourisme Tel: 04 93 23 15 15.

Cross-Country Skiing
Val Casterino, Tende; tel: 04 93 04 73 71.
Le Boréon, St-Martin-de-Vésubie; tel: 04 93 03 33 77.
FFS Côte d'Azur, Nice; tel: 04 93 18 17 18; www.stationsdumercantour.com

Spectator Sports

Watersports Events
There are all kinds of professional sailing and other watersports events for spectators, with most of the major competitions taking place at Mandelieu-la-Napoule, just west of Cannes, including the **Grand Prix de la Corniche d'Or** (April), and the **International Rowing Regatta** (August).

Other events are the **International Marathon** in the Baie des Anges, Nice, in April, the **Transgolfe Windsurf Regatta** in St-Tropez in July, **Les Voiles de St-Tropez** in October (and

Voiles Latines in May), the **Royal Regattas** in September in Cannes to coincide with the **International Pleasure Boat Festival**; there is also a **Boat Show** at Beaulieu-sur-Mer in May.

Grand Prix
Probably the most famous event in the whole region is the prestigious **Monte-Carlo Car Rally**, held in January. First staged in 1911, this road trial continues to attract the top names in the sport. The other big motoring event is the **Monte-Carlo Grand Prix** in May, one of the most decisive contests in the competition for the world motor-racing championship.

Tennis and Golf Tournaments
April is the time for the **International Tennis Championships** in Monte-Carlo, the **Monte-Carlo Open**, which is complemented by another "open", this time the **Golf Tournament**, which takes place in early July. Another golfing event is the **Professional Golf Open** at Mougins (Cannes), held every April. A new international tournament, the **Golf Classic**, takes place at Cannes in September.

Horse-racing Events
The major horse-racing venue is the **Côte d'Azur Hippodrome** at

SPAS

Spa centres *(thassalotherapie)* are a wonderful way to relax, whether for half a day or a whole week. The most reputable centres are found at L'Ile des Embiez, Bandol, Hyères, Fréjus, Antibes and Monaco. Information can be found by contacting: **Allô Thalasso**, tel: 01 53 21 86 95; www.allo-thalasso.com

Cagnes-sur-Mer, where meetings are held during the day from December to May and in the evenings in July and August. One of its major events takes place in February. There is also an international showjumping competiton in Cannes during May and an International polo event at St-Tropez in July. Hyères is popular for racing, and meetings are held at the Hippodrome there during the spring and autumn. Fréjus hosts a horse show in June.

SHOPPING

Shopping Areas

Over the years the powers that be in most major French towns have made the sensible decision to keep the town centre for small boutiques and individual shops. Many of these areas are pedestrianised, as some cars ignore the *voie piétonnière* signs.

Large supermarkets, hypermarkets, furniture stores and DIY outlets are grouped on the outskirts of the town, mostly designated as a *centre commercial*. This laudable intent is somewhat marred by the horrendous design of some of these centres – groups of garish functional buildings that make the town's outskirts very unattractive. In the case of Nice, for example, there are vast hypermarkets, out by the airport to the west of the town.

Centres commerciaux are fine for bulk shopping, self-catering or finding a selection of wine to take home at reasonable prices, but otherwise the town centres are usually far more characterful. It is here that you will find the individual souvenirs that give a taste of the region, alongside the beautifully dressed windows of delicatessens and patisseries.

What to Buy

You should have no trouble finding wonderful gifts and mementoes to take home from Provence, without having to spend a lot of money. The best things to buy are local crafts or products, for which the Provençals are so famous. Among these are: *santons* (little figures from clay or sometimes dough used together to create a Nativity scene); pottery (the pottery pictured left is from Vallauris, a famous centre for pottery); faience (fine ceramics decorated with opaque glazes); brightly coloured fabrics, as pictured left (the Souleiado stores carry the most famous examples, but they are also the most costly); handwoven baskets; and toiletries made with local herbs such as lavender. You might just want to pick up a bottle of lavender essence, a few bottles of delicately coloured olive oil or a little

bag of fresh *herbes de Provence* (usually a blend of dried herbs including thyme, sage, tarragon, rosemary, chervil and sometimes even lavender).

And there is the wine: from the celebrated Châteauneuf-du-Pape at Avignon to the pale pink rosés from Côtes-de-Provence. A good source of information for visiting wine producers, tastings and wine courses are: Maison des Vins des Côtes-de-Provence (Les Arcs; tel: 04 94 99 50 20) and Maison des Vins de Châteauneuf-du-Pape (8 rue Maréchal Foch, Châteauneuf-du-Pape; tel: 04 90 83 70 69; www.vinadea.com).

Some towns are inextricably linked with particular products, such as the wonderful hand-blown glass from Biot, the perfumes from Grasse or soap *(savon)* from Marseille, herbs from St Rémy-de-Provence or earthenware in Vallauris. The same goes for certain regions: honey is linked with the Alpes-Maritimes and Alpes-de-Haute-Provence; olive oil and *santons* with the Bouches-du-Rhône; and leather products are typical of the Camargue and the Alpes-de-Haute-Provence. And if you're on the Côte d'Azur – well, there really is no better place to buy a bikini.

Tax Refunds *(Détaxes)*

A refund (average 13 percent) of value-added tax (TVA) can be claimed by non-EU visitors if they spend over €180 in any one shop. The shop will supply a *détaxe* form, which you will need to have stamped by customs on leaving the country. Send a copy back to the shop, which will refund you by bank transfer or through your credit card. *Détaxe* does not cover food, drink, antiques or works of art.

Buying Direct

Across the region you may be tempted by signs by the side of the road for *dégustations* (tastings). A large number of wine pro-

MARKET ETIQUETTE

In a market all goods by law have to be marked with the price. Prices are usually by the kilo or by the *pièce*, that is, each item priced individually. Usually the stallholder *(marchand)* will select the goods for you. Sometimes there is a serve-yourself system – observe everyone else to see whether this is the case or not. With some foods, you may be offered a taste to try first: *un goûter*. Here are a few useful words:

bag	*le sac*
basket	*le panier*
flavour	*le parfum*
organic	*biologique*
tasting	*la dégustation*

ducers and farmers will invite you to try their wines and other produce with an eye to selling you a case, or maybe a few jars of pâté. This is a good way to try before you buy, and sometimes includes a visit to a wine cellar.

Farm produce can be more expensive to buy this way than in the supermarkets – but it is home-produced, not factory-processed, and should be extremely fresh.

Markets

If there is one thing that symbolises Provence more than anything else, it is probably the open-air market. After cafés, these markets are usually the centre of social activity for the locals, as well as where the Provençal cook obtains the multitude of fresh ingredients that make up the region's celebrated cuisine.

Vendors of locally produced vegetables, fruit, herbs, cheese, sausage, meat, honey, flowers, soaps, lavender essence and fresh-baked breads set up their stands at daybreak. In addition, some towns have a *marché au brocante* (literally meaning "junk market"), offering a range of items, from valuable antiques to brand-new wares (often clothing and shoes) to bric-a-brac. If you want to get to know Provence, you should visit one of the markets listed below.

Alpes-de-Haute-Provence

Barcelonnette: Wed, Sat
Castellane: Wed, Sat
Colmars-les-Alpes: Tues
Digne: Wed, Sat
Forcalquier: Mon
Manosque: Sat
Moustiers: Fri
Sisteron: Wed, Sat

Alpes-Maritimes

Grasse: Sun
St-Etienne-de-Tinée: Fri
St-Jeannet: Thur
Sospel: Thur, Sun
Tende: Wed
Vallauris: Tues, Sun
Vence: Tues, Fri

Bouches-du-Rhône

Aix-en-Provence: main market: daily; flower market: Mon, Wed, Fri, Sun
Arles: Wed, Sat
Barbentane: Wed
Cassis: Wed, Fri
Fontvieille: Mon, Fri
Jouques: Wed afternoon, Sun
La Ciotat: Tues, Sun
Maillane: Thur
Marseille: daily
St-Etienne-du-Grès: daily
Stes-Maries-de-la-Mer: Mon, Fri
St-Rémy-de-Provence: Wed, Sat
Salon-de-Provence: Wed, Fri
Tarascon: Tues

Côte d'Azur

Antibes: daily except Mon
Cannes: daily except Mon
Menton: daily
Nice: daily except Mon
St-Tropez: Tues, Sat

Var

Bormes-les-Mimosas: Wed, Thur
Colobrières: Sun, Thur
Draguignan: Wed, Sat
Fayence: Tues, Thur, Sat
Hyères: Tues, Sat

Le Lavandou: Thur
Salernes: Sun
Sanary-sur-Mer: Wed
Toulon: Tues–Sat

Vaucluse

Apt: Sat
Avignon: main market: daily; produce and flea market: Sat and Sun am
Bollène: Mon
Cavaillon: Mon
Châteauneuf-du-Pape: Fri
Gordes: Tues
Isle-sur-Sorgue: Thur, Sun
Roussillon: Wed
Vaison-la-Romaine: Tues

SIZE CONVERSION CHART

WOMEN

France	UK	US
38	10	8
40	12	10
42	14	12
44	16	14
46	18	16
48	20	18

MEN

France	UK	US
32	32	42
34	34	44
36	35	46
38	36	48
40	37	51
42	38	54

TRANSPORT

ACCOMMODATION

ACTIVITIES

A – Z

LANGUAGE

A - Z

A HANDY SUMMARY OF PRACTICAL INFORMATION, ARRANGED ALPHABETICALLY

A dmission Charges

The entrance fees for visiting museums and galleries generally fall between €4–6 per adult, with free admission for children – check on the qualifying age, since for some places it is under 18 and others under 12 or 7 years of age. Look out for special rates for students, over 60s and families of five or more. Usually admission is free every other Sunday and often during public holidays.

There are also passes on offer in the major towns which can be bought at a local tourist office or the museums themselves. The **Carte Musées Côte d'Azur**, which can be purchased at any of the sites, is valid for one (€10), three (€17) or seven (€27) days and provides unlim-

ited access to all museums and monuments from Thoronet to Menton. In the Var there is a **Pass Sites** valid for 24 sites and for one year. You pay for the first admission, the second site visited is then free. Avignon has a similar offer, the **Pass'ion**, where the second admission is offered at a reduced price, and which is also valid for tourist transport.

B udgeting for Your Trip

The tourist season starts around Easter and continues to the end of October. Many restaurants and hotels close at the end of the season, especially along the coast. At the peak period from 15 July to the end of August reservations are essential. Also reserve for the ski resorts in

winter, especially at weekends and during French school holidays.

For accommodation count around €20 for two people, a tent and a car, and €70 for a comfortable double room in a hotel. However, in high season the rates can be almost double. Often half board is obligatory, and reservations may only be accepted for periods of a week or more during the peak period. If you have a car, check the parking arrangements proposed by the hotel. Parking can be difficult and very expensive.

The average cost of eating out is around €20 per person at the coastal resorts and €15 in the Arrière Pays for lunch, and around €30 for dinner. Opt for a fixed-price menu, which is good value and often includes wine and coffee. Children's menus are readily available. At gastronomic restaurants count around €50, but children are not so readily catered for.

Transport by train: a full fare return ticket on the TGV Paris to Nice costs around €200–250, and local fares, for example, single Marseille to Nice costs around €30. Ask about special passes and rates at the train ticket offices *(see page 259)*.

Travelling by coach is less expensive: for example, TAM bus services have a single ticket costing €1.30 for any one-way destination. Car hire varies according to the type of car and the rental period, but on average runs to about €30/day.

Business Hours

The sacred lunch break is still largely observed in the south, which means that most shops and offices close at midday and do not reopen until 2pm or even 2.30pm. **Hypermarkets** *(grands surfaces)* usually remain open through lunch and normally until 7 or 8pm in the evening. Many shops close in the morning or all day on Monday or Wednesday.

Opening hours for **food shops** are generally 8.30am–1pm and 2.30–7pm. Most shops close on Sunday, but most **boulangeries** (bakers), **patisseries**, **bureaux de tabac** (for cigarettes, newspapers and stamps) and **maisons de la presse** (for newspapers, magazines, etc.) usually open on Sunday mornings. **Banks** tend to open 9am–noon and 1.30–5pm Mon–Fri, although these times can vary *(see also page 291)*.

Petrol stations usually open 8.30am–noon and 2 or 2.30–9pm (later on motorways). Supermarket petrol stations may stay open for credit card sales only.

Public offices usually open from 8.30am–noon, and 2–6pm.

Mairies (town halls) also tend to close for lunch, and in smaller places they may only open in the morning, typically from 9am–noon.

Business Travellers

The most important thing to know about doing business in France, and especially the south, is that people always prefer to meet in person. You will often be expected to go and see someone, even to discuss something that could easily be dealt with over the phone.

Most major banks can refer you to lawyers, accountants and tax consultants, and several US and British banks provide expatriate services, in Paris and locally. Chambres de Commerce et d'Industrie provide local details, and a calendar of trade fairs is available from the **Chambre de Commerce et d'Industrie de Paris**, 27 avenue de Friedland; tel: 01 55 65 55 65.
CCI Nice-Côte d'Azur, 20 boulevard Carabacel, Nice; tel: 08 20 42 22 22.
CCI Marseille-Provence, 9 La Canabière, tel: 04 91 39 33 33.

Business Information

BFM is a business radio station *(see Radio, page 290)*.
Les Echos gives stock quotes on the website www.lesechos.fr. Business directories **Kompass France** and **Kompass Régional** also give company details and detailed French market profiles on www.kompass.fr

C hildren

Sightseeing with children is only likely to be difficult in steep hill villages with lots of steps, which can be difficult to negotiate with a pushchair.

A wide range of activities can be found to suit children of all ages, from riding and cycling to river-bathing, rambling through the countryside and exploring castles. Most towns and villages have swimming pools, tennis courts and playgrounds.

The beach and the sea are of course the easiest way to amuse children, and private beach concessions with sun-loungers and parasols are the easiest of all.

Inflatables are often provided, and there are sometimes also bouncy castles.

Many seaside resorts have children's clubs on the beach, where, for a fee, children can be left under supervision for a few hours to take part in organised sports and fun events.

When hiring a car, be sure to book any baby seats in advance, although larger hire companies do usually have a few ready to go.

Hotels and Restaurants

Most hotels have family rooms so that children do not have to be separated from their parents, and a cot *(lit bébé)* can often be provided for a small supplement, although it is a good idea to check this in advance.

Eating out is easy, especially during the day, as all but the poshest restaurants welcome young children: just choose one with a terrace and they can run around while you have another glass of wine. Many restaurants offer a children's menu, will split a *prix-fixe* menu between two children, or even give you an extra plate to share your own meal.

Shopping

French shops are well provided with all child necessities. Disposable nappies *(couches à jeter)* are easy to find, and French baby food is often of gourmet standard – though watch out for added sugar.

Climate

Provence and its Côte d'Azur are renowned for their sunshine. Each year there are typically more than 300 sunny days and less than 850 mm (33½ inches) of rain. When it does rain, however, it pours. Average temperatures range from 48°F (8°C) in winter to 84°F (26°C) in summer. Winters are usually mild and sunny, and summers are typically hot and dry.

CLIMATE CHART

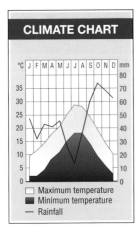

☐ Maximum temperature
■ Minimum temperature
— Rainfall

Climate varies between the high country and low country. However, the whole region experiences the sporadic virulence of the legendary northwest wind, the mistral, during the late autumn to early spring. There have also been violent storms in the area in recent years, causing major floods and damage.

When to Visit and What to Wear

The temperatures in Provence rise into the high 20°C in summer; it is therefore advisable to keep in the shade between noon and 3pm. However, if walking outside always wear a hat and carry plenty of drinking water. At the coastal resorts apply sunscreen regularly. In the winter, at the ski resorts and in the mountain areas, the temperatures are low, but again apply sunscreen and protect your eyes with sunglasses.

Weather Information

For weather information **in English**, tel: 08 36 70 12 34. Tel: 3250 gives 7-day weather forecasts. Alternatively, tel: 08 92 68 02 followed by the number of the *département*.
For **local forecasts** in Provence, tel: 08 36 68 02 04.
On **Minitel**, go to 3615 METEO.
On the **web** visit: www.meteo.fr

Temperatures are always given in Celsius (centigrade). To convert to Fahrenheit, see below:

0°C = 2°F	20°C = 68°F
10°C = 50°F	25°C = 77°F
15°C = 59°F	30°C = 86°F

Crime and Security

If you take the usual sensible precautions with your personal possessions you should be just as safe in France as at home. In cities, watch out for pickpockets, and be careful on trains, especially at night.

If you lose your credit card, notify the bank immediately: **Visa/Carte Bleue**, tel: 08 92 70 57 05; **Diner's Club**, tel: 08 10 31 41 59; **American Express**, tel: 01 47 77 72 00; **MasterCard**, tel: 08 00 90 23 90. For any debit card tel: 08 92 70 57 05.

Disabled Travellers

It is not particularly easy for disabled visitors to travel in Provence, and access to some sites can be a problem. Even if it is claimed that hotels, restaurants, museums, monuments and other places have access for disabled people, it's always wise to check beforehand exactly what is meant by this.

Small villages with steep streets and inaccessible clifftop castles can be difficult to negotiate with a wheelchair. Cities are sometimes better equipped with facilities but this is not always the case. The best approach is to check out your route as much as possible in advance.

Disabled parking is available in most places – it is indicated with a blue wheelchair sign. The international blue disabled parking disc scheme is recognised in France. To hire a wheelchair or other equipment enquire at the local pharmacy.

Rick Steves' Easy Access Europe is a useful book. For further information in the UK/US contact: **Tourism for All UK**, tel: 0845 124 9973 (9am–5pm, Mon–Fri; www.tourismforall.org.uk)

or **RADAR**, tel: 020 7250 3222; www.radar.co.uk. In the US contact **SATH**, tel: (121) 447 7284; www.sath.org

Useful Websites

www.guide-accessible.com
www.vita-vie.com
www.franceguide.com
www.tourisme-handicaps.org
www.access-tourisme.com
www.parisinfo.com has good links from its "Practical Paris" page.

Transport

EuroShuttle (in UK tel: 0870 535 3535) – the Channel Tunnel car-on-a-train service – allows disabled passengers to stay in their vehicle. **Eurostar** trains (UK special requests, tel: 0870 518 61 86) give special-rate wheelchair-user fares and a reduced rate for one travelling companion.

Most **ferry** companies offer facilities for disabled travellers if they are contacted in advance of travel.

For **rail** travel, *Le Guide du Voyageur à Mobilité Réduite* SNCF is available free in train stations. SNCF Accessibilité Service, tel: +33 (0) 8 00 15 47 53; www.voyages sncf.com/voyageurs_handicapes

Reduced tolls are charged on **autoroutes** for vehicles fitted to accommodate the disabled. An *autoroute* guide for disabled travellers *(Guides des Autoroutes à l'Usage des Personnes à Mobilité Réduite)* is available free from the Ministère des Transports, Direction des Routes, Service du Contrôle des Autoroutes, La Défense, 92055 Cedex, Paris; tel: 01 40 81 21 22; email: dma@equipmewnt.gouv.fr. For services see also: www.autoroutes.fr/voyage/servicesmob.php

If you are disabled, **taxi** drivers in France cannot refuse to take you, help you into the vehicle or transport a guide dog for a blind passenger.

Accommodation

Gîtes Accessibles à Tous lists *gîte* accommodation that is equipped for the disabled. It is available from: Maison de Gîtes de France, 59 rue St-Lazare, 75009 Paris; tel: 01 49 70 75 75; www.gites-de-france.fr

The *FFCC Guide Officiel Camping et Caravaning*, produced by the Fédération de Camping-Caravaning (www.ffcc.fr), indicates which campsites have facilities for disabled campers. It is obtainable from www.campingfrance.com or www.amazon.fr

The *Michelin Green Guide – Camping/Caravanning France* lists sites with facilities for the disabled. The Association des Paralysés (APF) publishes *Où Ferons-§Nous Etapes?*, which lists accommodation suitable for disabled travellers: APF Alpes-Maritimes, Nice, tel: 04 92 07 98 00; APF Var, tel: 04 98 01 30 50; www.apf.asso.fr

E lectricity and Gas

The electric current is generally 220/230 volts. It alternates at 50 cycles, not at 60 cycles as in the US, so American visitors will need a transformer for electric shavers, travel irons, hairdryers, etc. Plugs are "Type E" round pin plug with male grounding pin from socket.

Electricity in rural areas occasionally fails, so ensure that you have candles or torches.

In many rural areas butane gas is used for cooking and heating water. Campers and caravanners needing replacement gas canisters will find them on sale at local shops, garages and supermarkets (return the empty one).

Embassies and Consulates

Call before going along to your consulate or embassy, in case an appointment is necessary.

Consulates in Provence
UK
24 avenue Prado, 13006 Marseille; tel: 04 91 15 72 10; fax: 04 01 37 47 06; www.british

embassy.gov.uk. Open Mon–Fri 9am–noon and 2pm–4pm.
US
Place Varian Fry, 13006 Marseille; tel: 04 91 54 92 00; www.amb-usa.fr/marseille
7 avenue Gustave V, 06000 Nice; tel: 04 93 88 89 55; www.amb-usa.fr/marseille/nice
Canada
10 rue Lamartine, 06000 Nice; tel: 04 93 92 93 22; www.international.gc.ca
Ireland
152 boulevard J.F. Kennedy, 06160 Cap d'Antibes; tel: 06 77 69 14 36; http://foreignaffairs.gov.ie

Entry Requirements

Visas and Passports
All visitors to France require a visa except for citizens of EU countries. Citizens of the US, Canada, Australia or New Zealand only need a visa for stays of more than three months. Check with the French consulate in your country.

If you intend to stay in France for more than 90 days you should apply for a *carte de séjour* (or *titre de séjour*). EU citizens with ID and proof of

EMERGENCY NUMBERS

The following services operate 24 hours daily:
Police: 17
Fire (Sapeurs-Pompiers): 18
Ambulance (SAMU): 15
European Emergency Number: 112

Other Useful Numbers
In rural areas the local taxi service often doubles as an ambulance, so it is worth getting their number from the tourist office or *mairie* (town hall).
SOS Médecins: 04 93 85 01 01
Nice Médecins: 04 93 52 42 42
Drug Info: 08 00 23 13 13
SOS Helpline: 01 46 21 46 46 (3–11pm).

former address are no longer required to get one, but it may be easier to do so, especially if you intend to work.

Travelling with Pets
It is possible to re-enter Britain with your pet without it having to go through quarantine. Conditions are stringent, however, and points of entry are restricted. For further details you should call 0870 241 1710 or see www.defra.gov.uk, or the French consulate if you are abroad. To travel between European countries with your pet you will only need a valid vaccination certificate.

Customs
You may take any quantity of goods into France from another EU country as long as they are for personal use and you can prove that tax has been paid on them in the country of origin. Customs officials still have the right to question visitors.

Quantities accepted as being for personal use are as follows:
• up to 3,200 cigarettes, 400 small cigars, 200 cigars or 1 kg of loose tobacco.
• 10 litres of spirits (more than 22 percent alcohol), 90 litres of wine (under 22 percent alcohol) or 110 litres of beer.

For goods from outside the EU, recommended quantities are:
• 200 cigarettes or 100 small cigars, 50 cigars or 250 g of loose tobacco.
• 1 litre of spirits (over 22 percent alcohol) and 2 litres of wine and beer (under 22 percent alcohol).
• 50 g of perfume.
Visitors may also carry up to €7,600 in currency.

G ay & Lesbian

The main hotspots for gay and lesbian travellers are around St-Tropez and along the coast. To find out more see regional listings magazines, such as *L'Excès* (www.exces.com) or visit www.gay.com for all gay travel information.

Health & Medical Care

EU nationals staying in France are entitled to use the French social security system, which refunds up to 70 percent of medical expenses (but sometimes less than this, eg for dental treatment). UK visitors need to provide a European Health Insurance Card (EHIC) at each medical visit in order to obtain this refund: call 0845 606 2030, visit www.ehic.org.uk or obtain an application form from the Post Office.

Nationals of non-EU countries are well advised to take out insurance before leaving home. Consultations and prescriptions have to be paid for in full in France and are reimbursed, in part, on receipt of a completed *fiche* (form).

Pharmacies

Pharmacies in France are good, but expensive. The staff in pharmacies are well qualified, however, and should be able to advise on many minor ailments. All pharmacies can be identified by a neon green cross. Most open from 9 or 10am until 7 or 8pm. If the pharmacy is closed there will be a sign giving details of a "*pharmacie de garde*", which will offer a night-time service.

Hospitals and Doctors

For a complete list of hospitals consult the *Pages Blanches* directory under "Hôpital Assistance Publique". Hotel staff should be able to provide the names of local doctors. Non-French speakers may like to request an English-speaking doctor – not always possible, but worth asking.

Lost Property

To report a crime or loss of belongings, go to the local police station *(gendarmerie* or *commissariat de police)*. Telephone numbers can be found at the front of local telephone directories. If you lose your passport, you should report it firstly to the police and then to the nearest consulate.

Maps

A first essential for touring is a good map. The large-format **Michelin** atlases or sheet maps are good for driving. For walking or cycling, **IGN** (Institut Géographique National) maps are invaluable. The 1:100,000 and 1:50,000 maps have all roads and most footpaths marked. For greater detail, go for the IGN blue series 1:25,000 maps. Town plans are often given away free at local tourist offices. Most good bookshops should have a range of maps, but they may cost less in hypermarkets or service stations.

Stockists of French maps in the UK include: **The Travel Bookshop**, 13 Blenheim Crescent, London W11, tel: 020 7229 5260; www.thetravelbookshop.co.uk; **Stanfords** (www.stanfords.co.uk) have stores in Covent Garden, London (tel: 020 7836 1321), Bristol and Manchester. Online, try www.mapkiosk.com or www.-amazon.co.uk

Media

Newspapers and Magazines

The French press is very regional. Popular papers in the south include *Nice-Matin*, *La Provence*, *Var-Matin*, *Le Dauphiné Vaucluse* and *La Marseillaise*. Foreign newspapers are widely available. The local English-language magazine *Riviera Reporter* is good for regional information and politics.

Television

France has six terrestrial TV channels. **TF1**, privatised since 1987, features movies, game shows, dubbed soaps, audience debates and the main news at 8pm.

France 2 is a state-owned station showing a mix of game shows, documentaries and cultural chat.

F3R is more heavyweight and shows local news, sports, excellent wildlife documentaries and a late-night Sunday Cinema.

Canal+ offers a roster of satellite and cable subscription channels with movies (sometimes in *VO*) and exclusive sport.

Arte is an excellent Franco-German hybrid, specialising in intelligent arts coverage and films in their original language.

M6 shows mainly American films and soaps dubbed into French, magazine programmes covering topical issues as well as pop music and celebrity gossip.

Radio

The following is just a selection of what is available (wavelengths are given in MHz):

87.8 France Inter. A state-run, middle-of-the-road channel offering music and international news.

90.9 Chante France. French song.

91.7–92.1 France Musique. Another state-run channel, offering classical music and jazz.

93.5–93.9 France Culture. A highbrow state culture station with the stress on literature, poetry, history, cinema and music.

BFM. Business and economics news. Aix-en-Provence 93.8, Cannes and Nice 104.4, Hyères 87.9, Marseille 93.8.

93.4 Radio FG FM. Gay station with music and lonely hearts: www.radiofg.com

101.5 Radio Nova. Serves a mix of hip hop, trip hop, world music and jazz; www.novaplanet.com

RTL. The most popular French station, providing a mix of music and talk programmes. Cannes and Nice 97.4, Avignon 107.2, Marseille 101.4.

Europe 1. News, press reviews and sports. Avignon 94.6, Cannes and Nice 101.4, Marseille 104.8.

105.5 France Info. Tune in for 24-hour news, economic updates and sports news.

107.7 Radio Trafic. Gives regular traffic bulletins in English.

BBC World Service. This can be received in France on shortwave between 6.195 and 12.095 MHz.

Local radio stations include: **Radio Côte d'Azur**: 103.4 FM; **Cannes Radio**: 91.5 FM; **Kiss FM**: 90.9 FM and 94.6 FM for Cannes.

Money

French banks usually open 9am–5pm Mon–Fri (some close for lunch noon–1.30pm). Some banks also open on Saturdays. All banks are closed on public holidays, sometimes from noon on the day prior to the bank holiday. In rural areas banks are often closed Mondays and foreign currency may need to be ordered.

Credit Cards and Cash Machines

Credit and debit cards issued from many European banks can be used as payment in many shops and restaurants. Most establishments have card readers that accept foreign credit and debit cards with a valid PIN number.

You can withdraw money from automatic cash machines using cards from foreign banks and PIN number, as long as the card and machine show either a Visa or Cirrus symbol.

Tipping

You do not usually need to add service to a restaurant bill in France. A charge of 10 percent is added automatically as part of the bill. (To be sure, check it says "service compris" on the menu, or ask "Est-ce que le service est compris?")

Taxis also include service charges. Doormen, porters, guides, hairdressers, etc, are usually given a tip of €1.50. Note that in bars and cafés you pay less at the counter than if you sit at a table. It's normal to leave some small change as a tip.

P ostal Services

Post offices (PTTs; www.laposte.fr) open Mon–Fri 9am–noon and 2–6pm, Sat 9am–noon. In large towns they may not close for lunch, but in small villages they may only be open for a short time in the morning.

In larger post offices, each counter has specific services, so check you are in the right queue (look for "Timbres" if you only want stamps. You can also buy stamps at tobacconists (bureaux de tabac) and some shops selling postcards. A €0.55 stamp is standard for letters within EU.

Urgent post can be sent par exprès. The Chronopost system is also fast but is expensive.

Poste Restante

Mail can be kept for collection when addressed to you at: Poste Restante, Poste Centrale (for the main post office) plus the town postcode and name. A small fee will be charged and you will need to show your passport to collect.

Public Holidays

Banks, post offices and public offices close on public holidays. Food shops, in particular boulangeries (bread shops), open in the morning, even on Christmas Day. It is common practice if a public holiday falls on a Thursday or Tuesday for French businesses to faire le pont ("bridge the gap") and take the Friday or Monday as a holiday as well.

Details of closures should be posted outside banks, etc, a few days before the event, but it is easy to be caught out, especially on days such as 15 August (Assumption), which is the climax of the summer and the biggest holiday of the year. While the shops may be shut, there will almost certainly be a fête in every town and village.

Foreign embassies and consulates observe French public holidays as well as their own.

1 January: New Year's Day (Nouvel An)
March/April: Easter Monday (Lundi de Pâques)
1 May: Labour Day (Fête du Travail)
May: Ascension Day (Ascension), on a Thursday 40 days after Easter
8 May: Victory Day (Fête de la Libération) to commemorate the end of World War II

14 July: Bastille Day (Quatorze Juillet)
15 August: Assumption Day (Fête de l'Assomption)
1 November: All Saints' Day (Toussaint)
11 November: Armistice Day (Fête de l'Armistice)
25 December: Christmas Day (Noël)

T elecommunications

French telephone numbers are all 10 figures including two-digit regional prefixes as follows: Paris, Ile de France region 01; Northwest 02; Northeast 03; Southeast and Corsica 04 and Southwest 05 (when dialling from outside France, omit the initial zero). They are always written and spoken in two-digit numbers (eg 01 25 25 25 25).

Public Phones

You should be able to find telephone boxes (cabines publiques) in every sizeable village. Most take only phonecards (télécartes), available from post offices, stationers, railway stations, some cafés and bureaux de tabac. Some cafés have metred phones, but these may cost more.

Phone Directories

You can find telephone directories (annuaires) in all post offices and in most cafés: Pages Blanches (White Pages) lists

TIME ZONE

France is always one hour ahead of the UK (i.e. Greenwich Mean Time +1 in winter, and GMT+2 in summer).

people and businesses alphabetically, while *Pages Jaunes* (Yellow Pages) lists business services. Both are also available on the Internet at: www.pagesblanches.fr and www.pagesjaunes.fr

Since 2006 one **directory enquiries** number has been replaced with over 20 operating companies. The numbers all start 118, for example:
Le Numéro 118 218
France Télécom 118 711
Pages Jaunes 118 008

International Calls

The international code for France is 00 33. For Monaco, tel: 00 377 plus an eight-figure number.

To make an international call dial 00 followed by the country's international call number. This can be found in the front of the *Pages Jaunes* section of the phone directory or on the information panel in a telephone box.
International directory enquiries: 3212.

Reverse-Charge Calls

To make a reverse-charge/collect call within France call 3006 and ask to make a PCV (pronounced "pay-say-vay") call. Collect calls can only be received at call boxes displaying the blue bell sign.

Free Calls

Numéros verts ("green numbers"), usually beginning with 08, are free. You still need to insert money or a card in a public phone, but coins will be returned and your card will not be debited.

Faxes

Most hotels, large post offices and *maisons de presse* also offer **fax** and **photocopying** services; many supermarkets also have coin-operated photocopiers.

Internet

Good hotels usually have Internet access, as do many libraries and post offices. Internet cafés are popular in main towns.
Avignon: Webzone, 2 rue St-Jean Le Vieux; tel: 04 32 76 29 47.
Cannes: Cyber Internet, 32 rue Jean Jaurès; tel: 04 93 38 85 63.
Marseille: Bluesincoffee, 83 rue Rabelais; www.bluesincoffee.com
Nice: Panini and Web, 25 promenade des Anglais; tel: 04 93 88 72 75.
Toulon: Webcafé, 33 rue des Boucheries; tel: 04 94 22 95 16.

Tourist Information

Every town and city, and almost every small village has its own **office de tourisme**, sometimes also referred to as the *maison* (or *bureau*) *de tourisme*, or the *syndicat d'initiative*. These are usually located on or near the main square, and sometimes also at main stations, and they can invariably be relied upon to supply the best available map of the locality as well as information about restaurants, accommodation, sights and events. Tourist office staff should be able to give you impartial advice or point you to the piles of free advertising leaflets, which are left by hotels, shops, museums and the like. Note that – especially in small places – these offices often close at midday, and some may not open again in the afternoon.

If there is no tourist office in a town you can get a wide range of help and information from the local *mairie* (town hall).

Regional Tourist Offices

Comité Régional du Tourisme de Provence-Alpes-Côte d'Azur
Les Docks, Atrium 10.5, BP 46214, 10 place de la Joliette, 13567 Marseille, Cedex 2; tel: 04 91 56 47 00; www.regionpaca.fr
Details of city/town tourist offices are also available here.
Comité Régional du Tourisme Riviera Côte d'Azur

55 promenade des Anglais, BP 602, 06011 Nice, tel: 04 93 37 78 78; www.guideriviera.fr.
Office de Tourisme et des Congrès de la Principauté de Monaco
2a boulevard des Moulins, 9800 Monaco, tel: 00 377-92 16 61 16; www.monaco-tourisme.com

Maisons de France

See www.franceguide.com
UK
178 Piccadilly, London W1V 0AL; tel: 0906 8244 123.
USA
444 Madison Avenue, New York, NY 10022; tel: 514 288 1904.
Canada
1800 Avenue McGill College, Suite 1010, Montreal, Quebec; tel: 514 288 2026.
Australia
Level 13, 25 Bligh Street, Sydney, NSW 2000; tel: 02 9231 5244.
Ireland
10 Suffolk Street, Dublin; tel: 1635 1008.

Tour Operators

Ace Study Tours
Tel: 01223 835 055; www.study-tours.org
Cultural tours.
Allez France
www.allezfrance.com
Gastronomic holidays.

TOILETS

Anyone may use the toilet in a bar or café, whether they are a customer or not, unless there is a sign specifying that this is not allowed. (Ask for *les toilettes* or *le WC*, which is pronounced "vay-say"). Many public toilets are still old-fashioned squat toilets and men and women sometimes use the same facilities.

Alternative Travel Group
Tel: 01865 315 679
Visits to wine estates.
Arblaster and Clarke
Tel: 01730 262 111
www.arblasterandclarke.com
Wine tours.
Cycling for Softies
Tel: 0161 248 8282
www.cyclingforsofties.co.uk
Cox and Kings
Tel: 020 7873 5006
www.coxandkings.co.uk
Botanical tours.
Erna Low Consultants
Tel: 0870 750 6820
www.ernalow.co.uk
Spa holidays.
French Life
Tel: 08704 448 877
www.frenchlife.co.uk
French holiday experts, for *gîtes*, hotel and apartment holidays.
Limosa Holidays
Tel: 01263 578 143
Birdwatching.
LSG Theme Holidays
Tel: 01509 231713
Language, painting and walking trips.
NatureTrek
Tel: 01962 733051
www.naturetrek.co.uk
Fauna and flora holidays.
Prospect
Tel: 01227 773 545
www.prospecttours.com
Music and art tours.
VFB Holidays
Tel: 01242 240 310
www.vfbholidays.co.uk
Skiing and walking holidays.

Websites

www.visitprovence.com
French government tourism website. Information in French and English on sights, tours, specialist walks, hotels and restaurants, plus essential practical information.
www.provence-beyond.com
English-language website with details on lesser-known places. Personally tailored tours may be arranged.
www.riviera-reporter.com
Local English-language magazine site with archive of articles on a variety of practical and political subjects and links to other relevant government and advice sites.
www.sunfrance.com
French government tourist site (in French and English) with online brochures and links.
www.luberon-news.com
Newspaper site offering links to restaurants and hotels, plus a variety of local information for the Languedoc-Roussillon area.
www.sncf.fr
French Railways website with timetables and booking online.
www.theanglophonebook.com
English-speaking businesses.
www.holidayfrance.org.uk
General tourist site on holidays in France compiled by the Association of British Travel Organisers.
www.tourisme.fr
General tourist site.
www.provence-azur.com
Maison de Tourisme de la Provence d'Azur.
www.provenceverte.com
Maison de Tourisme de la Provence Verte.
www.riviera-explorer.com
Information on sports, transport and general tourist information.
www.provenceweb.com
Helps you prepare your trip to Provence with useful maps and themed circuits.
www.cotedazur-en-fetes.com
Information on the festivals and concerts, places to stay, local cuisine, and list of tourist offices.

Weights and Measures

The metric system is used in France for all weights and measures. For a handy reckoning, 80 km is about 50 miles, thus 40 km equals 25 miles.

What to Bring

You should be able to buy anything you need in France. Pharmacies offer a wide range of drugs, medical supplies and toiletries, along with expert advice, but you should bring any prescription drugs you might need. A second pair of spectacles or contact lenses is recommended (which drivers are required by law to carry). Sunscreen and anti-mosquito products are advisable in summer. Remember to bring an adaptor if you have electrical equipment *(see page 289)*.

The clothing you bring depends on your destination and when you travel; you will only need to dress up for chic restaurants in the cities or casinos. Dress appropriately for visiting churches; a scarf or shirt are always useful cover-ups. Most sports equipment can be hired but you should bring personal gear such as walking boots with you.

In the larger cities you will find English-language newspapers and magazines and English bookshops, but elsewhere you will need your own reading matter. Ensure that you have up-to-date local guides, phrase books and maps, though these items are increasingly available in supermarkets. Electronic translators can be really useful.

TRANSPORT

ACCOMMODATION

ACTIVITIES

A – Z

LANGUAGE

L ANGUAGE

KEY FRENCH WORDS AND PHRASES

Words and Phrases

yes/no *oui/non*
OK *d'accord*
I'm sorry *Excusez-moi/Pardon*
please *s'il vous/te plaît*
thank you (very much) *merci (beaucoup)*
you're welcome *de rien*
excuse me *excusez-moi*
hello *bonjour* ("*allo*" on telephone)
goodbye *au revoir*
good evening *bonsoir*
here/there *ici/là*
today *aujourd'hui*
yesterday *hier*
tomorrow *demain*
now *maintenant*
later *plus tard*
this morning *ce matin*
this afternoon *cet après-midi*
this evening *ce soir*
What is your name? *Comment vous appelez-vous?*
My name is… *Je m'appelle…*
Do you speak English? *Parlez-vous anglais?*
I am English/American *Je suis anglais(e)/américain(e)*
I don't understand *Je ne comprends pas*
Please speak more slowly *Parlez plus lentement, s'il vous plaît*
Can you help me? *Voulez-vous m'aider?*
I'm looking for… *Je cherche*
Where is…? *Où est…?*
I don't know *Je ne sais pas*

On Arrival

airport *l'aéroport*
train station *la gare (SNCF)*
bus station *la gare routière*
Métro stop *la station de Métro*
bus *l'autobus, le car*
bus stop *l'arrêt*
platform *le quai*
ticket *le billet*
return ticket *aller-retour*
toilets *les toilettes/les WC*
I want to get off at… *Je voudrais descendre à…*
Is there a bus to…? *Est-ce qui'il y a un bus pour …?*
What street is this? *A quelle rue sommes-nous?*
Which line do I take for…? *Quelle ligne dois-je prendre pour…?*
How far is…? *A quelle distance se trouve…?*
Validate your ticket *Compostez votre billet*
I'd like a (single/double) room… *Je voudrais une chambre (pour une/deux personnes) …*
….with shower *avec douche*
….with a bath *avec salle de bain*
Does that include breakfast? *Le prix comprend-il le petit déjeuner?*
washbasin *le lavabo*
key *la cléf*
elevator *l'ascenseur*
air-conditioned *climatisé*

On the Road

Where is the nearest garage? *Où est le garage le plus proche?*
Our car has broken down *Notre voiture est en panne*
I want to have my car repaired *Je veux faire réparer ma voiture*
left/right *gauche/droite*
straight on *tout droit*
far/near *loin/près d'ici*
at the end *au bout*
on foot *à pied*
by car *en voiture*
road map *la carte*
street *la rue*
give way *céder le passage*
motorway *l'autoroute*
toll *le péage*
speed limit *la limitation de vitesse*
petrol *l'essence*
unleaded *sans plomb*
diesel *le gasoil*
water/oil *l'eau/l'huile*
puncture *un pneu de crevé*

Shopping

Where is the nearest bank/ post office? *Où est la banque/ Poste la plus proche?*
I'd like to buy *Je voudrais acheter*
How much is it? *C'est combien?*
Do you take credit cards? *Est-ce que vous acceptez les cartes de crédit?*

NUMBERS

0	*zéro*	**11**	*onze*	**30**	*trente*
1	*un, une*	**12**	*douze*	**40**	*quarante*
2	*deux*	**13**	*treize*	**50**	*cinquante*
3	*trois*	**14**	*quatorze*	**60**	*soixante*
4	*quatre*	**15**	*quinze*	**70**	*soixante-dix*
5	*cinq*	**16**	*seize*	**80**	*quatre-vingts*
6	*six*	**17**	*dix-sept*	**90**	*quatre-vingt-dix*
7	*sept*	**18**	*dix-huit*	**100**	*cent*
8	*huit*	**19**	*dix-neuf*	**1000**	*mille*
9	*neuf*	**20**	*vingt*	**1,000,000**	
10	*dix*	**21**	*vingt-et-un*	*un million*	

Have you got…? *Avez-vous…?*
I'll take it *Je le prends*
size (clothes) *la taille*
size (shoes) *la pointure*
cheap *bon marché*
expensive *cher*
a piece of *un morceau de*
each *la pièce* (eg *ananas, €0.5 la pièce*)
bill/receipt *la note/le reçu*

Dining Out

Table d'hôte (the "host's table") is one set menu served at a set price. **Prix fixe** is a fixed-price menu. **A la carte** means dishes from the menu are charged separately.
breakfast *le petit déjeuner*
lunch *le déjeuner*
dinner *le dîner*
meal *le repas*
first course *l'entrée/les hors d'oeuvre*
main course *le plat principal*
drink included *boisson compris*
wine list *la carte des vins*
the bill *l'addition*
plate *l'assiette*
glass *le verre*

Breakfast and Snacks

beurre **butter**
confiture **jam**
crêpe **pancake**
croque-monsieur **ham-and-cheese toasted sandwich**
croque-madame **ham-and-cheese toasted sandwich with a fried egg on top**
galette **type of pancake/cake**
oeufs **eggs**
oeufs à la coque **boiled eggs**
oeufs sur le plat **fried eggs**
oeufs brouillés **scrambled eggs**
pain **bread**
sucre **sugar**

L'Entrée (Starters)

anchoïade **sauce of olive oil, anchovies and garlic, served with raw vegetables**
assiette anglaise **cold meats**
potage **soup**
rillettes **rich fatty paste of shredded duck, rabbit or pork**
tapenade **spread of olives and anchovies**

Viande (Meat)

bleu **rare**
à point **medium**
bien cuit **well done**
grillé **grilled**
agneau **lamb**
bifteck **steak**
blanquette **stew of veal, lamb or chicken with a creamy egg sauce**
…à la bordelaise **with red wine and shallots**
…à la bourguignonne **cooked in red wine, onions and mushrooms**
boeuf en daube **beef stew with red wine, onions and tomatoes**
brochette **kebab**
canard **duck**
carbonnade **casserole of beef, beer and onions**
carré d'agneau **rack of lamb**
cassoulet **stew with beans, sausages, pork and duck, from southwest France**
cervelle **brains (food)**
confit **duck or goose preserved in its own fat**
contre-filet **cut of sirloin steak**
coq au vin **chicken in red wine**
côte d'agneau **lamb chop**
dinde **turkey**
entrecôte **beef rib steak**
escargot **snail**
faisan **pheasant**
farci **stuffed**
faux-filet **sirloin**
foie **liver**
foie gras **goose/duck liver pâté**
gardiane **rich beef stew with olives and garlic**
cuisses de grenouille **frog's legs**
grillade **grilled meat**
hachis **minced meat**
jambon **ham**
lapin **rabbit**
lardons **small pieces of bacon**
moelle **beef bone marrow**
oie **goose**
porc **pork**
poulet **chicken**
poussin **young chicken**
rognons **kidneys**
rôti **roast**
sanglier **wild boar**
saucisse **fresh sausage**
saucisson **salami**
veau **veal**

Poissons (Fish)

Armoricaine **made with white wine, tomatoes, butter and cognac**

EMERGENCIES

Help! *Au secours!*
Stop! *Arrêtez!*
Call a doctor *Appelez un médecin*
Call an ambulance *Appelez une ambulance*
Call the police *Appelez la police*
Call the fire brigade *Appelez les pompiers*
Where is the nearest telephone? *Où est le téléphone le plus proche?*
Where is the nearest hospital? *Où est l'hôpital le plus proche?*
I am sick *Je suis malade*
I have lost my passport/purse *J'ai perdu mon passeport/ porte-monnaie*

anchois **anchovies**
anguille **eel**
Bercy **sauce made with
fish stock, butter, white wine
and shallots**
bigorneau **sea snail**
bouillabaisse **traditional fish
soup, served with grated
cheese, garlic croutons and
rouille, a spicy sauce**
calmars **squid**
coquillage **shellfish**
coquilles St-Jacques **scallops**
crevette **shrimp**
fruits de mer **seafood**
homard **lobster**
huître **oyster**
langoustine **large prawn**
moule **mussel**
moules marinières **mussels in
white wine and onions**
raie **skate**
saumon **salmon**
thon **tuna**
truite **trout**

Légumes (Vegetables)

ail **garlic**
artichaut **artichoke**
asperge **asparagus**
aubergine **aubergine (eggplant)**
avocat **avocado**
céleri **grated celery**
rémoulade **with mayonnaise**
champignon **mushroom**
cornichon **gherkin**
chips **potato crisps**
chou **cabbage**
chou-fleur **cauliflower**
cru **raw**
crudités **raw vegetables**
frites **chips, French fries**
gratin dauphinois **sliced
potatoes baked with cream**
haricot **dried bean**
haricots verts **green beans**
lentilles **lentils**
maïs **corn**
navet **turnip**
noix **nut, walnut**
oignon **onion**
panais **parsnip**
poireau **leek**
pois **pea**
poivron **bell pepper**
pomme de terre **potato**
salade niçoise **egg, tuna,
olives, onions and tomato
salad**

Fruits (Fruit)

ananas **pineapple**
cerise **cherry**
citron **lemon**
citron vert **lime**
figue **fig**
fraise **strawberry**
framboise **raspberry**
groseille **redcurrant**
mangue **mango**
pamplemousse **grapefruit**
pêche **peach**
poire **pear**
pomme **apple**
raisin **grape**
prune **plum**
pruneau **prune**

Sauces (Sauces)

aioli **garlic mayonnaise**
béarnaise **sauce of egg, butter,
wine and herbs**
forestière **with mushrooms and
bacon**
hollandaise **egg, butter and
lemon sauce**
lyonnaise **with onions**
meunière **fried fish with butter,
lemon and parsley sauce**
meurette **red wine sauce**
Mornay **sauce of cream, egg
and cheese**
Parmentier **served with potatoes**
paysan **rustic style, ingredients
depend on the region**
pistou **Provençal sauce of basil,
garlic and olive oil; vegetable
soup with pistou sauce**
provençale **sauce of tomatoes,
garlic and olive oil**
papillotte **cooked in paper**

Dessert (Puddings)

Belle Hélène **fruit with ice
cream and chocolate sauce**
clafoutis **baked pudding of
batter and cherries**
coulis **purée of fruit or
vegetables**
gâteau **cake**
île flottante **meringue in custard**
crème anglaise **custard**
pêche melba **peaches with
ice cream and raspberry sauce**
tarte tatin **upside-down tart of
caramelised apples**
crème caramel **caramelised
egg custard**
crème Chantilly **whipped cream**

I am a vegetarian Je suis
végétarien(ne)
I am on a diet Je suis au
régime
What do you recommend?
Que'est-ce que vous recom-
mandez?
**Do you have local speciali-
ties?** Avez-vous des spécial-
ités locales?
I'd like to order Je voudrais
commander
That is not what I ordered
Ce n'est pas ce que j'ai
commandé
Is service included? Est-ce
que le service est compris?
May I have more wine?
Encore du vin, s'il vous plaît?
Enjoy your meal Bon appétit!

In a Café

coffee café
...with milk/cream au lait/crème
...decaffeinated déca/décaféiné
...black/espresso noir/express
...filtered coffee filtre
tea thé
herb infusion tisane
hot chocolate chocolat chaud
milk lait
mineral water eau minérale
fizzy gazeux
**fresh lemon juice served with
sugar** citron pressé
freshly squeezed orange juice
orange pressé
fresh or cold frais, fraîche
beer bière
...bottled en bouteille
...on tap à la pression
with ice avec des glaçons
neat sec
red rouge
white blanc
rose rosé
dry brut
sweet doux
house wine vin de maison
local wine vin de pays
glass verre
pitcher carafe/pichet
...of water/wine d'eau/de vin
half-litre demi-carafe
cheers! santé!

FURTHER READING

History

France in the New Century: Portrait of a Changing Society by John Ardagh (Penguin). Weighty tome on modern France.
Côte d'Azur: Inventing the French Riviera by Mary Blume (Thames & Hudson). Excellent account of *emigré* Riviera.
The Identity of France by Fernand Braudel (HarperCollins). Unputdownable analysis, weaving major events with everyday life, by one of France's best historians.
France on the Brink: A Great Civilization Faces the New Century, by Jonathan Fenby (Arcade). Controversial, personal and witty account of French politics and life.
The French by Theodore Zeldin (Random House). Irreverent, penetrating analysis of the French character.

Art

France: A History in Art, by Bradley Smith (Weidenfeld & Nicolson). The history of France seen through the eyes of artists.
Letters of Van Gogh, ed. Ronald de Leeuw (Penguin). Correspondence revealing a subtle side of the celebrated Dutch painter.
A Life of Picasso. Vols I and II by John Richardson (Cape).
The Unknown Matisse by Hilary Spurling (Knopf). Well-researched biography.

Fiction

The Avignon Quintet by Lawrence Durrell (Faber). Classic travel writing from Durrell.
Bonjour Tristesse by Françoise Sagan. (Penguin). The story of a teenager and her father, living the hedonistic Riviera life.

The Count of Monte-Cristo by Alexandre Dumas (Various editions). Gripping account of prison life and revenge at the Château d'If, near Marseille.
The Horseman on the Roof by Jean Giono (Harvill). Provence in the 1830s.

FEEDBACK

We do our best to ensure the information in our books is as accurate and up to date as possible. The books are updated on a regular basis, using local contacts, who painstakingly add, amend and correct as required. However, some mistakes and omissions are inevitable, and we are ultimately reliant on our readers to put us in the picture.

We would welcome your feedback on any details related to your experiences using the book "on the road". Maybe we recommended a hotel that you liked (or another that you didn't), or you have come across interesting new attractions or facts you could tell us about. The more details you can give us (particularly with regard to addresses, emails and telephone numbers), the better.

We will acknowledge all contributions, and we'll offer an Insight Guide to the best letters received.

Please write to us at:
Insight Guides
PO Box 7910
London SE1 1WE
United Kingdom
Or send email to:
insight@apaguide.co.uk

Jean de Florette and **Manon of the Springs** by Marcel Pagnol (Picador). Peasant struggles in rural Provence. Novels that inspired award-winning films.
Perfume by Patrick Süskind (Picador). Sinister but gripping tale of an 18th-century Grasse perfumer.
The Rock Pool by Cyril Connolly (Persea). Satirical novel set in 1930s Riviera.
Tender is the Night by F. Scott Fitzgerald (Penguin). Wealth and decadence on the Riviera.
A Year in Provence by Peter Mayle (Penguin). Enjoyable, if clichéd, account of Mayle's first 12 months in Maillane.

Food and Wine

Flavours of France by Alain Ducasse (Artisan). Recipes from the Provençal masterchef.
The Food Lover's Guide to France by Patricia Wells (Workman). Regional dishes, restaurants, shops, markets and more.
A Table in Provence by Leslie Forbes (Penguin). Recipes.
Touring in Wine Country: Provence ed. Hugh Johnson (Mitchell Beazley). Tours of the Provençal vineyards, plus maps.

Other Insight Guides

Insight Guides to France include *Southwest France* and *the French Riviera* among other regions.
Insight Pocket Guides, containing route-based itineraries and a large fold-out map, cover *Paris, Provence* and *The French Riviera*.
Insight Compact Guides and the new **Insight Smart Guides**, fact-packed easy-reference guides, cover a number of French regions.
Insight Fleximaps. Durable maps. French regions include Provence.

ART & PHOTO CREDITS

INDEX